Design for Living

By the same author

Dr. Bob's Library

Anne Smith's Journal, 1933-1939

The Akron Genesis of Alcoholics Anonymous

The Books Early AAs Read for Spiritual Growth

New Light on Alcoholism:
  The A.A. Legacy from Sam Shoemaker

Courage to Change (with Bill Pittman)

Design for Living

*The Oxford Group's
Contribution to Early A.A.*

Dick B.

With a Foreword by T. Willard Hunter

Paradise Research Publications
San Rafael, California

Paradise Research Publications, 247 Bret Harte Rd., San Rafael, CA 94901

This Paradise Research Publications Edition is published by arrangement with Good Book Publishing Company, 2747 S. Kihei Rd., D-110, Kihei, Maui, HI 96753

Cover Design: Richard Rose (Sun Lithographic Arts, Maui)

We gratefully acknowledge permission granted by Alcoholics Anonymous World Services, Inc., to quote from Conference Approved publications with source attributions. The publication of this volume does not imply affiliation with nor approval or endorsement from Alcoholics Anonymous World Services, Inc.

Publisher's Cataloging in Publication $^7/_{95}$
(Prepared by Quality Books Inc)
B., Dick.
  Design for living : the Oxford Group's contribution to early
A.A. / Dick B. ; with a foreword by T. Willard Hunter. -- Rev.
Paradise ed.
  p. cm.
  Includes bibliographical references and index.
  ISBN: 1-885803-02-8
  1. Oxford Group. 2. Alcoholics Anonymous--History. 3. Alcoholism--
Treatment--United States. I. Title
  HV5278.B17 1995   362.29287'092
            QBI94-1697

(previously published by Good Book Publishing Company, ISBN: 1-881212-02-5; and Glen Abbey Books, ISBN: 0-934125-30-9; previous title: The Oxford Group & Alcoholics Anonymous: An A.A.-Good Book Connection)

Library of Congress Catalog Card Number: 94-068063

As I grew, however, I began to find the reality of religion. And as I found that I not only could be born in Christ but could grow in Him day by day and hour by hour, I saw that this reality provided an "escape" . . . not from life, but from death . . . not from the reality of life, but from the ugliness, delusion, and sin of life—an escape from the *un*realities of life and a finding of the underlying beauty, truth and goodness which go to make up God's real *"design for living"* [emphasis added].

Victor C. Kitchen
I Was a Pagan

We, in turn, sought the same escape [a vital spiritual experience] with all the desperation of drowning men. What seemed at first a flimsy reed, has proved to be the loving and powerful hand of God. A new life has been given us or, if you prefer, *"a design for living"* [emphasis added].

Alcoholics Anonymous, 3rd ed.

Contents

Foreword

Dick B. has pulled together a most amazing piece of research on the spiritual origins of the Twelve Step movement, particularly as found in the Oxford Group, from which it sprang.

This volume is of particular relevance in the decade of the 1990's when both Alcoholics Anonymous and Moral Re-Armament (the name by which the Oxford Group has been called since 1938) are in a stepped-up search for their spiritual roots and for the personal renewal that has been their historic contribution.

A.A. separated from the Oxford Group in two stages, in 1937 and in 1939. Separation is always painful, and usually regretted. But history has borne out the wisdom of Bill W. and Dr. Bob in finding their own milieu in the 1930's, separate from the parent Oxford Group movement. They had a divine calling, and they obeyed, which after all, the Oxford Group's initiator, Frank Buchman, held as his aim for every one. The heart of his message was: "When a person listens, God speaks; when a person obeys, God acts." God certainly acted in an extraordinary way through Bill and Bob. The miracle could probably not have happened had they stayed in the other fold.

Still, we are all in the same family and dedicated to people becoming different. We also have the wider confidence, as Lois W. believed, that "these principles will one day save our troubled world."

Dick B. is making a most important contribution, and I am honored to have been included in a small way. The way of life he describes in *Design for Living* makes everything new for those who really try it. Let us pray that the words between these covers will reach many hearts and stir many wills to action: action that will result in new directions for people, for communities, and for our troubled world.

T. WILLARD HUNTER

Mr. Hunter is a newspaper columnist, platform orator, and ordained minister. In the 1940's and 1950's, he was a close associate of Frank Buchman, initiator of the Oxford Group (and Moral Re-Armament), and has written and spoken extensively on related matters. He is co-author of "AA's Roots in the Oxford Group," a brief account issued to inquirers by A.A. General Services in New York. His latest publication is *It Started Right There*, subtitled "Behind the Twelve Steps and the Self-Help Movement." He is also the author of *The Spirit of Charles Lindbergh*. He and his wife Mary Louise live in Claremont, California.

Preface

This title revises the earlier study I wrote on the Oxford Group aspect of the spiritual history of early A.A. Over four years ago, I set out, at A.A.'s International Convention in Seattle, to learn the specific content of A.A.'s basic spiritual ideas and why they were so successful in the earliest years. In the late 1930's, these ideas produced a seventy-five percent success rate with "medically incurable" alcoholics who really tried to recover. I felt and feel the information is worth investigating in depth and passing on to others. And the quest took me to libraries; archives; A.A. points of origin such as Calvary Church, Calvary House, Hartford Seminary, Princeton University, Stepping Stones in New York, and Dr. Bob's Home in Akron; *and* to the families and survivors of A.A.'s founders, the Oxford Group's founders, and the many A.A. and Oxford Group oldtimers I have met.

A.A. co-founder, Dr. Bob, was the Bible student and reader. Therefore, I started with his family and the books he owned, studied, and circulated. Hence, my first title: *Dr. Bob's Library*. Then, I discovered that Dr. Bob's wife, Anne, had actually recorded and shared with Bill W., Dr. Bob, the early Akron AAs, and their families the material all were studying in the Bible, Christian literature of the day, and the Oxford Group, of which A.A. was an integral part in its formative years in New York and Akron. Hence, my second title, *Anne Smith's Spiritual Workbook* (now revised and titled, *Anne Smith's Journal*). At that point, I turned my efforts to the Oxford Group itself. Hence, *The Oxford Group & Alcoholics Anonymous*, of which this current title is a revision. This title was followed by *The Akron Genesis of Alcoholics Anonymous*, *The Books Early AAs Read*, and *New Light on Alcoholism: The A.A. Legacy from Sam Shoemaker*, plus a short work, *Courage to Change*, which Bill Pittman and I did involving primarily quotes from Sam Shoemaker's books.

But there was need for much more work on the Oxford Group. Many of the Oxford Group people, who were much involved with Frank Buchman, Sam Shoemaker, and Oxford Group activities in the 1930's, are still alive, but growing old. They needed to be contacted and interviewed. There were many more Oxford Group titles of the 1920's and 1930's than I first knew about; and these needed to be dug out and studied. The murky historical details about Sam Shoemaker, Bill Wilson, and early A.A. needed to be unearthed, studied, and correlated with other historical facts—and while Shoemaker's family still survived. And I did these things.

The objective was to learn where the Oxford Group came from, what it believed, the nature and extent of early A.A.'s participation in it, the influence it had on A.A. founders, and the words, phrases, and ideas that reached A.A. from the Oxford Group. And the study needed to be correlated with the material learned on the other aspects of A.A. history. A.A. needs to know where it came from and what its own expressions meant to those for whom it worked so well in the beginning.

I believe this revised title brings a major part of A.A.'s early spiritual history and successes into proper focus. The first chapter summarizes the roots of early A.A. ideas which came from sources other than Dr. Frank Buchman himself—sources such as the Bible, Sam Shoemaker, Anne Smith, the Bible devotionals AAs used, and the Christian literature of the day that they read. You will find much new material on Oxford Group mentors; much more information on the Oxford Group, Shoemaker, and Oxford Group activists; and much new information on Oxford Group meetings, houseparties, teams, and A.A. influence. Finally, we have included a completely new section on the tremendous number of Oxford Group ideas you can find in the Twelve Steps, the Big Book, and the actual language in A.A.

Acknowledgements

We here record our debt of gratitude to the many who made this work possible. We've listed most in our other titles; but our helpful resources keep growing in number.

First and foremost, there is my son, Ken, Biblical scholar, computer consultant, communications specialist, editor, and patient co-worker.

Then there are the leaders in the Oxford Group who know their own history and literature and contributed immensely to the author's efforts. They are the Rev. Harry Almond; K. D. Belden; Terry Blair; the Rev. Howard Blake; Charles D. Brodhead; Sydney Cook; Charles Haines; Michael Henderson; James Houck; T. Willard Hunter; Michael Hutchinson; Garth D. Lean; Dr. Morris Martin; Dr. R. C. Mowat; Eleanor Forde Newton; James D. Newton; Richard Ruffin; L. Parks Shipley, Sr.; George A. Vondermuhll, Jr.; and Ted Watt.

There are those connected with my research on the Rev. Sam Shoemaker, Jr. They include Dr. Shoemaker's wife, Helen; his daughters, Nickie Shoemaker Haggart, and Sally Shoemaker Robinson; the widow of Shoemaker's former assistant minister, Mrs. W. Irving Harris (a great admirer and associate of Sam Shoemaker's); the Rev. Dr. Thomas Pike, rector at The Parish of Calvary/St. George's; the Rev. Steve Garmey, Vicar at Calvary Church in New York; the Reverend Dr. Norman Vincent Peale; and David Sack at the Department of Religion in Princeton University. Also Messrs. Blake, Haines, Houck, Shipley, and Mr. and Mrs. Newton.

xvii

Special thanks to: the Reverend Richard L. McCandless, rector of St. Paul's Episcopal Church in Akron; Martha Baker; Dr. John Campbell; Leonard Firestone; Raymond Firestone; Robert Koch; the Thomas Pike Foundation; L. Parks Shipley, Sr.; Mrs. Walter Shipley, and R. Brinkley Smithers. Also to Beverly Kitchen Almond; Marjory Zoet Bankson at Faith at Work; the Rev. David Else at the Center for Spirituality in Pittsburgh; the Rev. Paul Everett at The Pittsburgh Experiment; the Rev. Tom Gray at NECAD; Mary Lean at *For A Change*; the Rev. Vern Myers at CECAD; Sarah Mullady at CASA; Dennis Wholey, and Dr. Paul Wood at NCADD.

Next there are A.A. leaders, archivists, historians, and scholars who have worked with the author and encouraged him all the way: Nell Wing, A.A.'s first archivist; Frank M., A.A.'s current archivist at General Services in New York; Ray G., archivist at Dr. Bob's Home; Gail L., Akron Founders Day archivist; Paul L., archivist at Stepping Stones, Bill and Lois W.'s home in New York; together with other dedicated archivists, historians, and oldtimers: David A., Mel B., Lyle B., Charlie B., Paul B., Dennis C., Earl H., Mitch K., Mike K., Dr. Ernest Kurtz, Joe McQ., Merton M., Tim M., Charlie P., Bob P., Bill Pittman, Ron R., Bill R., Robert R., Dave S., Sally S., Joe S., George T., Berry W., Charles W., Jim W., Bruce W., and Fay and Bob W.

There are the surviving families of A.A.'s founders: Dr. Bob's son, Robert R. Smith, and his wife, Elizabeth, and Dr. Bob's daughter, Sue Smith Windows. Also the children of Henrietta Seiberling—former Congressman, John F. Seiberling, and his sisters, Dorothy Seiberling, and Mary Seiberling Huhn; and Mrs. Dorothy Culver, daughter of T. Henry Williams.

There have been others in A.A. and elsewhere—particularly those in my own family: My daughter-in-law, Cindy, has been of immense help. My younger son, Don, and his wife, Julia, have been very supportive. My Bible fellowship friends and sponsees on Maui have provided much help for this edition: Chuck, Craig, Jeff, Matt, and Nathanael. Special thanks go to my sponsor, Henry B.

Many research resources have been provided by Hawaii public libraries in Honolulu, Kahului, Kihei, Makawao, and Wailuku; by the Seeley G. Mudd Manuscript Library at Princeton University; by the public library in Princeton; by the Enoch Pratt library in Baltimore; by the archives at Hartford Seminary; by Calvary Church Archives; by the archives at A.A. General Services, Dr. Bob's Home, Founders Day, and Stepping Stones; and by the seminary libraries at The Graduate Theological Union in Berkeley, Golden Gate Baptist Seminary in Tiburon, and San Francisco Theological Seminary in San Anselmo, California.

1

The Roots of Early A.A.'s Success Rate

As A.A. moves toward its 60th Anniversary and its International Convention at San Diego, California, in 1995, is there any value in looking back to the nature and origins of its spiritual roots and early successes? Can something be learned about how and why early A.A. achieved a seventy-five percent success rate among its first "medically incurable" alcoholics who really tried to recover? Can Twelve Step programs, recovery workers, therapists, public agencies, churches, and clergy work more successfully with those who want to recover today if the facts about the early spiritual sources are known? Can the principles and practices which Dr. Bob, the "Prince of Twelfth Steppers;" his wife, Anne, the "Mother of A.A.;" and the other Akron oldtimers used to help more than 5,000 alcoholics still be applied today? Or, is there a "new," "universal" recovery program that has evolved in Alcoholics Anonymous and other "self help" groups which no longer has use for information as to how A.A. began?

We'll try to provide some evidence on these subjects and let the reader decide on the answers. And, in this particular title in our series, we will focus primarily on what early A.A. took from "A First Century Christian Fellowship" (the Oxford Group)—of which A.A. was an integral part during its formative period beginning in January, 1933, and lasting until mid-1939.

"Nobody invented Alcoholics Anonymous." "Everything in A.A. is borrowed from somewhere else." So said Bill Wilson, the co-founder of Alcoholics Anonymous. And he said it frequently.[1]

Bill believed A.A.'s Twelve Steps were a group of principles—spiritual in their nature—which, if practiced as a way of life, could expel the obsession to drink and enable the sufferer to become happily and usefully whole.[2] The basic principles, he said, were borrowed mainly from the fields of religion and medicine.[3] He admonished that, as a society, AAs should never become so vain as to suppose they had been the authors and inventors of a new religion. Each of A.A.'s principles, he said, "every one of them, has been borrowed from ancient sources."[4]

This is a book about one of A.A.'s major sources: "A First Century Christian Fellowship," also known as the "Oxford Group," and later as "Moral Re-Armament." The Oxford Group spawned most of A.A.'s spiritual principles—a fact accepted by A.A.'s founders and its "Conference Approved" literature.

About A.A.'s Oxford Group source, Bill Wilson said, "The basic principles which the Oxford Groupers had taught were ancient and universal ones, the common property of mankind."[5] And our book describes what the Oxford Group and Bill Wilson both characterized as a "design for living."[6] A design for living

---

[1] See *The Language of the Heart: Bill W.'s Grapevine Writings* (New York: The AA Grapevine, Inc., 1988), pp. 195-202; *As Bill See's It: The A.A. Way of Life...selected writings of A.A.'s co-founder* (New York: Alcoholics Anonymous World Services, Inc., 1967), p. 67; *Twelve Steps and Twelve Traditions* (New York: Alcoholics Anonymous World Services, 1952), p. 16; and Nell Wing, *Grateful to Have Been There: My 42 Years with Bill and Lois and the Evolution of Alcoholics Anonymous* (Park Ridge, IL: Parkside Publishing Corporation, 1992), p. 25.

[2] *Twelve Steps and Twelve Traditions*, p. 15.

[3] *Twelve Steps and Twelve Traditions*, p. 16.

[4] *Alcoholics Anonymous Comes of Age: a Brief History of A.A.* (New York: Alcoholics Anonymous World Services, Inc., 1957), p. 231.

[5] *A.A. Comes of Age*, p. 39.

[6] *Alcoholics Anonymous*, 3d ed. (New York: Alcoholics Anonymous World Services, Inc., 1976), p. 15. Compare pp. 28, 229, 381. Hereafter we refer to this title as the "Big Book," the name affectionately bestowed on their basic text by AAs themselves.

that really works, said Bill.[7] "God's real 'design for living'," said a popular American Oxford Group writer in the early A.A. days of the 1930's.[8]

Our first edition was titled *The Oxford Group & Alcoholics Anonymous*. We have revised that original material to include what we have learned from four years of additional research. In recent months and years, we have acquired new information and gained new insight about: (1) The Oxford Group itself; (2) The Reverend Sam Shoemaker, one of its major American leaders; (3) The reading and studies of A.A. co-founder, Dr. Bob (Robert H. Smith); (4) The writings and teachings which Dr. Bob's wife, Anne Smith, shared with early AAs and their families; and (5) The large amount of spiritual reading, practices, and activities of the early AAs in their meetings, homes, and personal lives as they developed their practical program of recovery.

A.A.'s Successes—Yesterday and Today

The importance of *all* early A.A.'s spiritual roots lies in the tremendous success rate the first AAs achieved as they utilized their root sources.

In the early 1930's, "real" alcoholics were often told of their general hopelessness and that they were "medically incurable."[9] The noted Swiss psychiatrist, Dr. Carl G. Jung, said to one of A.A.'s founding friends, Rowland Hazard, that he (Jung) had never seen "one single case (with the mind of a chronic alcoholic such as Hazard's) recover."[10] Several early AAs were told by the

---

[7] Big Book, p. 28.

[8] Victor C. Kitchen, *I Was a Pagan* (New York: Harper & Brothers, 1934), p. 167.

[9] See report of Frank Amos to John D. Rockefeller, Jr., in *DR. BOB and the Good Oldtimers* (New York: Alcoholics Anonymous World Services, Inc., 1980), p. 131; Big Book, pp. 7, 11, 27, 30, 307-08. The Big Book often refers to those who admit powerlessness over alcohol as "real alcoholics." See pp. 21, 23, 30, 31, 34, 35, 92, 109.

[10] Big Book, p. 27; *Pass It On* (New York: Alcoholics Anonymous World Services, Inc., 1984), pp. 381-86.

staff member of a world-renowned hospital, "There is no doubt in my mind that you were 100% hopeless, apart from divine help."[11]

Despite such imposing obstacles in those early, formative years, Alcoholics Anonymous achieved a remarkable success *rate*. Its Big Book said, "Of alcoholics who came to A.A. and really tried, 50% got sober at once and remained that way; 25% sobered up after some relapses, and among the remainder, those who stayed on with A.A. showed improvement."[12]

In his famous March 1, 1941, *Saturday Evening Post* article on Alcoholics Anonymous, Jack Alexander wrote:

> One-hundred-percent effectiveness with non-psychotic drinkers who sincerely want to quit is claimed by the workers of Alcoholics Anonymous. . . . As it is impossible to disqualify all borderline applicants, the working percentage of recovery falls below the 100-percent mark. According to A.A. estimation, fifty percent of the alcoholics taken in hand recover almost immediately; twenty-five percent get well after suffering a relapse or two; and the rest remain doubtful. This rate of success is exceptionally high. Statistics on traditional medical and religious cures are lacking, but it has been informally estimated that they are no more than two or three percent effective on run-of-the-mine cases.[13]

But A.A.'s early success rate was completely dependent upon the spiritual aspects of its program. This was a fact that Bill Wilson learned by comparing the results of his work in New York with the spirituality of A.A.'s program in the midwest.[14] Bill wrote:

---

[11] Big Book, p. 43.

[12] Big Book, p. xx; *DR. BOB*, p. 174.

[13] See reprint in full of the Jack Alexander article in A.A.'s *the Jack Alexander Article about AA* (New York: Alcoholics Anonymous World Services, Inc., 1991).

[14] When the author visited Bill's home at Stepping Stones, he located a fact sheet by Bill Wilson, dated November 2, 1954, which vividly portrayed Bill's frustration over failures. At page 2 of his fact sheet, Bill reported that in the three years from August 25,

(continued...)

I explain this at some length because I want you to be successful with yourself and the people with whom you work. We used to pussyfoot on this spiritual business a great deal more out here [in the New York area] and the result was bad, for our record falls quite a lot short of the performance of Akron and Cleveland, where there are now about 350 alcoholics, many of them sober 2 or 3 years, with less than 20% ever having had any relapse. Out there they have always emphasized the spiritual way of life as the core of our procedure and we have begun to follow suit in New York for the simple reason that our record was only half as good, most of the difficulties being directly attributable to temporizing over what it really takes to fix the drunks, *i.e., the spiritual.*[15]

However, the phenomenal seventy-five or eighty percent success rate in early A.A. was not to be the success rate of A.A.'s later years and certainly not the rate that exists today.

A.A.'s current archivist, Frank M., was recently the principal speaker at a large meeting in Marin County, California, at which the author also spoke. Frank estimated that, of those pouring into A.A. today, one-third are on their way out of A.A. within their first ninety days of participation. In 1961, ten years after his partner, Dr. Bob, had died, Bill Wilson wrote:

---

[14] (...continued)
1935, until 1939, "not a single one of them made a recovery in our house but we learned a lot about drunks." This should be contrasted with the successes Dr. Bob and Anne were having with the drunks they helped at the Smith home in Akron. In his fact sheet, Bill further stated, "By the close of 1936 a small but strong nucleus had been established at Akron and in New York. We had isolated out of towners like Fitz Mayo and Don McL., a banker who lived at Cohoes, New York. Scores, and I think hundreds were exposed to us. The failure rate was immense." Though Bill spoke of Akron *and* New York, the people he referred to [Fitz and Don McL.] were "New York" people. Elsewhere in this book, we quote Bill as to the successes he said Dr. Bob was achieving in the Akron area. See Bill Wilson, "Main Events: Alcoholics Anonymous Fact Sheet by Bill." November 2, 1954, Archives Room, Stepping Stones Archives, Bedford Hills, New York, p. 2.

[15] The foregoing quote is from private correspondence of Bill Wilson and is taken from Ernest Kurtz and Katherine Ketcham, *The Spirituality of Imperfection: Modern Wisdom from Classic Stories* (New York: Bantam Books, 1992), p. 110.

We can also take a fresh look at the problem of "no faith" as it exists right on our doorstep. Though three hundred thousand did recover in the last twenty-five years, maybe half a million more have walked into our midst, and then out again. No doubt some were too sick to make even a start. Others couldn't or wouldn't admit their alcoholism. Still others couldn't face up to their underlying personality defects. Numbers departed for still other reasons. Yet we can't well content ourselves with the view that all these recovery failures were entirely the fault of the newcomers themselves. Perhaps a great many didn't receive the kind of sponsorship they so sorely needed. We didn't communicate when we might have done so. So AAs failed them. Perhaps more often than we think, we still make no contact at depth with those suffering the dilemma of no faith.[16]

Charlie P. and Joe Mc.Q., two venerable AAs who conduct A.A. Big Book Seminars around the world, made some telling observations about the early statistics. They said:

If you look at the top of page xx in the Big Book, you'll see just how effective the book was when the fellowship's recovery program and the recovery program described in the book were the same. Page xx explains that AA grew by leaps and bounds. . . . Half of all the alcoholics who came to AA and seriously and sincerely tried to recover got sober immediately and stayed that way. Another 25 per cent sobered up a little more slowly. So in the beginning, when the fellowship program and the program of the Big Book were the same, it is estimated that 75% of the people who used the Twelve Step program and really tried to recover from the disease of alcoholism actually did. We wonder what the percentage is today. We doubt seriously if it's 50 percent, let alone 75 per cent. . . . The only thing that has really changed is the fellowship itself.[17]

---

[16] *The Language of the Heart*, p. 252.

[17] *A Program for You: A Guide to the Big Book's Design for Living* (Minnesota: Hazelden, 1991), p. 15. See also Joe McQ., *The Steps We Took* (Little Rock, Arkansas: August House Publishers, 1990), pp. 11, 175-78.

Those observations are *very conservative*, as any currently active A.A. can affirm. The author has attended almost two thousand A.A. meetings in many states; and the number of people who rise to claim lengthy sobriety on "sobriety calls" is astonishingly low. Sobriety celebrations, or "birthday meetings," or "chip" meetings, as they are sometimes described, start with a request for those with "24 hours" (without a drink) to raise their hand or stand. Then for those with "30 days;" then "60 days;" then "90;" then six months; then a year; and so on. And the deathly silence at most "chip" meetings, which occurs upon the call for those with more than three or four years is appalling.

A.A.'s critics have reached similar conclusions. Some have estimated today's success rate at somewhere between 1.3 percent and 10.8 percent.[18] One current state A.A. archivist observed:

> One survey question revealed that out of 100 newcomers, only 4 to 6 were able to maintain their newfound sobriety for a year. The vast majority slipped! This was not the case in AA's early years.[19]

So, before we look back to "A.A.'s early *years*," we present this major reason for our study of A.A.'s *spiritual origins*. And that reason has been articulated over and over by A.A.'s current archivist, Frank M., who quotes Carl Sandburg as follows:

> Whenever a civilization or society declines, there is always one condition present. They forgot where they came from.[20]

---

[18] See Charles Bufe, *Alcoholics Anonymous: Cult or Cure* (San Francisco: Sharp Press, 1991), pp. 108-09; and William L. Playfair, *The Useful Lie* (Wheaton, IL: Crossway Books, 1991), pp. 22-23, 64-71.

[19] Charles Bishop, Jr. & Bill Pittman, *To Be Continued. . . . . The Alcoholics Anonymous World Bibliography 1935-1994* (Wheeling West Virginia: The Bishop of Books, 1994), p. xiii.

[20] The author has personally heard this quote by Frank M. at a number of different A.A. Conferences; and Frank recently informed the author on the phone that he believed his quote came from the national archives building in Washington, D.C.

The author is an active, recovered member of A.A. He has sponsored more than sixty men in their recovery. He still works with A.A. newcomers at almost every A.A. meeting he attends. And he believes, from his own sustained recovery in A.A., and from observing the life-changes in the men he has sponsored, that active participation in the A.A. Fellowship, a thorough knowledge of A.A.'s Big Book, a diligent effort to take and practice A.A.'s Twelve Steps, and a well-directed program of spiritual growth—based on the spiritual verities the early AAs learned from A.A.'s root sources—will still (1) expel the obsession to drink, (2) insure recovery, and (3) enable a life that is more than abundant.

Now to the roots.

The Varied Sources of A.A.'s Basic Ideas

A.A.'s spiritual roots were several in number. Not all that clear. Not separate and distinct. And not just in the Oxford Group. Hence before we study the Oxford Group as a major source of A.A.'s spiritual ideas, we need to summarize the *other* sources. Those that have been acknowledged. Those that have been mentioned. Those that have scarcely been mentioned. Those that may have had some impact, but probably not on the original form and content of A.A.'s Twelve Steps and Big Book. And those that have been claimed but, from an historical standpoint, we leave to others to prove or disprove because they lack of relevance to the original program of recovery which still stands virtually unchanged from the form set forth in A.A.'s basic text in the spring of 1939.

For it is the original recovery program, the one with the seventy-five percent success rate, that we will examine here from the perspective of its Oxford Group origins. We have left, and leave, to some of our other titles a thorough exploration and exposition of the other roots. Here we present the following outline of them.

The Bible

You cannot examine any of the sources of A.A.'s spiritual principles without examining the Bible as well.

Bill Wilson said, many times and in many ways, that the spiritual substance of almost all of A.A.'s Twelve Steps came from the teachings of the Reverend Sam Shoemaker, rector of Calvary Episcopal Church in New York.[21] Bill called Shoemaker a "co-founder" of A.A.[22] Shoemaker's long-time friend and assistant minister, the Reverend W. Irving Harris, described Shoemaker as a "Bible Christian." He said Shoemaker's church was the place to learn "How to find God. How to pray. How to read the Bible. How to pass faith on."[23] And Shoemaker himself wrote endlessly on the importance of the Bible and the study of it.[24] Hence Bill's frequent, early exposure to Sam Shoemaker, Shoemaker's meetings, and Shoemaker's circle of friends quite simply must have meant exposure to the Bible.

A similar situation existed as to other A.A. sources in the Oxford Group. Dr. Frank N. D. Buchman's biographer described Buchman (the Oxford Group's founder) as being "soaked in the Bible."[25] And the Reverend Sherwood Day's pamphlet, *The Principles of The Oxford Group*, stated, "The principles of 'The Oxford Group' are the principles of the Bible."[26]

---

[21] See Dick B., *New Light on Alcoholism: The A.A. Legacy from Sam Shoemaker* (Corte Madera, CA: Good Book Publishing Company, 1994), pp. 3-4, 9, 34-35.

[22] Letter from William G. Wilson to S.M. Shoemaker, dated April 23, 1963, quoted in full in Dick B., *New Light on Alcoholism*, p. 3.

[23] Irving Harris, *The Breeze of the Spirit: Sam Shoemaker and the Story of Faith-at-Work* (New York: The Seabury Press, 1978), pp. 15, 17-18, 25.

[24] Samuel M. Shoemaker, Jr., *Realizing Religion* (New York: Association Press, 1921), pp. 65-66; *The Conversion of the Church* (New York: Fleming H. Revell, 1932), pp. 49, 60, 79; *Children of the Second Birth* (New York: Fleming H. Revell, 1927), p. 97; and *Twice-Born Ministers* (New York: Fleming H. Revell, 1929), p. 184.

[25] Garth Lean, *On the Tail of a Comet: The Life of Frank Buchman* (Colorado Springs: Helmers & Howard, 1988), p. 157.

[26] Sherwood Sunderland Day, *The Principles of the Oxford Group* (Oxford University: The Oxford Group, n.d.), p. 1.

The daily meditation books which were so widely used in early A.A. were grounded on a Bible verse to be studied each day.[27] The Bible was also the principal subject matter of the other Christian literature that early AAs were reading as they developed their recovery program and sought spiritual growth.[28]

But it was the Bible itself—not the books about it—that was the principal focus of early A.A. reading and meetings. It was a major source of A.A.'s ideas. Following are remarks by A.A.'s founders and Conference Approved literature corroborating this fact.

A.A. co-founder, Dr. Bob, modestly said:

> It wasn't until 1938 that the teachings and efforts and studies that had been going on were crystallized in the form of the Twelve Steps. I didn't write the Twelve Steps. I had nothing to do with the writing of them. But I think I probably had something to do with them indirectly. After my June 10th episode, Bill came to live at our house and stayed for about three months. There was hardly a night that we didn't sit up until two or three o'clock talking. It would be hard for me to conceive that, during those nightly discussions around our kitchen table, nothing was said that influenced the writing of the Twelve Steps. We already had the basic ideas, though not in terse and tangible form. We got them, as I said, as a result of our study of the Good Book. We *must* have had them. Since then, we have learned from experience that they are very important in maintaining sobriety. We *were* maintaining sobriety—therefore, we must have had them.[29]

---

[27] See Dick B., *The Akron Genesis of Alcoholics Anonymous: An A.A.-Good Book Connection* (Corte Madera, CA: Good Book Publishing Company, 1994), p. 212. Excerpts from four of the principal devotionals, *The Upper Room, My Utmost for His Highest, Daily Strength for Daily Needs,* and *Victorious Living* will be found at pages 349-56 of *The Akron Genesis.*

[28] See Dick B., *Dr. Bob's Library: Books for Twelve Step Growth* (San Rafael, CA: Paradise Research Publications, 1994); *Anne Smith's Journal. 1933-1939: A.A.'s Principles of Success* (San Rafael, CA: Paradise Research Publications, 1994); and *The Books Early AAs Read for Spiritual Growth* (San Rafael, CA: Paradise Research Publications, 1994).

[29] *The Co-Founders of Alcoholics Anonymous: Biographical sketches. Their last major talks* (New York: Alcoholics Anonymous World Services, Inc., 1972, 1975), p. 10.

When we started in on Bill D. [A.A. #3], we had no Twelve Steps, either; we had no Traditions. But we were convinced that the answer to our problems was in the Good Book. To some of us older ones, the parts that we found absolutely essential were the Sermon on the Mount, the thirteenth chapter of First Corinthians, and the Book of James.[30]

Dr. Bob's wife, Anne Ripley Smith, whom Bill Wilson called a "founder" of A.A. and the "Mother of A.A.," kept a journal from 1933 to 1939 in which she recorded the spiritual ideas the founders were then studying.[31] Anne frequently shared the contents of this journal with the early AAs and their families who came to the birthplace of A.A. at the Smith home in Akron.[32] Both Anne and Dr. Bob read the Bible daily; and Anne shared the following from her journal with those she and Dr. Bob helped:

Of course the Bible ought to be the main Source Book of all. No day ought to pass without reading it.[33]

Quoting Bill Wilson as to Anne's emphasis on Scripture reading, A.A.'s *DR. BOB and the Good Oldtimers* said:

"For the next three months, I lived with these two wonderful people," Bill said. "I shall always believe they gave me more than I ever brought them." Each morning, there was a devotion, he recalled. After a long silence, in which they awaited inspiration and guidance, Anne would read the Bible. "James was our favorite," he said. "Reading from her chair in the corner, she would softly conclude, 'Faith without works is dead.'" This was

---

[30] *Co-Founders*, p. 9.

[31] As to Bill Wilson's remarks about Anne as an A.A. "founder" and as the "Mother of A.A.," see *The Language of the Heart*, pp. 353-54; Bob Smith and Sue Smith Windows, *Children of the Healer* (Illinois: Parkside Publishing Corporation, 1992), pp. 29, 43, 132; Dick B., *The Akron Genesis*, pp. 107, 108, 123; and *Anne Smith's Journal*, p. 10.

[32] Dick B., *The Akron Genesis*, pp. 110, 133.

[33] Dick B., *Anne Smith's Journal*, p. 60.

a favorite quotation of Anne's, much as the Book of James was a favorite with early A.A.'s—so much so that "The James Club" was favored by some as a name for the Fellowship.[34]

Wilson also has been quoted as stating:

We much favored the Apostle James. The definition of love in Corinthians also played a great part in our discussions.[35]

Wilson made some remarks about *himself* which illustrated the importance to him of the Bible as a source. He said:

[During an interview of T. Henry and Clarace Williams:] I learned a great deal from you people, from the Smiths themselves, and from Henrietta [Seiberling]. I hadn't looked into the Bible, up to this time, at all. You see, I had the [conversion] experience first and then this rushing around to help drunks and nothing happened.[36]

For a great many of us have taken to reading the Bible. It could not have been presented at first, but sooner or later in his second, third, or fourth year, the A.A. will be found reading the Bible quite as often—or more—as he will a standard psychological work.[37]

A.A.'s Conference Approved Literature said this:

This [from 1935 forward] was the beginning of A.A.'s "flying-blind period." They had the Bible, and they had the precepts of

---

[34] *DR. BOB*, pp. 71, 213.

[35] Ernest Kurtz, *Not-God: A History of Alcoholics Anonymous*. Exp. ed. (Minnesota: Hazelden, 1991), p. 320, n.11.

[36] From the transcript of Bill Wilson's taped interview with T. Henry and Clarace Williams on December 12, 1954, which transcript is on file in A.A. Archives in New York, and from which the author obtained the quote during his visit to the archives.

[37] W. W., Lecture 29, *The Fellowship of Alcoholics Anonymous* (Yale Summer School of Alcohol Studies: Quarterly Journal of Studies on Alcohol, 1945), p. 467.

the Oxford Group. They also had their own instincts. They were working, or working out, the A.A. program—the Twelve Steps—without quite knowing how they were doing it.[38]

The Bible was stressed as reading material, of course.[39]

Dr. Bob was the first group leader I heard refer simply and without ostentation to God. He cited the Sermon on the Mount as containing the underlying spiritual philosophy of A.A.[40]

Hence many Bible words, phrases, and ideas almost inevitably found their way directly into A.A.'s Big Book and other literature.[41]

Perhaps symbolic of this major A.A. source is the fact that Dr. Bob's own Bible is still, to this very day, brought to the podium of every meeting of A.A.'s first group, the King School Group in Akron. And it there remains throughout the meeting—a tradition the author personally observed when he attended the King School Group's meeting with Dr. Bob's daughter.[42]

The Reverend Samuel Moor Shoemaker, Jr.

Our own research has confirmed what Bill Wilson often said, but never really described in depth. The Reverend Canon Samuel

---

[38] *DR. BOB*, p. 96.

[39] *DR. BOB*, p. 151.

[40] *DR. BOB*, p. 228.

[41] See, for examples of these words and phrases, Dick B., *Dr. Bob's Library*, pp. 92-94.

[42] Dick B., *The Akron Genesis*, p. 210. *DR. BOB* states the following at page 228: "Dr. Bob donated the Bible to the King School Group where it still rests on the podium at each meeting. Inside is an inscription: 'It is the hope of the King School Group—whose sobriety [the actual inscription says *property*] this is—that this Book may never cease to be a source of wisdom, gratitude, humility, and guidance, as when fulfilled in the life of the Master.' It is signed 'Dr. Bob Smith.'" Dr. Bob's daughter, Sue Smith Windows, provided the author with a picture of this Bible and the inscription and called attention to the error mentioned above.

Moor Shoemaker, Jr., D.D., S.T.D., rector of Calvary Episcopal Church in New York City, was a major source of the spiritual ideas incorporated into A.A.'s Twelve Steps and Big Book.

Early on in our investigation, it had seemed to us that Bill Wilson credited Sam Shoemaker as a major source of A.A. ideas more to deflect attention from the Oxford Group than to pinpoint Shoemaker as the principal source of those ideas. Thus A.A.'s own Conference Approved biography of Wilson had said:

> While Bill was always generous in recognizing A.A.'s debt to the Oxford Group, he would always tie the Oxford Group connection to Dr. Shoemaker.[43]

And we can see from some of the following statements by Bill just how this approach was accomplished.

However, our research for *New Light on Alcoholism: The A.A. Legacy from Sam Shoemaker* showed the direct link between Sam Shoemaker, Bill Wilson, and the ideas developed in early A.A. before its Big Book and Twelve Steps were written.[44] Our investigation of Shoemaker's writing, his correspondence with Bill Wilson in the 1930's, and his personal journals, which were made available to us by his daughters, established a very close teacher-student relationship.

And that relationship was initiated by Bill; for Bill assisted Sam Shoemaker in Shoemaker's work with drunks from the earliest days of Bill's sobriety.[45] Shoemaker's personal journals recorded that Bill met and worked with Shoemaker from late December of 1934 to at least 1936.[46] Later in the 1930's, Bill met with

---

[43] *Pass It On*, p. 174.

[44] See Dick B., *New Light on Alcoholism*; also Samuel M. Shoemaker, *Courage to Change: The Christian Roots of the 12-Step Movement*. Compiled and edited by Bill Pittman and Dick B. (Grand Rapids, Michigan: Fleming H. Revell, 1994).

[45] Dick B., *New Light on Alcoholism*, p. 323.

[46] Dick B., *New Light on Alcoholism*, pp. 329-32. Since the publication of *New Light* in early 1994, the Shoemaker family have found still more of Shoemaker's journals; and

(continued...)

Shoemaker in Shoemaker's book-lined study and often discussed Christian principles relevant to A.A.[47] Bill participated in an Oxford Group businessmen's team in New York of which Shoemaker was the principal leader.[48] There were many other early Shoemaker-Wilson-A.A. links; and the examination of all of Shoemaker's writings shows the close parallels between their contents and the writings and ideas of Bill Wilson. A fact which commanded the attention of at least one earlier researcher.[49]

Shoemaker himself said:

> Bill Wilson found his spiritual change in this House [Calvary House adjacent to Shoemaker's church in New York City] when the Oxford Group was at work here many years ago. I have had the closest touch with Bill from that day to this.[50]

> It happens that I have watched the unfolding of this movement [the fellowship of A.A.] with more than usual interest, for its real founder and guiding spirit, Bill W., found his initial spiritual answer at Calvary Church in New York, when I was rector there, in 1935.[51]

> I never forgot that I was one of those who read the first mimeographed copy of the first book [*Alcoholics Anonymous*]—I

---

[46] (...continued)
we believe these, when examined and analyzed, may further confirm the close Shoemaker-Wilson relationship of the 1930's, extending through the 1939 publication of A.A.'s Big Book.

[47] Dick B., *New Light on Alcoholism*, pp. 325-27.

[48] Dick B., *New Light on Alcoholism*, pp. 333-36.

[49] See Charles Taylor Knippel, *Samuel M. Shoemaker's Theological Influence on William G. Wilson's Twelve Step Spiritual Program of Recovery (Alcoholics Anonymous).* Dissertation. St. Louis University, 1987.

[50] Letter from Samuel M. Shoemaker to H. H. Brown, March 13, 1952, a copy of which the author personally inspected during his August, 1992, research visit to Bill's home at Stepping Stones, Bedford Hills, New York.

[51] From a sermon by Samuel M. Shoemaker, titled, "What the Church Has to Learn from Alcoholics Anonymous," reprinted in *And Thy Neighbor* (Waco, Texas: Word Books, 1967), pp. 24-25.

am afraid with considerable skepticism, for I was then under the shadow of the old group feeling that unless a thing were done directly under the auspices of the group, it was as good as not done at all.[52]

And we will here list two of Bill's many tributes to Shoemaker which seem to us, at this point in our research, to have been well corroborated by the evidence we found. Bill said:

The Twelve Steps of A.A. simply represented an attempted to state in more detail, breadth, and depth, what we had been taught—primarily by you [Sam Shoemaker]. Without this, there could have been nothing—nothing at all. . . . Though I wish the "co-founder" tag had never been hitched to any of us, I have no hesitancy in adding your name to the list![53]

Where did early AAs find the material for the remaining ten Steps? Where did we learn about moral inventory, amends for harm done, turning our wills and lives over to God? Where did we learn about meditation and prayer *and all the rest of it?* The spiritual substance of our remaining ten Steps came straight from Dr. Bob's and my own early association with the Oxford Groups, as they were then led in America by that Episcopal rector, Dr. Samuel Shoemaker [emphasis added].[54]

The latter remark confirms Bill's accreditation of Shoemaker; but it also points to the Oxford Group link about which we shall have much to say in a moment and then in detail throughout the rest of this, our study of "The Oxford Group & Alcoholics Anonymous."

---

[52] Letter from Samuel M. Shoemaker to William G. Wilson, August 5, 1953, a copy of which the author personally inspected during his August, 1992, research visit to Bill's home at Stepping Stones.

[53] Letter from William G. Wilson to S. M. Shoemaker, dated April 23, 1963, a copy of which was supplied to the author by Shoemaker's daughter, Sally Shoemaker Robinson.

[54] *The Language of the Heart*, p. 198.

Meditation Books, Quiet Time and God's Guidance

The student of early A.A.'s spiritual history who merely looks to the Bible, to the Oxford Group, to Bill Wilson's friends in the clergy, and to Christian literature of the 1930's will miss an important part of the picture.

Early AAs believed they could be and were *directly* guided by God. They believed they could receive definite, accurate information from God. They had many guidance tools to help them on their way; and their convictions can still be found firmly embedded in the language of A.A.'s Eleventh Step and the Big Book's discussion of that step. The Eleventh Step states:

> Sought through prayer and meditation to improve our conscious contact with God *as we understood Him*, praying only for knowledge of His will for us and the power to carry that out.

The very titles of the guidance books used by early AAs give strong indication of the process they employed. Sam Shoemaker's parish magazine, *The Calvary Evangel*, contained an "Oxford Group Literature List" before, during, and after the years from 1933 to 1939. It recommended a tiny pamphlet by Hallen Viney, titled, *How Do I Begin?*[55] The Reverend Howard J. Rose wrote an equally tiny pamphlet titled *The Quiet Time*, and it was also included in Calvary's recommended literature list.[56] Eleanor Napier Forde had, in 1930, written for the Oxford Group *The Guidance of God*; and Miss Forde's thoughts were quoted by Dr. Bob's wife in her Journal.[57] Burnett Hillman Streeter, an Oxford theologian, had written *The God Who Speaks*.[58] Cecil Rose wrote

---

[55] Hallen Viney, *How Do I Begin?* (New York: The Oxford Group, 1937).

[56] Rev. Howard J. Rose, *The Quiet Time* (6 The Green, Slaugham, Hayward's Heath, Sussex, n.d.)

[57] Eleanor Napier Forde, *The Guidance of God* (Oxford: The Oxford Group, 1930). And see Dick B., *Anne Smith's Journal*, pp. 66, 76.

[58] Burnett Hillman Streeter, *The God Who Speaks* (London: Macmillan & Co., 1943). The first edition was published in 1936.

When Man Listens.[59] Jack Winslow wrote an article for *The Calvary Evangel*, titled "Vital Touch with God: How to Carry on Adequate Devotional Life;" and he also wrote *When I Awake.*[60] And Donald W. Carruthers wrote a pamphlet often mentioned by Sam Shoemaker and titled *How to Find Reality in Your Morning Devotions.*[61]

As we cover in much more detail later, early AAs usually observed "Quiet Time," which included morning Bible study, reading from a page of a daily Bible devotional, "two-way" prayer (which meant asking God for guidance and listening for His message), writing down the thoughts received, and "checking" (a procedure we'll discuss in some detail and which, at times, was much criticized in some early A.A. quarters).

In *The Akron Genesis of Alcoholics Anonymous*, we covered just how early AAs observed Quiet Time and utilized Bible study, meditation books, two-way prayer, notebooks, and so on.[62] The AAs sought and felt they received information from God; and the information they received cannot directly be verified in our study.

For their assistance, early AAs employed a number of daily Bible devotionals. Most contained a verse for study, some references to other Bible verses, a meditation thought, and a prayer. The principal devotionals were the Methodist quarterly known as *The Upper Room*, Oswald Chambers' *My Utmost for His Highest*, Mary Wilder Tileston's *Daily Strength for Daily Needs*, and *Victorious Living* by E. Stanley Jones.[63] None of this literature was "Oxford Group" or "Shoemaker," though some of it was used by both sources.

---

[59] Cecil Rose, *When Man Listens* (New York: Oxford University Press, 1937).

[60] Jack C. Winslow, "Vital Touch with God: How to Carry on Adequate Devotional Life," *The Evangel* (8 East 40th Street, New York, n.d.); and *When I Awake* (London: Hodder & Stoughton, 1938).

[61] Donald W. Carruthers, *How to Find Reality in Your Morning Devotions* (Pennsylvania: State College, n.d.).

[62] See, for example, Dick B., *The Akron Genesis*, pp. 203-15.

[63] For a discussion of the use of these daily Bible devotionals and a list of all of them, see Dick B., *The Akron Genesis*, pp. 181-215, 343-44, 349-55, 385.

The exact impact of these meditation books, of Quiet Time, and of God's direct guidance is seldom discussed in A.A. history studies. Yet A.A.'s Steps and literature contain recognizable evidence of early meditation, Quiet Time, and guidance ideas. And we have treated and will treat these important items at length in other titles.

Anne Smith's Journal: 1933-1939

As we've said, Bill Wilson frequently called Dr. Bob's wife, Anne Ripley Smith, the "Mother of A.A." On her death, Bill added, "In the full sense of the word, she was one of the founders of Alcoholics Anonymous."[64] He often spoke of morning devotions at the Smith home, during which Anne read to Bill and Dr. Bob from the "Good Book."[65] He said that, in the summer of 1935, when he was living with Dr. Bob and Anne, "Anne and Henrietta infused much needed spirituality into Bob and me."[66]

Yet with all these accolades directed at Anne Smith, a vital, detailed historical document, which contains sixty-four pages of information about Anne and her contribution, has lain virtually unnoticed for years. That source is the spiritual journal Anne compiled in the years between 1933 and 1939 and read to AAs and their families as those people came to A.A.'s Akron birthplace for "spiritual pablum."[67] This set of notes was referred to in a footnote of Dr. Ernest Kurtz's history of Alcoholics Anonymous.[68] It was mentioned in a title about Sister Ignatia, who worked with Dr. Bob in his later A.A. years.[69] And Dr.

---

[64] *The Language of the Heart*, p. 354.

[65] *The Language of the Heart*, p. 356.

[66] *The Language of the Heart*, p. 357.

[67] Dick B., *The Akron Genesis*, p. 110.

[68] Kurtz, *Not-God*, p. 331, n.32.

[69] Author Mary Darrah commented, "In addition to reading passages from Holy Scripture to the newly sober men, she [Anne Smith] read from her own Oxford Group notebook, disclosing the personally meaningful ideas and spiritual guidance she had

(continued...)

Bob's daughter, Sue Smith Windows, touched on the importance of Anne's Journal in the story Sue and her brother wrote about their own lives.[70] But the full significance of this journal was not apparent to us until a copy of it was made available to us by A.A. General Services in New York through the good offices of Dr. Bob's daughter.

Even then, our first discussion of the journal bought into the idea that it was an "Oxford Group" workbook or notebook.[71] Later, however, many readers asked us for more material on what Anne herself had actually said. We again reviewed the contents of the sixty-four page journal; and we saw from a new perspective how much of Anne's thinking, words, and language had, *in fact*, been infused into Bill and Dr. Bob and had *in fact* found their way into the Twelve Steps and Big Book of Alcoholics Anonymous.

Our revised edition of the Anne Smith notes and journal tells the full story.[72] We will not here repeat the material in that title. Suffice it to say, however, that Anne's words on the unmanageable life, lack of power, God "as you know Him," "one day at a time," self-examination, confession, conviction, conversion, restitution, the guidance of God, the "spiritual experience," passing on the message, and the practice of spiritual principles can be found throughout her journal and throughout A.A. language and literature.

Anne's journal, therefore, seems to us to be a major A.A. spiritual root which Anne herself culled from the Bible, the Oxford Group, the daily devotionals, the Shoemaker books, Christian

---

[69] (...continued)
gathered over the years." See Mary C. Darrah, *Sister Ignatia: Angel of Alcoholics Anonymous* (Chicago: Loyola University Press, 1992), pp. 115-16.

[70] Bob Smith and Sue Smith Windows, *Children of the Healer* (Illinois: Parkside Publishing, 1992) p. 29.

[71] See our earlier edition on Anne Smith's journal: Dick B., *Anne Smith's Spiritual Workbook: An AA-Good Book Connection* (Corte Madera, CA: Good Book Publishing Company, 1992).

[72] See Dick B., *Anne Smith's Journal 1933-1939: A.A.'s Principles of Success* (San Rafael, CA: Paradise Research Publications, 1994).

literature, and her own work with alcoholics and their families. It contains material she directly passed on to others in the Smith home and elsewhere in A.A.'s earliest formative days. Small wonder, then, that Bill Wilson referred to her as the "Mother of A.A." and a "co-founder."[73]

Other Possible Sources

Some AAs have believed their spiritual ideas can be found in non-Biblical and non-Christian sources. Yet even if that were the case, those were not the roots with which the founders worked or which they mentioned. There are, however, sources which did contribute ideas and which are not among those we've mentioned, and which do not involve the Oxford Group.

The first and most significant source involves the many Christian books, other than Oxford Group and Shoemaker books, which were read by early AAs.[74] Some of the titles were studied by Dr. Bob, Anne Smith, Henrietta Seiberling, and Mr. and Mrs. T. Henry Williams. Their probable influence lies not alone in the fact that they were read and circulated in early A.A., but in the fact that the Oxford Group people themselves did not have much of their own literature available in the formative years of A.A. There were a number of Sam Shoemaker books in the 1920's and early 1930's, but other significant Oxford Group books were not yet numerous in 1935. Hence Oxford Group adherents were themselves reading and "swapping" many other Christian titles, books by Oswald Chambers and other Christian writers of that day.

The most widely read authors [read by Oxford Group people and/or early AAs] were: James Allen, Oswald Chambers, Glenn Clark, Henry Drummond, Harry Emerson Fosdick, E. Stanley Jones, Toyohiko Kagawa, Charles Sheldon, and Leslie D.

---

[73] See Smith and Windows, *Children of the Healer*, pp. 29, 43.

[74] See Dick B., *The Books Early AAs Read for Spiritual Growth*; *Dr. Bob's Library*; and *The Akron Genesis*.

Weatherhead.[75] Some AAs also read the earlier Christian writers, St. Augustine, à Kempis, and Brother Lawrence, as well as works by writers on the life of Jesus Christ.[76]

A second possible source of A.A. ideas seems to us to have been given far too much attention. That source was Emmet Fox.[77] Emmet Fox was *not*, as many AAs believe today, a "member" of the Oxford Group; nor was Fox, despite the belief of some, in any way connected with the Oxford Group. Fox's ideas were, in fact, very contrary to those of Shoemaker, the Oxford Group, and the other Christian writers early AAs studied.[78] Both Dr. Bob and Bill Wilson studied or discussed Emmet Fox's books, but we found no mention of them in Anne Smith's Journal or during our investigation of Henrietta Seiberling's reading and beliefs. In other words, there was *interest* in Fox's writings, but not necessarily *input* from them. Many have possibly confused the "Sermon on the Mount," about which Dr. Bob spoke so much, and which can be found in Matthew, Chapters 5 to 7 of the Bible, with the book by Emmet Fox, *The Sermon on the Mount*.[79]

To be sure, AAs read Fox's books.[80] But they also read the Sermon on the Mount in the Bible. However, Dr. Bob studied a *number* of books on Jesus's Sermon on the Mount, including particularly those by Oswald Chambers, Glenn Clark, Emmet Fox, and E. Stanley Jones.[81]

Emmet Fox did not believe in the Biblical idea of salvation, or in the necessity of a decision to accept Jesus Christ as Lord and

---

[75] See Dick B., *The Books Early AAs Read for Spiritual Growth*.

[76] See Dick B., *Dr. Bob's Library*, pp. 25-28

[77] Note that, when Bill was writing "A Fragment of History: Origin of the Twelve Steps," in July of 1953, he never mentioned Emmet Fox. *The Language of the Heart*, pp. 195-202.

[78] See our discussion of this point in Dick B., *The Akron Genesis*, pp. 290-93.

[79] Emmet Fox, *The Sermon on the Mount* (New York: Harper & Row, 1934).

[80] See Dick B., *Dr. Bob's Library*, pp. 14, 21, 35, 36, 38, 39, 53, 59, 63, 64; and *The Books Early AAs Read*, pp. vii, 1, 6-7, 9-10, 26, 27.

[81] See Dick B., *The Akron Genesis*, p. 343; and *Dr. Bob's Library*, pp. 38-40.

Savior.[82] Yet these concepts were very much a part of early A.A. and Oxford Group-Shoemaker thinking.[83] We therefore believe that such influence as Fox may have had occurred *after* the battle over Big Book language which resulted in the elimination from the Big Book of all significant, specific mention of the Bible, Jesus Christ, and Christianity.[84]

Igor Sikorsky, Jr., attempted to make the case that Fox was one of A.A.'s "Godparents."[85] But Sikorsky cited no authority for any of influence he attributed to Fox. Sikorsky's evidence seems to rest on the fact that the mother of one of Bill Wilson's early alcoholic co-workers was also Emmet Fox's secretary. The problem is that Sikorsky was discussing a period *after* the writing and publication of A.A.'s Big Book.

A.A. historian Mel B. wrote of the influence of Fox on A.A.[86] Mel said: (1) Fox "influenced the pioneering AAs," (2) "the second AA member from Detroit, often mentioned the inspiration he received from Fox's book when he started his recovery in 1938," and (3) "*The Sermon on the Mount* became one of the society's most useful guides until the publication of *Alcoholics Anonymous* in 1939."[87] Mel added, "Bill Wilson freely acknowledged the importance of the book to AA. . . ."[88] Though this is strong language, we do not find the evidence in A.A.'s Big Book that backs up Fox's alleged influence.

That Fox has *had* an impact through the years seems undeniable. The author's own observations in A.A. establish that Fox's books are often read and that they are occasionally quoted

---

[82] See John 3; Romans 10:9-10. And compare Fox, *The Sermon on the Mount*, pp. 4-8, 13.

[83] As to early A.A., see Dick B., *The Akron Genesis*, pp. 118, 138, 140, 157-58, 187-88, 193-97, 209, 211, 219, 231-33, 250, 290-93, 318, 328-31.

[84] For discussion of the A.A. elimination process, see Kurtz, *Not-God*, p. 50.

[85] Igor Sikorsky, Jr., *A.A.'s Godparents* (Minnesota: CompCare Publishers, 1990).

[86] See Mel B., *New Wine: The Spiritual Roots of the Twelve Step Miracle* (Minnesota: Hazelden, 1991).

[87] Mel B., *New Wine*, pp. 5, 106, 111.

[88] Mel B., *New Wine*, p. 111.

in A.A. That Fox and his "new thought" ideas had any significant impact on A.A.'s Twelve Steps and Big Book is, however, a far more speculative and probably unproven idea.

We *have* found one expression which conforms to Fox's thinking. Fox said the Bible "teaches that every man or woman, no matter how steeped in evil and uncleanness, has always direct access to an all-loving, all-powerful Father-God, who will forgive him, and supply His own strength to him to enable him to find himself again; and unto seventy times seven if need be."[89] Coupled with Fox's assertion that there is no plan of salvation in the Bible, this establishes there is no need for accepting Jesus Christ as personal Lord and Savior or for being born again in the Biblical sense. And note that page 28 of the Big Book states, "[A]ll of us, whatever our race, creed, or color are children of a living Creator with whom we may form a relationship upon simple and understandable terms as soon as we are willing and honest enough to try." This idea seems popular in today's A.A.; and its appeal seems validated when AAs join together at the end of their meetings and commence the prayer, "Our Father."

But that was not the A.A. idea when Bill Wilson made a decision for Christ at Calvary Mission in 1934, when Bill and others in New York had their newcomers "give their lives to God," or when the alcoholic squad of the Oxford Group in Akron had newcomers "make surrender" in the years between 1935 and 1939.

The Oxford Group Roots Confirmed

In his last major address to A.A., Dr. Bob described his own and Bill's Oxford Group beginnings as follows:

> We had both been associated with the Oxford Group, Bill in New York for five months, and I in Akron, for two and a half years.

---

[89] Fox, *The Sermon on the Mount*, p. 5.

Bill had acquired their idea of service. I had not, but I had done an immense amount of reading they had recommended.[90]

Bill's biographer had the following to say about what Bill and Bob did with these roots:

They had both wound up trying to give shape and meaning to their lives by adhering to the excruciatingly high standards of the Oxford Group.[91]

All four of them [Bill and Lois Wilson and Bob and Anne Smith] were agreed that their efforts to find a practical program of recovery must be given top priority. They were agreed, but it was not an easy project. . . . But fortunately again—or so Bill and Bob believed at the time—there was the Oxford Group with its dynamic course of action all mapped out. They tried to base everything they did, every step they took toward formulating their program, on Oxford Group principles. And they both worked. They went daily to City Hospital, talked to drunks, brought some hopeful prospects back to live with them on Ardmore Avenue. They never stopped, and there were heady moments when their wildest hopes seemed justified.[92]

As Bill himself said, concerning this earliest trial and error period, he and Dr. Bob were tearing around, helping drunks, giving them "the Towns [Hospital] treatment," as to which Bill added, "That plus more oxidizing [probably short for "Oxfordizing"] has been magical."[93]

By 1940, Bill had developed a laundry list of reasons why he felt the Oxford Group presentation had to be abandoned. But he prefaced his statements with the following:

---

[90] *Co-Founders*, p. 7

[91] Robert Thomsen, *Bill W.* (New York: Harper & Row, Publishers, 1975), p. 239.

[92] Thomsen, *Bill W.*, p. 249.

[93] *DR. BOB*, p. 78.

I am always glad to say privately that some of the Oxford Group
presentation and emphasis upon the Christian message saved my
life.[94]

Bill later admitted that he had greatly feared Roman Catholic
critics, as far as disclosing Oxford Group origins was
concerned.[95] In his 1940 Oxford Group critique, Bill listed a bill
of particulars as to Oxford Group ideas which would not work. He
specified some eight Oxford Group "attitudes" which he felt had
required abandonment.[96] Then, despite his statement that he owed
a "very real debt of gratitude to the Oxford Group," Bill pointed
to a "vast and sometimes unreasoning prejudice [that] exists all
over this country against the O.G. and its successor M.R.A."
This, he said, was causing him to limit his public acknowledgement of the Oxford Group debt.[97]

Writing to Jack Alexander on January 6, 1941, about
Alexander's proposed *Saturday Evening Post* article on A.A., Bill
said, concerning "the Oxford Group situation":

I would give anything if you could avoid mentioning the matter
at all, but if it must be noted I'm quite anxious to avoid words

---

[94] *Pass It On*, p. 171. The material came from a letter Bill wrote to "Dear McGee,"
dated October 30, 1940.

[95] In a letter to the Reverend Sam Shoemaker, dated February 7, 1957, Bill spoke
of a talk he had had with his "spiritual sponsor," Father Ed Dowling. Bill said: "I told
him [Dowling] what you [Sam Shoemaker] and the O.G. had done for us and how
reluctant I had been all these years to publicly disclose it. Then I explained how prudence
had suggested that this be deferred because the Pope at one time had written off the O.G.
meetings for attendance of [Roman] Catholics." This same concern was evidenced in a
letter Bill wrote to "Dear Elmer," dated October 8, 1943, which stated: "In fact, I
believe the Pope, at about that time [the time the Big Book was being written] forbade
all [Roman] Catholics to go to Oxford Group meetings." In *Not-God*'s footnotes on pages
325 and 335, Dr. Ernest Kurtz disputed Bill's beliefs about the alleged *papal*
condemnation. Kurtz wrote: "According to John C. Ford, S.J., interview of 12 April
1977, as well as my reading of the Lunn book cited in note # 33, no such papal decree
existed, although there was strong [Roman] Catholic suspicion of the OG."

[96] *Pass It On*, pp 171-73.

[97] *Pass It On*, p. 175.

carrying criticism or sting. After all we owe our lives to the group.

In 1943, Bill said:

While I shall be eternally grateful to the Oxford Group for my own recovery, I cannot see the advantage of raising unnecessary prejudice.[98]

By 1955, Bill had begun to change his tune. He said at A.A.'s St. Louis Convention:

The basic principles which the Oxford Groupers had taught were ancient and universal ones, the common property of mankind. Certain of the former O.G. attitudes and applications had proved unsuited to A.A.'s purpose, and Sam's own conviction about these lesser aspects of the Oxford Groups had later changed and become more like our A.A. views of today. But the important thing is this: the early A.A. got its ideas of self-examination, acknowledgment of character defects, restitution for harm done, and working with others straight from the Oxford Groups and directly from Sam Shoemaker, their former leader in America, and from nowhere else.[99]

The Foreword to the Second Edition of the Big Book added a bit more to this picture, saying:

Though he [Bill Wilson] could not accept all the tenets of the Oxford Groups, he was convinced of the need for moral inventory, confession of personality defects, restitution to those harmed, helpfulness to others, *and the necessity of belief in and dependence upon God* [emphasis added].[100]

---

[98] Letter from Wilson to "Dear Elmer," dated October 8, 1943.

[99] *A.A. Comes of Age*, p. 39.

[100] Big Book, p. xvi.

Finally, in 1960, as we've previously written, Bill broadened his Oxford Group acknowledgement much further, stating that the spiritual substance of *almost all* the steps came from his and Dr. Bob's earlier association with the Oxford Group. Bill pointed out that AAs had learned about moral inventory, amends for harm done, turning wills and lives over to God, meditation and prayer "and all the rest of it" from the Oxford Group.[101]

A month after Oxford Group founder, Frank Buchman, died in 1961, Bill finally said, "Now that Frank Buchman is gone and I realize more than ever what we owe to him, I wish I had sought him out in recent years to tell him of our appreciation."[102]

When the time came for A.A.'s own "official" historians to report on Bill Wilson's utilization of Oxford Group principles and practices, they cast fear of "unnecessary prejudice" aside. In A.A.'s Conference Approved biography of Bill, the authors made observations like these:

> Criticism and rejection notwithstanding, Lois and Bill did not become immediately disillusioned with the Oxford Group or with its principles, *from which Bill borrowed freely* [emphasis added].[103]

> Bill was about to write the famous fifth chapter [of the Big Book], "How It Works." The basic material for the chapter was the word-of-mouth program that Bill had been talking ever since his own recovery. *It was heavy with Oxford Group principles. . . .* [emphasis added].[104]

> Bill's first three steps were culled from his reading of James, the teachings of Sam Shoemaker, *and those of the Oxford Group* [emphasis added].[105]

---

[101] *The Language of the Heart*, 198.

[102] *Pass It On*, pp. 386-87.

[103] *Pass It On*, p. 169.

[104] *Pass It On*, p. 197.

[105] *Pass It On*, p. 199.

We believe that when the reader has studied our book, he or she will realize precisely how, and to what a great extent Bill did in fact "borrow freely" and write a Big Book that was "heavy with Oxford Group principles."

A Summary of What the Oxford Group Is

In the early 1930's, the British journalist, A. J. Russell, wrote *For Sinners Only*.[106] This book immediately became extremely popular among Oxford Group adherents. And it also was widely used by Dr. Bob and the early Akron AAs to learn about the Oxford Group program. Russell had the following to say about the Oxford Group:

> God had a plan. They were trying to fit in with it. Knowledge of that plan, God's guidance and God's power were available for all who chose to work in with that plan. This guidance and power transcended every form of self-determination. God-guidance in God's strength could be the normal experience of everybody at all times (p. 23). . . .

> Not only has God a plan for every life, . . . but when, through sin we spoil that plan, God is always ready with another. . . . Unfortunately, most of us refused to follow the plan when we saw it, or, if unaware of it, to pray for the plan to be revealed. Our sin of sins, embodying all other sins, was independence towards God; doubting God's interest in us, that He had a plan for us, that He would show us the plan, and that He would help us to carry out the plan which was the only satisfactory plan for our lives (p. 27). . . .

> [T]hose who attempted to live without God's plan, as revealed by the Holy Spirit, were as certain to encounter disaster as those living under God's daily direction were certain of success. . . . My objection to this argument was human nature's chronic

---

[106] A. J. Russell, *For Sinners Only* (London: Hodder & Stoughton, Ltd., 1932).

inability to know when it was being guided. To that the Three [Troubadours] offered the answer of two-way prayer; petitions and quiet listening for the reply, especially in the morning when preparing for the day's work. They called this early morning listening to God "Quiet Times." The Oxford Group believed God spoke to them when they needed His guidance. . . . They emphasized that the condition of clear guidance was complete surrender of everything—will, time, possessions, family, ambitions—all to God. . . . It meant a handing over of our little in return for God's All-Sufficiency. . . . Accepting completely the discipline of God brought not bondage, but the fullest freedom to do what we wished—and that was always the Will of God. . . . I learned that it was a practice of the Group to keep a guidance-book and record in it those thoughts which came in periods of quiet listening to God. . . . Reaching back into the first century for their standards of Christian fellowship, they were ready to scrap any later practices they believed redundant or old-fashioned, and to substitute the earliest customs for something that met modern needs. They did much of their work through house-parties, where visitors shared their religious experiences and drew close to God (pp. 28-29).

. . . They were even so orthodox as to believe that everyone, parson as well as prodigal, must at some time come to himself, must experience the forgiveness of God through Jesus Christ. In short, the Cross was central in their teaching. At the Cross, man reached a turning-point when he decided to live as God directed and guided instead of according to his own human standards. Old-fashioned evangelicals called it conversion, but through misuse that word had for many minds lost its original potency, and so they preferred the simpler word "Change.". . . Those who sought to change others were called "Life-Changers" instead of evangelists (p. 30). . . .

They challenged the world to turn back to God, to cut out sin, to make restitution for past sins, and to let God take full command of every area of life, just as the early disciples challenged the world. . . . While the Group practiced social service, they felt man's deepest need was not money, but God, for those who truly sought first the Kingdom of Heaven had all other necessary things added unto them. That was their own experience. Men and women were keenly hungry for the true God, who was more ready to manifest Himself to them than they were to seek Him. The work of life-changing was never more necessary than now. . . . There was no joy in life so great as leading a prodigal home to his Heavenly Father, always half-way down the road to meet him. . . . Life-changing was contagious. . . . But How? . . . The best answer to the How of both sinner and potential Life-Changer was the Group custom of Sharing. Changed men might go wrong in trying to change others by argument, but they were on safe ground in recounting their own experiences as the Apostles recounted theirs. . . . Not emotional decisions, as witnessed in some of the old fashioned mass-revivals, but decisions taken in quiet heart-to-heart talks . . . telling their own experience of their indwelling Master . . . (pp. 31-33).

I was certainly getting the hang of what the Oxford Group were after. First, there was absolute Surrender, including Faith in the Cross of Christ, bringing Guidance by the Holy Spirit; then there was Sharing, bringing true Fellowship and shining faces; then Life-Changing, bringing in God's Kingdom and Joy, in Heaven, in the Sinner, and in the Life-Changer; then Faith and Prayer, bringing all things needful and helping forward God's plan to provide for everybody; also those four standards of Love, Honesty, Purity and Unselfishness on which Christ never compromised; and, of course, Restitution. Later I was to understand perhaps the strongest principle of all—Fearless Dealing with Sin. Meanwhile, there were two other principles easier to swallow—Teamwork and Loyalty. Jesus practiced teamwork. . . . Truth is presented more adequately through a team than through one individual. . . . Then there was the principle of Loyalty. First there must be supreme loyalty to Jesus Christ [and] . . . to those trying to live in loyalty to Christ. Above all, the Group was a Fellowship—a first-century Christian Fellowship controlled by the Holy Spirit (pp. 42-43).

Though several long-time Oxford Group activists have informed the author that the following title was not written by an

Oxford Group "member," *What Is The Oxford Group?* was owned
by Dr. Frank Buchman and circulated by him.[107] Several copies
were owned and circulated by Dr. Bob among early AAs.[108] And
the book had the following to say about the "structure" of the
Oxford Group:

> You cannot belong to the Oxford Group. It has no membership
> list, subscriptions, badge, rules, or definite location. It is a name
> for a group of people who, from every rank and profession, and
> trade, in many countries, have surrendered their lives to God and
> who are endeavoring to lead a spiritual quality of life under the
> guidance of the Holy Spirit. The Oxford Group is not a religion;
> it has no hierarchy, no temples, no endowments; its workers have
> no salaries, no plans but God's Plan; every country is their
> country. . . . Their aim is "A New World Order for Christ, the
> King." . . . The Oxford Group works within churches of all
> denominations, planning to bring those outside back into their
> folds and to re-awaken those within to their responsibilities as
> Christians. It advocates nothing that is not the fundamental basis
> of all Christian Faith, and takes no side in sectarian disputes.
> . . . The aims of the Oxford Group are to bring into the world
> the realization of the power of the Holy Spirit as a force for
> spiritual and material stability and betterment of the world; to
> awaken in us as individuals the knowledge that we are dissipating
> our spiritual inheritance and that Sin is the frustration of God's
> Plan for us all (pp. 3-6).

---

[107] See The Layman with a Notebook, *What Is The Oxford Group?* (London: Oxford
University Press, 1933). In a letter to the author of June 10, 1993, long-time Oxford
Group activist, K. D. Belden, wrote that he had met the "Layman with a notebook" on
two or three occasions. Belden said the author was a Roman Catholic writer who came
to an Oxford Group House Party in 1935 or 1936, and wrote *What Is The Oxford Group?*
Belden said, "The book was quite a competent, well written one within the limitations
of what the Layman had been able to gather on his fairly brief acquaintance, though it
was never one of our main books in those days." A.A. historian, Dennis C., wrote the
author that he had obtained a copy of the book with Buchman's inscription in it.

[108] The author has personally seen copies of this book in the possession of Dr. Bob's
family and also at Dr. Bob's Home in Akron. And two contain Dr. Bob's name and
address and one contains the request "Please return." All notations are in Dr. Bob's own
handwriting.

Some Oxford Group people have put together descriptions of the Group's early principles and program, and their work can be helpful in obtaining an adequate overview. Shoemaker's friend, the Reverend Sherry Day, wrote *The Principles of the Group*. Day's work was printed by the Oxford Group, and in Shoemaker's parish publication, *The Calvary Evangel*.[109] Jack Winslow wrote several pamphlets on the Group, including *Why I Believe in The Oxford Group*.[110] Clarence Benson, who was connected with the Group in the early 1930's, wrote *The Eight Points of the Oxford Group*; but the author has thus far discovered no evidence that Benson's book was widely read either by the people who influenced A.A. or by AAs themselves.[111] *What Is The Oxford Group?* also contains an accurate and succinct statement of the Oxford Group's principles and practices; but none of the present Oxford Group octogenarians has been able to come up with the name of "The Layman with a Notebook," its author.

The Oxford Group, A.A., and Finding God

AAs may have adopted some statements about finding God by Dr. Shoemaker and other Oxford Group writers. Page 59 of the Big

---

[109] Day, *The Principles of the Group*. See also a slightly different version of Day's principles in Harris, *The Breeze of the Spirit*, pp. 18-21. Commencing with the statement that The Oxford Group's principles were the principles of the Bible, Day then set forth the following seven Biblical principles: (1) God-Guidance; (2) Fearless dealing with Sin; (3) Sharing; (4) The necessity for adequate intelligent expressional activity; (5) Stewardship; (6) Team-work; and (7) Loyalty. And one can find Dr. Bob's wife, Anne Smith, discussing all of these ideas in the spiritual journal she read to early AAs. See Dick B., *Anne Smith's Journal*, pp. 40, 88, 112, 127-30.

[110] Jack C. Winslow, *Why I Believe in The Oxford Group* (London: Hodder & Stoughton, 1934).

[111] See Clarence Irving Benson, *The Eight Points of the Oxford Group* (London: Humphrey Milford, Oxford University Press, 1936). In his letter to the author of March 13, 1994, Dr. Morris Martin provided what little information about Benson that we have been able to locate.

Book stated emphatically: "But there is One who has all
power—that One is God. May you find Him now!"

Where did that come from?

In his first book, written in 1921, Dr. Sam Shoemaker wrote:

What you want is simply a vital religious experience. You need
to find God. You need Jesus Christ.[112]

Then at A.A.'s 20th Anniversary Convention at St. Louis, he said:

I would like to quote for those who believe themselves still to be
without faith in God a wonderful word from the Roman Catholic
Spanish philosopher Unamuno y Jugo, who said, "Those who
deny God deny Him because of their despair at not finding
Him."[113]

It is not surprising to find that Dr. Shoemaker was still, at the
end of his career, writing about *finding God*. Shoemaker devoted
an entire pamphlet to the subject, "How to Find God," reprinted
from the *Faith at Work* magazine. Shoemaker commenced:

How shall we find God? That means more than finding a belief
that God exists. It means knowing God for a certainty in our own
lives and experience.[114]

Dr. Leslie D. Weatherhead was a prolific writer in the 1930's.
His works on the Oxford Group and its principles can be found in
early A.A. collections.[115] In 1934, Weatherhead wrote:

---

[112] Shoemaker, *Realizing Religion*, p. 9.

[113] *AA Comes of Age*, p. 263.

[114] Samuel Moor Shoemaker, Jr., *How to Find God* (New York: Faith at Work, Inc.,
295 Madison Ave, New York, New York 10017, n.d.), p. 1. See also Shoemaker, "The
Way to Find God," *The Calvary Evangel*, August, 1935.

[115] We found a copy of Weatherhead's *Discipleship* in Bill Wilson's library at
Stepping Stones. The volume bore the name of Henrietta Seiberling, who apparently gave
it to Bill. Also, when we interviewed Nell Wing, Bill Wilson's secretary, we found that

(continued...)

Down through the centuries from one of the oldest dramas in the Bible, perhaps *the* oldest, comes that wistful cry of Job, "Oh that I knew where I might find Him!" [Job 23:3]; and the cry is taken up by modern writers. . . . In the main, those who complain that they cannot find God—who say that prayer is unreal, that it seems like talking to nobody, that they never feel anyone is there, that their prayer lacks reality, and that the experiences they read and hear concerning others never happen to them—are perfectly sincere in their quest for God; but since God is what He is, the thing that is hindering them is on their side, not on God's, though exactly what that hindrance is may not be discernible by them, standing just where they are standing at present. For, though we ask the question, "How can I find God?", a truer way of putting the question would be, "How can I put myself in the way of being found by Him?"[116]

AAs apparently responded to the challenge they heard from Shoemaker and from other Oxford Group people that they needed to find God. They not only made the suggestion in the Big Book—May you find Him now. They also incorporated further material on the "discovery" of God in various editions and drafts of that Big Book.

The First Edition of the Big Book contained the following about Professor William James:

The distinguished American psychologist, William James, in his book, "Varieties of Religious Experience", indicates a multitude of ways in which men have discovered God.[117]

---

[115] (...continued)
Nell had a copy of Weatherhead's *Psychology and Life* in her apartment. Bill Wilson had given it to her, and it also bore the name of Henrietta Seiberling.

[116] Leslie D. Weatherhead, *How Can I Find God?* (London: Hodder and Stoughton, 1943. First Printing, September, 1933), p. 7.

[117] *Alcoholics Anonymous* (New York City: Works Publishing Company, 1939), p. 38.

On the next page, the Big Book's First Edition said:

> Each individual, in the personal stories, describes in his own
> language and from his own point of view the way he established
> his relationship with God (p. 39).

An *earlier* multilith draft of the Big Book's First Edition,
which was circulated prior to publication of the First Edition in
1939, showed the Oxford Group origins more clearly. It stated as
to the same subject matter:

> The distinguished American psychologist, William James, in his
> book, "Varieties of Religious Experience," indicates a multitude
> of ways in which men have *found God* (emphasis added).

> Each individual, in the personal stories, describes in his own
> language, and from his own point of view the way he *found or
> rediscovered God* (emphasis added).[118]

This Book's Oxford Group Journey and Destination

In our book, we'll examine the source of Oxford Group ideas from
the perspective of their influence on early A.A. We'll look at the
life, beliefs, and activities of Oxford Group founder, Dr. Frank N.
D. Buchman, to see where he fit in the picture. We'll review the
role that Frank Buchman's long-time American associate, Sam
Shoemaker, played in the Oxford Group and in A.A.'s beginnings.
We'll see how A.A.'s roots began in the Oxford Group, how A.A.
departed from the Oxford Group, and how even Sam Shoemaker
later severed his Oxford Group connection. We'll look at the body

---

[118] Alcoholics Anonymous (New York: Works Publishing Co., 1939—multilith draft
on file in A.A. Archives in New York), p. 13. The origins of this earlier language; the
change itself from "finding God" to "discovering" God and "establishing a relationship
with God;" and the reasons for the change provide an important topic for further
research—something the author is challenged to do.

of Oxford Group ideas and practices which heavily influenced A.A.'s recovery program and still impact upon that program today. We'll review specifically the places in A.A.'s Big Book, Twelve Steps, and language where Oxford Group ideas and words can be found.

We'll conclude by asking just how useful this information can be to those today who, like the author, wish to utilize A.A.'s tremendous fellowship, great popularity, and simple program to continue to help alcoholics and addicts recover from their dread disease. A.A. did work. A.A. can work. And A.A. will work, despite today's diminishing success rate and heterogeneous membership. We believe A.A. will work, if those who participate in and with the Fellowship know how and why it worked when it drew so effectively on the Bible, the Oxford Group and Sam Shoemaker, the daily devotional books, other Christian literature, and revelation from God in the experimental, but heady recovery days of the 1930's.

2

Mentors Who Influenced
the Oxford Group's Founder

Some highly respected theologians, educators, and evangelists influenced the life-changing ideas of Oxford Group founder, Dr. Frank N. D. Buchman. Peter Howard, Buchman's successor, described life-changing as an "art," and said, "The art of changing men is ageless."[1] Buchman preferred to say of his own work, "It is not my art. It is God's art."[2]

In writing the popular Oxford Group book, *For Sinners Only*, A. J. Russell suggested that Buchman's "house-party religion" had been grounded in, but had departed from, "old-time evangelists," "old-fashioned evangelicals," and "old-fashioned revivalism."[3] Russell said the Oxford Group preferred the word "Change" to what he said "old-fashioned evangelicals" called "conversion."[4] "Those who sought to change others were called 'Life-Changers' instead of *evangelists*," he said (emphasis added).[5] He added that Oxford Group people felt the new age required different words and

---

[1] Peter Howard, *Frank Buchman's Secret* (New York: Doubleday & Co., 1961), p. 98.

[2] Howard, *Frank Buchman's Secret*, p. 15.

[3] A. J. Russell, *For Sinners Only* (London: Hodder & Stoughton, 1932), pp. 31-32.

[4] *For Sinners Only*, p. 30.

[5] *For Sinners Only*, p. 30.

less music, saying, "They believed that such phrases as 'Are you saved?' were unintelligible to the average man."[6]

Buchman himself, however, seemed to make very little effort to distance Oxford Group ideas and practices from those of the evangelists and religious leaders of the 19th Century who inspired him. As we will see, many of Buchman's most commonly used words and phrases were those made popular by his 19th Century mentors. And a number of "old-fashioned" evangelists and revivalists did make their mark on Frank Buchman and the Oxford Group. More important, perhaps, a number of religious leaders, Bible scholars, theologians, and professors—who cannot be written off as "old-fashioned" or unduly impassioned—also made their contributions to the thinking of Frank Buchman and the Oxford Group's principles and practices.

Dr. Horace Bushnell

One of the Oxford Group mentors least mentioned in present-day accounts of the Oxford Group is Yale divinity professor, Dr. Horace Bushnell.[7] We begin with Bushnell, not claiming that Bushnell himself was the originator of some very important ideas that influenced Frank Buchman, but rather that Bushnell was the first prestigious Christian writer, in point of time, who was quoted by Oxford Group people as a source for Oxford Group ideas.

Dr. Bushnell wrote much on the God of the Scriptures as Creator, a God of love, and a God who cares. In 1868, in his book, *The New Life*, Bushnell wrote eloquently of this God of love and the paternal love of God.[8] Though the Biblical idea that God

---

[6] *For Sinners Only*, p. 30.

[7] For background on Bushnell's life, see Mary B. Cheney, *Life and Letters of Horace Bushnell* (New York: Harper & Bros., 1890); and Robert L. Edwards, *Of Singular Genius Of Singular Grace: A Biography of Horace Bushnell* (Cleveland: Pilgrim Press, 1992).

[8] Horace Bushnell, *The New Life* (London: Strahan & Co., 1868), p. 67.

has a plan was apparently not original with Bushnell, he seems to have authored the Oxford Group's use of that phrase.[9] The first chapter of Bushnell's *The New Life* is titled, "Every Man's Life a Plan of God" (pp. 1-15). Oxford Group writers and their mentors quoted Bushnell for this concept.[10]

Bushnell's writings discussed conviction, conversion, surrender of self, being born again, obedience, getting rid of self-will, unselfishness, and the concept of willingness found in John 7:17.[11] And Oxford Group writers referred to him as one of the sources of these and a number of the other ideas in which they believed.[12] Ideas which can be found today in Buchman's teachings and in A.A.'s literature and principles.[13]

---

[9] Note that A. J. Russell began his description of the Oxford Group by stating: "God had a plan." Russell, *For Sinners Only*, p. 23. Interestingly, when Sam Shoemaker's daughter, Nickie Haggart, wrote the Foreword to our Shoemaker title, she began: "When I was growing up, I often heard my Dad, Sam Shoemaker, say: 'God has a plan. You have a part. Find it. Follow it.'" Dick B., *New Light on Alcoholism: The A.A. Legacy from Sam Shoemaker* (Corte Madera, CA: Good Book Publishing Company, 1994), p. xiii. Reviewing the manuscript for our first edition of this Oxford Group title, A.A. historian Dr. Ernest Kurtz took issue with the word "authored" in our reference to Bushnell. Kurtz suggested reading a good commentary on Augustine's *City of God*. And we have since done so, finding ample discussion of the "plan" of God. However, we do not mention Buchman's mentors and their contributions to show that their particular writings and ideas about the Word of God were their own product or contained original matter. Rather, we believe we establish that Buchman's own points of emphasis had their origins, as far as Buchman was concerned, in the teachings or writings of some eight Christian writers, including Bushnell, whose works were available, or taught to, Buchman as he began his studies and ministry.

[10] Clarence Irving Benson, *The Eight Points of the Oxford Group* (London: Oxford University Press, 1936), pp. 3-5; and Henry Wright, *The Will of God and a Man's Lifework* (New York: The Young Men's Christian Association Press, 1909), pp. 3-12.

[11] Bushnell, *The New Life*, pp. 58-73, 26-27.

[12] Benson, *The Eight Points*, pp. 135-37; Wright, *The Will of God*, pp. 4-8, 64-75, 148-49, 153-57, 180-82, 198-200, 205, 222-36, 239-40, 259, 272; Walter Houston Clark, *The Oxford Group. Its History and Significance* (New York: Bookman Associates, 1951), p. 126; and Douglas Clyde Macintosh, *Personal Religion* (New York: Charles Scribner's Sons, 1942), pp. 365-66.

[13] For example, in the Big Book, as to: (1) "getting rid of self," pp. 62, 63; (2) Problems of "self-will," pp. 60, 62; (c) Problems of "selfishness," pp. 61, 62, 67, 69; (d) "Willingness," pp. 47, 57, 59-60, 69, 76, 77, 79, 570.

Evangelist Dwight L. Moody

Dwight L. Moody was born February 5, 1837, and died December 22, 1899. His life touched that of Oxford Group Founder, Frank Buchman, in a number of different ways. And there are a number of parallel ideas which Moody and Buchman both shared and which point to the Moody influence.[14]

For one thing, there was the way Moody thought of the Bible and what should be done with its message. Moody held "tenaciously to the Bible as the inspired Word of God," stating: "Take the Bible; study it . . . feed on the Word . . . pass on the message."[15] Buchman often said of Bible study, "Read accurately, interpret honestly, apply drastically."[16] Buchman also said, "Read it through. Pray it in. Write it down. Work it out. Pass it on."[17] The "pass it on" idea was used by Buchman in other contexts. He said, for example, "The best way to keep an experience of Christ is to pass it on."[18] And it is not

---

[14] For our sources on Moody, see William R. Moody, *The Life of D. L. Moody* (New York: Fleming H. Revell, 1900); James F. Findlay, Jr., *Dwight L. Moody American Evangelist* (Chicago: University of Chicago Press, 1969); J. C. Pollock, *Moody: A Biographical Portrait of the Pacesetter in Modern Mass Evangelism* (New York: Macmillan, 1963); Paul D. Moody, *My Father: An Intimate Portrait of Dwight Moody* (Boston: Little, Brown, 1938); Edgar J. Goodspeed, *The Wonderful Career of Moody and Sankey in Great Britain and America* (New York: Henry S. Goodspeed & Co., 1876); J. Wilbur Chapman, *Life and Work of Dwight L. Moody* (Philadelphia, 1900); and Emma Moody Fitt, editor, *Day by Day with D. L. Moody* (Chicago: Moody Press, n.d.). See also R. C. Mowat, *Modern Prophetic Voices: From Kierkegaard to Buchman* (Oxford: New Cherwell Press, 1994).

[15] William Moody, *The Life of D. L. Moody*, pp. 497, 19.

[16] Garth Lean, *On the Tail of a Comet* (Colorado: Helmers & Howard, 1988), p. 157; Harry Almond, *Foundations for Faith* (London: Grosvenor, 1980), p. 31; and Miles G. W. Phillimore, *Just for Today* (privately published pamphlet on the occasion of Buchman's Lake Tahoe, California meeting, 1940—copy in possession of the author, n.d.), p. 67.

[17] Almond, *Foundations for Faith*, p. 31.

[18] Frank N. D. Buchman, *Remaking the World* (London: Blandford Press, 1961), p. x.

unreasonable to assume that the Buchman "pass it on" expression impacted upon the common use of "pass it on" language in A.A.[19]

Moody and Buchman were both evangelists.[20] James Findlay called Moody the most widely heralded representative of evangelical Protestantism after 1870 . . . a "professional revivalist."[21]

Findlay also made these additional comments about Moody:

Jesus as the Christ stood as the divine instrument by which individuals were brought to God and transformed into the people of faith. . . . The dealings of God compel men to turn to the man Christ Jesus for sympathy, to the Savior Christ Jesus for atonement and pardon, to the intercessor Christ Jesus for an answer to prayer, and to the glorified Christ for an heavenly inheritance (p. 231).[22]

Moody (chose) to place himself alongside those who stressed primarily the efficacy of God's love as saving power over men (p. 236).[23]

---

[19] Bill Wilson's A.A. biography was titled *Pass It On* (New York: Alcoholics Anonymous World Services, Inc., 1984). And see the letter to A.A. General Services Office, from which letter the title was taken and in which Bill used the expression. *Pass It On*, p. 7.

[20] As to Buchman, see Walter Houston Clark, *The Oxford Group: Its History and Significance* (New York: Bookman Associates, 1950), pp. 53-61.

[21] Findlay, *Dwight L. Moody*, pp. 19-21, 136.

[22] Frank Buchman was noted for the expression: "Sin is the disease. Jesus Christ is the cure. The result is a miracle." See H. W. "Bunny" Austin, *Frank Buchman As I Knew Him* (London: Grosvenor, 1975), p. 110; Howard, *Frank Buchman's Secret*, p. 130; and Almond, *Foundations for Faith*, pp. 9-30. Buchman also often repeated and taught a number of simple prayers and anagrams having to do with Jesus and his power. Almond, *Foundations for Faith*, pp. 21, 44.

[23] See Austin, *Frank Buchman As I Knew Him*, pp. 81-82. Austin stated: Buchman often said, "The greatest lines in the English language were from Charles Wesley's hymn, 'Jesus, lover of my soul'" (pages 81-82). Buchman also often used the expression: "Jesus, stand amongst us In Thy risen power." See Phillimore, *Just for Today*.

The were other comments by Findlay about Moody's beliefs. And these beliefs seem to have appealed to Buchman. Findlay said:

> There appeared to be three steps to salvation. First, one had to be "convicted" of sin; that is, one must become conscious of wrongdoing. . . . Conviction was followed by repentance—turning face to face with God. It was only one short step into the circle of faith, by believing in Christ and accepting him as a personal savior. This was the act of regeneration (p. 239).[24]

> Moody was "saturated" with Scripture, in its spirit and aim. . . . The Bible is continually in his hands. He believed that the Bible not only claims a Divine authority for all of its teachings, but vindicates its own claims. . . . When you read the Bible, the Word of God talks to you. . . . There are depths in the Bible no one, however acute his theology, can sound (pp. 257-58).[25]

> Through the years Moody remained firm in his advocacy of . . . the verbally inspired Bible. . . . [He said:] I cannot understand what these people mean who come to me and say that they cannot believe in the Old Testament, but can believe in the New. Now, both Testaments come from the Lord, and both are entitled to the same credence. . . . If you can't rely on this book, what can you rely on? (p. 409).[26]

---

[24] Compare Harold Begbie, *Life Changers* (London: Mills & Boon, Ltd., 1932), pp. 169-74, discussing Buchman's views on Sin, the 5 C's (Confidence, Confession, Conviction, Conversion, and Continuance), and Surrender.

[25] Compare the comment of Frank Buchman's friend, J. P. Thornton-Duesbury, who described Frank Buchman as "soaked in the Bible." See Lean, *On the Tail of a Comet*, p. 157.

[26] There are endless examples in Oxford Group writings of Buchman's belief in the verbally inspired Bible. One of his simplest statements was, "It is thoughts from God which have inspired the prophets all through history." See Buchman, *Remaking The World*, p. 36. Compare 2 Timothy 3:16, "All scripture *is* given by inspiration of God, and *is* profitable for doctrine, for reproof, for correction, for instruction in righteousness."

Moody founded his Moody Bible Institute in Chicago in 1889.[27] Traces of Moody's beliefs can certainly be found in the words and practices of Oxford Group Founder, Frank Buchman. And will appear as we move along.

As shown, Moody held to verbal inspiration of the Bible, and so did Buchman.[28] Moody urged "Crucify the great 'I.'"[29] This expression can be found in Frank Buchman's speeches and in Oxford Group books.[30] Moody presented the 32nd Psalm as seven words: Conviction, Confession, Forgiveness, Prayer, Protection, Guidance, Joy.[31] And these words also have counterparts in Oxford Group language—particularly in Frank Buchman's Five C's—Confidence, Confession, Conviction, Conversion, and Conservation.[32] Moody propounded two other ideas which later were of extreme importance in Oxford Group ideology. They concerned honest sharing and restitution. Moody said:

---

[27] Pollock, *Moody: A Biographical Portrait*, pp. 267-71.

[28] Paul D. Moody, *My Father*, p. 191. In *Remaking the World*, Buchman is quoted as saying: "God spoke to the prophets of old. He may speak to you. God speaks to those who listen" (p. 41).

[29] Goodspeed, *The Wonderful Career of Moody and Sankey*, p. 46.

[30] See Russell, *For Sinners Only*, p. 60: "For light and direction had come at last. As Frank puts it, he had turned the Big 'I' of Self on to its beam end thus (-), which left him with only a big minus. He saw that Christ must be the Big 'I' to turn that minus back into a mighty + and by continuing the line of Christ the symbol was now the Cross." *What Is The Oxford Group?* said, "In the 'I' in the word Sin, the Oxford Group tells us, lies the secret of Sin's power. The 'I', or the ego, is more important to sinners than spiritual health. . . . If we can surrender that 'I' to God, Sin goes with it; when we live without that 'I' in our lives, we are without Sin" (pp. 23-24). See also Almond, *Foundations for Faith*, p. 21; Howard, *Frank Buchman's Secret*, p. 43; *The World Rebuilt: The True Story of Frank Buchman and the Achievements of Moral Re-Armament* (New York: Duell, Sloan and Pearce, 1951), p. 242; Bremer Hofmeyr, *How to Change* (New York: Moral Re-Armament, n.d.), p. 3, stating, "The basic problem is my self-will—the big 'I'"; and Paul Campbell and Peter Howard, *Remaking Men* (New York: Arrowhead Books, 1954), p. 75.

[31] Chapman, *Life and Work of Dwight L. Moody*, p. 451.

[32] For early references to these 5 C's, see: Begbie, *Life Changers*, p. 169; Howard A. Walter, *Soul Surgery: Some Thoughts on Incisive Personal Work*, 6th ed (Oxford: at the University Press, 1940); Clark, *The Oxford Group*, p. 28; and Samuel M. Shoemaker, *Realizing Religion* (New York: Association Press, 1923), pp. 79-82.

If you have ever taken money dishonestly, you need not pray God to forgive you and fill you with the Holy Ghost until you make restitution. Confession and restitution are the steps that lead to forgiveness.[33]

And by what means did Moody influence Buchman, either through his writings and beliefs, or in other ways? First of all, Buchman actually met Moody at the Northfield Student Conference in Massachusetts, in 1901. Moody had founded the conference which was then run by John R. Mott, the Assistant General Secretary of the YMCA. Buchman said the visit "completely changed his life" in that he there decided that winning people to Christ must be his main objective in life.[34]

Moody touched Buchman's life in another way through Buchman's mentor, Professor Henry Wright of Yale Divinity School. While lecturing at Hartford Seminary, Buchman attended Wright's lectures at Yale. On the wall of Wright's lecture room, Buchman was confronted with Moody's words:

The world has yet to see what God can do in, for, by and through a man whose will is wholly given up to Him.[35]

Wright began all lectures with two minutes of silent consideration of Moody's words. Then Wright would say, "Will you be that man? Will you be that man?" Wright would always link this challenge by Moody with the Bible verse, "I, if I be lifted up, will draw all men unto me" [See John 12:32]. Buchman said of those sessions, "It took me six weeks until I came to absolute conviction and yielded myself to that principle." Buchman's biographer, Garth Lean, said Buchman then made a profound commitment to

---

[33] Emma Moody Fitt, *Day By Day With D. L. Moody*, p. 93. Compare *What Is The Oxford Group?*, pp. 27-35, 55-64; and Russell, *For Sinners Only*, pp. 119-35 (the latter dealing with confession and restitution).

[34] Lean, *On the Tail of a Comet*, p. 17.

[35] Lean, *On the Tail of a Comet*, pp. 77-78; and Austin, *Frank Buchman As I Knew Him*, p. 24.

break out from a narrow to a universal conception of Christianity. Lean also believed Buchman then acquired the quality in Buchman that showed, according to Henry van Dusen of Union Theological Seminary, that Buchman was in the tiny company of men who have known themselves to be summoned to the surrender of all to the exacting demand of the Divine Will.[36]

Moody also exerted an indirect influence on Buchman through Buchman's other mentors, Professor Henry Drummond of Edinburgh and Professor Henry B. Wright of Yale. Historian Walter Houston Clark observed:

The most important source of the [Oxford] Group's ideas and practices was the American collegiate evangelism of the early twentieth century, when Buchman was at Penn State and Hartford Seminary, and until 1922, when he severed connections with institutions and pursued his way alone. The particular tide of college religious work whose ebb coincided with the beginning of his own movement was that which may be said to have begun with the founding of the student Y.M.C.A. in 1858. In this movement, the great American evangelist Dwight L. Moody played an important part, aided by some cross-fertilization with members of the great British universities. Two men whom Moody influenced were destined to leave their mark on Buchman. The first was Henry Drummond of Edinburgh University, whom Buchman probably never saw but knew through his writings; the second was Henry B. Wright of Yale, who was converted by Moody in 1898.[37]

---

[36] Lean, *On the Tail of a Comet*, pp. 77-78. See also, Austin, *Frank Buchman As I Knew Him*, p. 24.

[37] Clark, *The Oxford Group*, p. 122. A.A. historian, David A. of Connecticut, provided the author with an inventory of the books in Frank Buchman's home on 11th Street, in Allentown, Pennsylvania. Included among Buchman's books were: *The Life of Henry Drummond*, Drummond's *Natural Law in the Spiritual World*, and an address by Henry Drummond. Oxford Group writer, T. Willard Hunter, wrote the author that Buchman often quoted Drummond as follows: "God can change the furniture of a person's soul in a single hour."

Clark pointed to four early aims of the College Christian Associations: (1) Religious meetings, (2) Bible study, (3) Personal evangelism, and (4) Intercollegiate visitation and correspondence. Clark said that, as a college YMCA secretary at Penn State, Buchman was expected to and did promote these activities. Students were challenged to "make a decision" or "dedicate their lives to Christ" or, in other words, to make a "decision for Christ." We would add that "religious" meetings, Bible study, and personal evangelism became an important part of the Oxford Group life-changing art. The inter-association visitation brought to Penn State campus and to Buchman such religious leaders as Henry B. Wright; and it brought to the inter-collegiate student conferences, at such places as Northfield, the evangelist, Professor Henry Drummond, of whom Henry Wright—and Frank Buchman, as well—became a great admirer.[38]

Evangelist F. B. Meyer

A few sprigs exist here and there in accounts of the Oxford Group concerning Frank Buchman's contacts with a noted evangelist and Congregational minister, F. B. Meyer.[39] But a reading of Meyer's book, *The Secret of Guidance*, makes clearer the reason for Buchman's interest in this man.[40] First, the sprigs; then Meyer's title, *The Secret of Guidance*.

---

[38] For further views on the Moody-Oxford Group influence, see Mark O. Guldseth, *Streams* (Alaska: Fritz Creek Studios, 1982), pp. 25-36; and Mel B., *New Wine: The Spiritual Roots of the Twelve Step Miracle* (Minnesota: Hazelden, 1991), pp. 136-38.

[39] See Lean, *On the Tail of a Comet*, pp. 30, 35, 74; Guldseth, *Streams*, pp. 108-109; Theophil Spoerri, *Dynamic out of Silence: Frank Buchman's Relevance Today* (London: Grosvenor, 1976). p. 30; K. D. Belden, *Reflections on Moral Re-Armament* (London: Grosvenor Books, 1983), p 38; Benson, *The Eight Points*, pp. 14-15; and Frank H. Sherry and Mahlon H. Hellerich, *The Formative Years of Frank N. D. Buchman* (an article produced at Frank Buchman's memorial service held at the First Presbyterian Church in Allentown, Pennsylvania—copy in author's possession), pp. 250-51, 256.

[40] See F. B. Meyer, *The Secret of Guidance* (New York: Fleming H. Revell, 1896).

Meyer had written *Reveries and Realities, or Life and Work in London.* Frank Buchman had a copy in his personal library. It was sent to Buchman by Meyer in 1907 with this flyleaf inscription: "With the author's warmest regards." Buchman received it while he was working with a Lutheran youth hospice early in his career.[41] Buchman had met Meyer at a Northfield Student Conference in Massachusetts.[42] And Meyer had visited Penn State campus while Buchman was YMCA secretary there. Garth Lean gave the following account of what transpired at Penn State:

> At this point he [Buchman] consulted a visitor to the college—almost certainly the F. B. Meyer he had sought in Keswick—about his inner questionings. "You need to make personal, man-to-man interviews central, rather than the organizing of meetings," said Meyer. "Since that time," remarked Buchman later, "I no longer thought in terms of numbers but in terms of people." Meyer also asked, "Do you let the Holy Spirit guide you in all you are doing?" Buchman replied that he did indeed pray and read the Bible in the morning, and sometimes received inspirations then and at other times in the day. "But," persisted Meyer, "do you give God enough uninterrupted time really to tell you what to do?" Buchman thought this over and decided to give at least an hour each day in the early morning to listening to God, a period which he came to refer to as a "quiet time."[43]

Garth Lean said that this conversation can be seen as the time when Buchman decided to give his will, as distinct from his life in general, to God and now must do God's work not in his way, but in God's.[44]

---

[41] Sherry and Hellerich, *The Formative Years of Frank N. D. Buchman*, p. 256.

[42] Lean, *On the Tail of a Comet*, p. 30.

[43] Lean, *On the Tail of a Comet*, pp. 35-36. See also Spoerri, *Dynamic Out of Silence*, pp. 30-31; and Guldseth, *Streams*, pp. 98, 108-09.

[44] Lean, *On the Tail of a Comet*, p. 74. See also Sherry and Hellerich, *The Formative Years*, p. 250.

An idea of Meyer's convictions and their influence on Buchman can be obtained by examining Meyer's *The Secret of Guidance.* Historian Mark Guldseth said Buchman cited Meyer's book as one which had helped him.[45] Meyer had quoted a number of Bible verses showing that God promises Guidance.[46] And the Oxford Group later also cited these.[47] Meyer wrote on the necessity for surrender of the will to God, stating that Jesus was constantly insisting on a surrendered will as the key to perfect knowledge. Meyer quoted several Bible verses to support this proposition.[48] And the Oxford Group relied on these—particularly John 7:17.[49]

Meyer's *The Secret of Guidance* also spoke to the vital necessity for Bible study, prayer, and waiting upon God.[50] We cannot be sure Oxford Group people obtained those ideas from Meyer, but they certainly utilized them. Meyer wrote a chapter titled, "Where am I wrong?"[51] And this stress on looking for one's own part in a wrong is fundamental in the Sermon on the Mount, Oxford Group thought, and in A.A.'s Big Book, as far as

---

[45] Guldseth, *Streams*, p. 108.

[46] Meyer, *The Secret of Guidance*, p. 7. For example, Meyer quoted Proverbs 3:6: "In all thy ways acknowledge him, and he shall direct thy paths;" and Psalm 32:8: "I will instruct thee and teach thee in the way which thou shalt go: I will guide thee with Mine eye." Other quoted verses included Isaiah 58:11 and John 8:12.

[47] For Proverbs 3:6, see Benson, *The Eight Points*, p. 81; B. H. Streeter, *The God Who Speaks* (London: Macmillan & Co., 1943), p. 135; and Philip M. Brown, *The Venture of Belief* (New York: Fleming H. Revell, 1935), p. 40. For Psalm 32:8, see Streeter, *The God Who Speaks*, p. 115; Benson, *The Eight Points*, p. 80; and Wright, *The Will of God*, p. 141.

[48] Meyer, *The Secret of Guidance*, p. 11, citing John 5:30: "My judgment is just; because I seek not mine own will, but the will of the Father which hath sent me;" and John 7:17: "If any man will do his will, he shall know of the doctrine, whether it be of God, or whether I speak of myself."

[49] At a later point in our book, we discuss at length the importance of John 7:17 in Oxford Group and Shoemaker writings. Here, we simply cite as examples: Streeter, *The God Who Speaks*, p. 126; Russell, *For Sinners Only*, p. 211; and Samuel M. Shoemaker, *Religion That Works* (New York: Fleming H. Revell, 1928), pp. 58, 64.

[50] Meyer, *The Secret of Guidance*, pp. 14-18.

[51] Meyer, *The Secret of Guidance*, Chapter II.

self-examination is concerned.[52] We believe this concept of looking for and correcting one's own wrongdoing, rather than focusing on that of another, is a major aspect of A.A.'s Fourth and Tenth Step procedures.[53] Hence Meyer could, directly or indirectly, have influenced those ideas. In any event, enough has been said to warrant including Meyer as a Buchman mentor.

Professor Henry Drummond

Henry Drummond was born August 17, 1851, and died on March 11, 1897. He became Professor of Natural Science, at Free Church College, Glasgow, Scotland.[54] On ordination, he declared his "belief in the Scriptures of the Old and New Testaments as the Word of God and the only rule of faith and manners."[55]

Several of Drummond's written works are important for this study. They are: (1) *Natural Law in the Spiritual World.*[56] (2) *The Changed Life.*[57] (3) *The Ideal Life.*[58] (4) *The New Evangelism.*[59] (5) *Essays and Addresses*, which contains Drummond's *The Greatest Thing in the World.*[60] Frank Buchman's biographer,

---

[52] See Matthew 7:3-5: Look for the log in your own eye, rather than the speck in your brother's; and see Geoffrey F. Allen, *He That Cometh* (New York: The Macmillan Company, 1933), p. 140; Buchman, *Remaking The World*, p. 46; and Big Book, pp. 67, 69, 70, 79, 84, 86.

[53] See also Benson, *The Eight Points*, p. 7.

[54] George Adam Smith, *The Life of Henry Drummond* (New York: McClure, Phillips & Co., 1901), p. 264. See also R. C. Mowat, *Modern Prophetic Voices: From Kierkegaard to Buchman* (Oxford: New Cherwell Press, 1994), pp. 32, 83.

[55] Smith, *The Life of Henry Drummond*, p. 266.

[56] Henry Drummond, *Natural Law in the Spiritual World* (Potts Edition). The author recently discovered, during a visit to the home of one of Dr. Bob's children, that Dr. Bob had owned and studied this volume. Dr. Bob's family still has the title.

[57] Henry Drummond, *The Changed Life* (New York: James Potts and Company, 1891).

[58] Henry Drummond, *The Ideal Life* (New York: Hodder & Stoughton, 1897).

[59] Henry Drummond, *The New Evangelism* (New York: Hodder & Stoughton, 1899).

[60] Henry Drummond, *Essays and Addresses* (New York: James Potts and Company, 1903).

Garth Lean, Dr. Samuel M. Shoemaker, and a number of scholars have confirmed the great influence, both direct and indirect, that Henry Drummond had on the thinking of Frank Buchman.[61] Mark Guldseth reported in *Streams* that Frank Buchman steered his friends toward Drummond's *The Greatest Thing in the World* and widely recommended the book for study and absorption.[62]

Dwight Moody brought Henry Drummond to Moody's second student summer conference at Northfield, Massachusetts, in 1887; and Drummond there delivered his talk *The Greatest Thing in the World*.[63] Essays and pamphlets containing this address—which was a study of Love as it is portrayed in 1 Corinthians 13—sold over a million copies. Drummond paid another visit to the Northfield conference in 1893 and made a tour of some of the Eastern colleges in the United States.[64] What Drummond said in several different speeches greatly influenced Professor Henry B. Wright and, in turn, Wright's protege, Frank Buchman.[65] Drummond's influence can be seen particularly by the frequent references to him in Wright's book, *The Will of God and a Man's Lifework*.[66]

Several ideas which found their way to Henry Wright and then to Frank Buchman were treated at great length by Professor Drummond. A number can be found Howard Walter's *Soul Surgery*, the Oxford Group title on which Walter collaborated with Wright and Buchman. The subjects were:

---

[61] Lean, *On the Tail of a Comet*, p. 78; Belden, *Reflections on Moral Re-Armament*, p. 82; Shoemaker, *Religion That Works*, pp. 54-65; Clark, *The Oxford Group*, pp. 124-25; and Douglas C. Macintosh, *Personal Religion* (New York: Charles Scribner, 1942), pp. 366-67.

[62] Guldseth, *Streams*, pp. 113-14.

[63] Henry Drummond, *The Greatest Thing in the World and other addresses* (London: Collins, 1953).

[64] Clark, *The Oxford Group*, p. 124.

[65] Macintosh, *Personal Religion*, p. 367.

[66] Wright, *The Will of God*, pp. xi, 10, 15, 16, 50-51, 64, 73-74, 78, 83-85, 107, 110-11, 119-52, 161-62, 173-74, 208, 223, 266.

1. *The thirteenth chapter of 1 Corinthians*—discussed and analyzed by Drummond in his address, *The Greatest Thing in the World*. In this analysis of *love*, Drummond asked:

> How many of you will join me in reading this chapter once a week for the next three months? A man did that once and it changed his whole life.[67]

The importance of 1 Corinthians 13, of Drummond's *The Greatest Thing in the World*, and of Drummond's suggestion about reading this "love" chapter to change a life may directly have reached A.A.'s Dr. Bob. Dr. Bob said early AAs considered 1 Corinthians 13 "absolutely essential" to their program.[68] One writer claimed Dr. Bob specified Drummond's book as "required reading" for the alcoholics with whom he worked.[69] Drummond's book was very popular with early AAs and was furnished to early AAs in Akron by Lucy Galbraith, who also gave them *The Upper Room*.[70] In fact, Dr. Bob once recommended for an alcoholic going into the D.T.'s:

> When she comes out of it and she decides she wants to be a different woman, get her Drummond's "The Greatest Thing in the World." Tell her to read it through every day for 30 days, and she'll be a different woman.[71]

---

[67] Drummond, *The Greatest Thing in the World*, p. 53. See Wright, *The Will of God*, pp. 161-62.

[68] *DR. BOB and the Good Oldtimers* (New York: Alcoholics Anonymous World Services, Inc., 1980), p. 96.

[69] See Bill Pittman, *AA The Way It Began* (Seattle: Glen Abbey Books, 1988), at page 197. We do not agree, however, since Dr. Bob probably *never* "required" reading, though he did highly recommend a great many books for growth, including Drummond's. See Dick B., *Dr. Bob's Library: Books for Twelve Step Growth* (San Rafael, CA: Paradise Research Publications, 1994), pp. 12-13.

[70] See *DR. BOB*, p. 151, and page 310, where Dr. Bob's son said that his father "put a lot of stock in 'The Greatest Thing in the World' by Drummond."

[71] *DR. BOB*, p. 310.

2. *The Changed Life*. It is not amiss to observe, as did Walter Houston Clark, that the title of Drummond's 1891 book, *The Changed Life*, bears close resemblance to the *life-change* and *life-changers* ideas so much popularized by Frank Buchman and the Oxford Group.[72] In *The Changed Life*, Drummond emphasized the importance of the will in conversion.[73]

3. *Conversion*. Drummond stressed the value of conversion in his major work, *Natural Law in the Spiritual World*. A conversion experience—a religious experience—a vital spiritual experience—was an Oxford Group *must*; and that "spiritual experience" idea became a foundation stone for A.A. recovery.[74]

4. *The Will of God: How to learn His Universal Will from the Bible and His Particular Will for man through Guidance*. Henry Wright is credited as the direct source of this Buchman concept. But Henry Wright himself makes clear from his endless references to Drummond's book, *The Ideal Life*, that it was Henry Drummond who spelled out the Biblical authority for these ideas as far as Wright was concerned.[75]

5. *John 7:17 and willingness to obey and do God's Universal Will as a condition to knowing His Particular Will*. Drummond articulated this important idea in *The Ideal Life*.[76] F. W. Robertson had delivered a sermon on John 7:17 (under the title

---

[72] See Clark, *The Oxford Group*, p. 124; and, for example, Buchman, *Remaking The World*, pp. 24, 37, 46, 160; Austin, *Frank Buchman As I Knew Him*, p. 26; Howard, *Frank Buchman's Secret* , pp. 16, 17, 62, 118, 132, 142; and Begbie, *Life Changers*.

[73] Compare Shoemaker, *Realizing Religion*, pp. 28-29.

[74] See Shoemaker, *Realizing Religion*, pp. 9, 22-28; *What Is The Oxford Group?*, pp. 41-48. And see Bill Wilson's letter to Dr. Carl Jung, quoted in part in *Pass It On* (New York: Alcoholics Anonymous World Services, Inc., 1984), pp. 382-83.

[75] Drummond, *The Ideal Life*, pp. 227-320; Shoemaker, *Religion That Works*, pp. 54-65; Wright, *The Will of God*, pp. 102-207; Lean, *On the Tail of a Comet*, p. 74; and Macintosh, *Personal Religion*, pp. 367-73.

[76] Drummond, *The Ideal Life*, pp. 302-20.

"Obedience the Organ of Spiritual Knowledge"); and it was this sermon which deeply influenced Henry Drummond. Robertson's sermon caused Drummond and Moody to lead Henry Wright's thoughts along these John 7:17 lines, and Wright gave much credit both to Robertson and Drummond for their origin.[77] As to how one learned God's particular will, Henry Wright modified Robertson's *obedience* concept to the idea that there must simply be "*Willingness* to do God's will the Necessary Condition for knowledge of it" (emphasis added).[78] But Wright did quote Drummond's *The Ideal Life* as authority for his thesis.[79]

6. *Spiritual Diagnosis, soul-surgery, and personal evangelism.* In 1899, Drummond wrote *The New Evangelism* and proposed a science of spirituality which involved personal evangelism—the duty of a pastor to get "over God towards man."[80] Drummond's ideas are much quoted in Howard Walter's *Soul Surgery*, which was a major Oxford Group "manual" in the 1930's.[81] As stated, Walter wrote *Soul Surgery* in collaboration with Henry Wright and Frank Buchman. And the "art" of soul surgery became a Buchman trademark.[82]

---

[77] Wright, *The Will of God*, pp. 19, 119, 125, 130, 133, 139, 143, 153, 159; Macintosh, *Personal Religion*; Russell, *For Sinners Only*, p. 211; Shoemaker, *Religion That Works*, pp. 54-65; and *Living Your Life Today* (New York: Fleming H. Revell, 1947), pp. 101-09.

[78] Wright, *The Will of God*, p. 117.

[79] Wright, *The Will of God*, pp. 120-21.

[80] Drummond, *The New Evangelism*, pp. 258-84.

[81] See Walter, *Soul Surgery*, pp. 9-10, 17, 24, 28, 31-32, 35, 39, 47-48, 65-67, 73-74, 91-96. K. D. Belden, a long-time Oxford Group activist and writer, wrote the author about the principal Oxford Group books that were used in Great Britain in the 1930's; but Belden did not mention *Soul Surgery*. In the United States, however, *Soul Surgery* was a title recommended in Sam Shoemaker's parish publication, *The Calvary Evangel*. It was owned and much circulated by Dr. Bob. See Dick B., *Dr. Bob's Library*, pp. 23, 44, 76, 78. And the author personally found a copy of *Soul Surgery* in the binder located at Stepping Stones which contains a copy of Anne Smith's Journal.

[82] See Austin, *Frank Buchman As I Knew Him*, p. 19; Begbie, *Life Changers*, pp. 24-41 (being a chapter entitled "The Soul Surgeon"); and Howard, *Frank Buchman's Secret*, p. 112.

Dr. Robert E. Speer

For the Oxford Group, obeying and doing the will of God certainly meant that one must start by trying to live by certain moral standards laid down by Jesus Christ. There had to be a complete renunciation of *self*-will and a *willingness*, evidenced by sincere effort, to conform to *God's will* as expressed in Jesus's standards.[83] The moral standards were summarized in the Oxford Group's "Four Absolutes"—Absolute Honesty, Absolute Purity, Absolute Unselfishness, and Absolute Love. The Four Absolutes are mentioned in Frank Buchman's speeches.[84] They can be found in books about Buchman.[85] They are usually mentioned in descriptions of the Oxford Group.[86] They are frequently mentioned in Dr. Sam Shoemaker's writings.[87] They are often mentioned in A.A.'s conference approved books.[88] They are still

---

[83] See Wright, *The Will of God*, pp. 31, 77, 125-28; Romans 6:16; and John 7:17.

[84] Buchman, *Remaking The World*, pp. 36, 40, 96, 131.

[85] Russell, *For Sinners Only*, pp. 319-29; Lean, *On the Tail of a Comet*, pp. 76-77; Howard, *Frank Buchman's Secret*. p. 117; Mowat, *Modern Prophetic Voices*, pp. 59, 75; and William Grogan, *John Riffe of the Steelworkers* (New York: Coward-McCann, Inc., 1959), p. 94.

[86] *What Is The Oxford Group?*, pp. 7-8; Stephen Foot, *Life Began Yesterday* (New York: Harper & Brothers, 1935), pp. 6, 55, 57, 62; Cecil Rose, *When Man Listens* (New York: Oxford University Press, 1937), p. 32; Benson, *The Eight Points*, pp. 44-57; Almond, *Foundations for Faith*, pp. 10-13; Belden, *Reflections on Moral Re-Armament*, pp. 29, 46, 49, 51, 53, 70; and Jack Winslow, *Why I Believe in the Oxford Group* (London: Hodder & Stoughton, 1934), pp. 24-32.

[87] Samuel M. Shoemaker, *The Church Can Save the World* (New York: Harper & Brothers, 1938), p. 113; *Twice-Born Ministers* (New York: Fleming H. Revell, 1929), p. 150; *One Boy's Influence* (New York: Association Press, 1925), p. 7; *God and America* (New York: The Oxford Group, 61 Gramercy Park, North, n.d.), p. 21; and see Helen Smith Shoemaker, *I Stand by the Door* (New York: Harper & Row, 1967), pp. 24-26.

[88] *DR. BOB*, pp. 54, 163; *Pass It On*, pp. 114, 172; *Alcoholics Anonymous Comes of Age* (Alcoholics Anonymous World Services, Inc., 1957), pp. 68, 75, 161; *The Language of the Heart* (New York: The AA Grapevine, Inc., 1988), pp. 198-200; and *The Co-Founders of Alcoholics Anonymous; Biographical Sketches; Their Last Major Talks* (New York: AA World Services, Inc., 1972, 1975), pp. 12-14.

practiced in some geographical A.A. areas today.[89] And it is often stated that they originated with Dr. Robert E. Speer's reconstruction of the principles of Jesus Christ's Sermon on the Mount.[90]

Dr. Speer spelled out Jesus Christ's four standards in his title, *The Principles of Jesus*.[91] Speer cited specific Bible verses containing Jesus's teachings, which proved to Speer that his (Speer's) four standards were those taught by Jesus.[92] Some, including Sam Shoemaker, believed that Speer's standards came directly from the Sermon on the Mount; but we will show, at a later point, that Speer selected the foundational Bible teachings from several of the Gospels.

Professor Henry B. Wright credited Speer as the originator of the Four Standards. Wright then further documented the standards as Christian teachings by referring to many verses in the New Testament—both in the Gospels and in the Epistles which contained the principles.[93] Wright called Speer's Four Standards the "Four Absolutes." However, Oxford Group writers still often refer to Wright's "Absolutes" as the "Standards."[94]

---

[89] Mel B., *New Wine*, pp. 76, 138. See particularly the pamphlet published by the Cleveland Central Committee of A.A., titled *The Four Absolutes*, a copy of which the author has in his possession and may be obtained in the Cleveland or Akron A.A. offices with ease.

[90] Samuel M. Shoemaker, *How to Become a Christian* (New York: Harper & Brothers, 1953), p. 57; Wright, *The Will of God*, pp. 167-218; and Lean, *On the Tail of a Comet*, p. 76.

[91] Robert E. Speer, *The Principles of Jesus* (New York: Fleming H. Revell, 1902), pp. 33-36.

[92] See Robert H. Murray, *Group Movements Throughout the Ages* (New York: Harper & Brothers, 1935), pp. 339-41.

[93] See Wright, *The Will of God*, pp. 165-218.

[94] See Grogan, *John Riffe*, p. 94; Howard, *Frank Buchman's Secret*, p. 117; Almond, *Foundations for Faith*, p. 11; Belden, *Reflections on Moral Re-Armament*, pp. 46, 49, 51, 53, 70; Garth Lean, *Cast Out Your Nets* (London: Grosvenor, 1990), p. 9; and T. Willard Hunter, *World Changing Through Life Changing* (Newton Center, Mass: Andover Newton Theological School, 1977), p. 16.

Professor William James

Professor William James of Harvard University figures in present-day A.A. discussions as the person whose writings on religious experiences validated A.A. co-founder Bill Wilson's own remarkable conversion experience (which occurred when Wilson recovered from alcoholism at Towns Hospital in New York in 1934).[95]

Immediately following Bill's oft-mentioned spiritual experience, Bill's "sponsor," Ebby Thacher, or possibly Rowland Hazard, had given Bill a copy of William James's *The Varieties of Religious Experience*.[96] Both Thacher and Hazard had achieved their own religious or conversion experiences through, and as "members" of, the Oxford Group.[97] And Bill concluded from his reading of the William James book that his [Bill's] conversion experience was a valid religious experience similar to experiences described in William James's title. Bill later described William James as a "founder" of Alcoholics Anonymous.[98]

---

[95] *Pass It On*, p. 124; Mel B., *New Wine*, pp. 77-79; Robert Thomsen, *Bill W.*(New York: Harper & Row, 1975), pp. 230-31; Kurtz, *Not-God*, pp. 20-24; Nell Wing, *Grateful to Have Been There* (Illinois: Parkside Publishing Corporation, 1992), pp. 21, 25; *and* Big Book, p. 28.

[96] See William James, *The Varieties of Religious Experience* (New York: Vintage Books/The Library of America, 1990). *The Varieties* is included in the inventory of the books in Frank Buchman's library at Allentown, Pennsylvania.

[97] In the past four years of research, we have frequently seen the last name of Bill's sponsor, Ebby, spelled "Thatcher." In fact, we found the name so spelled in the records of Ebby's baptism at, and becoming a communicant of, Shoemaker's Calvary Episcopal Church in New York. See Dick B., *New Light on Alcoholism*, pp. 348, 350. However, we have also seen Ebby's last name spelled "Thacher." As our book was going to press, we telephoned A.A. historian and old-timer, Mel B., at his home in Toledo, Ohio. And we are now able to resolve the spelling with "finality." Mel B. reported to us that he had seen the name "Thacher" on Ebby's tombstone at the family plot. Mel also said he had confirmed the "Thacher" spelling through correspondence with Ebby's nephew, through review of Ebby's personal correspondence, and through examination of public records in Albany, New York. Henceforth, in this book and elsewhere, we will report Ebby's full and correct name as "Edwin Throckmorton Thacher."

[98] *Pass It On*, p. 124.

But the influence of William James on the Oxford Group and on Alcoholics Anonymous involved much more than the validation of Bill's religious experience.[99] Bill thought he had learned from the James book that "deflation" of the ego was a necessary condition of a religious experience.[100] A.A. historian, Dr. Ernest Kurtz, challenged Bill's conclusion as to what Bill thought he had read in William James's book. Kurtz wrote:

> Yet Wilson also seemed to attribute the phrase "deflation at depth" to William James. The problem: neither this expression nor the bare word *deflation* appears anywhere in *Varieties*. On the other hand, Wilson apparently did *not* note and certainly did *not* cite what *was* in James: the openness to explicit religion. Two examples, one minor, the second major. First, in one of the briefer notes in *Varieties*, James approvingly cited evidence that the only cure for "dipsomania" was "religiomania." Given the circumstances in which Bill Wilson, painfully sobering up founder of Alcoholics Anonymous, read this simultaneously profound and diffuse writing of James' Gifford Lectures, it is difficult to imagine that his eye did not pause for relaxation if not refreshment at the scattered mentions of drinking and alcohol. Yet he never adverted to this clearly unwelcome idea—an idea that, bare weeks before, he had himself at first used to explain away Ebby on that first fateful visit. Second, if there is one key word as well as concept in *Varieties*, it is not "deflation" but "conversion." Yet this term, so suggestive in America of a certain style of religion, never passed Bill Wilson's lips or writing hand—at least not for publication—until many years later.[101]

Kurtz rightly observed that Bill Wilson may have had fuzzy thinking in the earliest days of his sobriety. But Kurtz possibly

---

[99] See, for example, the frequent mention of William James and his ideas in Begbie, *Life-Changers*, pp. 32, 139, 176; Walter, *Soul Surgery*, pp. 78-84; and Shoemaker, *Realizing Religion*, pp. viii, 4, 22, 26, 35, 62.

[100] *Pass It On*, pp. 124-25, 197-99.

[101] Kurtz, *Not-God*, p. 23.

missed the significance of James's emphasis on *self-surrender* (which seems to us to involve ego deflation), something which James called the "turning point" and which A.A. adopted as the starting point for its action steps. But Kurtz's remarks do set the stage for examining the real contributions of William James to the Oxford Group and to A.A.—whether the contributions were known and publicized or not.

James, a leader in the field of psychology, *defined conversion*. His definition was utilized over and over by religious writers including Oxford Group writers and even by Dr. Bob's wife, Anne Smith. James's definition of conversion appeared in Sam Shoemaker's first book as follows:

> The process, gradual or sudden, by which a self, hitherto divided and consciously wrong, inferior, and unhappy, becomes unified, consciously right, superior and happy.[102]

It was the foregoing concept of *change* and its *nature* (as defined above by James), and the validation of such a change (when occurring through a religious transformation or regeneration or conversion experience), that really captivated Oxford Group writers and Bill Wilson.

Then, having had twenty-five years of A.A. experience, Wilson wrote about another aspect of what Bill believed to be William James's contribution to A.A. Wilson said:

> Who, then, first told us about the utter necessity for such an awakening, for an experience that not only expels the alcohol obsession, but which also makes effective and truly real the practice of spiritual principles "in all our affairs?" Well, this life-

---

[102] See Shoemaker, *Realizing Religion*, p. 22; Walter, *Soul Surgery*, p. 80; Harold Begbie, *Twice-Born Men* (New York: Fleming H. Revell, 1909), pp. 16-17; "The Study of Christian Evangelism," in *Education for Christian Service*, by Yale Divinity School Faculty, New Haven, 1922, p. 334; Shoemaker, *Twice-Born Ministers*, p. 10; and Dick B., *Anne Smith's Journal*, pp. 27-28.

giving idea came to us of AA through William James, the father
of modern psychology.[103]

We have a good deal of difficulty with this Bill Wilson statement,
much as Dr. Kurtz had with Wilson's attribution of "deflation" to
William James. But our reason is different. The necessity for, and
validation of an "awakening" via a conversion experience, *is*
certainly the heart of William James's treatise. But we believe the
foregoing statement by Bill ignored the fact that Bill's own Oxford
Group "mentors," Rowland Hazard, Shep Cornell, Victor Kitchen,
and Ebby Thacher—along with countless thousands of others—had
frequently experienced a "spiritual awakening" and conversion and
then release from alcoholism in the Christian confines of the
Oxford Group and, often, at Calvary Rescue Mission where Bill
himself had first "given his life to God."[104]

In other words, Bill's reading of the William James book *after*
Bill had undergone his religious or conversion experience
apparently did validate that experience *for Bill*.[105] But it was
something else for Bill to claim that *James* was the *author* of A.A.
ideas about the necessity for a spiritual awakening which in turn
gave rise to the idea of "practicing the principles." For these two
ideas (an awakening and practicing spiritual principles) were
clearly present in the Oxford Group literature and teaching long
before Bill associated himself with the Oxford Group. And Bill
must have been saturated with talk about conversion and about
practicing the principles of the Four Absolutes from the day Ebby

---

[103] *The Language of the Heart*, pp. 297-98.

[104] See Samuel M. Shoemaker, *Calvary Church Yesterday and Today* (New York:
Fleming H. Revell, 1936), pp. 247-50; *Children of the Second Birth* (New York:
Fleming H. Revell, 1927), pp. 14-16, 121-25, 127-28; Cuyler, *Calvary Church In
Action*, pp. 61-70; V. C. Kitchen, *I Was a Pagan* (New York: Harper & Brothers,
1934); and Charles Clapp, Jr., *The Big Bender* (New York: Harper & Brothers, 1938),
pp. 105-52. In fact, in a letter to the author, dated October, 1994, Kitchen's daughter
wrote the author that, whether Kitchen was an alcoholic or not, he indeed had a serious
problem with alcohol and was relieved of it and died sober years later.

[105] See observations in *Pass It On*, pp. 124-25.

Thacher first carried the Oxford Group message to Bill to the day Bill left the Oxford Group in 1937.[106]

Ideas pertaining to Conversion and the Four Standards were in place and articulated long before the William James book was written.[107] It is likely they had been learned and absorbed by Bill through his Calvary Mission and Oxford Group contacts before he had had, in later years, an opportunity to reflect on the fine points he might have read in James's book as he came out of early "detox."

We do believe there are at least four A.A. ideas which could possibly have come to Bill Wilson from William James via the Oxford Group:

1. Deflation or "hitting bottom," an idea whose presence in Oxford Group thought might *possibly* be found as the result of the relationship of Harold Begbie to Frank Buchman. Begbie wrote *Twice-Born Men* in 1909, dedicated it to William James, and described the "born again" changes which occurred when wretches turned from despair and misery to Christ and changed through a

---

[106] At pages 113-16 of *Pass It On*, there is a lengthy discussion of: (1) Dr. Carl Jung's having told Rowland Hazard that he must have a "spiritual awakening" to recover from his obsession with alcohol, (2) Jung's telling Rowland he should align himself with a religious movement, (3) Rowland's "joining" the Oxford Group and receiving a thorough indoctrination in Oxford Group teachings, (4) Rowland's impressing upon Ebby Thacher the four principles of the Oxford Group—absolute honesty, purity, unselfishness and love—with particular emphasis on absolute honesty ("Honesty with yourself, honesty with your fellowman, honesty with God"), and (5) the fact that Rowland and Ebby each had a religious experience through the Oxford Group, had been relieved of the obsession to drink, and had received a peace of mind and happiness not known for years prior to their respective experiences. For clear statements that the necessity for religious experiences or awakenings were part of the Oxford Group teachings and that the principles of the Four Absolutes were "standards" to be practiced, see Shoemaker, *Realizing Religion*, pp. 9, 22-31; Buchman, *Remaking the World*, pp. 19, 24, 35; *What Is The Oxford Group?*, pp. 7-9; Wing, *Grateful to Have Been There*, pp. 20-21; and Big Book, pp. 13-15.

[107] See, for example, James H. Leuba, "A Study in the Psychology of Religious Phenomena," *The American Journal of Psychology*, Volume VII, No. 3, April, 1896.

conversion experience.[108] Later, Begbie wrote *Life Changers*, (also published as *More Twice-Born Men*), in which Begbie described Frank Buchman's "art" of soul-surgery and how his life-changing personal work enabled men, through Jesus Christ, to be relieved of sin.[109] In other words, Begbie certainly dramatized the origins of some conversion experiences in those besotted with alcoholism and/or with "sin" and who had lost all.[110]

2. Validation of conversion experiences by which men were "changed" and "found or discovered God." In this area, there is little doubt of the James influence on some Oxford Group writers, particularly Shoemaker, and little doubt that these James ideas were transmitted to Bill Wilson via Ebby Thacher after Bill Wilson had his dramatic Towns Hospital religious experience.[111]

3. Definition of what a conversion experience is. In this realm, we can certainly find the James definition quoted in Oxford Group books. We can also find Bill Wilson attributing conversion experience information to James.[112] But the actual description of the change itself was, as A.A. years rolled on, very much left to individual definition and description.[113]

4. Bill's apparently belated attribution to James of the idea of "practicing the principles" in the sense that Bill felt they could not be practiced without being preceded by the spiritual awakening thoughts he attributed to James. As we have said, we find this last thesis—that James was a major source of "practicing the principles"—difficult to buy.

---

[108] Begbie, *Twice-Born Men.*

[109] Begbie, *Life Changers*, pp. 13-41.

[110] See also the lengthy James H. Leuba study mentioned above.

[111] See, for example, the views of Mel B., *New Wine*, pp. 24-25; and Big Book, p. 28.

[112] Mel B., *New Wine*, p. 25.

[113] See *Came To Believe* (New York: Alcoholics Anonymous World Services, Inc., 1973).

In any event, the William James book was a favorite of A.A. co-founder, Dr. Bob; was on his supposed "required reading list;" and was frequently read by early AAs.[114] Thus the thinking of William James must have been paramount in the minds of Shoemaker, Bill Wilson, and Dr. Bob as the thinking of a distinguished scholar who, along with psychologists James H. Leuba and Edwin Diller Starbuck, documented religious conversion as a cure for alcoholism.[115]

Dr. John R. Mott

By the time of his death, John R. Mott had become President of the World Alliance of YMCA's, the World Student Christian Federation, and the Student Volunteer Movement.[116] Frank Buchman's biographer, Garth Lean, said Mott was Buchman's "old friend and mentor."[117]

Buchman's first encounter with Mott was in the summer of 1901 when Buchman had been to the Northfield Student Conference in Massachusetts, founded by Dwight L. Moody, and then run by Mott. Mott was then the Assistant General Secretary of the YMCA, and Lean called him "perhaps the dominant figure in the student evangelical movement."[118] About 1909, John Mott's office at YMCA headquarters arranged for Buchman to be YMCA Secretary at Penn State College and be in charge of the religious work at the college.[119]

---

[114] *DR. BOB*, pp. 306, 310; Pittman, *AA The Way It Began*, pp. 192, 197; and Dick B., *Dr. Bob's Library*, pp. 12, 51-52, 68.

[115] See discussion in Pittman, *AA The Way It Began*, pp. 72-81; and the Leuba article we cited above.

[116] C. Howard Hopkins, *John R. Mott, A Biography* (Grand Rapids: William B. Erdmans Publishing Company, 1979), pp. 698-99.

[117] Lean, *On the Tail of a Comet*, p. 417. For further insight on Buchman and Mott, see Mowat, *Modern Prophetic Voices*, pp. 32, 50, 67-68, 87-88.

[118] Lean, *On the Tail of a Comet*, p. 17.

[119] Lean, *On the Tail of a Comet*, p. 33.

In 1915, Mott—very pleased with Buchman's work at Penn State—arranged for Buchman to go abroad; and Buchman went to India with Dr. Sherwood Eddy to help prepare a large-scale religious campaign.[120] Buchman was not happy with the YMCA secretaries in India and ultimately went to China with Mott's son (John), Howard Walter (who was to become the author of *Soul Surgery*), and Sherwood Day (who became one of Sam Shoemaker's closest friends).[121] Mott went on to become General Secretary of the American YMCA, but Buchman was to leave his YMCA connection and his post at Hartford Seminary and go out to remake the world, feeling a higher calling.[122]

Yet the impact of Mott's twenty-year relationship with Buchman remained. As stated, Buchman, Henry Wright, and Howard Walter collaborated on Walter's book, *Soul Surgery*.[123] And that book is replete with references to John R. Mott's ideas and books.[124] The Mott books and pamphlets Walter mentioned were *The Present World Situation*, *Individual Work for Individuals*, *Personal Work How Organized and Accomplished*, and *Constructive Suggestions for Character Building*. Most were published by the Association Press.

Mott's major contribution to Buchman, reflected in the Walter book, concerned the technique for carrying the Christian message to individual people.

Before leaving Mott, we should point to some observations made in his biography. First, Mott was an effective advocate of world outreach, but also embodied the evangelical ideals of enthusiasm, dedication, Bible study, the life of prayer, and full

---

[120] Austin, *Frank Buchman As I Knew Him*, p. 18.

[121] Lean, *On the Tail of a Comet*, pp. 45-46, 50. The point about Shoemaker's friendship with Day was conveyed to the author by Shoemaker's younger daughter, Nickie Shoemaker Haggart, in a personal interview in Florida in 1993.

[122] Lean, *On the Tail of a Comet*, pp. 81-96; and Austin, *Frank Buchman As I Knew Him*, pp. 38-40.

[123] Austin, *Frank Buchman As I Knew Him*, pp. 18-19.

[124] Walter, *Soul Surgery*, pp. 11-13, 18, 87.

commitment to Christ.[125] These ideals were embodied in YMCA practices which found a counterpart in Oxford Group ideals and activities. Second, the concept of "Morning Watch" was significant in the Bible study and prayer realms, and Mott promoted it at every opportunity.[126] The Morning Watch practice—ultimately to be known in the Oxford Group as Quiet Time—became a very definite part of the lives that Mott touched. Henry B. Wright practiced it.[127] Oxford Group writer Jack Winslow practiced it, moved by John Mott.[128] The Reverend Sam Shoemaker practiced it.[129]

Jack Winslow had this to say of Mott's enthusiasm for the Morning Watch:

> But, amid much else that has been forgotten, one sentence spoken by Mott proved revolutionary. He said something of this kind: "If you wish to make your life effective and useful for God and your fellow-men, it is essential that you should put aside unhurried time every day for a morning watch with God."[130]

Mott had a thirteen-year association with evangelist Dwight Moody who, as we have stated, had great impact on Drummond, Wright, and Buchman.[131] When Frank Buchman first headed for the Northfield, Massachusetts, summer conference in 1901, the conference—founded by Moody—was then under the leadership of

---

[125] Hopkins, *John R. Mott*, p. 214.

[126] Hopkins, *John R. Mott*, p. 218. Oxford Group writer, T. Willard Hunter, wrote the author, "Morning Watch was part of the daily program at YMCA youth conferences like the one I attended at Lake Geneva, Wisconsin, in 1933."

[127] See Macintosh, *Personal Religion*, p. 362.

[128] Jack C. Winslow, *When I Awake* (London: Hodder & Stoughton, 1938), pp. 5, 9-11.

[129] Shoemaker, *Realizing Religion*, pp. 60-61.

[130] Winslow, *When I Awake*, p. 9. See also the Morning Watch comment in Harry Emerson Fosdick, *The Meaning of Prayer* (New York: Association Press, 1915), p. xi. Fosdick's book contains an introduction by John R. Mott.

[131] Hopkins, *John R. Mott*, p. 223.

John R. Mott and Robert E. Speer.[132] All of these men—Moody, Drummond, Speer, Mott, and Henry B. Wright—were, through the student movement, a vital part of Buchman's training in personal work. And Buchman ultimately shared the training with Samuel M. Shoemaker, first in China, and then, for some 20 years thereafter, in America.

Professor Henry B. Wright

Oxford Group writer and long-time Buchman associate, Reverend T. Willard Hunter, wrote of Professor Henry B. Wright:

> The key to Buchman's life and methods during these years [1909 to 1915] was Henry B. Wright. The Yale professor was probably the most influential single individual in Frank's entire life, outside his mother. From Wright, Buchman heard of the four absolute standards of honesty, purity, unselfishness, and love. The two men were almost of an age, although Wright (1877-1923) lived hardly more than half as long, dying at 46 of tuberculosis. Wright taught classics at Yale and developed an undergraduate Christian work of widespread influence. Some say they still feel it in New Haven. Buchman also learned from Wright how to conduct a meeting, follow up individuals with intensive care, and pursue one-to-one life changing through warm personal friendship. Together they were planning to bring out a book on personal evangelism [ultimately Walter's *Soul Surgery*], a project prevented by Wright's death.[133]

In the face of such a statement, one would expect to find much writing about the details of Wright's influence on Buchman. And much has been written. But the fact is that Wright's ideas came largely from the mentors we have already discussed. Wright

---

[132] Guldseth, *Streams*, p. 87.

[133] Hunter, *World Changing Through Life Changing*, pp. 15-16.

generously credits all these mentors in his *The Will of God and a Man's Lifework.*

Wright gave Professor Bushnell full acknowledgement for Bushnell's ideas as to God's Plan.[134] Wright credited Dr. Speer for the moral standards of Jesus and the Four Absolutes.[135] Wright pointed to Drummond in connection with "Thy will be done" as an expression of self-surrender, and with the idea of "giving everything to God."[136] Wright extensively quoted Drummond and F. W. Robertson in connection with the concept of *willingness* to do God's Will as the necessary condition for knowledge of it, and obedience as the organ of spiritual knowledge.[137] Wright quoted Drummond for the vital idea that the Bible is the embodiment, in written words, of God's Universal Will.[138] Wright discussed at great length the writings of Bushnell, Drummond, and Speer on the subject of knowing the "particular will" of God.[139] And Wright credited Moody in connection with the "Secret Power."[140]

What, then, are some of the Wright contributions to the Oxford Group that were more clearly the product of Wright's own thinking?

Buchman's biographer, Garth Lean, emphasized the encouragement Buchman received through study of Wright's book, *The Will of God and a Man's Lifework.*[141] Lean pointed out that the central theme of Wright's book was that an individual could, through "two-way-prayer"—listening for guidance as well as talking to God—find God's will for his life and for the ordinary

---

[134] Wright, *The Will of God*, pp. 5-12.

[135] Wright, *The Will of God*, pp. 15-20, 167-220.

[136] Wright, *The Will of God*, pp. 50-51, 74.

[137] Wright, *The Will of God*, pp. 118-19, 125-26, 234-40.

[138] Wright, *The Will of God*, pp. 132-38.

[139] Wright, *The Will of God*, pp. 119-246.

[140] Wright, *The Will of God*, p. 256.

[141] See also Spoerri, *Dynamic out of Silence*, pp. 39-40.

events of the day.[142] And Buchman very much picked up on and practiced Wright's ideas of: (1) setting aside time each day for "listening" prayer, (2) receiving "that arresting tick," and (3) writing down the thoughts received. While Henry Wright got his ideas for the "Four Standards" from, and credited Dr. Robert E. Speer for, the absolutes of "honesty, purity, unselfishness, and love," it was from Henry Wright's book that Buchman found those standards summarized and then realized their importance.[143] Finally, Lean emphasized the part that Henry Wright played in placing before Buchman, during Wright's lectures at Yale, Dwight Moody's challenge to man to give up his will to God.[144]

Professor Douglas Clyde Macintosh made a comprehensive survey of the influence of Wright upon the thought and methods of Frank Buchman.[145] Macintosh mentioned "Expert Friendship" as an important Wright influence. He said that, for Wright, the Christian life was the life more abundant, and evangelism the art of influencing men and women to lay hold on this more complete life.[146]

The "art" was that of personal evangelism and was no doubt embodied in the Wright-Buchman-Walter effort set forth in *Soul Surgery*. This personal evangelism had "decision for Christ as its objective."[147] Macintosh also suggested Wright was making a plea for self-revelation as an instrument of personal evangelism

---

[142] Lean, *On the Tail of a Comet*, pp. 74-76.

[143] Lean, *On the Tail of a Comet*, pp. 76-77.

[144] Lean, *On the Tail of a Comet*, pp. 77-78.

[145] See Macintosh, *Personal Religion, supra.*

[146] Macintosh, *Personal Religion*, pp. 348-49. See Austin, *Frank Buchman As I Knew Him*, pp. 82-83. See John 10:10: "I am come that they might have life, and that they might have it more abundantly;" and Ephesians 3:20: "Now unto him that is able to do exceeding abundantly above all that we ask or think, according to the power that worketh in us." Both these verses were, according to Austin, a part of the Buchman working vocabulary. Phillimore's *Just for Today* confirms Bunny Austin's assertion.

[147] George Stewart, Jr., *Life of Henry B. Wright* (New York: Association Press, 1925), pp. 100-01, 104, 107-08, 110, 200. See Austin, *Frank Buchman As I Knew Him*, pp. 80-83. Compare Brown, *The Venture of Belief*, pp. 26-28, emphasizing the importance of "decision" in the surrender process.

and that self-revelation required "confession and witnessing."[148] Macintosh pointed to Wright's view that *decision* for the Christian life was a drastic experience, a major operation in the life of the spirit; it involved absolute surrender to the will of God.[149]

Wright's own decision to surrender was made shortly after his graduation from Yale College when he attended the Northfield Student Conference and heard Dwight L. Moody comment simply and briefly on John 7:17.[150] At that time, said Wright, "without anyone knowing what was going on, I gave myself to God, my whole mind, heart, and body; and I meant it."[151] Wright very definitely observed the "morning watch"—with quiet time, Bible reading, and prayer.[152] And Wright was very much taken with the concept of "willingness," expressed in John 7:17, as a condition of knowing God's will.[153] As we have pointed out, however, these ideas preceded Wright.

Historian Walter Houston Clark summarized seven ideas he believed came to the Oxford Group from Henry Wright. Clark felt these justified his calling Wright "the spiritual father of the Oxford Group movement."[154]

However, an examination of Wright's writings, as well as those of people Wright cited, make it clear that most of Clark's seven concepts derived from the other mentors we have discussed. The seven are: (1) God's plan and man's obligation to surrender himself to that plan (God's Will).[155] (2) The Four Absolutes as the substance of God's will and the standards by which the Christian life is to be measured.[156] (3) Confession (with attendant

---

[148] Macintosh, *Personal Religion*, p. 352. Compare *What Is The Oxford Group?*, pp. 26-38, discussing "Sharing For Confession And Witness."

[149] Macintosh, *Personal Religion*, p. 354.

[150] Macintosh, *Personal Religion*, pp. 355-56.

[151] Stewart, *Life of Henry B. Wright*, p. 18.

[152] Stewart, *Life of Henry B. Wright*, p. 111.

[153] Macintosh, *Personal Religion*, p. 365.

[154] Clark, *The Oxford Group*, pp. 128-29.

[155] Derived from Bushnell and Drummond.

[156] Derived from Speer.

"soul-surgery" when required).[157] (4) Restitution.[158] (5) "Quiet Time" with emphasis on "two-way prayer" and Guidance.[159] (6) "Life-changing."[160] (7) Fellowship as a means of realizing the Christian life by the act of influencing a single human will or the corporate will of a group to make that decision which leads to greater fulness of life through the process of friendship.[161]

The foregoing summaries omit one of the most important Wright contributions, *if* the contribution came from Wright. That contribution is the 5 C's—Confidence, Confession, Conviction, Conversion, and Continuance. These five concepts are discussed in detail in Howard A. Walter's *Soul Surgery*, the book Walter prepared in 1919 in collaboration with Wright and Buchman.[162] The Five C ideas became a part of early A.A. talk and thinking.

Clark reported that, as early as 1910, Buchman was using Wright's manual, *The Will of God and a Man's Lifework* in his [Buchman's] classes.[163] Clark said any influence between Wright and Buchman was chiefly from Wright to Buchman and not vice versa.[164] But did the 5 C's originate with Wright or with Buchman?

It appears that the nomenclature, at least, is something Buchman got directly through the guidance of God. In *Group Movements Throughout the Ages*, R. H. Murray wrote:

---

[157] Derived primarily from James 5:16 and from Moody.

[158] Derived from Moody and, particularly, from several Bible verses in the Sermon on the Mount [Matthew 5:23-24], Luke 15 [containing the story of the "Prodigal Son"], Luke 19:1-10 [containing the story of Zacchaeus], and the Book of Numbers [Numbers 5:6-7].

[159] Derived from Drummond, Meyer, and Mott.

[160] Derived in part from Moody and in part from Drummond.

[161] See Shoemaker, *Religion That Works*, p. 67.

[162] Walter, *Soul Surgery*, pp. 30-100. In April of 1992, Garth Lean wrote the author that the collaboration was actually made impossible due to the deaths of Walter in 1918 and Wright in 1924. Lean said Walter deserved the credit, as he was the author of the soul-surgery book, while Wright and Buchman only supplied ideas and corrected the final draft.

[163] Clark, *The Oxford Group*, p. 129.

[164] Clark, *The Oxford Group*, p. 129.

In 1917 Frank Buchman was crossing the Pacific and a fellow-passenger listened to his statement that normal Christianity enabled the ordinary person to do the extraordinary thing. She asked him one evening how an ordinary person like herself could win others to Christ. "But," she added warningly, "if you tell me, you must tell it very simply." Next morning during his quiet time five words came to him, and he wrote them down—confidence, confession, conviction, conversion, and continuance—words he passed on to her (p. 317).

Howard Walter said the art of soul-winning had been described as "Woo, Win, Warn;" but that Buchman had suggested the 5 C nomenclature.[165] We mention the 5 C's at this point because we believe they had much to do with the form the A.A. Steps took; and we are not sure whether the 5 C's themselves [as distinguished from the five descriptive words] were put together by Buchman himself as the result of direct guidance he received, or whether he had been given the personal evangelism procedures by a mentor such as Wright and, by guidance, simply gave them alliterative expression. The foregoing account of Buchman's receipt of the 5 C's in his "quiet time" also appears in *Life Changers*. It was accompanied there by a discussion of how the principles of Christian work with individuals were forming in Buchman's mind. Thus we believe the five words—Confidence, Confession, Conviction, Conversion, and Continuance (the five C's)—which described the "art" of "soul-surgery"—were a product Buchman himself received—the product, as Buchman would put it, of writing down Divine thoughts received.[166] The words described the personal evangelism "art" Buchman was then developing, however he may have received and fleshed out the specifics.

---

[165] Walter, *Soul Surgery*, p. 30.
[166] Begbie, *Life Changers*, pp. 168-71.

3

Frank Buchman and His
First Century Christian Fellowship

Some Chapters in Frank Buchman's Life[1]

Frank Nathan Daniel Buchman was born in Pennsburg, Pennsylvania, on June 4, 1878.[2] When Buchman was eight, his parents

---

[1] Most of the biographical material which follows was taken from Garth Lean, *On the Tail of a Comet* (Colorado Springs: Helmers & Howard, 1988). Lean's title was first published in Great Britain as *Frank Buchman: A Life* (London: Constable and Company Limited, 1985). We added some brief additional material, at the suggestion of Garth Lean, from a letter to us, dated October 21, 1991, after Lean had reviewed the Oxford Group and Shoemaker portions of the author's basic research manuscript. Lean suggested the Oxford Group portion include as to Buchman "something of his growing vision and sense of calling." In view of some early events in Buchman's career and his later worldwide renown, this seemed a useful and important suggestion. After Garth Lean's death, Garth's long-time associate, Michael B. Hutchinson (who joined the Oxford Group with Garth in the early 1930's) wrote the author on July 18, 1994, suggesting some corrections for this revised edition. Additional information on Buchman's life, written by Oxford Group people, was taken from H. W. "Bunny" Austin, *Frank Buchman As I Knew Him* (London: Grosvenor Books, 1975); Peter Howard, *Frank Buchman's Secret* (New York: Doubleday, 1961); Theophil Spoerri, *Dynamic out of Silence: Frank Buchman's Relevance Today*. Translated by John Morrison (London: Grosvenor Books, 1976); and R. C. Mowat, *Modern Prophetic Voices: From Kierkegaard to Buchman* (Oxford: New Cherwell Press, 1994).

[2] Buchman died on August 7, 1961, at Freudenstadt in the Black Forest of Germany. He was laid to rest in Allentown, Pennsylvania, the location of his family home.

sent him to Perkiomen Seminary (later Perkiomen School), in Pennsburg. The seminary was run by a liberal German sect that favored Bible study and the concept of "the inner light" which they considered came through the direct inspiration and rule of the Holy Spirit. The sect, known as Schwenkfelders, may well have had an impact on Buchman's life.[3]

Buchman's family moved to Allentown, Pennsylvania, where Buchman attended Allentown High School. He later entered Muhlenberg College which was run by the Lutheran Ministerium and was designed to provide the Lutheran Church with a steady flow of ministers. From there, he went to Mount Airy Theological Seminary, a Lutheran theological institution, at Mount Airy in Germantown, Pennsylvania.

In 1901, Buchman attended a meeting of the Lutheran Church's Inner Mission Society and became interested in missionary social work. In the summer of 1901, he attended the Northfield Student Conference in Massachusetts. Buchman believed this conference "completely changed" his life. He graduated from Mt. Airy in the summer of 1902 and also studied abroad at Westminster College at Cambridge.

On September 10th, 1902, he was ordained to the Gospel Ministry at St. John's Lutheran Church in Allentown by the

---

[3] In his doctoral thesis, "The Origins and Development of the Oxford Group (Moral Re-Armament)," St. Edmund Hall, Oxford, Submission for D. Phil Thesis, January, 1976, Dr. David C. Belden spoke of "The Schwenkfelders" and said, "An additional element in Buchman's upbringing . . . was the influence of the Schwenkfelder sect. From the age of 8 until the move to Allentown, Buchman attended Perkiomen Seminary. It was a new school of only 17 pupils, whose parents clubbed together to pay the teachers. The latter were Schwenkfelders. This sect owed its origins to Caspar von Schwenkfeld (1489-1561), though it had not been his intention to found a sect. He stressed the spreading of conventicles, or groups of 'saints', throughout the churches, claiming to belong to no church himself; he rejected the sacraments and believed in the direct inspiration and rule of the Holy Spirit. . . . Any definite idea of the Schwenkfelder's influence on Frank Buchman must await further knowledge . . . . [But] some attitudes may have [had an influence]. . . . These would probably have included the belief that religion was primarily an interior matter between the individual and the Holy Spirit, that church and sacraments were of secondary importance, and that the Spirit could rule congregations as well as individuals" (pp. 86-87).

Evangelical Lutheran Ministerium of Pennsylvania and Adjacent States. He was immediately asked to start a new church in Philadelphia.

There he began to "discover" his spiritual principles as he went along. In his first parish, there was the principle that God was reliable and that, in a life of "faith and prayer," practical needs were met. By 1908, Buchman had formed a Lutheran Hospice for Young Men under authority of the Church's Home Mission Board; but he got in a dispute with the Board members and resigned.

On a trip abroad, he underwent a spiritual transformation experience during his attendance at a conference at Keswick in the Lake Country of North England. He called it the turning point of his life. For the first time, he found he was effective in the lives of other individuals. At this point, he apparently learned that winning people to Christ must be his main objective in life. This Keswick experience, of which we shall later speak in more detail, gave rise to important ideas on elimination of resentment, the Cross, restitution, and forgiveness.[4]

On his return to America, Buchman became aligned with, and later became the full-time secretary of, the Penn State YMCA for seven years. During this period, he received a visit at the college from the Congregational preacher, Dr. F. B. Meyer. Meyer told Buchman he needed to make personal, man-to-man interviews central; and Buchman began thinking in terms of people rather than numbers. After Meyer's visit, Buchman began the habit of the early morning Quiet Time in which he wrote things down.[5]

---

[4] For a description of this Keswick experience and what Peter Howard called the first landmark in Buchman's life (1908), see Howard, *Frank Buchman's Secret*, pp. 22-25. Howard quoted Buchman: "With an experience of the Cross, you will shrink from nothing. I learned at Keswick that I was as wrong as anybody else. I was most in need of change. I was the one to begin" (p. 25). See also Mowat, *Modern Prophetic Voices*, pp. 76-78.

[5] Peter Howard believed a second landmark in Buchman's life was at State College, Pennsylvania. At Penn State, Howard said, Buchman "learned the secret of full obedience to the voice of God." See Howard, *Frank Buchman's Secret*, pp. 26-30.

In 1912, Buchman was struck with the conviction that Christianity has a moral backbone. He felt those who professed faith but lived filth denied before men the power of God as a force in their nature.[6]

From 1916 to 1922, Buchman was connected part-time with the Hartford Theological Seminary in Connecticut and traveled widely on personal evangelical work. In January of 1921, he invited three evangelical Cambridge undergraduates to join him in America. Two came, and they told of being convinced of three fundamental and practical facts concerning the leading of God: (1) God does guide. (2) Where He guides, He also provides. (3) He works at the other end, confirming and preparing the way. They spoke of getting their air and food—prayer and the Bible—but being short on exercise; really getting down to where men live and diagnosing a man's trouble.

By May of 1921, Buchman was in Cambridge and began to have the sense that God was calling him to a wider task. He was, with all humility, struck with a sudden thought: "You will be used to remake the world."[7] Even at Penn State, Buchman had begun to think with a global perspective. "Think in continents" and "be a world power," he told students.

In his travels, Buchman met Samuel Moor Shoemaker, Jr., in Peking, China. On January 19, 1918, Buchman came to Peking on a personal work campaign. He brought with him convictions about the Four Absolutes—Honesty, Purity, Unselfishness, and Love. On visiting with Shoemaker in China, Buchman helped bring Shoemaker to a "crisis of self-surrender." Shoemaker believed this religious experience was, as he described it, "the greatest turning point in my life."

---

[6] To Howard, this conviction indicated another Buchman landmark. Howard, *Frank Buchman's Secret*, p. 30.

[7] Howard believed this period in 1921, in which Buchman had these thoughts, was another landmark. See Howard, *Frank Buchman's Secret*, p. 30-32; and Loudon Hamilton, *MRA: How It All Began* (London: Moral Re-Armament, n.d.).

Shoemaker's conversion story has been told, from several viewpoints, by several authors.[8] But all make clear that, from that point on, and for the next twenty-plus years, Buchman and Shoemaker worked in company in many ways.[9]

There are a couple of important Buchman ideas which escaped us in the writing of our first edition. Both ideas seemed to have had a major influence on A.A. principles and language as these Buchman ideas filtered down from their Oxford Group sources.

Both ideas come from an often-related story about Buchman and a boy he met in the Himalayas. Buchman had met Gandhi in India in 1915 and then was invited by the headmaster of a famous public school to come to the school camp. The master complained about a boy called Victor. The boy was very rebellious; and the master asked Buchman to talk to him. Buchman agreed. Buchman shared with Victor some of his own rebelliousness. The boy then shared honestly about his (the boy's) own wrong behavior. Buchman shared with the boy about Jesus and the big "I" in sin which comes between a person and God or between the first person and another.

Buchman then told the boy how he himself had gone on his knees and *given all of himself that he knew to all that he knew of God.* Victor told Buchman, "I'd like to do that." The boy then went on his knees with Buchman and said, *"Lord, manage me, for I can't manage myself."* Later, the boy told Buchman, "It's as if a lot of old luggage had rolled away that was no good. I must go

---

[8] Lean, *On the Tail of a Comet*, pp. 54-57; A. J. Russell, *For Sinners Only* (London: Hodder & Stoughton, 1932), pp. 208-11; Helen Smith Shoemaker, *I Stand by the Door* (New York: Harper & Row, 1967), pp. 24-27; and Irving Harris, *The Breeze of the Spirit* (New York: The Seabury Press, 1978), pp. 2-6.

[9] As the author and his son, Ken, reviewed Shoemaker's personal journals at the home of Jim Newton in Florida (in the presence of Shoemaker's younger daughter, Nickie Haggart), all noticed that every year, in the journals we examined, Shoemaker made a notation as to the importance of the decision he made on January 19, 1918, during Buchman's visit to China. Shoemaker often wrote on January 19 of each year that he had made, on that date, his "great decision to surrender all to God." See Dick B., *New Light on Alcoholism: The A.A. Legacy from Sam Shoemaker* (Corte Madera, CA: Good Book Publishing Company, 1994), pp. 40-42.

and tell my friends what has happened to me." Buchman said, "If Jesus is your best friend, then it's plain bad manners not to introduce him to other people."

Victor changed, and people began talking about that change. The story spread throughout India. Later, a Bishop met Buchman and said to him, "I don't need any introduction to you. I've seen Victor."

The "Victor" story contains a number of elements of Buchman's life-changing art; and those should become apparent as our study of the Oxford Group proceeds. But the important point, we believe, is that the seeds were sown for two vital A.A. ideas seldom credited to an Oxford Group source.

The first A.A. idea involved the concept of surrendering to God as one understands Him. As we document in the following footnote, and will later discuss in more detail, the Victor story marks the origin, we believe, of the concept that one need only surrender as much of himself as he knows (or understands) to as much of God as he knows (or understands) in order to begin the path to a relationship with God. Oxford Group people often spoke of "surrendering as much of yourself as you understand to as much of God as you understand."[10] Or, in the alternative, of surrendering all one knows of self to all one knows of God.[11] Bill Wilson used such surrender-to-God-as-you-understand-Him language at the very beginnings of his Oxford Group association.[12] And Anne Smith suggested it as a prayer of

---

[10] Samuel M. Shoemaker, *Children of the Second Birth* (New York: Fleming H. Revell, 1927), pp. 27, 47; *How to Become a Christian* (New York: Harper & Brothers, 1953), p. 72; *How to Find God* (Reprint from *Faith at Work* magazine, n.d.), p. 6; "In Memoriam" (Princeton: The Graduate Council, June 10, 1956), pp. 2-3; and Dick B., *New Light on Alcoholism*, pp. 45, 350.

[11] Stephen Foot, *Life Began Yesterday* (New York: Harper & Brothers, 1935), pp. 12-13, 175; and James D. Newton, *Uncommon Friends* (New York: Harcourt Brace, 1987), p. 154.

[12] See full discussion in Dick B., *Anne Smith's Journal: A.A.'s Principles of Success* (San Rafael, California: Paradise Research Publications, 1994), pp. 24-29.

decision for the people she helped in A.A.'s birthplace at Akron, Ohio.[13]

The second A.A. idea involved the concept of the unmanageable life, epitomized by the prayer of surrender, "Lord, manage me, for I can't manage myself."[14] Dr. Bob's wife, Anne, three times utilized this prayer in the spiritual journal she read to early AAs.[15] And A.A. seems to have incorporated this idea in its First Step and in its well-known "a,b,c's."[16]

Before leaving this brief review of Buchman's basic religious and evangelical background, we should mention some of the early world events in Buchman's life that were to result in Buchman's working with a "drunken world," as he called it, while his long-time colleague, Sam Shoemaker, came to focus on individual work within the church framework.[17]

As the years rolled by, Buchman received an honorary Doctor of Divinity degree at Muhlenberg College and an honorary LL.D degree from Oglethorpe University. He was twice nominated for the Nobel Peace Prize. And he was decorated by the governments

---

[13] Dick B., *Anne Smith's Journal*, pp. 25, 29.

[14] For the innumerable times in which the Victor story was told in company with the "Lord, manage me, for I can't manage myself" prayer, see Lean, *On the Tail of a Comet*, pp. 47-48, 113; Howard, *Frank Buchman's Secret*, pp. 41-44; Spoerri, *Dynamic out of Silence*, pp. 34-37; Russell, For *Sinners Only*, p. 79; and Cecil Rose, *When Man Listens* (New York: Oxford University Press, 1937), pp. 19-22. Sam Shoemaker used a similar prayer. See Harris, *The Breeze of the Spirit*, p. 10; and Shoemaker, *How to Find God*, p. 6; and *How You Can Help Other People* (New York: E. P. Dutton & Co., 1946), p. 60.

[15] Dick B., *Anne Smith's Journal*, pp. 20-22.

[16] A.A.'s First Step language states: "We admitted we were powerless over alcohol—that our lives had become unmanageable" (Big Book, p. 59). The "a,b,c's" state: "Our description of the alcoholic, the chapter to the agnostic, and our personal adventures before and after make clear three pertinent ideas: (a) That we were alcoholic and could not manage our own lives. (b) That probably no human power could have relieved our alcoholism. (c) That God could and would if He were sought" (Big Book, p. 60).

[17] See T. Willard Hunter, *AA & MRA "It Started Right There": Behind the Twelve Steps and the Self-help Movement* (Washington, D.C.: Moral Re-Armament, 1994), pp. 18-19; and Dick B., *New Light on Alcoholism*, p. 49.

of France, Germany, Japan, Republic of China and others. Dr. Hans Koch, adviser to Chancellor Konrad Adenauer of Germany, outlined five reasons why Buchman might have qualified for the Nobel Peace nominations: (1) foundations for new trust between Germany and France; (2) unity between Japan and her neighbors in southeast Asia; (3) interracial unity and moral basis of self-government in Africa; (4) moves helping the Islamic World to build a bridge between East and West; and (5) racial teamwork in the United States.[18]

Garth Lean, Buchman's biographer, pointed the author to some significant growth periods in Buchman's life: (1) In South America, in 1931, the Communist bid for world power brought home a new challenge to Buchman. He concluded Communism was built on moral relativism in an advanced form but was also militantly anti-God. He noted, "Communism is the most organized and effective leadership abroad today. . . . Vital Christianity is the only cure."[19] (2) By 1933, Buchman perceived the need to redirect the forces let loose in Germany. His speeches and broadcasts were in part drafted with Hitler in mind. Lean wrote, "Where Hitler demanded the 'leadership principle' and 'the dictatorship of the Party', Buchman called for God-control and the 'dictatorship of the living Spirit of God.'"[20] (3) Though Buchman failed in Germany in the thirties, he achieved victory in the post-war period and had a part in laying foundations for democracy in Japan.[21] (4) In his last years, Buchman prophesied that Commun-

---

[18] These five are set forth in T. Willard Hunter, *World Changing Through Life Changing* (Newton Center, Mass.: Andover Newton Theological School, 1977), pp. 169-70. See also Lean, *On the Tail of a Comet*, discussing national revivals in South Africa (pp. 137-38, 140-43); Canada (pp. 192-202); Norway (pp. 215-25); Denmark (pp. 225-30); and Britain (p. 161). And see Austin, *Frank Buchman As I Knew Him*, pp. 92-197.

[19] Lean, *On the Tail of a Comet*, pp. 147-48.

[20] Lean, *On the Tail of a Comet*, pp. 203-14.

[21] Lean, *On the Tail of a Comet*, pp. 348-84, 498-501.

ism would disappear in our life-time and quested for "the next step ahead for the Communist and the non-Communist world alike."[22]

Lest it be thought that the foregoing views about Buchman and the Oxford Group are the only ones when the Oxford Group is examined in light of its association with Alcoholics Anonymous, one need only turn to two recent historical accounts. The first had to do with Roman Catholic concern about A.A.'s connection with the Oxford Group.[23] The second, from an entirely different source, contained an openly hostile view.[24]

It is beyond the purview of this study to discuss the question of Roman Catholic opposition to early A.A. when A.A. was an integral part of the Oxford Group. Or to discuss the Roman Catholic Church's earlier objections to the Oxford Group and Moral Re-Armament. But substantial information on this issue is available.[25] However Roman Catholic opposition to A.A. itself seemed to melt away for a number of possible reasons: (1) AAs themselves left the Oxford Group in the late 1930's. (2) The Big Book was submitted to the Catholic Committee on Publications in the New York Archdiocese at the time of its proposed publication. There, the book itself and its message were given high praise; there were some minor suggested changes; and the book received

---

[22] Lean's letter to the author, dated October 21, 1991; and Frank N. D. Buchman, *Remaking the World*, New and Rev. ed (London: Blandford Press, 1961), p. 306.

[23] See Mary C. Darrah, *Sister Ignatia: Angel of Alcoholics Anonymous* (Chicago: Loyola University Press, 1992), pp. 28-37.

[24] Charles Bufe, *Alcoholics Anonymous: Cult or Cure?* (San Francisco: Sharp Press, 1991), pp. 16-33.

[25] See the Reverend Clair M. Dinger, *Moral Re-Armament: A Study of Its Technical and Religious Nature in the Light of Catholic Teaching* (Washington, D.C.: The Catholic University of America Press), 1961; the Right Reverend Monsignor Suenens, *The Right View of Moral Re-Armament* (London: Burns and Oates, 1954); the Reverend Ronald A. Knox, "The Group Movement: Second-Hand Impressions of Buchmanism," *The Clergy Review* V (1933), pp. 265-74; Edward J. Mahoney, "Moral Re-Armament-Lawfulness for Catholics," *The Clergy Review* XXXVII (1952), pp. 157-59, 253; and Francis J. Connell, C.Ss.R, "An Important Roman Instruction," *American Ecclesiastical Review*, CXXII (1950), pp. 321-30.

"unofficial" endorsement.[26] (3) In Akron, Dr. Bob and Sister Ignatia managed to obtain the blessings of Father Vincent Haas, a newly ordained priest; then from the monsignor of the Akron Catholic deanery; and finally from the Reverend Mother Clementine, administrator of St. Thomas Hospital. And work with alcoholics proceeded there on Roman Catholic premises.[27] (4) Bill Wilson began to work with Father Ed Dowling as his "spiritual sponsor;" and Dowling told Wilson he was fascinated by the parallels he felt he had discovered between the Twelve Steps of Alcoholics Anonymous and the Exercises of St. Ignatius, the spiritual discipline of his Jesuit order.[28] (6) Bill Wilson began taking Roman Catholic instructions from Monsignor Fulton J. Sheen in 1939.[29] (7) The percentage of Roman Catholics in later Alcoholics Anonymous membership became very substantial.[30] (8) Wilson intentionally withheld public recognition of A.A.'s debt to the Oxford Group in order to assuage Roman Catholic critics.[31] (8) Wilson actually had Roman Catholic Theologian, John C. Ford, S.J., edit Wilson's *Twelve Steps and Twelve Traditions* and *Alcoholics Anonymous Comes of Age*, both of which became A.A. "Conference Approved" literature.[32]

There are various views about the Roman Catholic position as to the Oxford Group and Moral Re-Armament today.[33] However,

---

[26] *Pass It On* (New York: Alcoholics Anonymous World Services, Inc., 1984), pp. 201-02.

[27] *DR. BOB and the Good Oldtimers* (New York: Alcoholics Anonymous World Services, Inc., 1980), pp. 188-90.

[28] *Pass It On*, p. 242.

[29] *Pass It On*, p. 280-81, 335.

[30] Ernest Kurtz, *Not-God: A History of Alcoholics Anonymous*, Exp. ed. (Minnesota: Hazelden, 1991), p. 47.

[31] Kurtz, *Not-God*, pp. 51-52.

[32] See the Foreword by John Cuthbert Ford, S. J., in Darrah's, *Sister Ignatia*, p. x.

[33] See *True Dialogue: Two Addresses at Harvard University by His Eminence Franz Cardinal Koenig, former Archbishop of Vienna* (London: Grosvenor, 1986); Peter Orglmeister, *An Ideology for Today* (Moral Re-Armament Pamphlet, 1965) with Foreword by Cardinal Agnelo Rossi, Archbishop of Sao Paulo, Brazil; and Mowat,

(continued...)

we are not prepared at this point to express an opinion on that matter.

The Development of the Oxford Group

For a description of what "membership" in the Oxford Group *is*, we previously quoted a passage from *What Is The Oxford Group?*[34] In this portion, we will cover how the Oxford Group Fellowship itself developed.

Beginning at Cambridge in 1921, Frank Buchman had a sense of specific mission to remake the world.[35] He resigned his connection with Hartford Theological Seminary, and decided to step out alone; but there were hundreds of people scattered around America, Britain, and the Far East to whom he had brought a basic experience of Christ. He had shown, in miniature, that his idea—contagion through traveling teams—worked. But the only cohesive groups which had developed were at Princeton and, in a very small way, at Oxford. Some of those he had helped in America said they would raise some $3000. per year to support him.[36]

In the autumn of 1922, Buchman and a few friends formed what they called "A First Century Christian Fellowship."[37] Buchman said it was to be "a voice of protest against organized, committeeised and lifeless Christian work" and "an attempt to get

---

[33] (...continued)
Modern Prophetic Voices, pp. 28, 69; and K. D. Belden, *Reflections on Moral Re-Armament* (London: Grosvenor Books, 1983), pp. 98-99.

[34] And see The Layman With a Notebook, *What Is The Oxford Group?* (London: Oxford University Press, 1933), pp. 3-6.

[35] Lean, *On the Tail of a Comet*, p. 93.

[36] Lean, *On the Tail of a Comet*, pp. 96-97.

[37] In Part I of his five-part history of Faith at Work, Karl Olsson dated the beginning of "A First Century Christian Fellowship" at 1921 and specifically mentioned Dr. Sam Shoemaker's part in the fellowship. Karl A. Olsson, "The History of Faith at Work," *Faith at Work News*, 1982-1983.

back to the beliefs and methods of the Apostles."[38] Garth Lean (Buchman's biographer) wrote that "A First Century Christian Fellowship" was never much more than a name; and Lean added that it was composed mainly of supporters rather than people with a commitment equal to Buchman's.[39] But the name and concept very definitely stuck.[40]

Harold Begbie's *Life Changers*, first published by G. P. Putnam's Sons in 1927, said that Frank Buchman wrote Begbie that he [Buchman] was entering with others into "A First Century Christian Fellowship."[41] In the foreword to his book, *Twice-Born Ministers*, Dr. Samuel Shoemaker wrote:

> The First Century Christian Fellowship is now a movement of international proportions, and we at Calvary are a part of it. . . . I am glad to be able through this book to pay a little of my debt to the First Century Christian Fellowship, and to record again my wholehearted and unconditional identification with it.[42]

---

[38] Lean, *On the Tail of a Comet*, p. 97.

[39] Lean, *On the Tail of a Comet*, p. 97.

[40] See Walter Houston Clark, *The Oxford Group Its History and Significance* (New York: Bookman Associates, 1951), p. 35; James D. Newton, *Uncommon Friends* (New York: Harcourt Brace Jovanovich, 1987), p. 157; and Spoerri, *Dynamic out of Silence*, p. 79. It appears that Clark's dating of the name at 1927 is at variance with that of Buchman's biographer, Garth Lean. The name and identity had real significance at Rev. Sam Shoemaker's Calvary Church. See Samuel M. Shoemaker, *Twice-Born Ministers* (New York: Fleming H. Revell, 1929), pp. 23, 90, 95, 100, 122, 147, 148; *Calvary Church Yesterday and Today* (New York: Fleming H. Revell, 1936), p. 270; John Potter Cuyler, Jr., *Calvary Church in Action* (New York: Fleming H. Revell, 1934), p. 11; and Harris, *The Breeze of the Spirit*, pp. 47, 58. Compare Foot, *Life Began Yesterday*, p. 139. In fact, the name "A First Century Christian Fellowship" may have had more significance in America than at Oxford or elsewhere in the world. For Shoemaker's colleague, Olive Jones, said her book, *Inspired Children*, "presents the first detailed description of the Oxford Group Movement (in America called A First Century Christian Fellowship)." See Olive M. Jones, *Inspired Children* (New York: Harper & Brothers, 1933), p. ix.

[41] Harold Begbie, *Life Changers* (London: Mills & Boon, Ltd., 1932), p. 122.

[42] Shoemaker, *Twice-Born Ministers*, p. 23. For other references by Shoemaker in this same title to the Oxford Group as "A First Century Christian Fellowship," see pp. 46, 90, 148.

Pass It On said of "A First Century Christian Fellowship" that, "In the late 1930's, Dr. Bob, co-founder of A.A., and the other Akron, Ohio, AAs continued to refer to it [the Oxford Group] in that way" [as the First Century Christian Fellowship].[43] In fact, Dr. Bob often referred to A.A.'s own early Akron meetings as "a Christian fellowship."[44]

About 1927, the center of gravity of Buchman's fellowship had shifted to England.[45] Frank Buchman was in no way connected with Oxford University, either officially or unofficially.[46] But a number of Oxford Group activities and adherents were. In 1928, when a "team" was touring South Africa, the team were called by the press the "Oxford Group." The name really just described the composition of the party of seven, six of whom were from Oxford. But the name met with favor among themselves.[47]

By the early 1930's, the name "Oxford Group" was in common usage, exemplified by the frequency with which A. J. Russell spoke of the Oxford Group, as such, in his book *For Sinners Only*, published in 1932.[48] In 1937, a legal matter in connection with receiving bequests arose, which made it important for the fellowship to incorporate as a non-profit, charitable enterprise and, of course, to have a corporate name. Buchman favored the name

---

[43] *Pass It On*, p. 130.

[44] *DR. BOB and the Good Oldtimers*, pp. 118-19. Dr. Bob's daughter, Sue Smith Windows, informed the author in a personal interview at Akron, Ohio, in June of 1991, that Dr. Bob described every King School Group meeting (of A.A.) as a "Christian Fellowship." Early Akron AA, Bob E., wrote a note to Lois Wilson, Bill Wilson's wife, on a "Four Absolutes" pamphlet, of which the author has a copy. Bob E. said Dr. Bob referred to A.A. as a "Christian Fellowship."

[45] Clark, *The Oxford Group*, p. 75.

[46] See Alan Thornhill, *Best of Friends: A Life of Enriching Friendships* (United Kingdom: Marshall Pickering, 1986), p. 64.

[47] Clark, *The Oxford Group*, p. 35-36.

[48] Russell, *For Sinners Only*, pp. 17, 20, 21, 28, 31, 42, 82-96. See also Austin, *Frank Buchman As I Knew Him*, p. 42; *What Is The Oxford Group?*; Clarence Benson, *The Eight Points of The Oxford Group*, 6th ed (London: Humphre Milford, Oxford University Press, 1940), and Jack Winslow, *Why I Believe In The Oxford Group* (London: Hodder & Stoughton, 1934).

"Oxford Group;" and, after some legal wrangling, the Oxford Group became a non-profit entity with charitable purposes. In Great Britain, the name "Oxford Group" remains today the legal name of the incorporated body.[49]

Garth Lean wrote, in *On the Tail of a Comet*, that Frank Buchman took a new turn in 1938. Buchman felt that many who had found a rich personal experience of faith through the Oxford Group were hugging it to themselves. Buchman wanted to persuade them to enter the struggle to answer the problems of the wider world.[50] With World War II approaching, there had also been talk of "pacificism" connected with the Oxford name.[51] So Buchman launched his world outreach under the name "Moral Re-Armament."[52]

The corporate name of the Oxford Group in the United States today is "Moral Re-Armament, Inc." The group has centres in the United States, the British Isles, Australia, Canada, India, Kenya, New Zealand, Nigeria, South Africa, and Zimbabwe. There is a legal entity at Caux, Switzerland.[53]

The centre in the United States is located at 1156 Fifteenth Street, N.W., Suite 910, Washington, D.C. 20005-1704. In September of 1994, MRA announced opening of a new reconciliation center in the Dag Hammerskjold Tower near the United Nations in New York. MRA publishes a newsletter, titled

---

[49] For discussion of the name squabble, the incorporation, and British status, see Lean, *On the Tail of a Comet*, pp. 280-83.

[50] Lean, *On the Tail of a Comet*. p. 261.

[51] In April, 1992, Lean wrote the author, "This false association of pacifism was owing to the fact that the Oxford Union, the famous debating society, passed a motion in 1933 that 'We will not fight for King and country.' In America, as a result, anything to do with Oxford was regarded as pacifist. The Oxford Group, which had nothing to do with the Union, got contaminated in the American mind."

[52] Lean, *On the Tail of a Comet*, pp. 186, 238n, 261-66.

[53] K. D. Belden, *Reflections on Moral Re-Armament*, p. 18.

"Breakthroughs." And the group in Great Britain publishes "For A Change" six times a year.[54]

Concerning the various names used through the years by Buchman and his supporters, Garth Lean suggested to the author that the idea of the Oxford Group and Its Work of Moral Re-Armament, as exemplified by an Oxford Group book, perhaps best expresses where the movement is today.[55]

Oxford Group Meetings

When Bill Wilson first met Dr. Bob in Akron on Mother's Day of 1935, Bill had been going to Oxford Group meetings in New York from almost the day of Bill's release from Towns Hospital on December 18, 1934.[56] At some point very soon after that, Bill began keeping company with some very knowledgeable Oxford Group business people—Victor C. Kitchen, F. Shepard Cornell, Hanford Twitchell, Rowland Hazard, and a good many others.[57] Bill also went to Oxford Group houseparties that these men attended. We know too that Dr. Bob had been attending Oxford Group meetings in Akron with his wife, Anne, Henrietta Seiberling, and others from the date of the departure of Dr. Frank Buchman and his team from Akron, Ohio in early 1933. We believe it important to dwell briefly on the probable format of those meetings in New York and in Akron because it was that

---

[54] The foregoing information was furnished to the author courtesy of George Vondermuhll, Jr., who has been connected with M.R.A. some 40 years as a field worker and, for many years, as corporate secretary. Additional facts were supplied by Richard Ruffin, Executive Director of MRA in Washington, D.C., and by Michael B. Hutchinson, who lives at Oxford in the United Kingdom.

[55] Lean said Sir Lynden Macassey struck the right note when he titled his book *The Oxford Group and its work of Moral Re-Armament* (published by the Oxford Group in 1954).

[56] Dick B., *New Light on Alcoholism*, pp. 241-45.

[57] Dick B., *New Light on Alcoholism*, pp. 319-41.

format which had much to do with the sharing of experience, strength, and hope that is the heart of A.A.'s meetings today.

East Coast U.S. Meetings

We will not attempt to state that this or that specific thing happened at the meetings Bill, Lois, Ebby Thacher, and Shep Cornell were attending in New York area. But we can list a few elements known to have been involved. From Julia Harris, friend of Bill W., and wife of Shoemaker's assistant minister, the Reverend W. Irving Harris, came the details that most meetings involved "Sharing," also called witnessing. Sometimes they were led by Sam Shoemaker. Shoemaker would welcome people. Those present would sing a song or two. And the leader would call on people to share their spiritual experiences. Meetings would close with the Lord's Prayer.[58]

The Reverend John Potter Cuyler, Jr., gave more details through his description of some of the sharing meetings:

> [Speaking of the Advent Mission of Personal Witness:] Every night during the first week in Advent, six or eight lay-people told at a simple service held at the church, the story of their own experience of Christ, relating it to the larger problems of the world in such a way as to show how new individuals are the only possible foundation for a new world. Those who came to hear the evidence (and there were two to three hundred every night) saw instanced in the lives of those who spoke many of their own problems and the solution of them, and some passed that week from a religion of aspiration to one of possession. Possibly greater value, however, lay in the training of those who spoke. To convey a real experience of Christ to others in these days requires naturalness rather than forensic ability; evidence rather than argument; experience rather than theology. A man must learn to recognize the significance of what has happened to

---

[58] Telephone interview by the author with Julia Harris at her New Jersey home on October 5, 1991.

himself before he can proceed to estimate and record it with sensitiveness, with humour, and in a language "understanded [*sic*] of the people." Excerpts from what was said may bring out some of this quality: one man said, "Surrender costs you something; and since I thought a whole lot of myself, it cost me a whole lot." "Religion is like a talent," said another, "if you don't use it, you lose it; I find that I have to keep witnessing to people I meet every day." One woman confessed that the summer before she had "unbuckled the whole armour of God, and just relaxed." Another declared that she had found that "Sin was not just an inconvenience to me, but an insult to God."[59]

Week after week, during 1932 and 1933, the capacity of Calvary Hall was taxed, with an average attendance of 232 persons in the first of these years and 301 in the second. They came to give and to receive the quality of life that derives from full commitment to our Lord Jesus Christ. Ordinarily there are about ten speakers, of varied type, mostly lay people, who tell in simple terms what He has done in their own lives and in the situations where they are placed. On any given night, one is likely to hear from a staff-member or two, some of the guests in the house, the telephone-girl or engineer or housekeeper or Rector, visitors from Oxford Group centres elsewhere, and a constant stream of new people, business, professional, young and old, employer and employee and unemployed, who have found in Christ the answer to their needs and want to "speak that they do know and testify that they have seen.". . . In quiet and in sharing, the plan of the Holy Spirit emerges; the emphasis varies from week to week, but there is always one theme, illustrated in experience after concrete experience, that Jesus Christ changes lives, and builds a new world with them.[60]

Sam Shoemaker had these things to say about some of the early meetings:

---

[59] Cuyler, *Calvary Church in Action*, pp. 32-33.

[60] Cuyler, *Calvary Church in Action*, p. 56.

For here was found the sharing of spiritual experience by ordinary individuals, confronted with the common problems and situations of life; they talked about these things naturally; the emphasis was on the will being given to God, and on what He could do to guide and use a life so given to Him.[61]

Advent Missions have been held before in Calvary parish as this record attests; but in 1926, we held one where the speaking was done by laymen. . . . Through seven successive nights a simple service of hymns, prayers and Scripture led on to the witness of three or four men and women who spoke out of their experience. There was no preaching, no exposition—just the sharing of experience. The sequence of themes of the services was:

> Spiritual Hunger
> The Failure of Conventional Christianity
> Sin, the Hindrance to Christ
> The Living Christ
> Self-surrender, the Turning Point
> Witness from Those Changed at the Mission.[62]

Lois Wilson said this of Oxford Group meetings:

The Oxford Group meetings on Sunday afternoons were usually led by Sam Shoemaker or one of his two assistants, and various members of the congregation were asked to speak. One Sunday Bill had been chosen to "share" or "witness," as it was often called. He recounted his alcoholic story, ending with his dramatic spiritual awakening. When he had finished, a big, florid-faced

---

[61] Shoemaker, *Calvary Church Yesterday And Today*, p. 245.

[62] Shoemaker, *Calvary Church Yesterday And Today*, p. 251. For an interesting comparison with "Self-surrender, the Turning Point," see Big Book, p. 59, "We stood at the turning point. We asked His protection and care with complete abandon."

man jumped up and said he would like to talk to Bill later. . . .
He needed Bill's help.[63]

For accounts of how Oxford Group meetings were conducted in
early A.A. at the A.A.'s birthplace in Akron, when AAs were an
integral part of the Oxford Group and called themselves, "the
alcoholic squad of the Oxford Group," see Dick B., *The Akron
Genesis of Alcoholics Anonymous.*[64]

Oxford Group House Parties

Lois Wilson (Bill's wife) had the following to say about Oxford
Group houseparties:

> Occasionally we [Lois and Bill] went to OG weekend house-
> parties. A house-party was a cross between a convention and a
> retreat. People came from far and near to be with one another,
> to worship, to meditate, to ask God's guidance and to gain
> strength from doing so together. Usually two or three well-known
> persons would lead the meetings, inspiring the rest of us to do as
> they had done.[65]

As to these Oxford Group houseparties, Julia Harris said to the
author, in her telephone interview in 1991, that houseparties
usually had choir time in the morning; then small groups; and then

---

[63] *Lois Remembers* (New York: Al-Anon Family Headquarters, Inc., 1988), pp. 93-
94. See also our discussion of Lois Wilson's Oxford Group Notebook, which contained
a number of the points that were made by the Oxford Group at meetings attended by Bill
and Lois. Lois's notes are set forth in full in Dick B., *New Light on Alcoholism*, pp. 337-
41.

[64] Dick B., *The Akron Genesis of Alcoholics Anonymous* (Corte Madera, CA: Good
Book Publishing Company, 1994), pp. 181-216.

[65] *Lois Remembers*, p. 103. See Dick B., *The Akron Genesis*, pp. 135-80. In her
"Oxford Group Notes," Lois Wilson specifically mentioned that F. Shepard Cornell had
led one meeting and that the Rev. Garrett Stearly had led a meeting at the Pocono House
Party. Dick B., *New Light on Alcoholism*, pp. 338-39.

a big chunk on the Bible each morning. Bible studies, lasting one and a half hours, were often led by Cleve Hicks [who was one of those on the Oxford Group team that went to Akron in January, 1933].[66] Then there would be reading with individual people questioning and sharing.

The Church of England Newspaper published a little pamphlet by The Bishop of Leicester, Chancellor R. J. Campbell, and its own Editor, titled "Stories of our Oxford House Party." The event occurred in 1931. Dr. Cyril Bardsley, the Bishop of Leicester, had the following to say of the emphasis:

> Three words are specially emphasized by the Groups—surrender, sharing, guidance. Complete surrender to Christ is urged if any person is to receive in fulness God's gifts of life and power. It is taught that this surrender involves absolute and unhesitating obedience—that the surrendered and consecrated life day by day is only possible through use of the means of grace, and great emphasis is laid upon the importance of the morning watch. "Sharing" is the word that has attracted most attention and called forth most criticism. . . . By "sharing" is meant the making known to others of personal failures and defeats, and of help and strength received in Christ. I must immediately say that any confession of acts—e.g., immoral acts or habits—at a group meeting is not allowed. . . . The possibility and need of constant guidance by the Holy Spirit is much stressed. This is to be sought and looked for in daily life and work.

Chancellor R. J. Campbell, D.D., said:

> Being intensely in divine guidance they are accustomed to begin the day with what they call a "quiet time," wordless waiting upon God. They believe, and with good reason, that we spend too much time in asking God for things and too little listening to what He may have to say to us. . . . They practice daily Bible

---

[66] Lois Wilson mentioned in her notes Charles Haines and the Bible; and she mentioned Cleveland Hicks. See Dick B., *New Light on Alcoholism*, pp. 337-39.

study for the nurture of the spiritual life. I listened to the conducting of one such study circle by a young clergyman. . . .' He did very little talking himself. With the Greek Testament on his knees he would give the literal meaning of a passage and then wait for members of the circle to give their several ideas of its spiritual value before adducing his own. . . . The most distinguishing feature of the gathering was what its members called "sharing"—in other words the frank and unreserved statement of what faith in Christ and experience of the operation of the Holy Spirit had done for them severally in changing their lives. It is this changing of lives that is the chief aim of the movement. The name we all know it by is conversion, but it is conversion that goes to the very root of what is morally wrong.

Jim Newton provided the author with an invitation to an Oxford Group houseparty at The Hotel Hawthorne in Salem, Massachusetts. The event took place between January 25 and 31, 1929. The following description of houseparties was contained in the invitation:

For the past decade or so there has been developing a unique variety of religious gathering known as a "houseparty." The name has held because it best describes the atmosphere of these gatherings, which, in their general setting, more closely resemble a secular houseparty than the "religious conference" or "convention." A prominent editor has called these meetings "the church in the house." They range in size from twenty to one hundred and fifty or more people. The place is a country inn, a hotel, or a private residence according to the demand for space. The period of time extends from a week-end to a week or ten days. They are attended by people of all ages and all professions—young people, parents, teachers, younger business men, men and women in every walk of life. Group meetings are held and people are free to go or not as they choose. There is time for quiet with one's self, for conversation with one's friends, and for the larger meetings. The object of the houseparty is frankly to relate modern individuals to Jesus Christ in terms which they understand and in an environment which they find convenient. The fundamentals of the principles of the message are covered in a series of informal talks. Bible study takes up an important part of each day. Separate groups for men and women, often divided as to age and profession, provide an opportunity for discussion of various problems relating to different aspects of the Christian life. Each morning opens with a time of united quiet during which thought is directed toward God in full conviction that, to a mind and heart eager to discover it, He can make known His will. The evening provides a period when anyone can talk who wants to.

Jim and Eleanor Forde Newton furnished us with another houseparty invitation by "The Groups—A First Century Christian Fellowship." The invitation was to a houseparty at Briarcliff Lodge at Briarcliff Manor, in New York. The event was scheduled for May 2-12, 1930; and the invitation said:

Emphasis will be laid on methods of Bible study. To this end, Miss Mary Angevine, of the biblical seminary in New York, will conduct Bible classes during the conference.

The movement of the houseparty will include a consideration of the following problems as related to the main topics:

Spiritual diagnosis.
The place of the guidance of God in human lives.
The principles of sharing Christian experiences.
The methods of helping those in difficulties.
The place of possessions.
The principles involved in developing a national and international fellowship.

Bill Wilson gave this description of some of the things he had heard at such meetings:

[*Pass It On* said that it appeared to Bill that social, class, and racial barriers were almost nonexistent in the Oxford Group, and even religious differences had been forgotten. Bill said:] Little was heard of theology, but we heard plenty of absolute honesty, absolute purity, absolute unselfishness, and absolute love. . . . Confession, restitution, and direct guidance of God underlined every conversation. They were talking about morality and spirituality, about God-centeredness versus self-centeredness.[67]

Oxford Group Teams

The Oxford Group relied heavily on "teams" to accomplish its life-changing objectives. Writing on the Biblical principle involved, the Reverend Sherwood Day said:

Jesus Christ believed in teamwork. He gathered a small group about Him and set the example for all His followers in this respect. . . . Individuals were members of a living body whose Head was Jesus Christ. . . . Truth is presented more adequately through a group than through an individual.[68]

Historian Walter Clark commented:

Key men and the *Team.* While not given prominence in the literature, the term "key men" is often heard in the counsels of the Group. Dr. Buchman, or "Frank," as he is always known to his followers, always made special efforts to convert the leaders in any group on which he had designs on the sound theory that the prestige of such people would enable them to touch others and so to spread the influence of the movement. He would then attempt to persuade the most impressive of these key men to accompany him on his evangelical trips. This group would be known as the "team." In the early days of the movement the members of the teams were usually young men in college or recent graduates. . . . It was Buchman's habit to remain in the background at meetings as much as possible, calling on the team members and

---

[67] *Pass It On*, p. 127.

[68] See discussions in Dick B., *New Light on Alcoholism*, p. 71; *Anne Smith's Journal*, pp. 88, 129; and Ephesians 2:12-19; 3:2-6, 9; 4:4-6, 15-16; 5:20-30; Colossians 1:18; 2:17-19; 3:11.

others to do the talking. Many times attendants at house-parties brought away a much more vivid remembrance of team members than of Buchman himself. Membership in a team did not always signify complete dedication to the movement, but a place was often offered to "key men" who were thought to be on the road to conversion because their participation was likely to speed the process. . . . Today the activities of teams and the interest in key people are as green as in days gone by. But instead of an interest in a football captain or president of the student body, the modern quarry is a foreign minister or the head of a state; instead of a team visit to a neighboring campus, a modern team may circle the globe.[69]

Longtime Oxford Group activist and writer, K. D. Belden wrote a whole chapter, from the perspective of an Oxford Group adherent, on Frank Buchman's teamwork ideas. It was titled "Teamwork: God in community."[70] The following are some useful descriptions:

> The day after I first gave my life to God, I went to talk to the friend in my college who had helped me decide. "Well," he said when I told him I had taken the decisive step, "that means you're on the team now." "The team," I asked, "What's that?" No one had mentioned this before. . . . "What do you do there?" I asked. " We give the news of what we have been doing the day before," he told me, "and we share the lessons we are learning, and what God is showing us about how to live the life." It appeared that they usually studied the Bible together and the principles of the Christian life. . . (p. 62).

> This was my introduction to the fact that the Christian life is designed to be lived in teamwork. The norm, from the earliest days, I came to realize, is the action of a team. It may be two

---

[69] Clark, *The Oxford Group*, pp. 31-32.

[70] Belden, *Reflections on Moral Re-Armament*, pp. 62-72. See also Garth Lean, *Cast Out Your Nets: Sharing your Faith with others* (London: Grosvenor, 1990), p. 121-28. Leans's Chapter Fourteen is titled, "Building a Team."

people, it may be twenty, it may be two hundred, but it is in the team that the faith is demonstrated. . . . Jesus created a team from the first and seldom moved without one (p. 63).

Frank Buchman re-emphasized the concept of teamwork as normal Christian living. As a young man he learned to take teams of students up and down the universities of the eastern states of America and later, too, across the Atlantic, training them in action to live the life, give their message, win men and move together. . . . He always felt that a team, of whatever size, was more effective and gave a wider picture of God's action than any individual could give (pp. 65-66).

Another necessity of teamwork and life in community is a united goal on which all are agreed without reservation. . . . "Unity is the grace of rebirth." The difference between a team and a committee is usually commitment—to God and to the goal to which He is calling us (p. 68).

Teamwork and the life of a community are impossible without absolute moral standards which keep every relationship redemptive. Honesty is one great key—about my own sins, not the other person's (p. 70).

Living in a community or working with a team in the field is not a *method* that will make our work more effective, still less a duty to conform to, so much as a desire of the heart, a gift of grace and love, because wherever a team gathers, united in honesty and care for one another and centred on the divine purpose, then, in a unique way, "there am I in the midst of them" (p. 72).[71]

We could include much more on Oxford Group "team" ideas; but we shall just cite a few significant A.A.-related events that occurred in connection with Oxford Group teams.

---

[71] In Matthew 18:20, Jesus Christ stated, "For where two or three are gathered together in my name, there am I in the midst of them."

In 1933, when Harvey Firestone's son, Russell ("Bud"), briefly recovered from alcoholism, it was an Oxford Group "team," headed by Dr. Frank N. D. Buchman, that came to Akron to witness to Bud's deliverance and to the changes in the lives of other Oxford Group people.[72] The events of 1933 marked the beginning of early A.A.'s association with Oxford Group activities. And we have recently discovered that another Oxford Group "team" returned to Akron in 1934 in the interest of "continuance"—helping the Akronites to further spiritual growth in their changed lives.[73]

In Akron, from 1935 to 1939, the idea of "team" life-changing efforts may well have spilled over *directly* into A.A. For "teams" of AAs would visit alcoholics in the hospital in an alcoholic's first days of recovery; and the Akron A.A. teams called themselves "the alcoholic *squad* of the Oxford Group" (emphasis added).[74]

Bill Wilson's wife, Lois, indicated that Bill belonged to an Oxford Group "team."[75] And our recent research has established the names of many members of the Oxford Group team to which Wilson belonged.[76] In fact, the author has several times corresponded, spoken on the phone, and met in person with L. Parks Shipley, Sr., who recalls Bill's team participation in the mid-1930's. Furthermore, our recent examination of the Reverend Sam Shoemaker's personal journals disclosed Shoemaker's remarks

---

[72] See Dick B., *The Akron Genesis*, pp. 25-51.

[73] See Dick B., *New Light on Alcoholism*, pp. 348-50. With the assistance of former U.S. Congressman John F. Seiberling, the author recently obtained copies of the *Akron Beacon Journal* for February 12, 1934, recounting that an audience of more than 500 persons turned out at the Mayflower Hotel to hear seven of the visiting team members and Mrs. F. A. Seiberling (Congressman Seiberling's grandmother) "bear witness to the importance of the [Oxford Group] movement in their lives. . . " The February 10th *Akron Beacon Journal* announced that the team would include an attorney, a clergyman, a physician, a college professor, as well as two figures who were to become well-known to students of A.A. history, F. Shepard Cornell and Victor C. Kitchen.

[74] See Dick B., *The Akron Genesis*, pp. 188, 200-01; and *DR. BOB and the Good Oldtimers*, pp. 117, 137, 156, 100.

[75] *Lois Remembers*, p. 93.

[76] Dick B., *New Light on Alcoholism*, p. 333-36.

about Bill's participation in a major team event on the East Coast of America. The event involved Carl Hambro, President of the Norwegian Parliament and then President of the League of Nations, who was the featured Oxford Group meeting speaker.[77]

The importance of the "team" and "teamwork" in early A.A. is further underscored by Anne Smith's lengthy discussion of "teams" and "teamwork" in her Journal.[78]

Story-telling; The Sharing of Experience; News, Not Views

Recently, when the author was visiting James D. and Eleanor Forde Newton at the Newton home in Fort Myers Beach, Florida, Mrs. Newton ("Ellie") told a story. Ellie is, as her husband puts it, "ninety something or another." And she's worked with and for the Oxford Group, Frank Buchman, and Sam Shoemaker since the Group's earliest days.

At the Newton home in Florida, and again on the telephone during our writing of this revised edition, Ellie vividly recalled one of her stories.[79] She told of her early affiliations, in the 1920's, with Sam Shoemaker, Frank Buchman, and with the Oxford Group, the latter association continuing to this day.[80]

---

[77] Dick B., *New Light on Alcoholism*, pp. 249-50; 329-32. In Victor Kitchen's *I Was a Pagan* (New York: Harper & Brothers, 1934), Kitchen discussed his businessmen's team (of which Wilson was probably a member) and Oxford Group business men groups meeting all over the world to "discuss our various business problems as God has guided us to work them out. . . [to] seek and check guidance on the next steps God wants us to take in our own business affairs and in wining other business men. . . [and to be] used by God to aid each other's growth, economically and well as spiritually" (pp. 123-24).

[78] See Dick B., *Anne Smith's Journal*, pp. 7, 19, 37, 88, 129.

[79] Telephone conversation by Jim and Eleanor Newton with the author on October 10, 1994, from the Newton home at Fort Myers Beach, Florida, to the author's office in Maui, Hawaii.

[80] See also Eleanor Forde Newton, *I Always Wanted Adventure* (London: Grosvenor Books, 1992); and Dick B., *The Akron Genesis*, pp. 22-27.

In the late 1920's, Frank Buchman approached Ellie and said, "I've arranged for you to go out into the country to have lunch with Queen Sophie of Greece."[81] Ellie said, "Oh, Frank, I wouldn't know what to do with a queen." Buchman replied, "You would curtsy." Ellie said Frank then showed her how to curtsy. Ellie asked, "What would I say to her?" And Buchman replied, "Tell her how God changed your life."

And that was the trademark of the Oxford Group. "Give news, not views!"[82] From the earliest days, the personal life-changing work in the Oxford Group started with the sharing of experience. The confidence of a new person was gained. The life-changer's experience was shared. The newcomer was encouraged to similar honest self-examination and confession. A "decision" was suggested. Then, by whatever form he or she chose, the new person was urged to "give his or her life to God."

Sometimes, the prayer was similar to that uttered by Bill Wilson prior to his spiritual experience.[83] Kenneth Belden, who was one of a hundred men and women commissioned by the Archbishop of Canterbury, in 1933, in a chapel at Lambeth Palace, for work with the Oxford Group, recalled his (Belden's) own Oxford Group beginnings.[84] When he reached Oxford in 1931, Belden had no faith at all. To all intents, he was, as he described himself, "a practising atheist, and a dishonest one at that."[85] Others shared with him when and how this or that experience had happened to them; when God freed them from an ingrained habit;

---

[81] Queen Sophie was one of the many daughters of Queen Victoria.

[82] See Dick B., *The Akron Genesis*, pp. 99, 237-38; and *DR. BOB and the Good Oldtimers*, p. 55. In her October 10, 1994 telephone conversation with the author, Eleanor Forde Newton said, "Frank Buchman frequently said, 'Give news, not views.'" Ellie's husband, Jim Newton (also a friend and associate of Shoemaker and Buchman from the 1920's) joined the phone conversation and said, "Frank often said that [give news, not views]. He taught us, 'Don't go beyond your own experience. You may win your argument and lose the man.'" Compare Shoemaker, *Twice-Born Ministers*, p. 54.

[83] One version of Bill's surrender prayer is reported as follows in *Pass It On*, at page 121: "If there be a God, let Him show Himself!"

[84] Belden, *Reflections on Moral Re-Armament*, p. 7 *et. seq.*

[85] Belden, *Reflections*, p. 15.

when God led them to an apology which restored a broken relationship and liberated them from bitterness; when they decided to commit their whole lives and futures into His hands; when He told them, Speak to so-and-so, and another man's life was changed; and when God made clear what their life's work was to be and they took it up. Belden recalled, "The moment I committed myself unreservedly on 29 January, 1933, even though it was still at the level of 'God, if there is a God, I give you my life,' Christ became real, and day by day I became increasingly aware of His presence in my life. At the same time I was delivered from some of the most deep-seated fears and flaws in my character, the ones that seemed most impossible to deal with."[86]

You can find Belden's story, and thousands like it, in page after page of Oxford Group literature, beginning with Buchman's own story of his experience of the Cross at Keswick.[87] Then the story of Sam Shoemaker's conversion experience in Peking, China in January of 1918.[88] Many of those who helped the author with this book have recounted similar stories.[89] And the record of these life-changing stories can be found in the many books Anne Smith recommended to early AAs and their families for reading.[90] The titles Anne recommended contained groups of stories of conversion and deliverance and included Begbie's *Life Changers* and *Twice-Born Men*; Shoemaker's *Children of the Second Birth* and *Twice-Born Ministers*; Russell's *For Sinners Only*; and Reynolds's *New Lives for Old*.[91] And, during the

---

[86] Belden, *Reflections*, p. 16.

[87] See Buchman, *Remaking The World*, pp. 312-15.

[88] See Harold Begbie, *Life Changers* (London: Mills & Boon, Ltd, 1932), pp. 164-68.

[89] See Garth Lean, *Cast Out Your Nets* (London: Grosvenor, 1990); James D. Newton, *Uncommon Friends* (New York: Harcourt Brace, 1987); Eleanor Forde Newton, *I Always Wanted Adventure*; and Belden, *Reflections on Moral Re-Armament*.

[90] See Dick B., *Anne Smith's Journal*, p. 81.

[91] Harold Begbie, *Life Changers* (London: Mills & Boon, Ltd., 1932); *Twice-Born Men* (New York: Fleming H. Revell, 1909); Samuel M. Shoemaker, Jr., *Children of the*
(continued...)

formative period of A.A.'s development as a part of the Oxford Group, a number of Oxford Group adherents, some including Bill Wilson's own friends, also wrote highly popular accounts of their life-change experiences. These writers included Victor C. Kitchen, Charles Clapp, Jr., and Stephen Foot.[92]

Interestingly, the earliest proposed form of A.A.'s Big Book was merely to contain "stories."[93] And though the move in A.A. today seems to be away from including personal narratives in the Big Book, even the most recently *abridged* edition of A.A.'s Big Book still begins with "Bill's Story" and ends with "Dr. Bob's Nightmare."

AAs share experience. One drunk tells another, or at least used to, just how God had changed the first drunk's life. And this sharing of experience, strength, and hope came directly from the sharing ideas in Oxford Group books, Oxford Group team activities, Oxford Group meetings, Oxford Group houseparties, and huge Oxford Group assemblies.

Just as Ellie Newton was advised to tell Queen Sophie of Greece "how God had changed her life" so have Oxford Group adherents, and the many AAs who succeeded them, done to this very day.[94]

---

[91] (...continued)
Second Birth (New York: Fleming H. Revell, 1927); *Twice-Born Ministers* (New York: Fleming H. Revell, 1929); A. J. Russell, *For Sinners Only* (London: Hodder & Stoughton, 1932); and Amelia S. Reynolds, *New Lives for Old* (New York: Fleming H. Revell, 1929).

[92] See V. C. Kitchen, *I Was A Pagan* (New York: Harper & Brothers, 1934); Charles Clapp, Jr., *The Big Bender* (New York: Harper & Row, 1938); and Stephen Foot, *Life Began Yesterday* (New York: Harper & Brothers, 1935). The first two authors were friends of Bill Wilson and participated in an Oxford Group businessmen's team with Wilson. See Dick B., *New Light on Alcoholism*, pp. 334-41.

[93] See Dick B., *The Akron Genesis*, pp. 233-39.

[94] In one sense, the very first A.A. "message" was shared when Bill Wilson's sponsor, Ebby Thacher, told Bill that "God had done for him what he could not do for himself" (Big Book, p. 11). See other, similar Big Book language at pp. 60, 84, 100, 116, 191, 395. In reviewing our manuscript, Willard Hunter recalled attending a huge Founders Day rally at which a speaker said she was invited to give "the message of
(continued...)

Buchman's Biblical Beliefs

In our first edition, we were content to list, in summary form, Frank Buchman's basic Biblical beliefs. We said that Lean's *On the Tail of a Comet* summarized Buchman's early background theological beliefs as follows: (1) Sovereignty and power of God; (2) Reality of sin; (3) Need for complete surrender to the will of God; (4) Christ's atoning sacrifice and transforming power; (5) The sustenance of prayer; and (6) The duty to witness to others.[95] We also said that, to the foregoing ideas, Buchman added basic elements from his own experiences—experiences in England, Penn State (which he called his early "laboratory"), and abroad. The elements were said to be: (1) "An experience of Christ that transforms the individual beyond anything it is possible for one to do for one's self; (2) Prompt restitution for the personal wrongs revealed by the experience; and (3) Immediate chain reaction, multiplier effect through sharing the experience with others."[96] We concluded with the statement that Buchman had often been described as "soaked in the Bible" and made certain that the Bible formed the basis for training given at Oxford. His recipe for Bible-reading was, "Read accurately, interpret honestly, apply drastically."

Buchman stated, "The Bible is a manual about fishing for fishermen."[97] We've previously pointed to Sherwood Sunderland

---

[94] (...continued)
A.A." When she asked what that was, she was told that Bill Wilson said the message of A.A. was "tell them what happened to you."

[95] Lean, *On the Tail of a Comet*, p. 73

[96] Hunter, *World Changing Through Life Changing*, p. 14.

[97] Lean, *On the Tail of a Comet*, p. 157. Sam Shoemaker began using this "fishing for men" idea in his first book, *Realizing Religion* (New York: Association Press, 1921), p. 82. Both Buchman and Shoemaker, of course, referred to Jesus's first call to Simon (called Peter) and Andrew, his brother, who were fishers. In Matthew 4:19, Jesus said to them, "Follow Me, and I will make you fishers of men."

Day's statement, "The principles of 'The Oxford Group' are the principles of the Bible."[98]

Since the writing of our first edition, we have come across some major Biblical ideas that frequently surfaced in the thinking, teachings, and daily life of Frank Buchman.[99] Frank's close friend, "Bunny" Austin, the famed British tennis star, said, "Psalms 23 and 121 . . . were his [Buchman's] daily diet, whatever else he read."[100] Buchman also frequently read and quoted Psalm 103.[101] From the writings of Paul, Buchman often quoted Romans 12, 1 Corinthians 6:9-11, and Ephesians 3:20-21.[102] And Buchman frequently tendered to his listeners the words in 1 John 1:7, ". . . and the blood of Jesus Christ his Son cleanseth us from all sin."[103]

Buchman was very fond of the following benediction from Numbers 6:24-26: "The Lord bless thee, and keep thee: the Lord make his face shine upon thee, and be gracious unto thee: the Lord lift up his countenance upon thee, and give thee peace."[104]

---

[98] Sherwood Sunderland Day, *The Principles of the Oxford Group* (Oxford Group Pamphlet printed in Great Britain at the Oxford University Press, Oxford, by John Johnson, printer to the University, n.d.), p. 3.

[99] For openers, see Dick B., *Dr. Bob's Library*, pp. 81-97.

[100] See Austin, *Frank Buchman As I Knew Him*, p. 192; Harry Almond, *Foundations for Faith* (London: Grosvenor, 1980), pp. 30, 38; and Miles G. W. Phillimore, *Just for Today* (privately printed pamphlet, 1940).

[101] Almond, *Foundations for Faith*, p. 31; and Phillimore, *Just for Today*, p. 3.

[102] See Spoerri, *Dynamic out of Silence*, p. 135; Phillimore, *Just for Today*, pp. 13, 37; Almond, *Foundations for Faith*, p. 27, 60; Howard, *Frank Buchman's Secret*, p. 40; and Belden, *Reflections on Moral Re-Armament*, p. 54.

[103] Howard, *Frank Buchman's Secret*, p. 109; Belden, *Reflections on Moral Re-Armament*, p. 51; Almond, *Foundations for Faith*, p. 15; and Phillimore, *Just for Today*, p. 7.

[104] Almond, *Foundations for Faith*, p. 61; and Phillimore, *Just for Today*, p. 51. Our quote is from the King James Version. Willard Hunter wrote us and said Buchman quoted the verses as follows: "The Lord bless you and keep you. The Lord make his face *shine* on you and be gracious unto you; the Lord lift up his countenance upon you, and give you—and the world—peace." Hunter added that Buchman generally emphasized "shine" and said it is important to let the Lord *shine*; too many want to do the *shining*.

(continued...)

As we previously covered, Buchman drew on the thinking and writing of eight distinguished earlier Christian thinkers for his own Biblical ideas and practices. These leaders were: Bushnell, Moody, Drummond, Meyer, Speer, Mott, James, and Wright.

To those names should be added three more: (1) Dr. L. W. Grensted, Oriel Professor of the Philosophy of the Christian Religion in the University of Oxford and Canon Theologian of Liverpool.[105] (2) Dr. Burnett H. Streeter, Provost of the Queen's College, Oxford, and formerly Canon of Hereford.[106] (3) The Reverend Julian P. Thornton-Duesbury, who enlisted with Buchman in 1924 and subsequently became Principal of Wycliff Hall (Oxford's leading theological college) and later Master (President or Provost) of St. Peter's College, Oxford. After retiring from Oxford, Thornton-Duesbury was Canon Theological for the diocese of Liverpool.[107] The foregoing three distinguished

---

[104] (...continued)

Hunter said Buchman used "you"—not "thee." And he always inserted "and the world" before "peace."

[105] See L. W. Grensted's Foreword to *What Is The Oxford Group?* Also L. W. Grensted, *The Person of Christ* (New York: Harper & Brothers, 1933). We recently discovered, during our 1993 trip to the Calvary Church archives in New York, that *The Person of Christ* was on the Calvary Church's list of recommended Oxford Group Literature. For Oxford Group comments on Grensted, see Russell, *For Sinners Only*, pp. 281-94.

[106] See Burnett Hillman Streeter, *The God Who Speaks* (London: Macmillan & Co., 1943); Lean, *On the Tail of a Comet*, p. 160; Mowat, *Modern Prophetic Voices*, pp. 7-18, 58-61, 72-73, 90; Alan Thornhill, *Best of Friends*, pp. 103-21; and *One Fight More* (London: Frederick Muller Ltd., 1943).

[107] In April, 1992, Garth lean wrote the author and suggested adding Duesbury's name. Duesbury wrote several books and booklets on the Oxford Group and Moral Re-Armament. Lean said, "Among the books or booklets written by Reverend Thornton-Duesbury are (a) he edited the first summary of Dr. Buchman's speeches in 1942; (b) *The Oxford Group: A Brief Account of Its Principles and Growth* (Oxford Group, 1947); (c) *A visit to Caux: First hand experience of Moral Re-Armament in action.* He avoided Buchman at Keswick in 1922, but was brought to a deeper experience of Christ in 1923." See Lean, *On the Tail of a Comet*, pp. 102, 135n, 157, etc.

theologian-teacher-writers gave Buchman's Biblical concepts intellectual authority at Oxford University.[108]

---

[108] For recollections on how the lives of these three distinguished men touched the life of Buchman, see Thornhill, *One Fight More, supra.*

4

Sam Shoemaker's Oxford Group Role

We have left to another of our titles a *detailed* study of the ideas, teachings, and writings of the Reverend Samuel Moor Shoemaker, Jr., as they bear on Shoemaker's contribution to Alcoholics Anonymous.[1] The sheer quantity of Shoemaker's books, articles, and pamphlets suggested separate treatment.[2]

However, we can, and in this book will, record Shoemaker's affirmation and espousal of the twenty-eight Oxford Group principles we believe influenced A.A. And the reader should also note that Shoemaker wrote very little about Oxford Group ideas that was not also covered by a host of other Oxford Group writers of the 1930's and earlier.

The author believes that Shoemaker's A.A. contribution is just part of a much richer and broader spiritual reservoir from which A.A.'s basic ideas were drawn by Bill W. and Dr. Bob. The Bible itself was paramount as a source. So also were the ideas of the eight Oxford Group mentors whose teachings and writings were in place and fixed in the minds of both Buchman and Shoemaker even

---

[1] Dick B., *New Light on Alcoholism: The A.A. Legacy from Sam Shoemaker* (Corte Madera, CA: Good Book Publishing Company, 1994). See also Samuel M. Shoemaker, *Courage to Change: The Christian Roots of the 12-Step Movement,* Compiled and edited by Bill Pittman and Dick B. (Michigan: Fleming H. Revell, 1994).

[2] See our Bibliography for list of books, articles, pamphlets by Shoemaker.

before the two worked together in Buchman's First Century Christian Fellowship from about 1920 to 1941.[3]

The jury is still out on exactly what Shoemaker's *direct* contribution was to A.A. and Bill Wilson, although our research for *New Light on Alcoholism* certainly made clear the very close relationship between the two men in the 1930's. Also, the vivid similarity of the language each used as he wrote on A.A.-related subjects. Therefore, our intent in this book is simply to fit Shoemaker into the Oxford Group picture—a picture in which he had a very large place.

Information on Shoemaker's Oxford Group role can be obtained from several major sources: (1) Shoemaker's own writings in the 1920's and 1930's. In these, Shoemaker made frequent reference to Frank Buchman, to A First Century Christian Fellowship, to the Oxford Group, and to Oxford Group principles and practices.[4] (2) Shoemaker biographies, and accounts of and by

---

[3] See Chapter Two of this book.

[4] See, for example: Samuel Moor Shoemaker, *Realizing Religion*, (New York: Association Press, 1923), pp. 56, 80-83; *A Young Man's View of the Ministry* (New York: Association Press, 1923), pp. 81-86; *Children of the Second Birth* (New York: Fleming H. Revell, 1927), pp. 73-76, 93-99, 160; *Religion That Works* (New York: Fleming H. Revell 1928), pp. 43-65; *Twice-Born Ministers* (New York: Fleming H. Revell, 1929), pp. 23, 90, 95, 101, 122, 147-48—note that the entire book is dedicated to Frank N. D. Buchman; *The Conversion of the Church* (New York: Fleming H. Revell, 1932), pp. 47-65, 75, 79-86, 111, 113, 123-25; *Confident Faith* (New York: Fleming H. Revell, 1932), pp. 16, 32-33, 57, 90-91, 110, 115, 117; *The Gospel According To You* (New York: Fleming H. Revell, 1934), pp. 10, 44-55, 81-93, 128-30; *National Awakening* (New York: Harper & Brothers, 1936), pp. 3, 5, 9, 18, 21, 40-44, 45-66, 78-88, 89-98; *Calvary Church Yesterday And Today* (New York: Fleming H. Revell, 1936), pp. 231, 256, 270-78; *The Church Can Save The World* (New York: Harper & Brothers, 1938), pp. 20, 25, 30, 32, 34, 40-42, 57, 63-64, 110-21, 124-45, 153-57; and *God's Control* (New York: Fleming H. Revell, 1939), pp. 9-16, 31-32, 57-59, 62-72, 120-21, 145.

him in his own Calvary Church in New York.[5] (3) Several books and articles about the Oxford Group.[6]

Opinions As to Sam Shoemaker's Role in the Oxford Group

The answer to where Sam Shoemaker fit in the Oxford Group seems to lie in the eye of the beholder.

Bill Wilson chose, in 1955, to dub Shoemaker "their [the Oxford Group's] former leader in America."[7] However, as *Pass It On* strongly suggested, Bill had chosen to stress A.A.'s tie with Shoemaker and down-play A.A.'s more basic Oxford Group roots.[8]

T. Willard Hunter, a younger Oxford Group activist and volunteer, called Shoemaker Frank Buchman's "chief American

---

[5] Helen Smith Shoemaker, *I Stand By The Door* (New York: Harper & Row, 1967), pp. 24-94; Irving Harris, *The Breeze of the Spirit* (New York: The Seabury Press, 1978), pp. 3-56, 70-80; John Potter Cuyler, Jr., *Calvary Church in Action* (New York: Fleming H. Revell, 1934), pp. 6, 11-29, 49-60; and Samuel M. Shoemaker, Jr., *Calvary Church Yesterday and Today*, pp. 231-84. And the author's personal examination of the issues of Shoemaker's parish publication, *The Calvary Evangel*, for the 1930's indicated that Shoemaker and other Calvary Church writers frequently mentioned Buchman, the Oxford Group, Oxford Group literature, and the work of A First Century Christian Fellowship.

[6] A. J. Russell, *For Sinners Only* (London: Hodder & Stoughton, Ltd., 1932), pp. 205-18; Garth Lean, *On the Tail of a Comet* (Colorado Springs: Helmers & Howard, 1988), pp. 55-57, 75, 83, 103, 104, 108, 110, 114-18, 152, 304-05; T. Willard Hunter, *World Changing Through Life Changing* (Newton Center, Mass: Andover Newton Theological School, 1977), pp. 18, 44-45, 58-59, 165-66; and Karl A. Olsson, "The History of Faith at Work" (five parts). *Faith at Work News*. 1982-1983.

[7] *Alcoholics Anonymous Comes of Age* (New York: Alcoholics Anonymous World Services, Inc., 1957), p. 39; and *The Language of the Heart* (New York: The AA Grapevine, Inc., 1988), pp. 298, 380. Interestingly, when the author introduced his Shoemaker title in Baltimore, Maryland, in April, 1944, one of Shoemaker's daughters gave the author a copy of a news article with a portrait of Sam Shoemaker which stated Shoemaker *was* "the American leader of the Oxford Group."

[8] *Pass It On* (New York: Alcoholics Anonymous World Services, Inc., 1984), p. 174.

lieutenant." [9]Recently, Hunter added, in a statement about Frank Buchman's contributions to alcoholics and others: "The chief liaison and catalyst was Reverend Samuel M. Shoemaker, one of Buchman's foremost lieutenants for twenty-two years . . . [whose] parish house at 61 Gramercy Park was the national center of Oxford Group activity."[10] Hunter, like Shoemaker, apparently had some questions about Buchman's leadership at the time when the Reverend Sherwood Day and Sam Shoemaker were bailing out of the Oxford Group. But Hunter stuck with the group on the premise, "Better wrong with the team than right without it."[11] Hunter's sympathy for Shoemaker's problems with Frank Buchman may have given him the ability to view Shoemaker's contribution over the entire Buchman-Shoemaker association, rather than for the period in the years just before the breakup.

Garth Lean, Frank Buchman's biographer and a long-time Oxford Group activist, wrote a letter to the author with the following perspective. Lean said Shoemaker was *not* "the American leader" of the Oxford Group, but "an American leader," or perhaps "the leader in New York." Lean said even this latter description was doubtful in 1936.

Lean said further:

> There were other outstanding people like Ray Purdy, Garrett Stearly, Cleve Hicks, Kenaston Twitchell, etc. In my two years, pre-war, mainly in New York, based in Calvary House, I only attended one team-meeting led or partly led by Sam Shoemaker. He lived on the top floor. We were seldom or never invited there. I do not remember him taking part in other states. Calvary Church, where, as you say, he was in charge for 26 years, and his writing, were his main tasks. Equally, I never went to the "mission" [Calvary Mission] nor knew it existed. We were working in Washington, New England, Detroit, Florida, etc. I

---

[9] Hunter, *World Changing Through Life Changing*, pp. 18, 44.

[10] T. Willard Hunter, *AA & MRA "It Started Right There": Behind the twelve steps and the self-help movement* (Washington, D.C.: Moral Re-Armament, 1994), p. 14.

[11] Hunter, *World Changing Through Life Changing*, pp. 58-59.

was in most of these, though not myself on the West Coast until after the war, and I never saw Sam anywhere except in New York, though that is not conclusive.[12]

Consider the probable individual perspectives from which each of the foregoing commentators viewed Shoemaker's Oxford Group position. Wilson was new to, not greatly interested in, and possibly knew little about the Oxford Group's world objectives and outreach. By contrast, Wilson knew a great deal about Shoemaker and his Calvary House Oxford Group centre. Also, Wilson was, for a number of years, attempting to distance A.A. from the Oxford Group itself. Hunter apparently had views of Buchman that somewhat coincided with those of Shoemaker at the time of the Buchman-Shoemaker breach.[13] Hunter could perhaps see Shoemaker's role as a longtime and staunch Buchman colleague and principal supporter in America over the period of the entire twenty-three year association. Lean, on the other hand, appeared not only to have become close to Buchman at a time when Buchman-Shoemaker views were diverging, but also to have been very active in the world outreach of Moral Re-Armament at a time when Buchman was moving away from personal work and toward "thinking in continents"— something which does not seem, by the time of the Shoemaker-Buchman breakup, to have been Shoemaker's major focus. Our last point is perhaps illustrated by

---

[12] In April of 1992, Willard Hunter reviewed this discussion and the Lean quote. Hunter wrote the author, "Lean is quite right about Purdy, Twitchell, and Stearly. Hicks was not in the same category. The three [not including Hicks] took more leadership nation wide and world wide than Shoemaker. My designation "chief American lieutenant" is perhaps misleading, influenced by the fact that Shoemaker was in charge of Calvary House during that period and host to the national headquarters of the Oxford Group/Moral Re-Armament, and Frank Buchman's national base when he was in the U.S. Sam was also considered a leader in his effectiveness as a personal life-changer. "A major American associate" might be better—"a leading spokesman of the Buchman idea."

[13] See the next chapter for the story of the Buchman-Shoemaker breakup.

Shoemaker's subsequent emphasis on "Faith at Work," small parish groups, and the ministry of the laity.[14]

What is important for our study is a brief look at Shoemaker's very close association with Buchman, A First Century Christian Fellowship, the Oxford Group, and even M.R.A. over a twenty-three year period. A good factual balance showing the real status of Calvary Church in the Oxford Group picture can be obtained from reading Samuel M. Shoemaker's own report to his church in *Calvary Church Yesterday and Today*.

Further, on July 1, 1932, the vestry of Calvary Church reported to its parishioners that the Oxford Group had become "one of the main movements of the Spirit in our time" and that the work of Calvary parish "is part of a much larger movement which is making a tremendous spiritual contribution in many countries today."[15] Shoemaker himself reported that a number of Sunday evening services had been made "Oxford Group services;" that Reverend Dr. Frank N. D. Buchman had preached to the largest single congregation gathered within its walls in many years; and that members of the parish, including the rector, had had part in two great national campaigns of the Oxford Group in 1935 in Denmark and in Switzerland.[16]

From Shoemaker's writings and from the Oxford Group materials emanating from Shoemaker's own parish publication, it is quite apparent that Shoemaker *did* thoroughly identify with, write about, and advocate twenty-eight Oxford Group principles which influenced or found their way to A.A.[17] And we will briefly cover here some details as to Shoemaker's association with Buchman, the Oxford Group, and the Oxford Group's early A.A. activities.

---

[14] See Helen Smith Shoemaker, *I Stand by the Door*, pp. 171-93; Karl A. Olsson, "The History of Faith at Work" (five parts), *Faith at Work News*, 1982-1983; and *The Pittsburgh Experiment Groups* (Pittsburgh, PA: The Pittsburgh Experiment, n.d.).

[15] Shoemaker, *Calvary Church Yesterday and Today*, pp. 270-72.

[16] Shoemaker, *Calvary Church Yesterday and Today*, pp. 276-77. See also Cuyler, *Calvary Church in Action*, pp. 11-29; and Harris, *The Breeze of the Spirit*, pp. 38-44.

[17] Dick B., *New Light on Alcoholism*, 1994), pp. 311-17.

Shoemaker and Buchman

Frank Buchman first met Sam Shoemaker during Buchman's visit to China on January 19, 1918.[18] During his visit with Buchman, Shoemaker had applied the tests of Buchman's Four Absolutes to his life and found himself wanting. Shoemaker went through his own crisis of self-surrender. Buchman had told him that he had to be honest about his failures with himself, with God, and with any persons they concerned. Shoemaker concluded that basic dishonesty, selfishness, want of love, and a kind of pervasive inferiority were holding him down. One by one Shoemaker tried to release them, and then, at Buchman's urging, began to relate his own new-found spiritual experience to the lives of the young men and boys around him. Before long, Shoemaker began to think his mission in life was to be something like Frank Buchman's, to spread the gospel of personal evangelism.[19]

In 1921, Shoemaker's titles, containing a great many Oxford Group-Buchman ideas, began to be published.[20] The two men were also much involved in YMCA activities on the Princeton campus. By 1923-1924, Shoemaker was traveling with Buchman. Then Shoemaker was called to be rector of the Calvary Episcopal Church in New York City. He became rector in May, 1925, and so remained for over twenty-six years. In the ensuing years, Shoemaker continued to write books containing his sermons and a good many of the Oxford Group principles he and Buchman had shared.

---

[18] Helen Smith Shoemaker, *I Stand By The Door*, p. 24. As we have previously noted, Shoemaker's personal journals highlighted this important event in each year's January 19th entry, every year thereafter.

[19] Helen Smith Shoemaker, *I Stand By The Door*, pp. 24-27.

[20] For a comprehensive look at Shoemaker's pre-1940 titles, see Dick B., *New Light on Alcoholism*; also, Shoemaker, *Courage to Change: The Christian Roots of the Twelve Step Movement*.

Calvary House and the Oxford Group

In 1928, Shoemaker opened Calvary House, which became, among other things, the virtual American headquarters for Frank Buchman's Oxford Group. Buchman lived in Calvary House when in New York. Many Oxford Group meetings were held there. Shoemaker's parish publication, *The Calvary Evangel*, almost literally became the American house organ for the Oxford Group, or M.R.A., for a number of years.[21] Oxford Group books, including those by Shoemaker, were stocked at Calvary House and sent out on order to those who wished to receive them.

Perhaps the best indications of the interrelationship of Buchman, the Oxford Group, Shoemaker, and Calvary House are the Oxford Group bookroom in the basement of Calvary House, and the list of "Oxford Group Literature" it sold. Dr. Shoemaker wrote about the beehive of individuals and teams of people with special commitment at Calvary House and said of its "bookstore":

> Downstairs is the book-room from which were sent out 144 orders, or 3291 items in a typical month to all parts of this country—this does not include what is sold locally in New York; and the press room where a team of people is working constantly on public relations, sending out positive and constructive views of a nationally significant character to every kind of publication.[22]

Mrs. W. Irving Harris, the wife of Shoemaker's assistant minister, was in charge of the "book-room" from 1936 to 1938. At the time we were writing our first edition of this title, Mrs. Harris furnished us with an Oxford Group Literature List, which was published in the March, 1939 issue of *The Calvary Evangel*, the Calvary Church's parish publication. Mrs. Harris stated that the list covered the Oxford Group titles being carried and disseminated

---

[21] Harris, *The Breeze of the Spirit*, p. 72.
[22] Shoemaker, *God's Control*, pp. 87-88.

by the American Headquarters of the Oxford Group at Calvary House during the late 1930's.

Since receiving Mrs. Harris's list, the author has visited Calvary Church archives in New York and reviewed copies of *The Calvary Evangel* for the entire formative years of A.A. in New York (1934 to 1939). The author discovered a number of titles, in addition to those listed in the March, 1939 *Evangel* issue, which were "Oxford Group" literature and had been specifically recommended for reading by *Evangel* recipients.

The following is the list of "Oxford Group Literature," as it was published in the March, 1939, issue of *The Calvary Evangel*, *supplemented* with the names of the other Oxford Group titles we found recommended by *The Calvary Evangel* between 1935 and 1939:

1. *Inspired Youth* by Olive Jones.[23]
2. *For Sinners Only* by A. J. Russell.[24]
3. *I Was a Pagan* by V. C. Kitchen.[25]
4. *Life Began Yesterday* by Stephen Foot.[26]
5. *The Church Can Save the World* by S. M. Shoemaker.[27]
6. *The God Who Speaks* by B. H. Streeter.[28]
7. *Children of the Second Birth* by S. M. Shoemaker.[29]
8. *Twice-Born Ministers* by S. M. Shoemaker.[30]

---

[23] Olive Jones, *Inspired Youth* (New York: Harper & Brothers, 1938).

[24] A. J. Russell, *For Sinners Only* (London: Hodder & Stoughton, 1932).

[25] V. C. Kitchen, *I Was a Pagan* (New York: Harper & Brothers, 1934).

[26] Stephen Foot, *Life Began Yesterday* (New York: Harper & Brothers, 1935).

[27] Samuel M. Shoemaker, *The Church Can Save the World* (New York: Harper & Brothers, 1938).

[28] Burnett Hillman Streeter, *The God Who Speaks* (New York: The Macmillan Company, 1936).

[29] Samuel M. Shoemaker, *Children of the Second Birth* (New York: Fleming H. Revell, 1927).

[30] Samuel M. Shoemaker, *Twice-Born Ministers* (New York: Fleming H. Revell, 1929).

9. *If I Be Lifted Up* by S. M. Shoemaker.[31]
10. *Confident Faith* by S. M. Shoemaker.[32]
11. *The Gospel According to You* by S. M. Shoemaker.[33]
12. *Inspired Children* by Olive Jones.[34]
13. *What Is The Oxford Group?* by The Layman with a Notebook.[35]
14. *Religion That Works* by S. M. Shoemaker.[36]
15. *The Conversion of the Church* by S. M. Shoemaker.[37]
16. *National Awakening* by S. M. Shoemaker.[38]
17. *The Venture of Belief* by Philip M. Brown.[39]
18. *Realizing Religion* by S. M. Shoemaker.[40]
19. *Church in Action* by Jack Winslow.[41]
20. *Why I Believe in the Oxford Group* by Jack Winslow.[42]

---

[31] Samuel M. Shoemaker, *If I Be Lifted Up* (New York: Fleming H. Revell, 1931).

[32] Samuel M. Shoemaker, *Confident Faith* (New York: Fleming H. Revell, 1932).

[33] Samuel M. Shoemaker, *The Gospel According to You* (New York: Fleming H. Revell, 1934).

[34] Olive Jones, *Inspired Children* (New York: Harper & Brothers, 1933).

[35] The Layman with a Notebook, *What Is The Oxford Group?* (London: Oxford University Press, 1933).

[36] Samuel M. Shoemaker, *Religion That Works* (New York: Fleming H. Revell, 1928).

[37] Samuel M. Shoemaker, *The Conversion of the Church* (New York: Fleming H. Revell, 1932).

[38] Samuel M. Shoemaker, *National Awakening* (New York: Harper & Brothers, 1936).

[39] Philip M. Brown, *The Venture of Belief* (New York: Fleming H. Revell, 1935).

[40] Samuel M. Shoemaker, *Realizing Religion* (New York: Association Press, 1923).

[41] Though we have made an extensive search for this book, and for information about it, we have not been able to obtain any information. We asked Oxford Group offices in the United States and in the United Kingdom. We have also made inquiry of long-time Oxford Group activists in the United States and abroad, and of Shoemaker associates, all to no avail.

[42] Jack C. Winslow, *Why I Believe in the Oxford Group* (London: Hodder & Stoughton, 1934).

21. *Soul Surgery* by Howard Walter.[43]
22. *When Man Listens* by Cecil Rose.[44]
23. *The Guidance of God* by Eleanor Napier Forde.[45]
24. *New Leadership* by Garth Lean and Morris Martin.[46]
25. *New Enlistment* by Wilfred Holmes-Walker.[47]
26. *How Do I Begin* by Hallen Viney.[48]
27. *The Quiet Time* by Howard Rose.[49]

28. *How to Find Reality in Your Morning Devotions* by Donald Carruthers.[50]

29. *The Person of Christ* by L. W. Grensted.[51]

30. *Calvary Church in Action* by John Potter Cuyler, Jr.[52]

31. *Seeking and Finding* by Ebenezer Macmillan.[53] This is one of the very few Oxford Group books the author found in Bill Wilson's library at Stepping Stones, Bedford Hills, New York.

32. *Christ's Words from the Cross* by Samuel M. Shoemaker.[54]

---

[43] Howard A. Walter, *Soul Surgery: Some Thoughts on Incisive Personal Work*, 6th ed. (Oxford at the University Press by John Johnson, 1940). The first edition of this work was published 1919).

[44] Cecil Rose, *When Man Listens* (New York: Oxford University Press, 1937).

[45] Eleanor Napier Forde, *The Guidance of God* (Oxford, The Oxford Group, printed at the University Press by John Johnson, 1930).

[46] Garth Lean and Morris Martin, *New Leadership* (London: Wm. Heinemann, Ltd., 1936).

[47] Volume not located by the author.

[48] Hallen Viney, *How Do I Begin?* (New York: Oxford Group at 61 Gramercy Park, North, 1937).

[49] Howard J. Rose, *The Quiet Time* (Sussex: Howard J. Rose, 6 The Green, Slaugham, Haywards Heath, n.d.).

[50] Donald W. Carruthers, *How to Find Reality in Your Morning Devotions* (Pennsylvania State College, n.d.).

[51] L. W. Grensted, *The Person of Christ* (New York: Harper & Brothers, 1933).

[52] John Potter Cuyler, Jr., *Calvary Church in Action* (New York: Fleming H. Revell, 1934).

[53] Ebenezer Macmillan, *Seeking and Finding* (New York: Harper & Brothers, 1933).

[54] Samuel M. Shoemaker, Jr., *Christ's Words from the Cross* (New York: Fleming H. Revell, 1933).

33. *The Meaning of Conversion* by J. Herbert Smith.[55]

To date, the author has been able to obtain copies of, review, and analyze all but three of the foregoing books and pamphlets on *The Calvary Evangel* "Oxford Group Literature" list.[56] Only a few of the Oxford Group books of the 1920's and 1930's, that seem relevant to this study, and that the author has reviewed, are missing from the foregoing *Evangel* list.[57]

We believe the *Evangel*'s recommendations are important as a guide to what Dr. Bob, Anne Smith, and Henrietta Seiberling may have been reading and discussing together with each other and with Bill Wilson in A.A.'s formative years between 1933 to 1939. In Dr. Bob's last major talk, delivered at Detroit in December, 1948, Dr. Bob said he had done "an immense amount of reading they [the Oxford Group] had recommended."[58] *The Calvary Evangel* list seems the most likely source, direct or indirect, of the

---

[55] J. Herbert Smith, *The Meaning of Conversion*, pamphlet, n.d. (not yet located by the author).

[56] The three not yet located are *Church in Action* by Winslow and *New Enlistment* by Holmes-Walker and *The Meaning of Conversion* by Shoemaker's Associate Rector at Calvary Church, J. Herbert Smith.

[57] The Oxford Group books that were not included are: Harold Begbie's *Life Changers* [read and recommended by Dr. Bob, Anne Smith, and Henrietta Seiberling]; A. J. Russell, *One Thing I Know*, (New York: Harper & Brothers, 1933) [owned and read by Dr. Bob. Earl H., an A.A. Oldtimer from Oklahoma, informed the author on February 9, 1992, that he owned a copy of this book with Anne Smith's signature in it.]; Philip Leon, *The Philosophy of Courage or The Oxford Group Way* (New York: Oxford University Press, 1939) [which *was* listed in a subsequent issue of the *Evangel*]; Jack C. Winslow, *When I Awake* (London: Hodder & Stoughton, 1938) [a copy of which was provided to the author by Mrs. Irving Harris]; Clarence Benson, *The Eight Points of the Oxford Group* (London: Humphrey Milford, Oxford University Press, 1936); Beverley Nichols, *The Fool Hath Said* (Garden City: Doubleday-Doran, 1936) [frequently read by Bill Wilson, and a copy of which the author found in Wilson's library at Stepping Stones]; and Amelia S. Reynolds, *New Lives for Old* (New York: Fleming H. Revell, 1929) [Her book was recommended by Anne Smith in her *Journal*].

[58] *The Co-Founders of Alcoholics Anonymous. Biographical sketches. Their last major talks* (New York: Alcoholics Anonymous World Services, Inc., 1972, 1975), p. 7. For a full discussion of the books Dr. Bob read, see Dick B., *Dr. Bob's Library: Books for Twelve Step Growth* (San Rafael, CA: Paradise Research Publications, 1994).

"recommendations" made to Dr. Bob. Though Dr. Bob may not have seen *The Evangel* issues for the 1933-1939 period, it seems probable that the Oxford Group literature it recommended was being read and probably being recommended by the Oxford Group teams that visited Akron, Ohio in 1933 and 1934. The books were also probably being read by Oxford Group residents of Akron such as Dr. Walter F. Tunks and T. Henry and Clarace Williams. The list also seems the most likely point of reference for Henrietta Seiberling's Oxford Group reading, of which former Congressman John F. Seiberling wrote, when he informed the author, "My mother, I am sure, read all the Oxford Group books of the 1930's."[59]

Shoemaker and Oxford Group Activities

Sam Shoemaker was very much involved in Oxford Group houseparties. He was the "guru" of the Oxford Group business men's team in New York. He frequently traveled with Oxford Group team members on their work throughout the United States and sometimes abroad. And he had endless contacts with Oxford Group leaders in America and abroad, people such as the Reverend Garrett Stearly, the Reverend Ray Purdy, Loudon Hamilton, Kenaston Twitchell (Shoemaker's brother-in-law), Professor Philip Marshall Brown, the Reverend Howard Blake, Charles Haines, Scoville Wishard, James D. Newton, Eleanor Forde, F. Parks Shipley, Sr., the Reverend W. Irving Harris, and many others. Almost all of these Oxford Group people were frequently mentioned in the personal journals of Dr. Shoemaker, which we have examined since the first edition of this work was published.[60]

---

[59] Letter from John F. Seiberling to the author, dated July 5, 1991.

[60] See Dick B., *New Light on Alcoholism*, pp. 329-41.

Shoemaker, Bill W., and the Oxford Group

As the first edition of this title was being written, a new and vitally significant piece of evidence surfaced in the form of a letter to the author from Mrs. Irving Harris, dated April 7, 1992. It was accompanied by a typewritten copy of a manuscript Mrs. Harris had just found in going through her husband's papers in connection with her intended move from her New Jersey home to her daughter's home in another state. Of the Harris manuscript, Mrs. Harris wrote:

> I thought it might confirm your [the author's] thinking in the Bill-Sam relationship. It's an eye witness account as I know Irv's [her husband, the Reverend Irving Harris's] way of writing.

In the typewritten manuscript itself, which was titled, "Bill Wilson and Sam Shoemaker," the Reverend Harris had written:

> While Bill never spent a single night at either Calvary House or at the Mission which Calvary Church maintained on East 23rd Street, New York, he owed much to the spiritual life generated at these places and even more to Sam Shoemaker, the man who headed up and fostered the activities at both centers.

> It was at a men's meeting at 61 Gramercy Park [Calvary House] that Bill's buddy, Ebbie Thatcher [*sic*] felt the power of fellowship and experienced the inner assurance that he could "move out of the dark tunnel" of alcoholism; and it was at a meeting at Calvary Mission that Bill himself was moved to declare that he had decided to launch out as a follower of Jesus Christ.

> Then as he was establishing guidelines which he believed to be basic in *maintaining* sobriety, he frequently turned to Sam Shoemaker to talk over the relation between these early formulations of the Twelve Steps and the principles of the New Testament. Sam's friend, "Sherry" Day, had already outlined several principles of basic Christian living with which Bill was

familiar.[61] As he discussed his counterparts to these he found that Sam's patient, quiet agreement put a seal on Bill's hope that these represented God's own truth. With a chuckle Sam would say something like, "Sounds like good old-fashioned Christian faith, Bill." And Bill would perhaps reply, "Yes, it looks that way . . . almost too good to be true." These talks took place in Sam's book-lined seventh floor study at Calvary House with the door closed and the telephone switched off.

At that time in New York the usual result of a full-blown experience like Bill's consisted of full-time participation in the activities of one of the several Oxford Group traveling teams. And Bill's new friends in the Group frequently urged him to get going in the customary team activity. Having shaken off the deadly grip of alcohol, he was consumed with a desire to spend his time not in general evangelism, or "life-changing," but in helping other alcoholics. He knew that many, many obsessive drinkers could find the same release and freedom which had come to him and it was to this work that he felt compelled to devote himself. And it was right here that Sam's counsel and backing proved so helpful. As one of the top American leaders of the old Group, Sam often had a deciding voice about where newly changed laymen might best tie in with the ever-extending work of the revival which was then taking place. And Sam was never personally persuaded that Bill should participate in the general team travel which was going on. He was impressed by the sincerity of Bill's own convictions about what he should do and advised him to follow his own deepest convictions even to the extent of incurring the disapproval of other leaders in the Group. In this Sam became Bill's special ally and "comforter", enabling him to withstand the pressures to conform. And by this, in God's providence, Sam shared in the steps which shortly led to the founding of Alcoholics Anonymous.

---

[61] See the seven principles of the Bible that Day had written at the request of Shoemaker. Harris included them in his book, *The Breeze of the Spirit*, pp. 18-21.

Several points should be made concerning the foregoing vital manuscript written by Reverend Irving Harris. It bears no date. Mrs. Harris stated it is an "eye witness" account. The account dealt with events that took place subsequent to November of 1934 and prior to December of 1938 (the date the actual Twelve Steps were written). In all likelihood, the events took place after Bill's return from his three month stay in Akron in the summer of 1935 and before the fall of 1937 since Bill and Lois severed their connection with the Oxford Group in the summer of 1937. There is a clear statement that Bill was familiar with Sherry Day's seven, biblical "Principles of the Group." Bill and Sam Shoemaker were definitely discussing and comparing notes on Christian-Bible principles. There is mention of Bill's involvement in Calvary House to the extent that his lay work on a team was considered.[62] There is no assertion that Sam Shoemaker *personally* "taught" Bill Wilson anything substantial, or that they discussed Sam's teachings, or that Sam "wrote," "participated in the writing of," "reviewed," or was in any way involved in the writing either of the Big Book or the Twelve Steps. Lois said, "Sam Shoemaker *ultimately* became an admirer of Bill's work and apologized for the lack of understanding by members of his staff and others in the OG [Oxford Group]"[63]

So—after reviewing this new piece of evidence and, more recently, Dr. Shoemaker's own personal journals—we believe history bears out these facts: (1) Bill Wilson participated substantially in Oxford Group work at Calvary House and elsewhere. (2) From at least the earliest days of January, 1935, Sam Shoemaker had personal knowledge of Bill Wilson's work

---

[62] *Lois Remembers*, p. 93 stated Bill belonged to a team; and we have since interviewed L. Parks Shipley, who remembers Bill's participation in teams. Also, Shoemaker's personal journals disclosed Bill's deep involvement in major Oxford Group team events in late 1935.

[63] *Lois Remembers*, p. 103 (emphasis added).

with alcoholics.[64] (3) Shoemaker had one-on-one conversations with Bill about Bill's work with alcoholics and also about broader Oxford Group ideas and objectives. (4) The personal conversations between Shoemaker and Wilson concerned the Oxford Group's Biblical principles and the basic ideas from the Bible that Bill had studied with Dr. Bob in Akron and was working into a recovery program. (5) There was a Christian and Biblical orientation to the recovery program that Shoemaker and Wilson discussed. We believe this, particularly because that Christian program—as far as its only effective implementation is concerned—was exemplified in the Frank Amos report to John D. Rockefeller, Jr. on early A.A.'s Akron program.[65] (6) Wilson was putting the Big Book and Twelve Step ideas together, not only from what he had learned from, participated in, and knew of the Akron program, but also from what he had learned at Calvary Church, Calvary House, and Calvary Mission from hearing and talking with Shoemaker, Shoemaker's staff, Calvary Church Vestrymen, and other Oxford Group people in and about Calvary.

---

[64] See Dick B., *New Light on Alcoholism*, p. 323, which sets forth in full a letter that Sam Shoemaker wrote to Bill Wilson on January 22, 1935, concerning what Bill did with an alcoholic named Breithut. Since the publication of *New Light on Alcoholism*, we have located in the pages of a fact sheet by Bill Wilson, dated November 2, 1954, the notation that sometime after Bill was discharged from Towns Hospital [12/18/34], Bill "attended an Oxford Group meeting at Calvary House, Calvary Episcopal Church, Fourth Avenue and Twenty-First Street, New York City . . . [and that] the first drunk, Fred Breithut, a professor of chemistry at Brooklyn University, appeared out of the audience." See Bill Wilson, "Main Events: Alcoholics Anonymous Fact Sheet by Bill." November 2, 1954, Archives Room, Stepping Stones Archives, Bedford Hills, New York, p. 1. At the archives at Calvary Episcopal Church in New York City, we located a copy of the 1935 issue of *The Calvary Evangel* which announced that Frederick E. Breithut was confirmed on March 24, 1935, as a member of Calvary Episcopal Church, having previously been sponsored at a baptism on March 14, 1935, by William G. Wilson as his godfather, with the Reverend Samuel Shoemaker performing the baptism. The foregoing facts convince us that even prior to January 1, 1935, Bill Wilson was, with Sam Shoemaker's knowledge, working with drunks at Shoemaker's Oxford Group meetings at Calvary House.

[65] *DR. BOB*, pp. 131-32.

Shoemaker's Oxford Group Friends and Bill W.

The Reverend J. Herbert Smith

The Reverend J. Herbert Smith was Associate Rector at Calvary Church during A.A.'s formative years. Smith was very much involved in working with Sam Shoemaker and in running the parish in Shoemaker's absences.[66] A good deal of the work in bringing people to Christ was in Smith's hands and in the hands of an Assistant Minister, the Reverend John Potter Cuyler, Jr.[67] Shoemaker frequently spoke of the importance of the work of both of these men.[68] Both these ministers and their wives lived at Calvary House and were actively involved in Oxford Group and parish work. Apparently Rev. Smith did not approve of Bill Wilson's work with alcoholics at Calvary; but the mention of "Jack" Smith in *Pass It On* indicates Smith must have had substantial contact with Bill Wilson.[69]

The Reverend and Mrs. W. Irving Harris

In Bill Wilson's letter in *Faith at Work*, which we quote below, Bill mentioned the contributions of the Reverend W. Irving Harris and his wife, Julia (both of whom were stalwart Oxford Group supporters in the 1930's). Beginning in 1933, Harris was a resident of Calvary House. He was a regular staff-member of Calvary Church, and he was in charge of the Oxford Group office at Calvary House.[70] Harris worked with Reverend Paul Musselman

---

[66] See Cuyler, *Calvary Church in Action*, pp. 30-44.

[67] See Cuyler, *Calvary Church in Action*, p. 33.

[68] Shoemaker, *Calvary Church Yesterday and Today*, pp. 259-60, 262, 272-74, 276. 279.

[69] See *Pass It On*, p. 169. Compare Harris, *The Breeze of the Spirit*, p. 27, where Reverend J. Herbert Smith is referred to as "Jack" Smith, just as he is in *Pass It On*. See also Mel B., *New Wine: The Spiritual Roots of the Twelve Step Miracle* (MN: Hazelden, 1991), p. 90.

[70] Cuyler, *Calvary Church in Action*, 53.

on *The Calvary Evangel*, later edited it, and frequently taught Bible. Harris wrote Oxford Group literature.[71] Mrs. Irving Harris gave the author a large number of the books in Harris's collection, many written by Sam Shoemaker. Most of Harris's Shoemaker titles contain a personal inscription to Harris in Shoemaker's hand. As we stated, Harris's wife, Julia, was in charge of the Oxford Group bookroom at Calvary House and evidenced to this author an intimate familiarity with Shoemaker's writings. The Reverend Harris and his wife, Julia, both had many direct contacts with Bill Wilson at Calvary.

Both Irving Harris and Bill Wilson have shed light on the Wilson-Shoemaker-Oxford Group link. Harris wrote in *The Breeze of the Spirit*:

> Besides that first Akron group, on Bill's return East, there soon developed a weekly meeting in the Wilson's Brooklyn parlor. When Bill visited Sam Shoemaker, who had been keenly following his progress, the two had a memorable reunion.[72]

When? The Reverend Harris's widow, Mrs. Julia Harris, contributed two items that might answer: (1) In a telephone interview with the author on November 5, 1991, Mrs. Harris said she was *sure* Bill Wilson checked the Twelve Steps with Sam Shoemaker at the time of their writing. She said Bill and Sam sat down and went over the Twelve Steps to see that they were Biblical and not offensive to other religions. (2) She sent the author an excerpt from an article in *Faith at Work* magazine, July-August, 1963, in which Wilson wrote:

> In our early days there were those who actually infused the breath of life into us. Speaking in the language of the heart, they brought us much of the grace in which our society today lives

---

[71] See, for example, Irving Harris, *An Outline of the Life of Christ* (New York: The Oxford Group, 1935).

[72] Harris, *The Breeze of the Spirit*, p. 55.

and has its being. There was my own doctor, William Southworth [*sic*]. . . . There was Dr. Carl Jung.
. . . From William James we learned. . . . But these cornerstones were only a part of the needed foundation. Who could furnish us the wherewithal to construct this spiritual edifice which today houses our world-wide brotherhood? Sam Shoemaker and his wonderful co-workers, among whom were Irving and Julie Harris, were the people who were given this critical assignment.

There is, then, a strong suggestion from Julia Harris's own comments and from the foregoing language by Wilson that Wilson consulted Shoemaker on the contents of the Twelve Steps. Shortly, we will see the suggestion that Bill also consulted Shoemaker as to the contents of the Big Book.

The Reverend Garrett R. Stearly

There is still much to be learned about Bill Wilson's relationship with the Reverend Garrett Stearly; and we will speak of him from time to time in this book. Stearly, an Episcopalian priest, first met Frank Buchman in 1924, became an Oxford Group leader, and then a Shoemaker associate.[73] In our review of Shoemaker's personal journals for the period of November, 1934 to January, 1936, we saw that Garrett Stearly's name sometimes appeared in company with the names of Bill Wilson, Rowland Hazard, Shepard Cornell, and Victor Kitchen. Lois Wilson's "Oxford Group Notes," which we personally inspected at the Wilson home at Stepping Stones, mentioned that Stearly led one of the Oxford Group Pocono House Party meetings. In our visit to the Calvary Church archives in 1993, we established that the two long-time Buchman associates, the Reverend Ray Foote Purdy and the Reverend Garrett R. Stearly, were members of the church corporation at Shoemaker's Calvary Episcopal Church.[74]

---

[73] See Garth Lean, *Frank Buchman: A Life* (London: Constable & Company, 1985), pp. 105, 184, 207, 240, and 526.

[74] See Dick B., *New Light on Alcoholism*, p. 351.

Then, from the Founders Day archives at Akron, Ohio, we unearthed an unpublished manuscript, which evidently was prepared by T. Willard Hunter in July of 1978 for publication by Alcoholics Anonymous. Hunter, an Oxford Group activist and an authority on Oxford Group history, wrote:

Frank [Buchman] had been drying out drunks since before Bill [Wilson] had his first cocktail. But he also discovered that his methodology was successful with non-alcoholics as well. In a way, they were tougher. It was harder for them to admit they were licked. . . . Recently I had lunch in Los Angeles with Mr. and Mrs. S. from Oakland. . . . With me was Garrett Stearly, long time veteran of the Buchman wars. An Episcopal clergyman, he was in the old days a close comrade in arms with Sam Shoemaker. We told our luncheon friends of the Oxford Group "links in the chain" of A.A. history. At the end of the tale, Garrett said, "Let me add just one more point. I recall vividly how we used to work with Bill [Wilson] down there at Calvary Church in New York—Frank [Buchman], Sam [Shoemaker], and I and others. We tried and tried to get him [Bill Wilson] away from concentrating so completely on this alcohol thing. We pleaded with him, with his great talents and his Wall Street experience, to help take on American business."[75]

There is another and far more important story pertaining to Garrett Stearly, Sam Shoemaker, and Bill Wilson. Our Oxford Group friend, James Draper Newton, who has been aligned with Buchman, Shoemaker, and the Oxford Group since the early 1920's, has repeatedly reminded us of two conversations he [Newton] had with Stearly. According to Newton, Stearly twice told him:

---

[75] Memorandum by T. Willard Hunter, "The Oxford Group's Frank Buchman," July, 1978, Founders Day archives, maintained by Gail L. in Akron, Ohio, pp. 9-10.

Bill Wilson asked Sam Shoemaker to write A.A.'s Twelve Steps. Shoemaker declined. Shoemaker told Bill that the Steps should be written by an alcoholic and that Bill was the one to do it.[76]

Tex Francisco and Calvary Mission

Another Shoemaker-Oxford Group influence on Wilson can be found in the personality of Taylor "Tex" Francisco, who became superintendent of Calvary Rescue Mission in 1933.[77] It was at Calvary Mission that Bill first made his "decision for Christ" and later spent much time working with drunks.[78] Bill spoke of this Tex Francisco as the person who "ran the mission."[79]

F. Shepard Cornell

There was also F. Shepard Cornell, whose name sometimes appears as "Shepherd." "Shep" was a member of the Calvary Church vestry.[80] Bill Wilson described him as "an active Oxford Group member."[81] Shep Cornell's name pops up frequently in the reminiscences of Bill Wilson and Lois Wilson.[82] Cornell had an active and effective contact with an Oxford Group alcoholic, Charles Clapp, Jr.; and this occurred about the time Bill Wilson

---

[76] Newton's recollection of these Stearly remarks is very clear. Newton has repeated the remarks to the author several times, both in person and on the telephone over the period from 1992 to 1994. In fact, Newton recently urged the author to undertake a search for Stearly's papers, if they still exist. And that search has begun.

[77] Cuyler, *Calvary Church in Action*, p. 67; and Harris, *The Breeze of the Spirit*, p. 49.

[78] See Dick B., *The Akron Genesis of Alcoholics Anonymous* (Corte Madera, CA: Good Book Publishing Company, 1994), pp. 146-47, 155-59.

[79] *Pass It On*, p. 117.

[80] This fact was given the author in a telephone interview with the Reverend Irving Harris's widow, Julia Harris, in October, 1991.

[81] *Pass It On*, p. 116.

[82] See *Pass It On*, pp. 113, 116, 122; Thomsen, *Bill W.*, pp. 211-212; Mel B., *New Wine*, p. 21; and Dick B., *New Light on Alcoholism*, 337-341.

was getting well through the Oxford Group activities at Calvary.[83] Shep was one of the leaders in Tuesday afternoon meetings at Calvary House which were held for sharing and witness. He also had a smaller "team" sharing work with him.[84] Cornell's Oxford Group work may have involved, on Tuesdays, what Mrs. Samuel Shoemaker called "Alcoholics Anonymous which, at this time met on Tuesday nights in the Great Hall of Calvary House."[85] Shep Cornell was an ardent Oxford Group "member" and a Calvary Church member who actually worked with alcoholics such as Ebby Thacher, Charles Clapp, Jr., *and* Bill Wilson. These are facts documented in Calvary Church records, Clapp's writings, Thacher's statements, A.A. literature, and Wilson's writings.[86] Lois Wilson specifically remembered that Ebby Thacher and Shep Cornell were companions of the Wilsons—joining them as all four "constantly" attended Oxford Group meetings.[87]

Rowland Hazard

We have frequently written in this book and in our other titles about Rowland Hazard.[88] It was Rowland Hazard's contact with Dr. Carl Jung in Switzerland that marked the beginning of A.A.'s East Coast link with the Oxford Group. At Dr. Jung's urging,

---

[83] See Charles Clapp, Jr., *The Big Bender* (New York: Harper & Brothers, 1938), pp. 105-14, 118, 125-28, 136, 150-52; and Pittman and Dick B., *Courage to Change*, pp. 22-23, 125-50.

[84] Cuyler, *Calvary Church in Action*, p. 57; and Dick B., *New Light on Alcoholism*, pp. 333-36.

[85] Helen Smith Shoemaker, *I Stand By The Door*, p. 177. We cannot tell for sure whether Cornell's work on Tuesdays at 5:15, of which the Reverend Cuyler wrote, is the same work on "Tuesday nights," of which Mrs. Shoemaker wrote.

[86] See Dick B., *New Light on Alcoholism*, pp. 347-51. As shown in these pages, Cornell and Tex Francisco sponsored the baptism of Ebby Thacher at Calvary Church as Ebby's godparents.

[87] *Lois Remembers*, p. 91.

[88] For details, see Dick B., *New Light on Alcoholism*, pp. 254-57, 263, 329-36, 347-51; and *The Akron Genesis*, pp. 141-44.

Rowland sought out the Oxford Group to attain and did attain a conversion experience.[89] Rowland became thoroughly conversant with Oxford Group ideas; and it was Rowland who taught Bill Wilson's "sponsor," Ebby Thacher, most if not all of the Oxford Group principles and practices Ebby passed on to Bill Wilson.[90] Rowland participated in Oxford Group teams that visited Ohio in the early 1930's and did so in company with Shoemaker, Victor Kitchen, and Shepard Cornell.[91] We observed, in our inspection of Shoemaker's personal journals for 1934-1936, that Rowland Hazard's name was frequently mentioned separately and in company with Bill Wilson's name. Hazard was a member of the Oxford Group businessmen's team to which Bill Wilson belonged.[92] Wilson met with Hazard many times.[93] Hazard was a member of the Calvary Church Vestry from 1937 to 1940; and, as Sam Shoemaker himself remarked to AAs at one of their international conventions, Hazard had two stained glass windows dedicated to him at Calvary Church.[94]

Victor C. Kitchen

An Oxford Group personality, as to whom more research is needed concerning his connection with Bill Wilson, is Victor C.

---

[89] See Bill Wilson's description of the Rowland Hazard story (where Rowland's name is not used) at Big Book, pp. 26-28.

[90] See *Pass It On*, pp. 113-15.

[91] In our inspection of 1933 and 1934 newspaper articles in *The Akron Beacon Journal*, we saw these names in company; and we also saw them mentioned in the articles in *The Calvary Evangel* which were written in 1935 issues by the Rev. John Potter Cuyler, Jr. and by Victor C. Kitchen.

[92] Dick B., *New Light on Alcoholism*, pp. 334-35.

[93] Thomsen, *Bill W.*, p. 230.

[94] During his 1933 visit to Calvary Church and to the Calvary Church archives in New York, the author saw Hazard's name listed as a vestryman and also inspected the stained glass windows, which are the subject of remarks in a Calvary Church pamphlet about the church's windows.

Kitchen.[95] Kitchen was a partner in the New York advertising firm of Doyle, Kitchen, and McCormick. Kitchen and his wife met the Oxford Group in the early 1930's. They soon decided to give their full time to the Oxford Group program. Both Kitchen and his wife were in close touch with Buchman, Shoemaker, and the Oxford Group people, such as Garrett Stearly and Ray Purdy, that we have mentioned, and that Bill and Lois Wilson mentioned.[96] Shoemaker's associate, Dubois Morris, Jr., was the editor of the Oxford Group page published weekly in *The Berkshire Eagle*; and Victor Kitchen collaborated with Morris and had a weekly column of "pithy ideas."[97] Kitchen was a member of the Oxford Group businessmen's team with Bill.[98] Whether or not Kitchen was a "real" alcoholic, one daughter specifically confirmed to the author that Kitchen "drank too much and quit drinking 100% soon after meeting the Oxford Group, and remained sober until he died." Kitchen wrote the popular Oxford Group title of the early 1930's, *I Was a Pagan*. If one reads that title with care, he or she can see a story development very similar to Bill Wilson's story in A.A.'s Big Book. There are also many words and phrases and ideas which Wilson seems virtually to have incorporated in A.A.'s Big Book. Kitchen was much involved in Calvary Church activities and wrote for *The Calvary Evangel*. He was also a leading figure in the Oxford Group team that returned to Akron in 1934 and very probably met Dr. Bob and Anne Smith, Henrietta Seiberling, T.

---

[95] For some details, see Dick B., *The Akron Genesis*, p. 153-54; and *New Light on Alcoholism*, pp. 319, 329-36, 339-40, 347-51.

[96] Much of this information on Kitchen was provided to the author in a letter, dated October 24, 1994, from Kitchen's daughter, Mrs. Harry Almond.

[97] Letter to the author, December 4, 1994, from Beverly Kitchen Almond which quoted her letter from Charles D. Brodhead. Brodhead was on the staff of Calvary House from 1936 to 1940. He presently lives in Brattleboro, Vermont.

[98] Charles D. Brodhead specifically recalls hearing Bill Wilson speak at Calvary House. Brodhead does not recall if Kitchen was present on that occasion but believes it probable that Shep Cornell, Garrett Stearly, and Sam Shoemaker *were* present. Brodhead added, in his correspondence with Beverly Almond Kitchen, that "the whole team of the Oxford Group who met there were in . . . close contact. . . ." Letter from Beverly Kitchen Almond to the author, 12/4/94.

Henry Williams and his wife, Clarace during the 1934 Oxford Group team visit.

James Houck, Hanford Twitchell, John Ryder, Parks Shipley, and Professor Philip Marshall Brown

There are several other Oxford Group people who had substantial connection with Frank Buchman, Sam Shoemaker, Calvary Church, the Oxford Group, and Bill Wilson. We have dealt with the specifics in our other titles.[99] James Houck recalls attending Oxford Group meetings with Bill Wilson. Houck is perhaps the A.A. member with the most sobriety in the world. Houck is presently a member of the board of directors of Moral Re-Armament, Inc. He lives in Maryland. Hanford Twitchell was Treasurer of Calvary Church, attended many Oxford Group functions, and often accompanied Bill Wilson when Bill was helping drunks. John Ryder was a long-standing friend of Wilson's and was active in the Oxford Group. Both Twitchell and Ryder are mentioned in Shoemaker's personal journals in connection with Bill Wilson. Parks Shipley was very much involved in the Oxford Group and the Oxford Group businessmen's team. He traveled abroad with Shoemaker. And he recalls attending Calvary Church, Oxford Group, and businessmen's team meetings with Wilson. Shipley lives in New Jersey. Professor Philip Marshall Brown was an Oxford Group scholar, a professor of international relations at Princeton, a frequent Oxford Group speaker, and the author of *The Venture of Belief*—a book highly recommended in the Oxford Group. As we pointed out in *The Akron Genesis of Alcoholics Anonymous*, Professor Brown frequently had conversations with Bill Wilson's friend, Rowland Hazard. Brown belonged to the businessmen's team to which Bill Wilson and Rowland Hazard belonged, and he frequently was listed on Oxford Group houseparty invitations and programs. In fact, Lois Wilson's Oxford

---

[99] For details, see Dick B., *The Akron Genesis*, pp. 43-44, 142-44, 146-50; and Dick B., *New Light on Alcoholism*, pp. 53-57, 247-57, 262-64, 319-51.

Group notebook mentions that she and Bill met Professor Brown; and Sam Shoemaker's personal journal contains an entry for June 25, 1935, which indicates that Shoemaker may have sent Bill Wilson a copy of Brown's *The Venture of Belief*, a book for which Shoemaker wrote the Foreword.

Shoemaker, A.A., the Steps, and the Big Book

The hard evidence thus far uncovered as to Bill Wilson's connections with Calvary Church, Calvary House, and Calvary Mission boils down to this: There certainly were Oxford Group meetings at Calvary House on Tuesdays, Thursdays, and Sundays.[100] Various accounts seem strongly to suggest that Bill and Lois Wilson, Shep Cornell, and Ebby Thacher probably attended most if not all of these meetings. Sam Shoemaker and his staff actively participated in the meetings, some of which were led by Sam and some by his staff.[101] Shoemaker led some of the Sunday afternoon meetings.[102] Shep Cornell was one of those who led the Tuesday meetings.

Calvary Church people who were mentioned by Bill Wilson and his wife, Lois, and with whom they had personal contact, were the Reverend J. Herbert Smith, the Reverend and Mrs. W. Irving Harris, the Reverend Garrett R. Stearly, the Reverend Ray Purdy, Shep Cornell, Superintendent Taylor Francisco, Rowland Hazard, Victor Kitchen, and Hanford Twitchell. And while the Reverend John Cuyler is not mentioned in any Wilson accounts we have read, Cuyler certainly was a resident of Calvary House and an important staff member. We later discovered that Lois herself

---

[100] Thomsen, *Bill W.*, pp. 229, 252; *Lois Remembers*, pp. 94, 98; *Pass It On*, pp. 132, 162; Harris, *The Breeze of the Spirit*, pp. 24, 47; and Cuyler, *Calvary Church in Action*, pp. 49, 55, 56, 57, 58.

[101] *Lois Remembers*, p. 94.

[102] *Lois Remembers*, p. 94.

had specifically recorded in her "Oxford Group Notes" the many Oxford Group people she and Bill had met.

Then there was Wilson's actual participation in an Oxford Group team. There are many specific remarks by Shoemaker that he was in close touch with Wilson from the very beginning of Wilson's sobriety. There are many specific remarks by Wilson that he was taught the A.A. spiritual principles by the Oxford Group as led in America by Shoemaker. And there are specific statements by Irving Harris that Shoemaker and Wilson did compare notes on spiritual matters and that Shoemaker took an interest in Bill's work but was not necessarily involved personally.

Our 1993 examination of Shoemaker's personal journals showed the close relationship between Shoemaker, Wilson, and Oxford Group people in 1935 and 1936; and we believe there is similar information in later Shoemaker journals we have not yet examined.[103]

As Garrett Stearly's remarks indicate, there is a strong possibility that Bill Wilson consulted Sam Shoemaker concerning the contents of the Twelve Steps. Shoemaker's own remarks indicate Wilson looked to Shoemaker for advice or suggestions at the time the Big Book was written. Shoemaker wrote to Bill: "I shall never forget that I was one of those who read the first mimeographed copy of the first book [*Alcoholics Anonymous*]. . . ."[104] This manuscript [a multilith] was circulated before the Big Book was put in final form and published.

We conclude this review knowing now that Wilson had a good deal of personal contact with Shoemaker himself between 1934 and 1939. Wilson was in close touch with many on the Calvary Church

---

[103] At the writing of this revised edition, the author learned from Shoemaker's younger daughter that the family has located some of Shoemaker's personal journals that had not been located when we wrote *New Light on Alcoholism*. These additional journals may record still more of the close and ongoing contacts between Shoemaker and Wilson that were recorded from 1934 to 1936 in the journals we read.

[104] See Charles Taylor Knippel, *Samuel M. Shoemaker's Theological Influence on William G. Wilson's Twelve Step Spiritual Program of Recovery* (Ph.D. dissertation, St. Louis University, 1987), p. 70.

staff and many in the Oxford Group teams. All these Oxford Group people were very much involved in passing on the ideas and teachings of the Oxford Group and Sam Shoemaker. Wilson was frequently present at Calvary House, Calvary Mission, and Oxford Group meetings and houseparties between late 1934 and mid 1937. On occasion, he consulted with Shoemaker in Shoemaker's own study at Calvary House.

5

The A.A. Links: Arrivals and Departures

A.A.'s Oxford Group Beginnings

Our previous titles cover most of the facts concerning A.A.'s beginnings in the Oxford Group.[1] Three of A.A.'s own "Conference Approved" titles deal with some of the history.[2] But a good deal of research has occurred since A.A.'s history titles were published. What we once called the "Shoemaker Puzzle" has now been largely resolved since the first edition of our first Oxford

---

[1] They are: Dick B., *The Akron Genesis of Alcoholics Anonymous* (Corte Madera, CA: Good Book Publishing Company, 1994); and *New Light on Alcoholism: The A.A. Legacy from Sam Shoemaker* (Corte Madera, CA: Good Book Publishing Company, 1994). See also: Dick B., *Anne Smith's Journal, 1933-1939: A.A.'s Principles of Success* (San Rafael, CA: Paradise Research Publications, 1994); *Dr. Bob's Library: Books for Twelve Step Growth* (San Rafael, CA: Paradise Research Publications, 1994): and *The Books Early AAs read for Spiritual Growth* (San Rafael, CA: Paradise Research Publications, 1994).

[2] See *Alcoholics Anonymous Comes of Age* (New York: Alcoholics Anonymous World Services, Inc.,1979); *DR. BOB and the Good Oldtimers* (New York: Alcoholics Anonymous World Services, 1980); and *Pass It On* (New York: Alcoholics Anonymous World Services, 1984).

Group title.[3] But no up-to-date integration of the various historical parts has yet been presented; and that is what we will set forth here in summary form.

The critical year was 1931.

The Oxford Group beginnings of Alcoholics Anonymous occurred in 1931. And they occurred in separate and totally unrelated settings and areas of the United States. Possibly the only common link was the Reverend Sam Shoemaker; and even Shoemaker could not have guessed how his Oxford Group activities in two different parts of the United States would wind up spawning A.A.'s own Oxford Group beginnings.

In the Central United States

Harvey Firestone, Sr.'s, son, Bud, had a serious drinking problem. Bud was an alcoholic. And Harvey Firestone's young protege, Jim Newton, befriended Bud and worked with him to help Bud change his life and achieve deliverance from alcoholism. Jim managed, in 1931, to bring Sam Shoemaker and the Firestone family together in Ohio, and then to get the young Firestone to an Episcopal Bishops Conference in Denver, Colorado. On the train ride back from Denver to Akron, in 1931, Sam Shoemaker brought Bud Firestone to a decision for Christ. And Bud was delivered from alcoholism for a while. In fact, for the next two years, Bud and his wife, Dorothy, were very much involved with Oxford Group teams and Group witnessing.

Finally, in January, 1933, Harvey Firestone, Sr., invited Dr. Frank Buchman and an Oxford Group team to Akron to witness to the changes God could make in people's lives, changes such as had occurred in the life of young Bud. Bud and Dorothy were among the principal witnesses. At public meetings, in the newspapers, in church pulpits, and in private conversations, Buchman, his Oxford Group team, and the Firestones related what had happened when

---

[3] Dick B., *The Oxford Group & Alcoholics Anonymous* (Seattle, WA: Glen Abbey Books, 1992).

they turned to Christ. And the events were widely heralded and widely attended.

Henrietta Seiberling, Clarace Williams, Delphine Weber, and Anne Smith (Dr. Bob's wife) participated in the 1933 events in Akron; and all were much taken with the Oxford Group program. Each of the four ladies, in her own way, saw an area of need and the possibility of deliverance. All wound up focusing on Dr. Bob and his drinking problem. All started attending Oxford Group meetings. And, as we recently discovered, an Oxford Group team returned to Akron in 1934 and again witnessed to the local populace and to Oxford Group adherents. The second Oxford Group team focused on further spiritual *growth*, known in Oxford Group parlance as "continuance."

We cannot be sure when Dr. Bob's wife, Anne Smith, heard some of these key Oxford Group people, whether it was in 1933, in 1934, or in both years. But we believe she did hear them. For she reported in her spiritual journal at some length on specific remarks by certain Oxford Group leaders. At pages 23 and 24 of her Journal, she wrote of a "Talk on Leadership by John Watt."[4] At page 34, she wrote about Eleanor Forde's ideas on leadership. At pages 25 to 30, she spoke of an Oxford Group house party and titled the section: "Oxford Group House Party, 1933 (Elinor Forde)." Also, on page 31, she set forth her "Notes From The Oxford England House Party."

Dr. Bob had been attending the Akron Oxford Group meetings, mostly at the home of T. Henry and Clarace Williams at 676 Palisades Drive, in Akron. Dr. Bob intensely studied the Bible, an immense amount of Oxford Group literature, and a good many other Christian books of the day. But his drinking problem persisted. Finally, Henrietta called a special Oxford Group meeting to help Dr. Bob deal with the alcohol problem. All shared their "costly" life experiences, from which they had been delivered.

---

[4] We have reported these and subsequent details in this chapter from the actual pages [as numbered by A.A. General Services archives in New York] of Anne's journal, a copy of which we have in our possession. See also, Dick B., *Anne Smith's Journal.*

They did this, in the Oxford Group manner, to bring Dr. Bob out of denial and into surrender to God. Dr. Bob shared that he was a "secret drinker"—a confession which shocked no one but Dr. Bob! And all, *including Dr. Bob*, knelt in prayer and asked for Bob's deliverance.

Within weeks, Bill Wilson showed up in Akron. Bill was in desperate need of finding another alcoholic with whom to work so that he (Bill) could maintain his new-found sobriety. Bill sought out Dr. Walter Tunks, an Episcopalian priest, who was also an Oxford Group adherent. Tunks put Wilson in touch with Henrietta Seiberling, who said Bill's call to her was "manna from Heaven." And Henrietta brought Bill and Dr. Bob together for their famous six hour visit at Henrietta's gatehouse home in Akron. After that, with but a brief drinking interlude on Bob's part, Bill and Dr. Bob began working together to help other alcoholics get sober.

Finally, on June 10, 1935, Dr. Bob had his last drink, and A.A. was born. Born at the Robert H. Smith home at 855 Ardmore Avenue, in Akron, Ohio, a place still open to the public for visits.

Details as to what occurred thereafter can be found in our *Akron Genesis* title. But the *significance* of the next four years of Oxford Group activity with Akron alcoholics lies in the fact that these early AAs called themselves a "Christian Fellowship" (which was one of the names for the Oxford Group). And they adopted the description of themselves as the "alcoholic squad *of the Oxford Group.*"

On the East Coast of the United States

Once again our starting date is 1931. But the starting *point* was Switzerland.

Rowland Hazard, a prominent New England businessman, and an alcoholic, had sought professional treatment for his alcoholism from the noted Swiss psychiatrist, Dr. Carl G. Jung. After working with Dr. Jung in Switzerland over an extended period of time, Hazard returned to America only to get drunk again. Hazard sought out Jung again and asked what the problem was. Jung told Hazard that he (Hazard) had the "mind of a chronic alcoholic." Jung opined, in substance, that there was little hope for Hazard's recovery without a conversion experience. Jung recommended that Hazard join some religious group, and seek such a religious experience—a "union with God," Jung later called it. Whether Hazard then established a relationship with the Oxford Group in Europe or in New England is a fact yet to be determined. But establish it he did. For Rowland became deeply and directly committed to the Oxford Group, had such a conversion experience, achieved sobriety, and, as far as we can determine, remained sober for the rest of his life.

In company with Oxford Group adherents, Cebra Graves and F. Shepard Cornell, Hazard sought out Edwin Throckmorton Thacher, who had a severe drinking problem. The three Oxford Group people worked with Thacher, shared Oxford Group principles and practices with him, and brought Thacher to a conversion experience. Thacher went to the Calvary Rescue Mission in New York City (a shelter, mostly for drunks, that was run by Sam Shoemaker's Calvary Church). Thacher, who came to be known as "Ebby," made a decision for Christ. Thacher was delivered from his alcoholism for a while. And, in the meantime, he made decision to carry the message of his Oxford Group religious recovery, and what God had done for him, to his (Ebby's) old drinking friend, Bill Wilson.

Persuaded that Ebby had what he, Bill Wilson, wanted, Wilson himself went to the Calvary Mission. There Bill also made a decision for Christ. Bill later reported he had been "born again."[5] Though he stayed drunk for several more days, Wilson then went to Towns Hospital in New York for help. He announced he had "found something." Shortly, Bill (with Ebby's help), applied the very Oxford Group principles that AAs apply today. Bill then had

---

[5] We have previously detailed Wilson's comments of his rebirth; and see Lois Wilson's observation about Bill's "rebirth." *Lois Remembers* (New York: Al-Anon Family Group Headquarters, 1987), p. 98.

what he called his "hot flash" conversion experience. And he never drank again.

Bill began working with drunks immediately. He constantly attended Oxford Group meetings with his wife (Lois) in company with Ebby Thacher, Shepard Cornell, and others. But Bill said he was unable to help one single person get sober.[6] Bill, however, did maintain his own sobriety.

As we've previously covered, Bill was in closest touch with Sam Shoemaker and with a host of thoroughly informed and experienced Oxford Group people. Bill went to Oxford Group meetings, particularly at Calvary House (adjacent to Shoemaker's Calvary Church). He joined an Oxford Group business men's team and is mentioned in that connection in Shoemaker's personal journals. He fellowshipped with Rowland Hazard, Shepard Cornell, Victor Kitchen, Hanford Twitchell, Charles Clapp, Jr., Charles Haines, L. Parks Shipley, and Ebby Thacher. And all these men were closely connected to Sam Shoemaker, his church, and the Oxford Group. All (except possibly Ebby) belonged to the Oxford Group businessmen's team. Bill attended Oxford Group houseparties where he met, among others, Buchman, Shoemaker, Shoemaker's wife (Helen), the Reverend Irving Harris and his wife (Julia), Professor Philip Marshall Brown, the Reverend Cleve Hicks, Eleanor Forde, Loudon Hamilton, Charles Haines, Jim Newton, Garth Lean, and the Reverend Ray Purdy, all of whom were leading Oxford Group activists of that day. Most were closely associated with both Buchman and Shoemaker.

As the Rev. Harris stated, Wilson began meeting with Shoemaker in Shoemaker's personal study and discussing the Christian principles which later were to be embodied in A.A.'s language and recovery program and practices.

---

[6] Such was Bill's report, but there is a letter written by Sam Shoemaker to Bill Wilson in the earliest days of Wilson's sobriety that indicate Bill did have some kind of success with at least one alcoholic named Frederick Breithut. See Dick B., *New Light on Alcoholism*, pp. 323, 347-51. See also our elaboration on the Breithut facts in footnote 63 in the previous chapter of this book.

Many of the foregoing facts, hanging together as they do, may come as a surprise to AAs and A.A. historians. For much of the evidence was only recently discovered by the author himself from archives at Calvary Church in New York; at Bill Wilson's home at Stepping Stones; in Shoemaker's own personal journals; from Lois Wilson's Oxford Group notes at Stepping Stones; from renewed study of Anne Smith's Journal; from Oxford Group businessmen team members such as Parks Shipley; from conversations with Shoemaker's wife and daughters; and from a number of long-time Oxford Group and/or Shoemaker associates such as Mrs. W. Irving Harris, James D. and Eleanor Forde Newton, Garth Lean, Michael Hutchinson, K. D. Belden, Dr. Morris Martin, George Vondermuhll, Jr., James Houck, the Reverend Harry Almond, the Reverend Howard Blake, Charles Haines, Dr. R. C. Mowat, Sydney Cook, Michael Henderson, Richard Ruffin, and the Reverend T. Willard Hunter.[7]

---

[7] *For A.A.'s own accounts* of A.A. beginnings and the Oxford Group connection, see Big Book, pp. xv-xvii, xxiv-xxx, 8-15, 26-29, 43, 153-60. 171-92; *Alcoholics Anonymous Comes of Age*, pp. vii-viii, 6-7, 10-11, 16, 19, 22, 38-40, 58-77; *DR. BOB and the Good Oldtimers*, pp. 53-121, 128-55, 228, 239, 306-15; *Pass It On*, pp. 101-206, 246-47, 381-88; *The Language of the Heart* (New York: The AA Grapevine, Inc., 1988), pp. 195-202, 276-86, 297-98, 53-380; *RHS* (New York: The AA Grapevine, Inc., 1951)—the memorial issue of The A.A. Grapevine, published at the time of Dr. Bob's death in 1951; and *The Co-Founders of Alcoholics Anonymous: Biographical sketches. Their last major talks* (New York: Alcoholics Anonymous World Services, 1972, 1975). *For other sources of details*, see James Newton, *Uncommon Friends* (New York: Harcourt Brace Jovanovich, Publishers, 1987), pp. 83-89, 157; Garth Lean, *On the Tail of a Comet* (Colorado Springs: Helmers & Howard, 1988), pp. 151-53; Helen Smith Shoemaker, *I Stand By The Door* (New York: Harper & Row, 1967), pp. 59, 79-94; 188-93; Irving Harris, *The Breeze of the Spirit* (New York: The Seabury Press, 1978), pp. 45-56, 70-72; *Lois Remembers* (New York: Al-Anon Family Group Headquarters, Inc., 1987), pp. 88-104; Ernest Kurtz, *Not-God: The History of Alcoholics Anonymous.* Exp. ed. (Minnesota: Hazelden, 1991); Mel B., *New Wine* (Minnesota: Hazelden Foundation, 1991), pp. 13-99; Dennis C. Morreim, *Changed Lives* (Minneapolis, Augsburg, 1991), pp. 11-94. And *see the author's own studies from the standpoint of Dr. Bob and Anne* in Dick B., *Dr. Bob's Library* (San Rafael, CA: Paradise Research Publications, 1994); *The Books Early AAs Read for Spiritual Growth* (San Rafael, CA: Paradise Research Publications, 1994); and *Anne Smith's Journal.*

The Collaboration at A.A.'s Birthplace

Henrietta Seiberling, Dr. Bob, Anne, T. Henry, and Clarace were all Oxford Group adherents. So were Bill and Lois Wilson. And the early AAs in Ohio considered themselves a part of the Oxford Group.[8] A.A. trustee-to-be, Frank Amos, reported to John D. Rockefeller, Jr. on the Christian technique the Akron AAs had used in helping alcoholics. Amos said that: (1) the alcoholics had to realize they were whipped from a medical standpoint, (2) had to surrender absolutely to God, (3) had to remove sins from their life, (4) had to have devotions every morning—a "quiet time" of prayer and some reading from the Bible and other religious literature, (5) had to help other alcoholics, (6) should meet with other "reformed" alcoholics in social and religious comradeship, and (7) should attend some religious service at least once weekly.[9]

Of major importance was the fact that the Akron AAs were achieving remarkable success. Akron AAs were essentially an important part, in fact, *the focus*, of the Akron Oxford Group meetings held at the T. Henry and Clarace Williams home from 1935 to 1939.

Departures from the Oxford Group

There were three connections which inextricably linked early Alcoholics Anonymous to the Oxford Group.

First, there was the close relationship of Oxford Group founder, Dr. Frank Buchman, with the Reverend Samuel Moor Shoemaker, Jr., Rector of the Calvary Episcopal Church in New York. Bill Wilson attended innumerable Oxford Group meetings led by Shoemaker, his assistants, and lay friends. Bill was involved in a good many other Oxford Group activities at Calvary Church and elsewhere. This occurred between December 18, 1934,

---

[8] *DR. BOB*, pp. 117, 137, 128, 100, 121.

[9] *DR. BOB*, pp. 131.

and August, 1937. Bill attributed the principles of the Twelve Steps to the Oxford Group, led (as Bill put it) in America, by Sam Shoemaker. But Oxford Group founder, Frank Buchman, was, of course, the root source.

Second, there were the large Oxford Group team meetings in Akron, Ohio, in January of 1933. These drew A.A.'s founders, Henrietta Seiberling, T. Henry and Clarace Williams, Anne Smith (Dr. Bob's wife), and ultimately Dr. Bob himself into the Oxford Group scene. All these A.A. founders regularly attended Oxford Group meetings at the T. Henry Williams home in Akron, and occasionally at other locations. This began two and a half years before Dr. Bob met Bill in May of 1935. Then an Oxford Group team returned to Akron in 1934. During and after the summer of 1935 and continuing through at least early 1940, the Akron AAs were an integral part of the Oxford Group.

Third, there was Bill Wilson's association with his old friend, Ebby Thacher, who had recovered from alcoholism as a participant in Shoemaker's Oxford Group program emanating from Calvary Episcopal Church in New York. Ebby was also involved in the Calvary Rescue Mission, run by Shoemaker's church. Ebby had brought Bill to the Rescue Mission and ultimately to the Oxford Group meetings held primarily at Calvary House, the American Oxford Group Headquarters at Gramercy Park North, in New York, adjacent to Shoemaker's Calvary Church.

And, almost in reverse, these three Oxford Group links disappeared from the A.A. scene, one-by-one, commencing in 1937.

The New York Scene

Bill Wilson began his participation in the Oxford Group at Calvary House and Calvary Mission in New York about five months before he met Dr. Bob in May of 1935. In little more than two years, however, Wilson and his wife, Lois, had become disenchanted with the goings-on at Calvary as far as alcoholics were concerned. They felt—and, according to Sam Shoemaker's own recollections, with some justification—that the Oxford Group people in New York were not much interested in working with alcoholics.[10] In August of 1937, Wilson and his few New York AAs severed their Oxford Group connection forever. Among other things, Wilson said: "We found that certain of their [the Oxford Group's] ideas and attitudes simply could not be sold to alcoholics."[11] Speaking quite bluntly, Bill's wife Lois once asserted, the "Oxford Group kind of kicked us out."[12]

The Akron Scene

On January 2, 1940, Dr. Bob wrote Bill: "Have definitely shaken off the shackles of the Oxford Group . . . and are meeting at my house for the time being. Had 74 Wednesday in my little house, but shall get a hall soon."[13] The exact reasons for the Akron A.A.-Oxford Group split are not clear and apparently have not been reduced to writing.[14] There have been many observations that, for Dr. Bob at least, the Akron A.A.-Oxford Group relationship was always a strong one. In fact, Bill Wilson wrote: "It was not until later, and well after the A.A. book was published [in the Spring of 1939] that our Akron members withdrew from the Oxford Group and finally from the home which had sheltered them so well."[15] Lois Wilson added at a later time: "The Akron alcoholics continued to call themselves Oxford Group after the New York bunch adopted the name Alcoholics Anonymous in 1939, when the book of that title was published. . . . To many in Akron it was a heartbreaking severance. . . and the Oxford Group's part in AA's beginnings can never be forgotten."[16]

---

[10] See Shoemaker's remarks that were quoted in *Pass It On*, p. 178.

[11] *A.A. Comes of Age*, p. 74. See also, A.A.'s own explanations for Bill's 1937 departure from the Oxford Group in *Pass It On*, pp 171-73.

[12] *Pass It On*, p. 174.

[13] *DR. BOB*, p. 218.

[14] *DR. BOB*, pp. 212-13.

[15] A.A. *Comes of Age*, p. 76.

[16] *Lois Remembers*, p. 104.

The Shoemaker-Buchman Breach in 1941

In 1941, Sam Shoemaker announced to the American and British press that he had decided to end his association with Buchman. Shoemaker asked Buchman to remove all personal and Oxford Group material and personnel from Calvary House. This was the large parish house attached to Calvary Church in New York, which had, for fifteen years, been the home and office of Buchman's work in America. The reasons for the break are not fully known.[17] For our purposes they can be described in terms of Shoemaker's desired focus on vital personal religion, working within the churches, and Buchman's desired focus on national and supernational change to save the world.[18]

During the author's visits to the archives of Calvary Episcopal Church in New York and the archives of Hartford Theological Seminary in Connecticut, the author was able to obtain copies of letters Shoemaker and his associate rector, J. Herbert Smith, addressed and sent to the parishioners of Calvary Church. Part of the November 1, 1941, Calvary Church letter to the parishioners stated:

> For many years the work of this parish has been closely associated with the work of the Oxford Group and Moral Re-Armament. Many members of the parish share with us a deep gratitude to Dr. Buchman and other leaders of the Movement,

---

[17] In April of 1992, Lean wrote the author, "The more I read the sources (for example, Irving Harris' *The Breeze of the Spirit*), the more I feel that your statement at the close of Chapter 3 [now set forth in the next sentence of the main text of this revised edition] gives the best explanation of the differences between Shoemaker and Buchman in 1941. Bishop Roots' statement at page 304 of *On the Tail of a Comet* defines it well. . . . Buchman once said to me—before the last war when I sympathized with him because one of our Oxford friends had hived off:—'It is not the first time. I have never withdrawn my love from anyone.' In this he was rather like John Wesley, when George Whitfield issued a pamphlet attacking him. Wesley said: 'You can read a pamphlet by Mr. Whitfield about Mr. Wesley. But you will never read a pamphlet by Mr. Wesley about Mr. Whitfield.'"

[18] See Lean, *On the Tail of a Comet*, p. 304.

from which we have learned great truths, and with whom we have enjoyed real fellowship. The Group has been of penetrating spiritual significance in America and in the world, and has made a great contribution to the life of this parish.

When the Oxford Group was, by its own definition, "a movement of vital personal religion working **within the churches** to make the principles of the New Testament practical as a working force today," we fully identified ourselves with it. Certain policies and points of view, however, have arisen in the development of Moral Re-Armament about which we have had increasing misgivings.

With this in mind, and also because it has become increasingly difficult to function as a parish church when the facilities of Calvary House were largely taken up by its use as a national headquarters for Moral Re-Armament, it has seemed advisable to us, after careful thought and prayer, that this house should cease to be used in this way, as of this date.

We are confident that our parishioners and all our friends will understand that we wholeheartedly adhere to the spiritual truths enunciated by the Oxford Group, which are fundamental Christian truths, and which transformed our lives and helped equip us to meet the needs of others. To those eternal verities we shall always be loyal. The life-changing principles which have been characteristic of our work at Calvary Church at its best will continue to be basic in carrying out our present program.

After the 1941 break with Buchman, Shoemaker continued for many years as Calvary Church Rector. He founded his own Faith-at-Work Movement. He was later called to be rector of Calvary Episcopal Church in Pittsburgh, Pennsylvania, where he remained until his retirement. Shoemaker there founded "The Pittsburgh Experiment."

And now it is appropriate for us to review the Oxford Group principles and practices we have unearthed. We will cite references showing Shoemaker's adherence to these principles and practices. We will also cite references showing their Biblical origins, cite references to *Anne Smith's Journal* containing them, and point to their probable resting places in A.A.'s Big Book and literature.

6

Twenty-eight Oxford Group Principles That Influenced A.A.

The people of the Oxford Group were concerned with aligning their lives with the Will of God. Their roots centered around studying the Bible to determine the Universal Will of God, and then listening to God and obeying His Universal Will in order to learn God's Particular Will for man.[1] Stress was laid on John 7:17

---

[1] See Horace Bushnell, *The New Life* (London: Strahan & Co., 1868), pp. 1-15; J. C. Pollock, *Moody: A Biographical Portrait of the Pacesetter in Modern Mass Evangelism* (New York: Macmillan, 1963), pp. 267-271; William R. Moody, *The Life of D. L. Moody* (New York: Fleming H. Revell, 1900), p. 496; Henry Drummond, *The Ideal Life* (New York: Hodder & Stoughton, 1897), pp. 268, 302—Drummond stating, "The Bible is God's will in words, in formal thoughts, in grace;" and then citing John 7:17 and stating "There is a will of God for me which is willed for no one else besides . . . a particular will;" F. B. Meyer, *The Secret of Guidance* (New York: Fleming H. Revell, 1896), p. 11; Robert E. Speer, *The Principles of Jesus* (New York: Fleming H. Revell, 1902), pp. 21-22; C. H. Hopkins, *John R. Mott: A Biography* (Grand Rapids: William B. Erdmans, 1979), pp. 223, 214; Henry B. Wright, *The Will of God and a Man's Lifework* (New York: Young Men's Christian Association Press, 1909), pp. 135, 146-47, 149; Garth Lean, *On the Tail of a Comet* (Colorado Springs: Helmers & Howard, 1988), p. 157; A. J. Russell, *For Sinners Only* (London: Hodder & Stoughton, 1932), pp. 23, 27-29; 35-36, 94, 211; Irving Harris, *The Breeze of the Spirit* (New York: The Seabury Press, 1978), p. 18; Samuel H. Shoemaker, *A Young Man's View of the Ministry* (New York: Association Press, 1923), pp. 78, 41; *Confident Faith* (New York: Fleming H. Revell, 1932), p. 106; *Religion That Works* (New York: Fleming H. Revell,

(continued...)

149

as the guide to knowing God's particular or private will. Our review of the thoughts of Frank Buchman's mentors points up a steady and consistent stream of Bible authority for every concept—from the writings of the earliest identified writer, Horace Bushnell, to the many books by the Oxford Group's most articulate and prolific expositor, Sam Shoemaker.[2]

There are two basic points which are the backdrop for our study. The first is the Bible-as-the-source emphasis in Oxford Group writings. The second are the "will of God" objectives of the Oxford Group principles. And it is in that light that we will review twenty-eight Oxford Group principles which we believe influenced the spiritual program of Alcoholics Anonymous.

Before his death, Garth Lean (Frank Buchman's biographer) reviewed the twenty-eight principles we constructed and noted that, while overlapping, they are valid as Oxford Group concepts. Reverend T. Willard Hunter, Oxford Group field worker, writer, and speaker in America, also validated the twenty-eight concepts in a personal interview with the author at Claremont, California. Hunter later suggested that the concepts be regrouped and consolidated for a more easy flow. And this we have endeavored to do.

Mrs. Irving Harris reviewed the author's research manuscript on Shoemaker and the twenty-eight principles and provided a similar validation. Dr. Ernest Kurtz is an A.A. historian and scholar and the author of *Not-God*.[3] Kurtz suggested to the author that the principles be condensed to a smaller number. That *would* ease recollection, but the problem we have is that too many writers have done just that and, we believe, omitted a number of ideas that

---

[1] (...continued)
1928), pp. 55, 58, 64; and *Living Your Life Today* (New York: Fleming H. Revell, 1947), pp. 101-09.

[2] And See our previous quotation from Sherwood Sunderland Day, *The Principles of the Group* (The Oxford Group, Printed at the Oxford University Press, n.d.), p. 3: "The principles of 'The Oxford Group' are the principles of the Bible."

[3] Ernest Kurtz, *Not-God: The History of Alcoholics Anonymous*, Exp. ed (Minnesota: Hazelden, 1991).

parallel, found their way to, or influenced A.A.'s basic spiritual ideas.[4]

We do not claim that the following twenty-eight concepts encircle all the Biblical concepts of the Oxford Group; but we do believe they adequately set the framework for a study of the Biblical roots of A.A.'s Twelve Steps and the Big Book's discussion about them. We found they served well for our analysis in *Anne Smith's Journal* and in *New Light on Alcoholism*.[5] And we believe they will serve well here and in ongoing research for other intended books.

When we interviewed former Congressman John F. Seiberling in his office at the University of Akron in Ohio, we asked about his familiarity with these twenty-eight concepts. Seiberling stated he would "have had to be deaf not to have heard them." Seiberling attended the early A.A.-Oxford Group meetings in Ohio. He personally knew Dr. Bob, Anne Smith, T. Henry and Clarace Williams, and Bill Wilson, who also attended the meetings. He remarked that his mother, Henrietta Seiberling, the leader at many early A.A. meetings, very frequently spoke of all the concepts. We therefore believe that Dr. Bob, Anne, and Bill would likewise "have had to be deaf not to have heard them." In other words, they were coin of the realm when early AAs were the "alcoholic squad of the Oxford Group."

---

[4] See for example The Layman with a Notebook, *What Is The Oxford Group?* (London: Oxford University Press, 1933), pp. 7-9, speaking of "four points" and "four practical spiritual activities;" *DR. BOB and the Good Oldtimers* (New York: Alcoholics Anonymous World Services, Inc., 1980), pp. 54-55, speaking of the "five C's" and the "five procedures;" Kurtz, *Not-God*, p. 49, speaking of the "five C's," the "Five Procedures," and "six basic assumptions;" Day, *The Principles of The Oxford Group*, pp. 5-11, speaking of "some" seven of the Bible principles; and Clarence Benson, *The Eight Points of the Oxford Group* (London: Oxford University Press, 1936)—which "Eight Points" were made the subject of examination in the recent book by Dennis C. Morreim, *Changed Lives. The Story of Alcoholics Anonymous* (Minneapolis: Augsburg, 1991), pp. 25-31.

[5] Dick B., *Anne Smith's Journal. 1933-1939: A.A.'s Principles of Success* (San Rafael, CA: Paradise Research Publications, 1994); and *New Light on Alcoholism: The A.A. Legacy from Sam Shoemaker* (Corte Madera, CA: Good Book Publishing Company, 1994).

The "squib" or introductory description we have used at the beginning of our discussion of each concept does not represent Oxford Group language, but rather our own summary of the concept as we believe the Oxford Group saw it. Before we begin, we suggest comparison of the Oxford Group's focus on the will of God with A.A.'s Big Book focus on "Thy Will be done," which, of course, is from the Lord's Prayer, taught by Jesus Christ in his sermon on the mount.[6]

In the Beginning, God

1.   *God—Biblical Descriptions of Him*

There is an Almighty, Loving God who has a personal interest in the well-being of every person.

When the Oxford Group spoke of God, they were speaking of God as He is described in the Bible. God is spoken of in the Bible as *Elohim*—Creator; *El Shaddai*—Almighty God; *Jehovah*—Lord; Father; Love; Spirit; and the Living God.[7] As *The Companion Bible* points out, God's names for Himself as Jehovah, in company with other words, reveal Him as Jehovah who will see, or provide; heals; is a banner or cover; sends peace; sanctifies; is Lord of hosts; is righteousness; is there; is most high; and is "my Shepherd."[8] In the New Testament, God calls and reveals Himself

---

[6] See Big Book pages 67, 85, 88. Compare pages 63, 76, 100, 164. See Matthew 6:10—"Thy will be done."

[7] See Andrew Jukes, *The Names of GOD in Holy Scripture* (Grand Rapids, Michigan: Kregel Publications, 1967); *The Companion Bible* (Grand Rapids, Michigan: Kregel Publications, 1990), Appendix 4; *New Bible Dictionary Second Edition* (Wheaton, Illinois: Tyndale House Publishers, 1987), pp. 427-31; and W. E. Vine, *Old and New Testament Words* (New York: Fleming H. Revell, 1981), pp. 160-61.

[8] *The Companion Bible*, Appendix 4, p. 6. See Genesis 22:14; Exodus 15:26; Exodus 17:15; Exodus 31:13; Judges 6:24; 1 Samuel 1:3; Jeremiah 23:6; Ezekiel 48:35; Psalm 7:17; Psalm 23:1.

as the God of peace, God of grace, God of patience and consolation, God of hope, God of all comfort, Father of mercies, and God of love.[9] Jesus Christ, God's only begotten son, called Him "your Father" and "Our Father" when speaking to the Judeans in the sermon on the mount.[10] The Bible often speaks of God as "the living God."[11]

Oxford Group scholar, Philip M. Brown, professor of international relations at Princeton, had this to say:

> The utter inadequacy of human speech to describe God leaves me almost inarticulate. I can fall back on the many *attributes* such as Omnipotent, Omniscient, All-Loving, King of Kings, Lord of Lords, Creator, Judge, Father of Mankind, to suggest in finite terms something of the Infinite. . . . So whether one prefers to speak of God, Jehovah, Father, Supreme Wisdom, Infinite, Power, Divine Providence, or any other designations, I do not much care. What does matter is the central fact of an identical experience.[12]

To this statement might be added those of William James and Horace Bushnell. James was highly thought of by both Bill W. and Dr. Bob.[13] And James, a self-described Christian, said this about God:

> God is the natural appellation, for us Christians at least, for the supreme reality, so I will call this higher part of the universe by

---

[9] Romans 16:20, 1 Peter 5:10, Romans 15:5, Romans 15:13, 2 Corinthians 1:3, 1 John 4:8.

[10] Matthew 6:8-9.

[11] See Acts 14:15 which speaks of "the living God, which made heaven and earth;" Isaiah 37:17, which calls God "the living God;" and *The Companion Bible* which discussed, at page 1614, the frequent use of the phrase "the living God" in both the Old and New Testaments.

[12] Philip M. Brown, *The Venture of Belief* (New York: Fleming H. Revell, 1935), pp. 24-25.

[13] *Pass It On* (New York: Alcoholics Anonymous World Services, Inc., 1984), pp. 124; *DR. BOB*, p. 306.

the name of God. We and God have business with each other; and in opening ourselves to his influence our deepest destiny is fulfilled. The universe, at those parts of it which our personal being constitutes, takes a turn genuinely for the worse or for the better in proportion as each one of us fulfills or evades God's demands. As far as this goes I probably have you with me, for I only translate into schematic language what I may call the instinctive belief of mankind: God is real since he produces real effects.[14]

Benson's *The Eight Points of the Oxford Group* quoted the following from a sermon by Dr. Horace Bushnell:

What do the Scriptures shew us, but that God has a particular care for every man, a personal interest in him, and a sympathy with him and his trials, watching for the uses of his one talent as attentively and kindly, and approving of him as heartily, in the right employment of it, as if He had given him ten. . . . How inspiring and magnificent to live, by holy consent. A life all discovery, to see it unfolding, moment by moment, a plan of God, our own life-plan conceived in His paternal love.[15]

The Oxford Group variously described God, saying: God is God, Almighty God, Creator, Maker, Father, Spirit, Omnipotent, Love—a loving God, a personal God, the living God, Sovereign over all, Infinite, and Reality.[16]

---

[14] William James, *The Varieties of Religious Experience* (New York: First Vintage Books/The Library of America Edition, 1990), p. 461.

[15] Benson, *The Eight Points*, pp. 3-4.

[16] See, for example, *What Is The Oxford Group?*, pp. 48, 110, 116; Geoffrey Allen, *He That Cometh* (New York: Macmillan, 1933), pp. 219-23; Benson, *The Eight Points*, pp. 46-47, 65, 73; Frank N. D. Buchman, *Remaking the World* (London: Blandford Press, 1961), pp. 13, 42, 67; Burnett Hillman Streeter, *The God Who Speaks* (London: Macmillan, 1943), pp. 11, 12, 13, 38, 84, 99, 101, 102, 104, 108, 109, 110; Philip Leon, *The Philosophy of Courage or the Oxford Group Way* (New York: Oxford University Press, 1939), pp. 26, 28, 30, 32-34, 48; Samuel Moor Shoemaker, *The Conversion of the Church* (New York: Fleming H. Revell, 1932), pp. 33, 49, 50, 51,

(continued...)

When Bill Wilson had his religious experience in Towns Hospital, he observed that he had been in touch with "the Great reality. The God of the preachers."[17] In an early draft of the Big Book, Bill wrote that each of the early AAs told "the way in which he happened to find the living God."[18] The *living God*—an expression used over and over in the Bible *and* in Oxford Group books.[19] Bill also remarked that alcoholics had "a form of lunacy which only *God Almighty* could cure" (emphasis added).[20] He wrote of "*God, our Father,* who very simply says, 'I am waiting for you to do my will.'" (emphasis added)[21] He referred to a

---

[16] (...continued)
124; *National Awakening* (New York: Harper & Brothers, 1936), pp. 48, 55, 97, 107, 108; *Confident Faith*, pp. 17-18, 38, 54, 59, 74, 83, 96, 106, 107, 152, 183; *Realizing Religion*, p. 35; *Children of the Second Birth*, p. 42; *Christ's Words from the Cross* (New York: Fleming H. Revell, 1933), p. 43; *Living Your Life Today*, pp. 18-19; *How to Become a Christian* (New York: Harper & Brothers, 1953), p. 39; and *The Experiment of Faith* (New York: Harper & Brothers, 1957), p. 53.

[17] *Pass It On*, p. 121.

[18] An early draft of the Big Book, which the author inspected during his visit to Stepping Stones in October of 1991, contains the statement, "In these accounts each person will describe in his own language and from his own point of view the way in which he happened to find the living God." The material, as changed, wound up on page 29 of the Big Book, speaking of a "relationship with God."

[19] See footnote 11, *supra*, and, for example, Buchman, *Remaking the World*, pp. 13, 67, 107; Stephen Foot, *Life Began Yesterday* (New York: Harper & Brothers, 1935), p. 161; and Shoemaker, *Twice-Born Ministers*, p. 185. Henry P. Van Dusen, head of the Union Theological Seminary, wrote an extensive appraisal of "The Oxford Group Movement." He said, concerning "guidance," that the Oxford Groups made a "most striking proclamation of a living and regnant God." Van Dusen believed there was clear logic for the Oxford Group position "that God is a living, guiding Power who knows intimately every human life in its every experience, who holds for each life at every moment a vision and a hope which are its highest possibility and His Purpose, and who is prepared to reveal that Purpose to those who earnestly desire it." Van Dusen deplored the fact "that the God of practical faith in our modern churches, even the God of the clergy, is no such Power, but a pitiful travesty upon the Majestic Sovereign of profound religion." Van Dusen, "The Oxford Group Movement: An Appraisal," *Atlantic Monthly* 154 (August, 1934): p. 250.

[20] See Dick B., *The Akron Genesis*, pp. 12-13.

[21] *A.A. Comes of Age*, p. 105; see Romans 1:7; 1 Corinthians 1:3; 2 Corinthians 1:2; Ephesians 1:2; Colossians 1:2; Philippians 1:2; 1 Thessalonians 1:1; 2 Thessalonians 1:1.

name for God, "Father of lights," which came from the Book of James.[22] And Bill and Dr. Bob both described God as their "Heavenly Father," just as Jesus Christ did in the sermon on the mount.[23]

To this author, it therefore seems clear that Bill Wilson's "God of the preachers" and "living God" was God as Bill had heard Him taught and described at the Oxford Group meetings he had attended in New York and later in Akron and as Anne Smith had read about God to Bill and Dr. Bob at the Smith home in Akron.

The name "God," spelled with a capital "G", appears at least 132 times through page 164 of the Big Book and the appendices to the Big Book; and pronouns for God such as "He", "Him", "His", etc., are mentioned eighty times.[24] A further examination of the Big Book will disclose use of the Biblical *names* for God—those used by the Oxford Group and, of course, other Judeo-Christian religions. See "Creator,"[25] "Maker,"[26] "Father,"[27] "Father of Light,"[28] "Friend,"[29] and "Spirit."[30] And A.A. language is also rich with descriptions of God as love.[31]

We would emphasize that the Oxford Group often mentioned the Ten Commandments, among which, in Exodus 20:3, was the commandment: "Thou shalt have no other gods before Me." We therefore think it fair to say that, at the time Big Book ideas were being drawn from the Bible, the Oxford Group, and

---

[22] James 1:17; see A.A. *Comes of Age*, p. 225; Big Book, p. 14.

[23] Matthew 6:32; *A.A. Comes of Age*, p. 234; Big Book, p. 181.

[24] Stewart C., *A Reference Guide To The Big Book of Alcoholics Anonymous* (Seattle, Wa: Recovery Press, Inc., 1986), pp. 115-116.

[25] Isaiah 40:28; Big Book, pp. 13, 76.

[26] Psalm 95:6; Big Book, pp. 57, 63.

[27] Matthew 5:45; Big Book, p. 62.

[28] James 1:17 (rendered "Father of lights"); Big Book, p. 14.

[29] James 2:23; Big Book, p. 13.

[30] John 4:24; Big Book, p. 84.

[31] 1 John 4:8, 16; *DR. BOB*, pp. 110, 117; *Pass It On*, p. 121; *Twelve Steps And Twelve Traditions* (New York: Alcoholics Anonymous World Services, Inc., 1987), p. 9; Big Book, p. 63.

Shoemaker—as Dr. Bob and Bill W. said they were—God, as He is described in the Good Book, found His way into the Big Book and the Twelve Steps. This is true, however much ideas about Him and choosing a conception of Him may have been modified to "as we understood Him," "power greater than ourselves," and later "Higher Power," as A.A. evolved.

Some seventeen years after A.A. was founded, Bill chose to write in *Twelve Steps and Twelve Traditions*, "You can, if you wish, make A.A. itself your higher power."[32] But that was not God as He is described in the Bible. And it was not even the Higher Power that some thought was mentioned in the Oxford Group and in the Big Book.[33]

Back in the 1930's, Dr. Bob's wife, Anne Smith, rejected unwillingness to use the word "Christ." She said that using the word "Group" instead of "Christ" was one of a person's "Funk Holes."[34]

Today A.A. has since traveled a long way from the early Biblical names for God that it used in the 1930's. The author has heard a good many strange names for a "god" at the more than 2000 A.A. meetings he has attended. So have others. And A.A. Conference Approved literature contains some of these names. They include: "Higher Power," a "Power Greater than ourselves,"

---

[32] *Twelve Steps And Twelve Traditions*, p. 27.

[33] Reverend T. Willard Hunter informed the author in an interview at Claremont, California, in the summer of 1991, that he had never heard the expression "Higher Power" used in the Oxford Group. The expression is used only twice in the Big Book text—both times in the context of God. See pages 43 and 100. The Big Book pointedly says at page 45, "it means, of course, that we are going to talk about God." Speaking at page 100 of following the dictates of a Higher Power, the Big Book introduces the statement with the phrase "when we put ourselves in God's hands." The author has found no convincing evidence that "power greater than ourselves," "God as we understood Him," or "Higher Power," as those terms were used in the Big Book and in early A.A., ever meant a "group." See, for example, Walker, *For Drunks Only*, pp. 22-26. See particularly V. C. Kitchen's *I Was a Pagan* (New York: Harper & Brothers, 1934), where Bill's Oxford Group friend wrote about a "Higher Power," but clearly was speaking about God (p. 85).

[34] Dick B., *Anne Smith's Journal*, pp. 89-90.

"Good Orderly Direction," "Group Of Drunks," the "Group itself," "Good," "It," "doorknob," "tree," "stone," "table," the "Big Dipper," "Santa Claus," and even "Ralph."[35]

2.   *God Has a Plan—His Will for Man*

God has a specific life-plan for every individual, with definite, accurate information for that individual if he wishes to see God's plan fulfilled.

Dr. Frank Buchman, the Oxford Group Founder, frequently spoke about "God's Plan."[36] So did Reverend Sam Shoemaker.[37] Early AA's picked up on this concept.[38] And there were a host of Oxford Group writings about God's Plan.[39]

---

[35] See Barnaby Conrad, *Time is all We have* (New York: Dell Publishing, 1986), p. 21; Nan Robertson, *Getting Better: Inside Alcoholics Anonymous* (New York: Fawcett Crest, 1988), pp. 124, 129; Jan R. Wilson and Judith A. Wilson, *Addictionary: A Primer of Recovery Terms and Concepts from Abstinence to Withdrawal* (New York: Simon and Schuster, 1992), pp. 181-183; *Twelve Steps and Twelve Traditions*, p. 27; *Alcoholics Anonymous Comes of Age*, p. 81; *Daily Reflections* (New York: Alcoholics Anonymous World Services, 1990): pp. 79 ("Good Orderly Direction"); 175 ("a table, a tree, then my A.A. group"); 334 ("Him, or Her, or It"); and Big Book, p. 248. A.A.'s Conference Approved pamphlet "Members of the Clergy ask about Alcoholics Anonymous" (New York: Alcoholics Anonymous World Services, 1961, revised 1992) states at page 12, "Some [members] choose the A.A. group as their 'Higher Power'; some look to God—*as they understand Him*; and others rely upon entirely different concepts."

[36] Buchman, *Remaking The World*, pp. 48, 53, 63, 77, 78, 101, 144.

[37] Shoemaker, *Children of the Second Birth*, p. 27; *Religion That Works*, p. 19; *National Awakening*, pp. 41, 83, 89-98; and Dick B., *New Light on Alcoholism*, p. xiii.

[38] *DR. BOB*, p. 145; *Lois Remembers* (New York: Al-Anon Family Group Headquarters, 1987), p. 100. See also Dick B., *Anne Smith's Journal*, pp. 43, 58, 88-90, 94, 103, 123, 140. Compare Big Book stories at pp. 208-09; 302-03.

[39] Wright, *The Will of God*, pp. 3-12; Eleanor Napier Forde, *The Guidance of God* (Oxford: The Oxford Group, 1930), pp. 18-19; Alan Thornhill, *One Fight More* (London: Frederick Muller Ltd, 1943), p. 20; R. C. Mowat, *Modern Prophetic Voices: From Kierkegaard to Buchman* (Oxford: New Cherwell Press, 1994), pp. 8-9; Peter Howard, *Frank Buchman's Secret* (New York: Doubleday & Co., 1961), p. 17; Russell, *For Sinners Only*, p. 23; Benson, *The Eight Points*, pp. 1-17; Cecil Rose, *When Man*
(continued...)

In fact, one cannot really understand the Oxford Group program without understanding this Biblical starting point. God has a plan. Its is beneficial. It can be learned—in its universal aspects—from the Bible; in its particular aspects through two-way prayer—praying and listening for guidance. The successful life-change involved complete surrender to and conformity with God's plan or will. When that was achieved through conversion, a new birth, surrender, or whatever it was called, there was "God-consciousness" and peace for the individual.

There were three major Bible sources quoted in the Oxford Group for this basic proposition. In one of his British broadcasts, Frank Buchman said, "Why not try God's Plan?"[40] At another point, he said, "The Holy Spirit is the most intelligent source of information in the world today. He [the Holy Spirit] has the answer to every problem. Everywhere when men will let Him, He is teaching them how to live."[41] In a speech in Norway, Buchman quoted the following from Jeremiah 7:23 to substantiate his point:

> Obey my voice, and I will be your God, and ye shall be my people; and walk ye in all the ways that I have commanded you, that it may be well unto you.[42]

Buchman stressed that God has a plan, and the combined moral and spiritual forces of the nation can find that plan.[43]

---

[39] (...continued)
Listens (New York: Oxford University Press, 1937), pp. 25-38; Brown, *The Venture of Belief*, pp. 39-41; The Layman with a Notebook, *What Is The Oxford Group?* (New York: Oxford University Press, 1933), p. 6; Howard Walter, *Soul Surgery: Some Thoughts on Incisive Personal Work*, 6th ed (Oxford at the University Press by John Johnson, 1940), pp. 26-27; Streeter, *The God Who Speaks*, pp. 7-17; Kitchen, *I Was a Pagan*, p. 122; and Stephen Foot, *Life Began Yesterday* (New York: Harper & Brothers, 1935), p. 173.

[40] Buchman, *Remaking The World*, p. 77.

[41] Buchman, *Remaking The World*, p. 12.

[42] Buchman, *Remaking The World*, p. 8.

[43] Buchman, *Remaking The World*, p. 48.

As authority for the idea of a plan of God, Bushnell cited Isaiah 14:5—"I girded thee, though thou has not known me."[44] And Philip Brown added these important comments, citing from Proverbs 3:5-6 which reads:

> Trust in the Lord with all thine heart; and lean not unto thine own understanding. In all thy ways acknowledge him, and he shall direct thy paths.

Brown wrote:

> Each day should be a day of high adventure. I must keep spiritually fit in order to be responsive, sensitive, alert, and aware of the significance of every act.
> . . . I cannot do this unless I "wait on God" and seek humbly and confidently to ascertain His will in my life. He does speak to those who listen. "In all thy ways acknowledge Him, and He shall direct thy paths." This is the "abundant life" which Christ revealed.[45]

3.   *Man's Chief End—To Do God's Will*

> Man's chief end is and ought to be to do the Will of God and thereby receive the blessings God promises to those whose lives are in alignment with His will.

Thy will be done! That's what A.A.'s Big Book says repeatedly. That's what the Lord's Prayer—which concludes almost every A.A. meeting—says. And that is the guide in much Christian prayer. From the Oxford Group approach, this concept follows logically from God's plan. If God has a plan—a universal and general will that He spells out in His Word, the Bible, and a

---

[44] Bushnell, *The New Life*, pp. iii, 1. See also, Wright, *The Will of God*, p. 3.

[45] Brown, *The Venture of Belief*. p. 40; see also Howard Rose, *The Quiet Time*, p. 2; and John 10:10.

particular will that He will tell man if man listens—then man should certainly do his best to learn and obey the plan.

Professor Henry Drummond laid the foundation for the Oxford Group concept in a chapter from one of his books. The chapter was titled, "The Man After God's Own Heart—A Bible study on the Ideal of a Christian life."[46] Drummond quoted from Acts 13:22 to show God desires "a man after Mine own heart, which shall fulfill all My will."[47] Drummond said these words are the definition and description of a model human life. They provide a key—that the end of life is to do God's will.[48] Drummond then cited eight ideas from the Bible which demonstrate the rewards for the man who has the will of God as his chief end:

> First, man asks, "What am I here for?" Hebrews 10:9 answers, "Lo, I am come to do Thy Will, O God." Second, man needs sustenance. Jesus responds that strength comes from the Almighty, saying in John 4:34, "My *meat* is to do the will of Him that sent me" (emphasis added). Third, man needs society; and Jesus offers him a family, saying in Matthew 12:50, "For whosoever shall do the will of My Father which is in heaven, the same is My brother, and sister, and mother." Fourth, man needs to communicate. Jesus gives him the ideal prayer in Matthew 6:10: "Thy will be done." Fifth, man does not always need to pray, but sometimes to praise. The Psalms show that the ideal praise is of the Will of God. Drummond quoted Psalm 119:54, "Thy statutes have been my songs in the house of my pilgrimage." Psalm 119:97, "O how I love Thy law. It is my meditation all the day." Psalm 40:8, "I delight to do Thy Will, O my God." Sixth, man needs education and thus asks in Psalm 143:10, "Teach me to do Thy Will; for Thou art my God." Seventh, man is promised results when he asks God in

---

[46] Henry Drummond, *The Ideal Life* (New York: Hodder & Stoughton, 1897), pp. 227-43.

[47] Acts 13:22 says in part: "He raised up unto them David to be their king; to whom also He gave testimony, and said, 'I have found David the son of Jesse, a man after Mine own heart, which shall fulfil all My will'."

[48] Drummond, *The Ideal Life*, p. 229.

accordance with His Will. 1 John 5:14-15 states, "If we ask anything according to His Will, He heareth us . . . and we know that we have the petitions that we desired from Him." Finally, there are the eternal rewards. 1 John 2:17 says, "He that doeth the will of God abideth for ever." In Matthew 7:21, Jesus's concluding statement in the sermon on the mount said, "Not every one that saith unto Me, 'Lord, Lord' shall enter into the kingdom of heaven, but he that doeth the will of My Father Which is in heaven."[49]

Oxford Group writers absorbed and elaborated upon Drummond's ideas.[50] Canon Streeter wrote:

The only sensible course for the individual is to ask what is God's Plan for him, and then to endeavor to carry out that plan. For if we can discern anything of God's Plan for us, common sense demands that we give ourselves entirely to it.[51]

Shoemaker taught that, "if we look after God's plan, He takes care of our needs." He cited the sermon on the mount where Jesus said in Matthew 6:32-33:

Your heavenly Father knoweth that ye have need of all these things. But seek ye first the kingdom of God, and his righteousness; and all these things shall be added unto you.[52]

Shoemaker also wrote the following on this subject:

All life's wisdom, all its power, all its grace lies in the will which cooperates with the Will of God; in the mind that thinks

---

[49] Drummond, *The Ideal Life*, pp. 232-43.

[50] See, for example, Wright, *The Will of God*, p. 9; Forde, *The Guidance of God*, p. 27; K. D. Belden, *Reflections on Moral Re-Armament* (London: Grosvenor Books, 1983), pp. 54-55; and Benson, *The Eight Points*, pp. 12-13.

[51] Streeter, *The God Who Speaks*, p. 11; Forde, *The Guidance of God*, p. 18; Thornhill, *One Fight More*, p. 50; and Mowat, *Modern Prophetic Voices*, pp. 8-9.

[52] Shoemaker, *National Awakening*, p. 42.

God's thoughts after Him; in the heart that loves Him and loves His Will.[53]

Give in, admit that God is, and that He has the great Answer to your life, and that your life never is nor will be complete without Him.[54]

Put your situation into the hands of God and take your hands off it. . . . And now just a word to carry with you all day: "Let go, and let God. . . . Let go, and let God."[55]

Note the language at the conclusion of the Big Book text on page 164, "Abandon yourself to God as you understand God." Similar language can be found in Anne Smith's Journal.[56] And compare the last words in Dr. Bob's story in the Big Book, "Your Heavenly Father will never let you down" (p. 181).

4.   *Belief—We Start with the Belief That He IS*

Man must start his journey in doing God's Will by believing that God IS.

Oxford Group people were neither atheists nor agnostics. They believed in God.[57] Frank Buchman did not preach the necessity

---

[53] Shoemaker, *Christ's Words From The Cross*, p. 50

[54] Shoemaker, *National Awakening*, p. 47.

[55] Shoemaker, *Living Your Life Today*, pp. 12-13.

[56] Dick B., *Anne Smith's Journal*, pp. 90-91.

[57] See our discussion in Chapter Seven under Step Two. *DR. BOB* stated at page 239, "As we have seen, early A.A. members were predominantly white, middle-class, and male. There were membership requirements—belief in God, making a surrender, and conforming to the precepts of the Oxford Group—in addition to having a desire (honest, sincere, or otherwise) to stop drinking. The requirements might be summed up by saying you had to believe before you began." From the Oxford Group and Bible requirements of "belief" as a condition of coming to God, acquiring Faith, and receiving deliverance, the author finds a very clear basis for the early A.A. attitude of "belief" described in the foregoing quote from *DR. BOB*. See Big Book, p. xvi, which (speaking of Bill Wilson)
(continued...)

for belief in God. He simply used such strong language about God that there could be no doubt about his belief. He talked: of the "miracle-working power of the living God," of "God-control," about the fact that "God spoke to the prophets of old. He may speak to you," and of his conviction that "When man listens, God speaks. When man obeys, God acts."[58]

Many in the Oxford Group, however, started with the concept of achieving "Faith by Experiment." Garth Lean wrote of this in his book, *Good God, It Works.*[59] You give God control of your life, the Oxford Group way, find that the experiment works, and wind up with belief in God resulting from the success of the experience. Essentials are praying and listening, a decision to obey God's will, and obedience to it. We will see, at a later point, how the Oxford Group emphasis on John 7:17 fits into this picture. Anne Smith made a very simple statement of belief: "It is not enough to surrender sin, but we must also claim the victory of the resurrection life. It is God that does it."[60]

Professor Philip Brown made his case for knowing God through a religious experience by starting with the fact that religious experiences throughout the ages have established contact with God and hence proved His existence. In *The Venture of Belief*, Brown wrote:

> *The Presence of God.* I find throughout the diverse testimonies of religious experiences a striking unity and identity. Whether it be Socrates heeding his "Daimon," Mohammed listening to his

---

[57] (...continued)
said: "Though he could not accept all the tenets of the Oxford Groups, he was convinced of the . . . necessity of belief in and dependence upon God." See also the last portion of Dr. Bob's story in the Big Book, where Dr. Bob states: "If you think you are an atheist, an agnostic, a skeptic, or have any other form of intellectual pride which keeps you from accepting what is in this book, I feel sorry for you" (p. 181).

[58] Buchman, *Remaking The World*, pp. 41, 42, 13, 24. See also, Cecil Rose, *When Man Listens*, p. 77; and Almond, *Foundations for Faith*. p. 23.

[59] Garth Lean, *Good God, It Works! an experiment of faith* (London: Blandford Press, 1974).

[60] Dick B., *Anne Smith's Journal*, p. 91.

"Voice," or Saint Francis and Marshal Foch in prayer, or Gandhi retiring into "the Silence," or simple Brother Lawrence at his ceaseless devotions in the kitchen: all testify to the irreducible minimum of religious experience, namely, the certainty of the "presence of God" in this universe. Men and women of all races, of different mental capacities, social and cultural backgrounds, unite throughout history in their common witness to the reality of God. They tell of the strength of heart and of mind, of the depth of knowledge of life, of the charity and love that are poured into human beings whenever they establish contact with God.[61]

But the underlying premise comes from Hebrews 11:6:

But without faith it is impossible to please Him [God]; for He that cometh to God must believe that He is, and that He is a rewarder of them that diligently seek Him.

The Oxford Group cited this verse for the proposition that one must start the experiment of faith by believing that God is.[62] Professor Philip Leon wrote, "The facts with which I propose to start here as undeniable are God and myself."[63] Canon Grensted, the Oxford theologian, wrote in his foreword to *What Is The Oxford Group?* that the book is "for those who can understand a piece of direct and first-hand evidence for the ways of God's working in a human life."[64] Dr. Shoemaker wrote:

Security lies in a faith in God which includes an experiment. It lies in believing that God is . . . There are three basic elements in the experiment. The first is a belief in God.[65]

---

[61] Brown, *The Venture of Belief*, p. 24.

[62] Leslie D. Weatherhead, *How Can I Find God?* (London: Hodder and Stoughton, 1933), p. 72; Shoemaker, *The Gospel According To You* (New York: Fleming H. Revell, 1934), p. 47; *National Awakening*, p. 40; *Religion That Works*, p. 55; and *Confident Faith*, p. 187.

[63] Leon, *The Philosophy of Courage or The Oxford Group Way*, p. 19.

[64] *What Is The Oxford Group?* Foreword.

[65] Shoemaker, *National Awakening*, pp. 40-41.

When we come to believe in God at all, we come to believe in Him as having something definite to say about our lives. To believe in the fact of the will of God is only to believe in God in the concrete. As you cannot pray without words, so you cannot imagine God apart from His desires which touch us.[66]

Note this language in A.A.'s Big Book at page 53:

Either God is everything or else He is nothing. God either is, or He isn't. What was our choice to be?[67]

Dr. Bob minced no words on this point. *DR. BOB and the Good Oldtimers* recorded this typical colloquy:

[Dr. Bob]: "Do you believe in God, young fella? . . ."

[Clarence]: "I guess I do."

[Dr. Bob]: "Guess, nothing! Either you do or you don't."

[Clarence]: "I do."

[Dr. Bob]: "That's fine. . . . Now we're getting someplace. All right, get out of bed on your knees. We're going to pray" (p. 144).

Sin—Estrangement from God—The Barrier of Self

5. *Sin As a Reality*

Sin is a reality—the selfishness and self-centeredness that blocks man from God and from others.

---

[66] Shoemaker, *Religion That Works*, p. 55.

[67] At a later point, we cover the fact that Dr. Shoemaker used almost identical language at page 187 of his book, *Confident Faith*, when he wrote: "God is, or He isn't. You leap one way or the other."

The Oxford Group had lots to say about sin. They believed in its reality. They defined it. They described it. They categorized it. And they asserted its power and deadliness in blocking man from God, from doing God's Will, and from bringing man's life into harmony with God's plan. Frank Buchman said of sin:

I don't know if you believe in it or not, but it is here. Don't spend the rest of the day arguing if it exists or not.[68]

What is the disease? Isn't it fear, dishonesty, resentment and selfishness? We talk about freedom and liberty, but we are slaves to ourselves.[69]

The root problems in the world today are dishonesty, selfishness and fear.[70]

It isn't any intellectual difficulty which is keeping you from God. It is sin.[71]

Sin is a word which denotes a choosing. The will chooses the bad. . . . This act of choosing constitutes the sin.[72]

Consciousness of God is the natural state of things. Sin is unnatural, and prevents the natural state of things from obtaining. Sin is unnatural in the sense that it is the will of the creature opposing itself to the will of the Creator. Always it is sin, and

---

[68] Buchman, *Remaking The World*, p. 54.

[69] Buchman, *Remaking The World*, p. 38. Cecil Rose said in *When Man Listens* that the word "barriers" expresses half the trouble of the world. He added, "Selfishness, fear, resentment, pride do not live in the air. They live in men . . . If we are to go on being honest with others we must go on being honest with ourselves" (pp. 41, 50). Compare the Big Book's Tenth and Eleventh Step discussions concerning "selfishness, dishonesty, resentment, and fear" (pp. 84, 86).

[70] Buchman, *Remaking The World*, p. 28.

[71] Begbie, *Life Changers*, quoting Buchman at page 14.

[72] Begbie, *Life Changers*, quoting Buchman at page 15.

only it is sin, which blinds the eyes and hardens the heart of mankind.[73]

Frank Buchman thus made clear his belief that Sin is a reality. So did a host of Oxford Group writers, including Sam Shoemaker.[74] And they provided some very simple definitions of sin:

Sin was anything done contrary to the Will of God, as shown in the New Testament or by direct guidance.[75]

The Best definition of sin that we have is that sin is anything in my life which keeps me from God and from other people.[76]

All selfishness is sin and all sin is a form of selfishness.[77]

The self is a self-defending system of habits over against other such systems. It is essentially separatist in relation to these other systems. Indeed, the defense is constituted by the separation, and this separation is itself the effect of the primal separation from God or unifying love.[78]

Sin is the thing that keeps us from being channels of God's power. Whatever keeps us from a living, loving relation with other people—or from a vital and open relationship with God—is sin.[79]

---

[73] Begbie, *Life Changers*, quoting Buchman at page. 16.

[74] Brown, *The Venture of Belief*, pp. 30-33; Day, *The Principles of the Group*, pp. 5-6; Russell, *For Sinners Only*, pp. 317-29; *What Is The Oxford Group?*, pp. 17-24; Begbie, *Life Changers*, pp. 14-17; Benson, *The Eight Points*, pp. 20-21; Walter, *Soul Surgery*, pp. 64-78; Shoemaker, *The Conversion of the Church*, p. 29; *If I Be Lifted Up* (New York: Fleming H. Revell, 1931), p. 131; *God's Control*, pp. 30, 57; *Twice-Born Ministers*, p. 30; and *They're on the Way* (New York: E. P. Dutton, 1951), p. 154.

[75] Russell, *For Sinners Only*, quoting Buchman at page 61.

[76] Russell, *For Sinners Only*, p. 319; *What Is The Oxford Group?*, p. 19; and Foot, *Life Began Yesterday*, p. 67.

[77] Benson, *The Eight Points*, pp. 20-21.

[78] Leon, *The Philosophy of Courage*, p. 129.

[79] Shoemaker, *How to Become a Christian*, p. 56.

> But if sin be looked upon as anything that puts a barrier between us and Christ, or between us and other people, then there are many things which we must call by the name of sin.[80]

One need not open many pages of the New Testament before reading about sin; so we need not document the Bible's references to it. However, *What Is The Oxford Group?* does point to Paul's statement in Romans 3:23 to demonstrate sin's commonality: "For all have sinned, and fall short of the glory of God" (p. 19). A.A.'s original steps referred to "sin."[81] A.A.'s Big Book certainly speaks of self, self-will, selfishness, ego-centricity, and self-centeredness (pp. 60-64, 76). And it makes clear that these are the roots of the "spiritual malady" which "blocks" or "shuts us off" from God (pp. 64, 66, 71).[82]

In his very first book, Shoemaker commented on the spiritual malady as follows:

> Now the thing which is striking about much of the misery one sees is that it is *spiritual* misery. It is the unhappiness of *spiritual* people very often—souls who are too fine-grained to get along without religion, yet who have never come to terms with it. . . . Rest cures and exercise and motor drives will not help. The only thing that will help is religion. For the root of the malady is estrangement from God—estrangement from Him in people that were made to be His companions.[83]

Leslie D. Weatherhead added this insight to the Oxford Group view:

> If God is seeking us and we are not found of him, the stop is on our side. . . . Let me indicate briefly some of the things which get in the way: 1. We can be quite sure that very often it is a

---

[80] Shoemaker, *They're on the Way*, p. 154.

[81] *Pass It On*, p. 197.

[82] See Dick B., *Anne Smith's Journal*, pp. 92-93.

[83] Shoemaker, *Realizing Religion*, pp. 4-5.

disguised selfishness. Self is too much in the picture. . . . 2. The second thing that gets in our way is a love of sin. . . . 3. Another door that we shut against God is the fear of what people will say and think.[84]

Finding or Rediscovering God

6.   *Surrender—The Turning Point*

Man can only do God's will and bring himself into alignment and harmony with God's plan when he has surrendered his will, his ego, and his sins to God. This is called self-surrender.

DR. BOB and the Good Oldtimers described "surrender" many times.[85] Obviously, early AAs were familiar with and practiced *surrender*. The discussions in *DR. BOB* suggest A.A.'s early "steps" began with a surrender (pp. 101-02). A surrender made on the knees, accompanied by prayer (pp. 101, 118). *DR. BOB* described the act as: "Surrender his will to God" (p. 110), "Surrender themselves to God" (p. 89), "surrender himself absolutely to God" (p. 131), and surrender of the life to God (p. 139). Bill W. said, as to his surrender at Calvary Mission, he was told [I had] "given my life to God."[86] Remnants of the practice could be found in Bill's early draft of the Twelve Steps which spoke of "on our knees."[87] Lois Wilson described the Oxford Group practice as "surrender your life to God."[88] Traces can be found in A.A.'s Big Book today where it says, "we could at last

---

[84] Leslie D. Weatherhead, *Discipleship* (New York: The Abingdon Press, 1934), pp. 23-24.

[85] See *DR. BOB*, pp. 77, 88, 89, 92, 93, 101, 102, 104, 110, 118, 131, 139, 141, 142.

[86] *Pass It On*, p. 118.

[87] *Pass It On*, p. 198.

[88] *Lois Remembers*, p. 92.

abandon ourselves utterly to him" (p. 63).[89] Also, "we decided to turn our will and our life over to God as we understood Him" (p. 60). Also, in the language of Step Three, "Made a decision to turn our will and our lives over to the care of God *as we understood Him*" (p. 59).

Talk of self-surrender began with the Oxford Group mentors. Bushnell and Drummond spoke of "regeneration" through being "born again."[90] Speer and Meyer spoke of the new birth and receiving "*Christ in you*."[91] There was also talk about "surrender of the will." Drummond discussed doing God's will and then said:

> Do you think God wants your body when He asks you to present it to Him? Do you think it is for *His* sake that He asks it, that He might be enriched by it. God could make a thousand better with a breath. He wants your gift to give you His gift—your gift which was just *in the way* of His gift. He wants your will out of the way, to make room for His will. You give everything to God. God gives it all back again, and more. You present your body a living sacrifice that you may prove God's will. You shall prove it by getting back your body—a glorified body.[92]

Meyer said, "Our will must be surrendered;" and he cited these two Bible verses:

> My judgment is just because I seek not mine own will, but the will of the Father which hath sent me (John 5:30).

> If any man will do his will, he shall know (See John 7:17).[93]

---

[89] See also, Big Book, pp. 59, 164.

[90] Bushnell, *The New Life*, pp. 59-73; and Drummond, *The Ideal Life*, pp. 212-26.

[91] Speer, *The Principles of Jesus*, pp. 204-08; and Meyer, *The Secret of Guidance*, pp. 31-32, 110-16. See John 3:1-9; Colossians 1:23. To the same effect are Weatherhead, *Discipleship*, pp. 146-47; and Streeter, *The God Who Speaks*, pp. 109-11.

[92] Drummond, *The Ideal Life*, p. 286. See 1 Thessalonians 4:3, 1 Peter 1:15-16, Hebrews 10:9, 10; Romans 12:1-2.

[93] Meyer, *The Secret of Guidance*, p. 11. Compare Streeter, *The God Who Speaks*, p. 126.

But it was William James who captured the attention of the Oxford Group with his talk of "surrender" and the "turning point." Dr. Shoemaker quoted from James:

> William James speaks with great emphasis upon this crisis of self-surrender. He says that it is "the throwing of our conscious selves on the mercy of powers which, whatever they may be, are more ideal than we are actually, and make for our redemption. . . . Self-surrender has always been and always must be regarded as the vital turning-point of the religious life, so far as the religious life is spiritual and no affair of outer works and ritual and sacraments. One may say that the whole development of Christianity in inwardness has consisted in little more than the greater and greater emphasis attached to this crisis of self-surrender."[94]

Henry Wright nailed down the James concept by writing an entire chapter in his *The Will of God and a Man's Lifework* on the principle of self-surrender involved in doing God's Will.[95] Wright cited Romans 6:16 for the principle of self-surrender. It reads:

> Know ye not, that to whom ye present yourselves as servants unto obedience, his servants ye are to whom ye obey; whether of sin unto death, or of obedience unto righteousness.[96]

The Oxford Group followed the lead of the Buchman mentors on the matter of surrender.[97] So did Anne Smith.[98] Benson's *The Eight Points* said:

---

[94] Shoemaker, *Realizing Religion*, p. 30.

[95] Wright, *The Will of God*, pp. 31-42.

[96] Wright, *The Will of God*, p. 31.

[97] See Russell, *For Sinners Only*, pp. 31, 143; Brown, *The Venture of Belief*, pp. 28-30; Olive Jones, *Inspired Children* (New York: Harper & Brothers, 1933), pp. 136, 142-44; Winslow, *Why I Believe in the Oxford Group* (London: Hodder & Stoughton, 1934), pp. 28-29; Weatherhead, *Discipleship*, pp. 15-30; and C. Rose, *When Man Listens*, p. 26.

[98] Dick B., *Anne Smith's Journal*, pp. 93-95.

The initial step and the indispensable step in the quest is *absolute surrender of our lives to God*. Surrender is "life under new management." . . . All that is in self, good, bad, and indifferent must be handed over to God. He will then give back whatever is fit for us to use. . . . Surrender is made possible by the operation of the Holy Spirit within us so that while we ourselves play our part in it, we can in no case suppose we are saving ourselves. . . . Repentance is the very breath of surrender (emphasis in original).[99]

What Is The Oxford Group? quoted several Bible verses in connection with surrender:

Know ye not that ye are the temple of God, and *that* the Spirit of God dwelleth in you (1 Corinthians 3:16).

God *is* a Spirit: and they that worship him must worship *him* in spirit and in truth (John 4:24).

For in him we live, and move, and have our being . . . (Acts 17:28a).

Repent ye therefore, and be converted, that your sins may be blotted out, when the times of refreshing shall come from the presence of the Lord (Acts 3:19).[100]

It then said:

Surrender to God is our actual passing from a life of Sin to a life God-Guided and Christ-conscious. It is the giving up of our old ineffective spiritual lives and taking on a life of spiritual activity in everything we do or say. . . . Surrender is our complete severance from our old self and an endeavoring to live by God's Guidance as one with Christ. . . . Surrendering our lives to God means a complete giving back to God of the will-power He gave

---

[99] Benson, *The Eight Points*, p. 5.
[100] See *What Is The Oxford Group?*, pp. 40-43.

us at Creation which, with the Ages, has separated itself by Sin from the Giver, and our taking, in its place, His will as He intended our will should be when He first made man in His own image (p. 41).

Dr. Shoemaker wrote:

Surrender is a handle by which an ordinary person may lay hold of the experience of conversion. It is the first step of the will. In order to make surrender the decision of the whole life . . . we must help people to see just what they are surrendering to God, their fears, their sins, most of all their *wills*, putting God's Will once and for all ahead of every other thing.[101]

William James said long ago that "self surrender has been and always must be regarded as the vital turning-point of the religious life." We need to help people see what goes into a decision of surrender: a complete break with sin . . . so that it is quite specific what they give to God—temper, fear, sex, inferiority, pride, etc; the readiness from now on to listen to God . . . the complete giving to God of the great trend of our lives.[102]

In the beginning was God.[103] The Oxford Group insisted on belief that God *is*. Also that God has a plan to which man must conform if he is to do well. Then, Biblically speaking, came sin—disobedience to God and separation from God.[104] Not surprisingly, the disobedience and estrangement from God occurred after man had been tempted by and succumbed to the lure that, in the act of disobedience, "ye shall be as gods."[105] We might add that people have been in a peck of trouble ever since—"playing God." And even A.A.'s Big Book addresses our

---

[101] Shoemaker, *The Conversion of the Church*, p. 78.

[102] Samuel M. Shoemaker, *The Church Can Save The World* (New York: Harper & Brothers, 1938), pp. 113-14.

[103] Genesis 1:1. See Streeter, *The God Who Speaks*, pp. 100, 48.

[104] Genesis 2:17; 3:15; 3:23-24.

[105] Genesis 3:5.

first move in returning to God: "First of all, we had to quit playing God. It didn't work" (p. 62).

William James called self-surrender the *turning point*.[106] This phrase commanded repeated attention in Oxford Group writings, particularly those of Sam Shoemaker.[107] And the phrase was apparently not lost in A.A. when the Big Book was written. For the Big Book's Twelve Step summary is preceded by these words:

> Half measures availed us nothing. We stood at the turning point.
> We asked His protection and care with complete abandon (p. 59).

7.   *Soul-surgery—The "Art" or Way*

> Man's sin of self-centeredness is a spiritual disease requiring cure of his "sick soul" by Frank Buchman's "soul-surgery" art, called, for short, *Confidence, Confession, Conviction, Conversion, Conservation.*

In *The Varieties of Religious Experience*, Professor William James wrote a chapter titled, "The Sick Soul."[108] James said evil is a disease; and worry over the disease is itself an additional form of disease which only adds to the original complaint. Evil facts, he said, are as genuine a part of nature as good ones. Christianity's answer is deliverance: man must die to an unreal life before he can be born into the real life. Sick souls must be "twice-born" to be happy. There are two lives, the natural and the spiritual. We must lose one before we can participate in the other. Man has a divided self. To be at peace, he must be rid of the evil one. The sick soul must be rid of the evil will and must be unified with the good will.

---

[106] See Shoemaker, *Children of the Second Birth*, p. 16—setting forth one of Shoemaker's many quotations of this William James expression.

[107] Weatherhead, *Discipleship*, p. 16; Kitchen, *I Was a Pagan*, p. 67; Shoemaker, *Realizing Religion*, p. 30; *A Young Man's View of the Ministry*, p. 55; *Children of the Second Birth*, p. 30; *Religion That Works*, p. 48; *The Church Can Save The World*, p. 113; *God's Control*, p. 138; and *The Experiment of Faith*, p. 25.

[108] James, *The Varieties of Religious Experience*, pp. 121-54.

This can be accomplished by a new birth through the process of conversion.

Frank Buchman bought this "sick soul" concept. Harold Begbie explained Buchman's thinking in *Life Changers*.[109] Buchman believed sin keeps man from God. The soul must be freed from the tyranny of sin and gain the liberty of a will in harmony with God's will. The will of the soul must be converted to the divine will. Jesus's prescription for healing was: "According to your faith, be it done unto you" [Matthew 8:29]. Sin robs a man's soul of its natural health. As Buchman put it, there can be no living and transforming unity with the divine will—no "God Consciousness," as he called it—so long as the heart is clogged by selfishness. There must be confession and restitution. Man's sin is "walling him in from God;" man's will is raised against the consciousness of God. But "God comes to us when we ask Him"—with the whole will.

Begbie called Buchman a "soul surgeon." Buchman got sin into the open and then eradicated the disease by cutting it out at the roots. Buchman led man to hate his sin, long to be rid of it, long for freedom and health, and passionately crave the consciousness of God in his soul. Then, when the surgeon had delivered from the disease; he became the physician—telling men how to *exercise* by helping others through becoming savers of souls. Life changers! Buchman's formula was: hate sin, forsake sin, confess sin, and make restitution. The heart was thus cleansed of iniquity. There would be a new sense of Jesus's declaration in Matthew 5:8 of the sermon on the mount, "Blessed are the pure in heart; for they shall see God."

Howard Walter wrote *Soul Surgery* to detail Buchman's life-changing art—"an art," as Professor Drummond called it—for healing the sick soul and cleansing the impure heart. Walter's book was about personal evangelism. The personal work was called "Cure of Souls."[110] Jesus was called the Great Physician because

---

[109] Begbie, *Life Changers*, pp. 31-41.
[110] Walter, *Soul Surgery*, p. 21.

He perfectly "knew what was in a man" [John 2:25].[111] The "New Evangelism" work began by laying siege to a particular soul. First, came early morning prayer. The worker's spirit became attuned to the Divine Spirit. The aim was to receive "leadings" through Divine Guidance. Howard Walter called the method, "Woo, Win, Warn;" but he deferred to Frank Buchman's soul-physician nomenclature which came to be known as the five C's: *Confidence, Confession, Conviction, Conversion, Conservation.*

Walter believed "the method comes from God."[112] Also, the Guidance as to how a particular soul should be helped.[113] Oxford Group writers often referred to the five C's and soul-surgery.[114] So did Anne Smith.[115] And Oxford Group writer Jack Winslow said:

> A third reason why my ministry so seldom bore fruit in transformed lives was that I lacked experience in what has been called the art of "soul-surgery." . . . And I cannot but pay this tribute to the Oxford Group, that it has taught me much that ought to have been taught to me in my theological college days as to the right ways of bringing men and women to the new life that is in Christ.[116]

Dr. Shoemaker also approved of Buchman's soul-surgery "art" and Five C's. In *The Conversion of the Church*, Shoemaker said:

> I think that the great practical apostasy of the Church in our time lies in her forsaking the great function of "the cure of souls" (p. 12).

---

[111] Walter, *Soul Surgery*, p. 24.

[112] Walter, *Soul Surgery*, p. 29.

[113] Walter, *Soul Surgery*, p. 28.

[114] Lean, *On the Tail of a Comet*, pp. 78-79; Spoerri, *Dynamic out of Silence*, p. 56; and Austin, *Frank Buchman as I knew him*, p. 19.

[115] Dick B., *Anne Smith's Journal*, pp. 96-97.

[116] Winslow, *Why I Believe In The Oxford Group*, pp. 60-61.

In his first book, Shoemaker explained the method of cure in the following way:

> And how do you do it? It may help to keep our object in view if we choose five words which will cover the usual stages of development: "Confidence; Confession; Conviction; Conversion; Conservation." You may feel this is a bit formidable and ready-made, but it is good to have the main points fixed. For these words I am indebted to Frank N. D. Buchman.[117]

We believe the five C's became the framework for A.A.'s Steps. "Confidence" became submerged in the method for working with others as well as the method for eliciting "Confession." "Confession" seems clearly to have wound up in A.A.'s Fifth Step.[118] "Conviction" may have been part of its Sixth Step. "Conversion" was certainly the process Bill Wilson discussed with Dr. Carl Jung as being the foundation of A.A.'s early success.[119] And "Conversion" was very possibly a part of the Third and Seventh Step ideas. Finally, "Conservation" seems to have comprehended the whole "maintenance," "growth," and "daily practice" ideas in Steps 10, 11, and 12.[120]

There is a good deal of scattered evidence in A.A. history that shows the Five C's and "soul surgery" were words used in early A.A. before the Steps were written—and even after. Early AAs spoke of "no pay for soul surgery."[121] And this idea may have been incorporated in the language of A.A.'s original six steps, where its fifth step said, "We tried to help other alcoholics, with no thought of reward in money or prestige."[122] There is negative evidence that "soul surgery" was a term bandied about early A.A.

---

[117] Shoemaker, *Realizing Religion*, pp. 79-80.

[118] Compare, *Pass It On*, pp. 128, 197.

[119] *Pass It On*. pp. 381-86. See also Nell Wing, *Grateful To Have Been There* (Illinois: Parkside Publishing, 1992), pp. 20-21.

[120] Compare Wing, *Grateful To Have Been There*, pp. 20-21.

[121] *DR. BOB*, p. 54.

[122] See Dick B., *The Akron Genesis*, pp. 256-58; and *Lois Remembers*, p. 92.

Dr. Kurtz reported in *Not-God* that both Lois Wilson (Bill's wife) and Henrietta Seiberling had an aversion to the term.[123]

The "five C's" are mentioned in *DR. BOB and the Good Oldtimers* (p. 54). Anne Smith wrote at length on each of the five in the pages of her Journal.[124] Richmond Walker, an early A.A. who wrote *Twenty-Four Hours A Day*, persisted in his references to the Five C's—Confidence, Confession, Conviction, Conversion, Continuance—as he called them. He mentioned them in his 1945 book, *For Drunks Only*.[125] And he mentioned them somewhat less explicitly in his last book in 1956.[126]

8. *Life-change—The Result*

> The Oxford Group was about Life-Changing. Man surrenders his life—past, present and future—into God's keeping and direction as part of a spiritual experience in which man's focus is then on changing others.

One can certainly read Harold Begbie's *Life Changers* and find Frank Buchman's concept of life-changing. The idea of "change," "life change," and "life changing" crops up again and again *in* Oxford Group writings and in writings *about* the Oxford Group.[127]

---

[123] Kurtz, *Not-God*, p. 324, note 36.

[124] See Dick B., *Anne Smith's Journal*, pp. 41, 42, 49, 96, 97, 100, 107, 141.

[125] Richmond Walker, *For Drunks Only* (Hazelden, reprint), pp. 45-46.

[126] Richmond Walker, *The 7 Points of Alcoholics Anonymous*, Rev. ed (Seattle, WA: Glen Abbey Books, 1989), pp. 91-93.

[127] Winslow, *Why I Believe in the Oxford Group*, pp. 33, 57-61; *What Is The Oxford Group?*, p. 37; Leon, *The Philosophy of Courage*, p. 93; Russell, *For Sinners Only*, pp. 53-69; Walter, *Soul Surgery*, pp. 25, 30; Austin, *Frank Buchman As I Knew Him*, p. 26; Weatherhead, *Discipleship*, pp. 125-38. Foot, *Life Began Yesterday* p. 174; Kitchen, *I Was a Pagan*, p. 145; Lean, *On the Tail of a Comet*, p. 79; Almond, *Foundations for Faith*, p. 25; and Bremer Hofmeyr, *How to Change* (New York: Moral Re-Armament, n.d.). Note the title of Reverend T. Willard Hunter's thesis on the life of Frank Buchman—"World Changing Through Life Changing." See also, Shoemaker, *God's Control*, pp. 21-22; and *The Church Can Save the World*, pp. 93, 118, 124, 153.

Benson's *The Eight Points of the Oxford Group* made these points:

1. Absolute surrender to which the Group witnesses includes all
    that the New Testament means by converting. It is conversion
    with a definite programme of world changing through life
    changing. The Group is insistent that every Christian must be
    a life changer. The New Testament knows nothing of a self-
    contained conversion (p. 158).

2. The Oxford Group is only a means of bringing men and
    women into vital relationship with Jesus Christ. He is the
    only Savior. No one in the Group ever changed anybody (pp.
    158-59).

3. Conversion, or what the Group calls "life changing," is the
    crisis when a man turns to Christ. That deep, initial
    experience cannot be skipped or slurred. Now while
    conversion is a crisis—salvation is a process. The Book of
    Acts (2:47, R.V.) says: "The Lord added to them day by day
    those that were being saved." . . . Conversion is a beginning,
    not a terminus. If we have converted—turned—changed, we
    need to ask ourselves whether our lives are "being
    saved,"—growing in grace and in likeness to Jesus Christ
    (pp. 162-63).

What Is The Oxford Group? said:

Those of us who have seen the wonders of the results of the life
changing of the Oxford Group can only describe them as modern
miracles. Men and women, who have never before realized that
Sin can kill not only the soul but the mind, talents, and happiness
as surely as the malignant physical disease, have found that the
surrender to God, in actuality as well as in theory, means a new
lease of life which brings with it a fuller joy of living than they
have realized was possible for them. They have been reborn to
the world as well as reborn to God. . . . Sinners who are

obsessed by their sins find that they can be set free and reborn into spiritual liberty (p. 6).

Anne Smith wrote in her Journal: "The axis of this group [the Oxford Group] is the changed life."[128]

The Path They Followed to Establish a Relationship with God

9. *Decision*

The first essential in the Oxford Group life-changing path is a decision—a voluntary action in which man verbalizes his surrender, usually with another, and gives in to God, essentially saying "Thy Will be done."

In *The Will of God and a Man's Lifework*, Wright included a chapter on "The Decision to Do God's Will" (pp. 41-114). Wright said self-surrender requires a definite, conscious, personal compact between man and God. Man voluntarily gives God absolute possession of his life, and God comes in. There is an energizing, life-giving impetus within of a "decision" to do God's will—often exemplified by the prayer, "Thy Will be done."[129] Absolute surrender was the "beginning" of "life under new management."[130] *What Is The Oxford Group?* said of the decision:

The Oxford Group recommend our making the initial act of Surrender to God in the presence of another person who is already a Changed Life, or in the presence of a person who has for some

---

[128] Dick B., *Anne Smith's Journal*, p. 96.

[129] Wright, *The Will of God*, pp. 50-51. See also Ebenezer Macmillan, *Seeking And Finding* (New York: Harper & Brothers, 1933), p. 273; Shoemaker, *Children of the Second Birth*, pp. 58, 175-87 (the latter pages containing an entire chapter on "Thy Will be done"); *If I Be Lifted Up*, p. 93; and *How to Find God*, p. 10.

[130] Benson, *The Eight Points*, p. 5.

time been an active Christian . . . to make our Surrender complete in the sight of God and Man; . . . it is a simple decision put into simple language, spoken aloud to God, in front of a witness, at any time and in any place, that we have decided to forget the past in God and to give our future into His keeping. . . . The Lord's Prayer is a perfect example of Surrender to God. . . . The essential point in studying the Lord's Prayer as Surrender in its complete form is to ask ourselves if we really are convinced that we believe in and act on every phrase in our daily lives. . . . "Thy will be done" are the four little words that give us the crux to the surrender of our will-power which is usually the last thing we wish to surrender to God (pp. 46-48).

The Oxford Group used the following kinds of surrender prayers:

O God, if there be a God, take command of my life; I cannot manage it myself.[131]

O Lord, manage me, for I cannot manage myself.[132]

O God, if there is a God, take charge of my life.[133]

O God, if there be a God, send me help now because I need it.[134]

---

[131] Brown, *The Venture of Belief*, pp. 26, 29-30.

[132] Russell, *For Sinners Only*, p. 80; Howard, *Frank Buchman's Secret*, p. 43; and Spoerri, *Dynamic out of silence*, pp. 36-37. Anne Smith suggested a similar prayer. See also Dick B., *Anne Smith's Journal*, pp. 20-22. Frank Buchman told the story in the 1920's about a student, George Moissides, who uttered the prayer, "O God, manage me because I cannot manage myself." This, said Buchman, occurred for Moissides "when God came into his life." And Buchman apparently invited an entire student body at Robert College in Constantinople to repeat the boy's prayer. See Lean, *On the Tail of a Comet*, p. 113. Perhaps unaware of the "Victor story" origins of the "manage me" prayer, the Reverend W. Irving Harris stated that a very similar prayer became known at Calvary Church as "Charlie's prayer." An "east-sider" named Charlie said "God, manage me, 'cause I can't manage myself." Harris, *The Breeze of the Spirit*, p. 10.

[133] Cecil Rose, *When Man Listens*, p. 22.

[134] Samuel M. Shoemaker, *How You Can Help Other People* (New York: E. P. Dutton, 1946), p. 60; and *How To Find God*, p. 6. See also Belden, *Reflections on Moral Re-Armament*, p. 16.

Compare Bill Wilson's cry of surrender at Towns Hospital just before he had his dramatic religious experience in 1934:

If there be a God, let Him show himself.[135]

Compare also this part of the Big Book's Third Step Prayer:

God, I offer myself to Thee—to build with me and to do with me as Thou wilt. . . . May I do Thy will always (p. 63).

Shoemaker wrote lots on the decision process. He said:

Of course, the mere externalizing of these difficulties does not banish them. . . . They must be gathered up in a new decision of the will and handed over to God in a new surrender . . . this step of decision. . . . It is true that only the Spirit of God converts any man: it is His direct action on the soul that alone converts. But we may draw near and put ourselves in a position to be converted by the simple act of self-surrender. . . . There must be a decision which the mind has collected, and the aspiration of the heart has felt, and pacts them into a moral choice. This is the act of self-surrender.[136]

You are all familiar with the words of the Forty-sixth Psalm, "Be still, and know that I am God: I will be exalted among the heathen." . . . Here is the meaning which Dr. Moffatt finds in these familiar words, "Give in, admit that I am God." . . . I believe they are the gateway to a true faith, and show us the way to find God. Now the place where our wills pass out of our own hands and into God's is the place of surrender, and surrender is our answer to this command from God, "Give in." . . . I began understanding it when I "gave in" to God in an act of the will called self surrender. . . . We need to know little about His nature, the completeness of His self-revelation in Christ to make this initial step towards Him. Understanding will come later:

---

[135] *Pass It On*, p. 121.

[136] Shoemaker, *The Conversion of the Church*, pp. 39-40, 77.

what is wanted first is relationship. That begins, as thousands will tell you from experience, at the point where we "give in" to God.[137]

God is God, and self is not God—that is the heart of it.[138]

He said he wanted to make a decision, and give himself completely to Christ, so we got down on our knees and he did it.[139]

I could give you a hundred instances of men and women whom, I have known, who have, at a critical place in their lives, made this momentous turning and have never retraced their steps or gone back on their decision.
. . . There are two elements in the complete experience of which I speak, if surrender grows into conversion: man's turn, and God's search. For some of us the critical element is the dedication of our own wills. For others it is the moment of God's invasion. Surrender is, then, not so much effort as is required in throwing ourselves over upon the mercy of God, but only so much as is needed to open the door of our life to Him.[140]

10.   *Self-examination—A Moral Inventory*

The surrender process requires that man make a moral inventory of himself—taking stock of his sins and their consequences.

The Oxford Group believed in self-examination. Man is not ready to give in to God until he is ready to flee from his own sins. To do this, he needs to examine himself and see the results of his

---

[137] Shoemaker, *National Awakening*, pp. 45, 46, 51.

[138] Shoemaker, *National Awakening*, p. 48. Compare Big Book, p. 62: "This is the how and why of it. First of all, we had to quit playing God. It didn't work."

[139] Shoemaker, *The Church Can Save The World*, p. 120. See also, Dick B., *Anne Smith's Journal*, pp. 27-19.

[140] Shoemaker, *Religion That Works*, pp. 46-47.

own feeble will-power. Oxford Group writers were fond of quoting from Jesus's sermon on the mount the proposition that one should "look for the log in his own eye before pointing to the speck in his brother's eye." Jesus Christ's actual words in Matthew 7:3-5 read:

> And why beholdest thou the mote [speck] that is in thy brother's eye, but considerest not the beam [log] that is in thine own eye? Or how wilt thou say to thy brother, "Let me pull out the mote out of thine eye;" and, behold, a beam is in thine own eye? Thou hypocrite, first cast out the beam out of thine own eye; and then shalt thou see clearly to cast out the mote out of thy brother's eye.[141]

Henry Drummond set the stage for what the Oxford Group was to call the "moral test."[142] In *The Ideal Life*, Drummond stressed "willingness" to do God's Will as essential to "knowing" God's Will, but said that willingness had to commence with man's "in-look."[143] He said man needs to "devote his soul to self-examination, to self examination of the most solemn and searching kind."[144]

Frank Buchman elaborated on the things to look *for*. He said:

1. International problems are based on personal problems of selfishness and fear.[145]

2. If you want an answer for the world today, the best place to start is with yourself.[146]

---

[141] See Geoffrey Allen, *He That Cometh*, pp. 81, 140; Kitchen, *I Was a Pagan*, pp. 110-11; Shoemaker, *The Church Can Save The World*, pp. 88-121; *God's Control*, pp. 62-72; and Dick B., *Anne Smith's Journal*, p. 141; Compare Russell, *For Sinners Only*, pp. 309-16.

[142] See Walter, *Soul Surgery*, p. 43-44; and see discussion of this in Dick B., *Anne Smith's Journal*, pp. 31-36.

[143] Drummond, *The Ideal Life*, pp. 313, 319, 316.

[144] Drummond, *The Ideal Life*, p. 316.

[145] Buchman, *Remaking The World*. p. 3

[146] Buchman, *Remaking The World*, p. 24.

3. You will find selfishness and fear everywhere.[147]

4. The root problems in the world today are dishonesty, selfishness and fear—in men, and consequently in nations.[148]

5. Moral recovery starts when everyone admits his own faults instead of spot-lighting the other fellow's.[149]

6. What is our real problem? . . . The symptoms may differ. . . . The disease remains the same. . . . What is the disease? Isn't it fear, dishonesty, resentment, selfishness? We talk about freedom and liberty, but we are slaves to ourselves.[150]

As stated, Walter's *Soul Surgery* likened Buchman's life-changing art to the work of the "soul physician" endeavoring to "cure" diseases of the soul through surgery that cuts them out and eradicates them. Walter said the soul surgeon must familiarize himself with the particular person, hear from the lips of the patient himself, and probe "to the root of the trouble."[151] To win the soul, the "physician" must "make the moral test," which requires the lost soul to make "entire self disclosure," that the spiritual surgeon may possess all the data for an accurate diagnosis. Walter even pointed to a leading Canadian pastor who conducted what he called his "Moral Clinic."[152]

To this imagery, *The Eight Points of the Oxford Group* added the idea of a businessman's taking an inventory—checking his financial position by having "taken stock."[153] Cecil Rose used a

---

[147] Buchman, *Remaking The World*, p. 24.

[148] Buchman, *Remaking The World*, p. 28.

[149] Buchman, *Remaking The World*, p. 46.

[150] Buchman, *Remaking The World*, p. 38. Compare Big Book pages 62, 84, 86.

[151] Walter, *Soul Surgery*, p. 69.

[152] Walter, *Soul Surgery*, pp. 41-48.

[153] Benson, *The Eight Points*, pp. 44, 162, 18, 7.

similar example, talking about "this business of looking into the books" with a pencil and paper and notes.[154]

The foregoing ideas—a moral test, a business inventory, and self-examination with pencil and paper—probably influenced the following ideas found in A.A.'s Fourth Step instructions:

1. "Made a searching and fearless moral inventory of ourselves" (Big Book, p. 59).[155]

2. "A business which takes no regular inventory goes broke. Taking a commercial inventory is a fact-finding and fact-facing process. . . . We did exactly the same thing with our lives. We took stock honestly" (Big Book, p. 64).

3. "In dealing with resentments, we set them on paper. . . . We reviewed our fears thoroughly. We put them on paper. . . . Now about sex. . . . We reviewed our own conduct over the years past. . . . We got this all down on paper and looked at it" (Big Book, pp. 68-69).

Sam Shoemaker spoke of a written check of conduct against the Four Standards. His remarks seem to have set the stage for A.A.'s Fourth Step process of reviewing one's life to find where it fails to measure up as to resentments, grudges, fears, dishonesty, and selfishness. Shoemaker said:

It would be a very good thing if you took a piece of foolscap paper and wrote down the sins you feel guilty of. Don't make them up—there will be plenty without that. . . . One of the simplest and best rules for self-examination that I know is to use the Four Standards which Dr. Robert E. Speer said represented the summary of the Sermon on the Mount—Absolute Honesty, Absolute Purity, Absolute Unselfishness, and Absolute Love. Review your life in their light. Put down everything that doesn't

---

[154] Cecil Rose, *When Man Listens*, pp. 17-19.

[155] See in Anne Smith's journal, the "moral test." Dick B., *Anne Smith's Journal*, pp. 30-32, 72, 98, 99.

measure up. Be ruthlessly, realistically honest. . . . You will be amazed at what a lift it gives you just to face up to these things honestly.[156]

Anne Smith made many comments of a similar nature in her Journal.[157] Several resembled the following comment by Shoemaker:

We thought we would take off the glasses, and begin to think about the fellow who was looking through them. As we talked, conviction developed that he was up against certain clearly defined sins in his own life. The first one was pride. . . . Finally, there was the sin of fear.[158]

I never learned more about religious work than I learned from Frank Buchman when he said, "The first and fundamental need is ourselves." It is so much easier to skip this first requirement and go on and to ask what comes next. The whole process has got to begin with us. For a good many it must begin with a fresh sense of sin, and we might question ourselves about professional ambition, discouragement and self-pity, grudges . . . intemperance, sins of the flesh and of the mind.[159]

Let us think of this also in connection with facing ourselves. . . . It is a real cross to face ourselves as we really are. How much better to take up that inescapable cross of having to find out about ourselves in the end—the whole, bitter, naked truth about our

---

[156] Shoemaker, *How to Become a Christian* (New York: Harper & Brothers, 1953), pp. 56-57. See also Cecil Rose, *When Man Listens*, pp. 18-19; Russell, *For Sinners Only*, pp. 20, 36; Olive Jones, *Inspired Children*, pp. 47-68; *Inspired Youth* (New York: Harper & Brothers, 1938), p. 41; Hofmeyr, *How to Change*, pp. 1-2; and Hallen Viney, *How Do I Begin?* (Copyright 1937 by The Oxford Group), pp. 2-4.

[157] Dick B., *Anne Smith's Journal*, pp. 30-36.

[158] Shoemaker, *The Conversion of the Church*, pp. 30-34.

[159] Shoemaker, *Twice-Born Ministers*, p. 182. As to "grudges" and the concept of a "grudge" list, see Big Book, p. 65; James 5:9 ("Grudge not, one against another, brethren, lest ye be condemned . . ."); Begbie, *Life Changers*, p. 38; and Shoemaker, *How to Become a Christian*, pp. 56-67. Oxford Group writer, Ebenezer Macmillan wrote at length on the importance of eliminating resentments, hatred, or the "grudge" that "blocks God out effectively" (See Macmillan, *Seeking and Finding*, pp. 98, 96-97).

pride, our self-will, our duplicity—how much better to take up that cross of our own volition, and let God, and the people who are close to God, help us face ourselves as we are, with a view to being different.[160]

11. *Confession—Sharing with God and Another*

Sharing in confidence the results of our own self-examination with another whose life has been changed is vital to the surrender process.

It is well documented that the Oxford Group confession idea rested largely on the following language in James 5:16:

Confess your faults one to another, and pray for one another that ye may be healed. The effectual fervent prayer of a righteous man availeth much.[161]

Oxford Group writers also cited Acts 19:18:

And many that believed came, and confessed, and shewed their deeds.[162]

Almost every Oxford Group book abounds in discussions of confession, which Oxford Group people called "Sharing" by confession.[163]

---

[160] Shoemaker, *God's Control*, pp. 104-05.

[161] J. P. Thornton-Duesbury, *Sharing* (Pamphlet of The Oxford Group, published at Oxford University Press, no date), p. 5; Day, *The Principles of The Group*, p. 6; *What Is The Oxford Group?*, pp. 29, 31; Almond, *Foundations For Faith*, p. 13; Benson, *The Eight Points*, p. 18; Garth Lean, *Cast Out Your Nets* (London: Grosvenor, 1990), p. 48; and Shoemaker, *The Conversion of the Church*, p. 35. See also *Pass It On*, p. 128; and Dick B., *Anne Smith's Journal*, pp. 36, 38, 40, 99, 129, 131-32, 142, 144.

[162] Thornton-Duesbury, *Sharing*, p. 5; and *What Is The Oxford Group?*, p. 27.

[163] Walter, *Soul Surgery*, pp. 41-64; Begbie, *Life Changers*, pp. 37, 102-04, 169; Benson, *The Eight Points*, pp. 18-29; *What Is The Oxford Group?*, pp. 25-35;

(continued...)

The emphasis was on Sharing with God and with another. There was to be absolute honesty, thoroughness, elimination of secrecy in a life, confessing one's own part in sin, and putting the past behind.[164]

The following are some of Sam Shoemaker's contributions on this important aspect of life-changing:

I have found a way to draw confession from others. It is to confess first myself. And this is the surest way for those who have not so wonderfully attuned themselves to others that they get the heart's secrets which have never been told to anyone else—the kind of secrets that are cleansed by being aired a bit. To draw souls one by one, to buttonhole them and steal from them the secret of their lives, to talk them clean out of themselves, to read them off like a page of print, to pervade them with your spiritual essence and make them transparent, this is the spiritual science which is so difficult to acquire, so hard to practice.[165]

If any man will to do His will, he shall know of the doctrine (John 7:17). We must get to the point of whether a man is willing to do His will in all areas. Take the four standards of Christ—absolute honesty, absolute purity, absolute unselfishness, and absolute love. When people's lives are wrong, they are usually wrong on one or more of these standards. Many quite respectable people have hidden things in their past and their present that need to come out in confidence with some one. A sin does not appear in all its exceeding sinfulness, until it is brought

---

[163] (...continued)

Weatherhead, *Discipleship*, pp. 31-44; Winslow, *Why I Believe in the Oxford Group*, pp. 27-31; Leon, *The Philosophy of Courage*, pp. 151-59; Thornton-Duesbury, *Sharing*, pp. 4-6; Day, *The Principles of the Group*, pp 6-7; Russell, *For Sinners Only*, pp. 41-42, 63-64, 284; Cecil Rose, *When Man Listens*, pp. 48-50; Brown, *The Venture of Belief*, pp. 33-36; Olive Jones, *Inspired Children*, p. 136; Shoemaker, *Realizing Religion*, pp. 80-81; *The Church Can Save the World*, pp. 110-12; and *The Conversion of the Church*, pp. 36-39.

[164] See for example, Benson, *The Eight Points*, pp. 18-29.

[165] Shoemaker, *Realizing Religion*, pp. 80-81.

into light with another; and it almost always seems more hopelessly unforgivable and the person who committed it more utterly irredeemable, when it remains unshared. The only release and hope for many bound and imprisoned and defeated people lies in frank sharing. It is not costly to share our problems, or even our comfortable sins, but it is costly to share the worst thing we ever did, the deepest sin of our life, the besetting temptation that dogs us. . . . By our frank honesty about ourselves, and our willingness, under God as He guides us to share anything in our own experience that will help another person . . . we shall get deep enough to know the real problem. At this point one of two things will probably happen. If the person is honest with himself and with God, he will be honest also with us and be ready to take the next step, which is a decision to surrender these sins, with himself wholly to God.[166]

We must find out how to go the rest of the way with our conversion. Personally, I am quite clear how this must start. It must start . . . by the sharing of these sins with another Christian who has found his way a bit farther than we have. . . . Of course, confession, in the absolute sense, is to God alone; but where there is a human listener, confession is found to be both more difficult and more efficacious. It is, as a matter of fact and experience, a relatively uncostly thing to fall on our knees and confess our sins to God . . . but it is a very costly thing to say these things out in the presence of a human being we can trust; and, as a matter of fact, this is extraordinarily effective in making the first break to get away from sins.
. . . Some of us prefer the word "Sharing" to the formal word confession; it has not quite such still and formal connotations. . . . It is my conviction and that of the Oxford Group with which I am associated, that the detailed sharing should be made with one person only. . . . We have known also the peculiar relief, having it something closely akin to the grace of God, which comes when "the worst" is known to at least one other human soul, when someone else carries with us in sympathetic

---

[166] Shoemaker, *The Church Can Save The World*, pp. 110-12.

understanding the secret which lay like lead in our hearts. . . .
He may have reason to think he knows what your difficulty is,
and he may share something parallel in his own life. . . . In any
case, he will create the sort of atmosphere in which you can talk
without fear, reserve or hurry.[167]

Note that A.A.'s Big Book says at page 73—after the person has
examined himself by means of a written inventory:

They only thought they had lost their egoism and fear; they only
thought they had humbled themselves. But they had not learned
enough of humility, fearlessness and honesty, in the sense that we
find it necessary until they had told someone else all their story.

12.   *Conviction—Readiness to Change*

Man needs to be convinced as part of the surrender process
that: (1) He has sinned against God. (2) Sin has Binding
Power, Blinding Power, Deadening Power, and Propagating
Power. (3) Christ can meet man's need to be rid of sin and
aligned with God.

Terms like "sin" and "conviction of sin" are foreign to today's
A.A. Such words will not be found in the Big Book text. But they
certainly were in common usage in the Biblically oriented meetings
the early AAs attended and also in the Oxford Group-Shoemaker
teaching and thinking to which they were exposed.[168] Shoemaker
and other Oxford Group sources were teaching that man would not
change, would not renounce his old self-willed, self-centered
behavior until he was "convicted of sin."[169] And one of Frank

---

[167] Shoemaker, *The Conversion of the Church*, pp. 35-39.

[168] See Lois Wilson's Oxford Group notes which are set forth in full in Dick B., *New Light on Alcoholism*, pp. 337-39. Lois spoke much of "sin."

[169] See Shoemaker, *Realizing Religion*, p. 81; Walter, *Soul Surgery*, pp. 64-78; and Olive Jones, *Inspired Children*, where Miss Jones defined the Oxford Group idea of
(continued...)

Buchman's five C's was "Conviction." Dwight Moody, one of Buchman's mentors, said being "convicted of sin" meant becoming conscious of wrongdoing—finding out that you are lost.[170] Shoemaker and Buchman both taught there must be a desire to "hate and forsake" the sin or wrongdoing.[171] Begbie discussed the five C's in *Life Changers* and, as to the third "C," said:

> Conviction of sin, is the normal result of the impact upon a man of a quality of life which he instinctively knows to be superior to his own, the lack of which he recognizes as an offense against God, and as his fault and only his (p. 169).

Almost every account of Frank Buchman tells of his "Keswick Experience."[172] Buchman went to England nursing a grudge against a Lutheran Mission Board. He heard a sermon on the "Cross." He was overwhelmed. He saw that to retain his consciousness of God, his heart must be empty of all sin and free from the angry past. He surrendered his life to Christ and wrote letters of apology to those he hated. He received relief, learning there can be no living and transforming sense of unity with the divine will, no "God Consciousness," while the heart nurses bitterness.[173] On his letters of apology, Buchman wrote this verse:

> When I survey the wondrous Cross
> On Which the Prince of Glory died,
> My richest gain I count but loss,
> And pour contempt on all my pride.[174]

---

[169] (...continued)
Conviction as follows: "*Conviction*, by which we come to the conscious realization of our sins which shut God away from us" (p. 135).

[170] William R. Moody, *The Life of D. L. Moody*, p. 239.

[171] Begbie, *Life Changers*, p. 38; and Shoemaker, *National Awakening*, p. 58. See also Hofmeyr, *How to Change*, p. 2.

[172] See, for example, Buchman, *Remaking The World*, pp. 312-15.

[173] See Begbie, *Life Changers*, p, 41; and Russell, *For Sinners Only*, pp. 166-67.

[174] For one of the countless quotations of this verse that Buchman used, see Buchman, *Remaking The World*, p. 315.

The Eight Points of the Oxford Group pointed out, concerning Buchman's Keswick experience:

1. He [Buchman] caught a vision of the Cross.
2. He had been convicted of sin in his life.
3. He had made an unreserved surrender to Jesus Christ.
4. He had made frank confession and restitution.
5. He had witnessed to the renewing power of Christ (p. xii).

Note the comment: "He had been convicted of sin in his life." *The Eight Points* said the Cross shows us to ourselves, exposes our excuses, unmasks our motives. The Cross makes us see the desperate nature of sin. The tragedy of Calvary was that ordinary people to whom little sins seemed harmless actually tried to murder "God." When the sight of what we are distresses us, we are then ready for the Gospel that there is forgiveness in Christ. For every "once" we look into our own hearts, said the author, let us look up twice to Christ.[175]

Soul Surgery had a chapter on Conviction.[176] Its author, Howard Walter, said Conviction is as closely related to Confession as Confession is to Confidence. It may come simultaneously with, or it may precede Confession. But confession of sin is not conviction of sin. "Conviction of sins means . . . a vision of his own personal guilt in the light of the revelation of God's holy love in Christ. It is the point where a man cries out to God, 'Against Thee only, have I sinned and done that which is evil in Thy sight.' Man is saying 'Father, I have sinned against heaven and in Thy sight, and am no more worthy to be called Thy son.'"[177]

Walter pointed to four things the sinner should realize:

1. Sin's Binding Power: My sins are mightier than I. Psalm 63:3 says, "Iniquities prevail against me."

---

[175] Benson, *The Eight Points*, pp. 17, 28.

[176] Walter, *Soul Surgery*, pp. 64-78.

[177] Walter, *Soul Surgery*, pp. 64-65. See Luke 15:21.

2. Sin's Blinding Power: Man suffers from moral myopia. He seems to say, "Evil, be thou my good." There is a gradual, tragic perversion of the moral vision.
3. Sin's Deadening Power: Man lacks the capacity for true moral indignation in the presence of the sin and wrong about him.
4. Sin's Propagating Power: Sin has the deadly power of passing on its taint to others in the family, the community, and even the next generation.[178]

Oxford Group writer Cecil Rose said:

Somewhere at the base of their life God is speaking to them, convicting them about the past and insistently pointing the new way. It is tremendously important that they should discover this themselves. . . . Christian revolution begins when a man is really willing for God to displace everything but Himself from a share in the control of life.[179]

Philip Brown wrote:

Surrender, as I see it, demands the expulsion of all conscious sin: the abject capitulation of pride, wilfulness, selfishness, the abandonment of all deceptions, and of all that is unclean. It is quite clear that the impure in heart cannot either see or hear God.[180]

Shoemaker wrote:

It was consciousness of personal sin which drew from my friend those pathetic and tremendously healthy words: Oh! to be made

---

[178] Walter, *Soul Surgery*, pp. 67-75; and Hofmeyr, *How to Change*, p. 2. See also Lois Wilson's own review of these qualities of sin. Dick B., *New Light on Alcoholism*, p. 338.

[179] Rose, *When Man Listens*, pp. 62, 74-78.

[180] Brown, *The Venture of Belief*, pp. 32-33. [See Matthew 5:8: "Blessed are the pure in heart; for they shall see God"]. And see Begbie, *Life Changers*, pp. 36-37, which discussed that verse.

over in the Spirit! I want a rebirth, but it comes not in one agony. Oh! how I want freedom from these deadening doubts, from this horrible, haunting sense, no "knowledge" of sin—this hopeless self-hatred and suffering. . . . By "conviction" two things are meant: conviction first of sin, and then a growing assurance that Christ can meet the need.[181]

We need to know how people behave under conviction of sin. We need to know what goes into a spiritual decision, and how to bring men to it. . . . We need the Cross, not as a theory, but as an experience of personal deliverance. We cannot evade some kind of pain: we can only choose between the pain of a divided mind and the pain of a crucified self. . . . We must let that Cross break us as it broke Him, cleanse and route the sin in us, bringing to us at last a united mind of forgiveness and peace.[182]

The heart of that problem is that many of us are wrong with God and wrong with each other: and what we need is to be right with God and right with each other. . . . The first step is not resurrection, it is crucifixion. . . . It is the crucifixion of pride, narrowness, stupidity, ignorant prejudice, intolerance. . . . There is no resurrection without crucifixion . . . either God's will is crucified on it [the Cross]; or our will is crucified on it so that God's will may prevail. Christ died to show us the everlasting victory and effectiveness of dying to self, that God might make His will prevail.[183]

Compare these two segments in A.A.'s Big Book:

Dr. Bob led me through all of these [six] steps. At the moral inventory, he brought up some of my bad personality traits or character defects, such as selfishness, conceit, jealously, carelessness, intolerance, ill-temper, sarcasm and resentments. We went over these at great length and then he finally asked me

---

[181] Shoemaker, *Realizing Religion*, pp. 21, 81-82.

[182] Shoemaker, *The Church Can Save The World*, pp. 153, 93-94.

[183] Shoemaker, *National Awakening*, p. 5.

if I wanted these defects of character removed. When I said yes, we both knelt at his desk and prayed, each of us asking to have these defects taken away. The picture is still vivid. If I live to be a hundred, it will always stand out in my mind. It was very impressive and I wish every A.A. could have the benefit of this type of sponsorship today. Dr. Bob always emphasized the religious angle very strongly, and I think it helped. I know it helped me (p. 292).

Are we now ready to let God remove from us all the things we have admitted are objectionable? . . . If we still cling to something we will not let go, we ask God to help us be willing (p. 76).

Mel B. made this observation about "Conviction" as it reached A.A.:

In describing his spiritual change, Buchman always used references to the problem of sin and acceptance of Christ that were widely employed in the Oxford Group but never took root in AA. What did take root in AA, however, was the focus on the dangers of resentment and self-pity, and the urgency of releasing these in order to find sobriety, happiness, and well-being. Learning from firsthand experience how resentment had blocked his own spiritual powers, Buchman developed an ability to target the same problem, and additional shortcomings in the lives of others. With modifications only in style and language, this became the essential method of AA when it began to form as part of the Oxford Group twenty-seven years later.[184]

13. *Conversion—The New Birth—Change*

Conversion occurs in the crisis of self-surrender in which man gives himself to God, is regenerated or reborn through the atoning and transforming power of Christ, and has part

---

[184] Mel B., *New Wine*, pp. 34-35.

of God's nature imparted to him. God is inwardly
experienced, and the barrier of sin is gone.

Everyone even remotely connected with the Oxford
Group—including Bill Wilson—had something to say about
conversion.[185] And the writers did not always approach the word
in the same way. Some spoke of conversion as Surrender.[186]
Some spoke of it as the new birth—being born again.[187] Some
spoke of it in terms of a spiritual or religious experience or
awakening.[188] It was often called an "experience of Christ" or
"experience of God."[189] Some talked in terms of salvation.[190]
But there was general agreement in the Oxford Group that
conversion involved a basic change in man—a change from self-
centeredness to God-centeredness, from sin "control" to "God-
Control."[191]

As we frequently mention, Oxford Group writers often used
William James's definition of conversion:

---

[185] We do not mention Dr. Bob, because the Akron AAs apparently spoke in terms
of making surrenders. However, Anne Smith certainly discussed conversion in her
workbook and quoted the William James definition of it. See Dick B., *Anne Smith's
Journal*, pp. 37-38.

[186] See Rose, *When Man Listens*, pp. 20-21; and *What Is The Oxford Group?*, pp. 43-
44.

[187] Allen, *He That Cometh*, pp. 19, 32, 48-49; Jones, *Inspired Children*, p. 136;
Shoemaker, *National Awakening*, p. 58; *How to Find God*, p. 7; and *How to Become a
Christian*, 65-82.

[188] Brown, *The Venture of Belief*, pp. 21-22; Shoemaker, *Realizing Religion*, pp. 4-9;
and Buchman, *Remaking the World*, pp. 19, 24, 35, 54.

[189] Buchman, *Remaking The World*, p. x; Benson, *The Eight Points*, p. 151; and
Leon, *The Philosophy of Courage*, pp. 89, 112-13.

[190] Winslow, *Why I Believe In the Oxford Group*, p. 17.

[191] Buchman, *Remaking The World*, pp. 3, 18, 24-25, 28-29, 30, 39, 42, 50, 63, 64,
69, 70, 95; Lean, *On the Tail of a Comet*, p. 83; Russell, *For Sinners Only*, pp. 324-29;
Leon, *The Philosophy of Courage*, pp. 129-49; Shoemaker, *God's Control*, pp. 9-10;
Foot, *Life Began Yesterday*, pp. 174-175; and Kitchen, *I Was A Pagan*, pp. 43-48; 89-
90.

The process, gradual or sudden, by which a self, hitherto divided and consciously wrong, inferior and unhappy, becomes unified, consciously right, superior and happy.[192]

---

[192] James, *The Varieties of Religious Experience*, p. 177; Shoemaker, *Realizing Religion*, p. 22; Walter, *Soul Surgery*, p. 80; and Kitchen, *I Was a Pagan*, p. 69. Compare Brown, *The Venture of Belief*, p. 23; and Weatherhead, *Discipleship*, p. 16. There has been a good deal of fuzzy thinking when the word "conversion" has been used. William James was talking, from a psychological standpoint, about change—the unifying of a divided self through a religious experience. In the Bible, the term "conversion" means "a turning or returning to God" through God's work in man; and in the New Testament, the securing, through faith in Christ, of the salvation which Christ brought [See *New Bible Dictionary*: Second Edition (Illinois: Tyndale House Publishers, Inc., 1982), pp. 228-29]. Hence there is no "process." There is a miracle by grace. Ephesians 2:8-9 states clearly, "For by grace are ye saved through faith; and that not of yourselves: *it is* the gift of God: Not of works, lest any man should boast." Bill Wilson used the term "conversion" in his correspondence with Dr. Carl Jung. See *Pass It On*, pp. 381-86. The Oxford Group preferred the word "surrender." *What Is The Oxford Group?* said, "The word 'converted' is much despised amongst us moderns. It savours of religious hysteria, dramatic penitent-form scenes—which serve a very useful purpose for those whom only such scenes can awaken to a living Christ—old-fashioned British revivalism or the latest American religious fervour. But the word conversion itself, although not in habitual use by the Oxford Group, is a good one and there is no reason why, if it is our idea of surrender, any of us who want to use it should refrain from doing so. But Absolute Surrender to God, as seen by the Oxford Group, is conversion with a definite constructive spiritual policy added which ensures it being of positive use and fertility for us and for others" (p. 43). In his dissertation, Charles Knippel pointed out that Shoemaker alternated between talking of conversion as a one-time act [See Romans 10:9] and conversion as a process—not unlike that of A.A.'s Twelve Steps—where there is an initial act or decision [a new birth] followed by some procedures such as self-examination, confession, restitution, and then conservation involving growth through Bible study, prayer, listening, Guidance, and so on. Early Akron AAs simply spoke of "surrender" and used the word frequently in speaking of their "surrender to God" on their knees. See *DR. BOB*, pp. 88-89, 92, 101, 110.

We suggest, for simplicity of understanding, that a distinction be drawn between two things: (1) The new birth—being "born again of the Spirit." The Bible teaches that in the new birth, when man is born again of the spirit, he is then and there—by the grace of God—changed. He becomes at once a son of God—not by his works but by his faith. The change is wrought by God (Romans 10:9; 1 John 3:1-2; e.g., Kitchen, *I Was A Pagan*, p. 43). Frank Buchman put the matter in simplest terms: Only three essential factors were involved in conversion—*Sin, Jesus Christ*, and (the result) *a Miracle*. See Walter, *Soul Surgery*, p. 86. (2) Fellowship with God through renewal of the mind. The Bible teaches that there is the additional problem of fellowship—the renewed mind walk to stay

(continued...)

Harold Begbie added to this definition the statement, "Conversion is the only means by which a radically bad person can be changed into a radically good person."[193]

Henry Wright referred to two Bible verses in speaking of the crisis of self-surrender involved in conversion:

> The gospel of the kingdom of God is preached, and every man entereth violently into it.[194]

> I beseech you therefore brethren, by the mercies of God that you present your bodies a living sacrifice holy, acceptable unto God, which is your reasonable service. And be not conformed to this world; but be ye transformed by the renewing of your mind, that

---

[192] (...continued)

in fellowship with God. This *does* involve works—the task of walking in love, behaving as God would have us behave, obeying His commandments in order to manifest the fruits of the power received in the new birth (James, Chapter 2; 1 John 4:7-5:5; Ephesians 4:22-5:21). "Faith without works is dead" [barren, useless] (James 2:17, 20). In other words, there is a distinction between the receipt of power through new birth and the utilization of the power and walking in fellowship. Both involve "change." In Vine's *Expository Dictionary of Old and New Testament Words*, the author says of the Greek noun, *anakainōsis*, "a renewal, is used in Rom. 12:2, 'the renewing (of your mind),' i.e., the adjustment of the moral and spiritual vision and thinking to the mind of God, which is designed to have a transforming effect upon the life; in Tit. 3:5, where 'the renewing of the Holy Spirit' is not a fresh bestowment of the Spirit, but a revival of His power, developing the Christian life; this passage stresses the continual operation of the indwelling Spirit of God; the Romans passage stresses the willing response on the part of the believer" (pp. 278-79). Garth Lean wrote the author, "When Michael and I met Buchman in 1931 and 1932, respectively, he much more used the word 'change.' The word 'conversion' had been cheapened and lost its content. Buchman was aware that 'change' happened in many different ways."

[193] Shoemaker, *Realizing Religion*, p.22, quoting Begbie. Harold Begbie, *Twice Born Men* (New York: Fleming H. Revell, 1909), p. 17.

[194] Luke 16:16b. Wright said there has to be a break from positive sin, plus a definite, conscious act of ethical decision between God and man personally, without reservation . . . "You give everything to God." See Wright, *The Will of God*, pp. 69, 74, 63-65, 50.

you may prove what is that good, and acceptable, and perfect will of God.[195]

Canon Streeter wrote at great length on the power of God that works through Christ. Streeter said the power is made effective primarily by the Cross in two quite different ways: (1) Christ died on the Cross to pay the price for man's disobedience. Christ's death effected the liberation of man from his sins. When man accepts Christ, he receives the spirit—Christ—and he is liberated from sin through the religion of faith in Christ. Streeter spoke of receipt of the spirit; and with that spirit, power; and with power, liberty; and the evidence of all this—the fruit of the Spirit—love, joy, peace.[196] (2) The Cross of Christ is the supreme example of surrender to the will of God, however great the humiliation or pain involved, with the result that we have the love of Christ when we

---

[195] Romans 12:1-2. See Wright, *The Will of God*, at pages 64 and 74 where he said, "You present your body a living sacrifice that you may prove God's Will. You shall prove it by getting back your body—a glorified body." Note: It is the author's view that this is a "renewed mind" verse referring to "fellowship" and not to "sonship." See, for example, *The Revised English Bible* (Oxford: Oxford University Press, 1989), p. 143, "Therefore, my friends, I implore you by God's mercy to offer your very selves to him: a living sacrifice, dedicated and fit for his acceptance, the worship offered by mind and heart. Conform no longer to the pattern of this present world, but be transformed by the renewal of your minds. Then you will be able to discern the will of God, and to know what is good, acceptable, and perfect." The *New Bible Dictionary* says, "The initiative in regeneration is ascribed to God (John 1:13); it is from above (John 3:3, 7); and of the Spirit (John 3:5, 8) . . . The divine act is decisive and once and for all . . . The abiding results given in these passages are doing righteousness, not committing sin, loving one another, believing that Jesus is the Christ, and overcoming the world. These results indicate that in spiritual matters man is not altogether passive. He is passive in the new birth; God acts on him. But the result of such an act is far-reaching activity; he actively repents, believes in Christ, and henceforth walks in the newness of life. . . . There is no change in the personality itself; the person is the same. But now he is differently controlled. . . . We may define regeneration as a drastic act on fallen human nature by the Holy Spirit, leading to a change in the person's whole outlook. He can now be described as a new man who seeks, finds and follows God in Christ" (pp. 1015-1016). See also *The Abingdon Bible Commentary* (Nashville: Abingdon Press, 1929), p. 1160.

[196] Streeter, *The God Who Speaks*, pp. 108-11. See Galatians 3:2; Acts 1:8; 2 Corinthians 3:17; and Galatians 5:22. And see Colossians 1:27—"Christ in you, the hope of glory;" and Weatherhead, *Discipleship*, pp. 146-47.

have his faith and are more than conquerors through Christ who loved us.[197]

Walter made the following points in *Soul Surgery*:

1. Conversion can be viewed from two sides: On man's side, it is an act of faith in which the sinner deliberately and finally turns from all known sin and identifies himself with Christ, for the future, in a saving, victorious moral unity and fellowship. On God's side, it is an act of God's free grace by which God is able, through bearing human sin—in suffering redemptive love—to forgive the sinner and so to effect in Christ a new relationship in which the barrier of sin no longer remains.[198]

2. The basis of conversion is the awakening of a new self, and the vital element in this new birth is the dawning of a new affection which henceforth dominates the heart.[199]

3. God outside of us is a theory. God inside of us becomes a fact. God outside of us is an hypothesis; God inside of us is an experience. God the Father is the possibility of salvation. God the Spirit is actuality of life, joy, peace, and saving power.[200]

Benson expressed the results of conversion in this way:

1. We become witness to the renewing power of Christ. Of Christ it says: I have overcome the world and I will come and put my overcoming Spirit in your weakness and fill you with my own victorious life and be in you the overcoming

---

[197] Streeter, *The God Who Speaks*, pp. 97-98. Streeter is clearly referring to Romans 8, particularly 35-37: "Who shall separate us from the love of Christ? shall tribulation, or distress, or persecution, or famine, or nakedness, or peril, or sword? . . . Nay, in all these things we are more than conquerors through him that loved us."

[198] Walter, *Soul Surgery*, p. 79.

[199] Walter, *Soul Surgery*, p. 82.

[200] Walter, *Soul Surgery*, p. 82.

and conquering power. Christ's victory is ours, and we are victorious in it.[201]

2. He [Christ] has overcome sin; therefore the very sin—the personal sin of ours has been overcome. The soul is charged with a strength not its own.[202]

3. Man breathes a new atmosphere and is vitalized with a Divine Energy. What the law could not do, is now fulfilled by the impulse and inspiration of the Spirit of Christ.[203]

4. He breaks the power of canceled sin. He sets the prisoner free.[204]

Weatherhead described the riches of the glory of the mystery in the new birth, speaking of "Christ in me the hope of glory . . . Christ in him the hope of glory."[205]

Shoemaker wrote a good deal on the "how" of conversion. He said:

But can one have a conversion at will? And what must we do to have it? Well, we must want it with all our hearts and put ourselves in the way of it. God on His part has longed to win us for years. It has been we who have been unwilling. We must open ourselves to Him, and be prepared to accept all it will mean to be a child of God. First, we have got to be willing to break finally with sin; it is accepting evils and wrongs in themselves as inevitable, and giving up the fight. In this there can be no

---

[201] Benson, *The Eight Points*, p. 119. See John 16:33.

[202] Benson, *The Eight Points*, p. 119.

[203] Benson, *The Eight Points*, p. 121-22.

[204] Benson, *The Eight Points*, p. 127. Benson seemed to refer to these Bible verses: Galatians 5:1; John 16:33; and 1 John 5:4-5.

[205] Weatherhead, *Discipleship*, pp. 146-147. Weatherhead obviously referred to Colossians 1:26-27, "Even the mystery which hath been hid from ages and from generations, but now is made manifest to his saints: To whom God would make known what is the riches of the glory of this mystery among the Gentiles; which is Christ in you, the hope of glory."

possible reservation or interpretation: we must embark on the business of cleansing ourselves through the grace of God, from top to bottom. And what the sum total of this means together with the absolutely yielded will, is best expressed in the old idea of self-surrender to God. . . . And this is primarily the business of the will—taking the Kingdom of Heaven by force. It takes will power to thrust out sin with one heave, even for a moment, and let God have place.

. . . Given this readiness to yield, the open mind, the hungering soul, the penitent heart, the surrendered will, the attitude of expectation, and the sense of abysmal need, the whole life given in earnest prayer—what then? . . . You and God are reconciled the moment you surrender. . . . Self recedes. God looms up. Self-will seems the blackest sin of all, rebellion against God the only hell. The peace that passes understanding steals over you. . . . This impartation of Himself to us is God's part in the conversion. Our part is to ask, to seek, to knock. His part is to answer, to come, to open. . . . The real witness of the Spirit to the second birth is to be found only in the disposition of the genuine child of God, the permanently patient heart, the love of self eradicated.[206]

But I would also like to say that something happens the first time the soul says "Yes" to God with its whole force, that never wholly disappears. As terrible sin does something to the human heart which may be forgiven, but leaves its trace, so, thank God, does tremendous surrender leave such an ineradicable mark.[207]

Except a man be born again, he cannot see the Kingdom of God. Nicodemus saith unto him [Jesus Christ], How . . . ? (John 3:3-4). . . . If the Christian Church is to be effective again in the affairs of men, it must begin by once more illuminating this great truth of rebirth. . . . A man is born again when the control of his life, its center and its direction pass from himself to God. . . . The how of getting rid of sin, if you are in earnest about doing

---

[206] Shoemaker, *Realizing Religion*, pp. 22-35.

[207] Shoemaker, *The Conversion of the Church*, p. 79.

it at all: face it, share it, surrender it. Hate it, forsake it, confess it, and restore for it.[208]

When A.A. began in Akron, Ohio, on June 10, 1935, there were no Twelve Steps. Bill and Dr. Bob simply had the Bible and the principles of the Oxford Group to which both belonged.[209] There was no Third Step prayer of "decision," nor was there a Seventh Step prayer of "humility."[210] The "alcoholic squad of the Oxford Group" in Akron simply got down on their knees and surrendered their lives to God. Prior to the Akron founding, Bill had simply gone to Calvary Church's rescue mission, knelt, and—as Mrs. Helen Shoemaker herself witnessed—"made a decision for Christ." In other words, the Oxford Group conversions in early A.A. usually involved a simple prayer of surrender. Sometimes the surrender emphasized "Thy will be done" from the Lord's Prayer.[211] Sometimes there were simple prayers asking God to take charge of an unmanageable life.[212] At least two Oxford Group writers (as well as Anne Smith) indicated their belief that God can "remove" the symptoms of sin.[213]

We close with this Big Book language in connection with Steps Three and Seven:

> As we felt new power flow in, as we enjoyed peace of mind, as we discovered we could face life successfully, as we became conscious of His presence, we began to lose our fear of today, tomorrow, or the hereafter. We were reborn (p. 63).

---

[208] Shoemaker, *National Awakening*, p. 55, 57, 58; and Allen, *He That Cometh*, pp. 19-43.

[209] *DR. BOB*, p. 96.

[210] See Dick B., *The Akron Genesis*, pp. 256-60, for the various forms the original "six" steps took.

[211] See *What Is The Oxford Group?*, pp. 47-48.

[212] See Dick B., *The Akron Genesis*, p. 263; *Anne Smith's Journal*, pp. 20-21; C. Rose, *When Man Listens*, pp. 22, 74-75; Brown, *The Venture of Belief*, p. 30; and Winslow, *Why I Believe in the Oxford Group*, pp. 36, 38.

[213] See Allen, *He That Cometh*, p. 147; Kitchen, *I Was A Pagan*, p. 73; and Dick B., *Anne Smith's Journal*, pp. 46-47.

Many of us said to our Maker, *as we understood Him*: "God, I offer myself to Thee. . . . May I do Thy will always!" (p. 63).[214]

When ready, we say something like this: "My Creator, I am now willing that you should have all of me, good and bad. I pray that you now remove from me every single defect of character which stands in the way of my usefulness to you and my fellows. Grant me strength, as I go out from here, to do your bidding, Amen." (p. 76).[215]

There was a common expression in the Oxford Group, which was repeated by Stephen Foot: "Surrender of all one knows of self to all one knows of God."[216] Anne Smith wrote similar language in her *Spiritual Journal*: "Try to bring a person to a decision to surrender as much of himself as he knows to as much of God as he knows."[217]

14.   *Restitution—Righting the Wrong*

The cord of sin which binds the convert to the past can only be cut by an amend—his act of restitution by which he acknowledges his faults to the people concerned and pays them back by apology or in kind for that which was taken from them.

Restitution was vital to Oxford Group life changing. Stories of Frank Buchman's life invariably mention two of his experiences. The first concerned "Keswick" which we have already discussed. In that situation, he was "released" when he wrote letters of

---

[214] This is a portion of what is commonly called the "Third Step Prayer."

[215] This is commonly called the Seventh Step Prayer.

[216] Foot, *Life Began Yesterday*, p. 175. See also, Shoemaker, *They're On The Way*, p. 156.

[217] See Dick B., *Anne Smith's Journal*, p. 25.

apology to the six ministers against whom he had a grudge.[218] The second account concerned "Bill Pickle at Penn State."[219]

Pickle was an alcoholic bootlegger on the college campus where Buchman was sent to teach the Bible and convert students to Christianity. Pickle was supplying the booze to potential converts. So Buchman went to work on Pickle first. The long and the short of the story is that Pickle decided to, and did become, a Christian. He was able to give up liquor and lead a model life. With Buchman's assistance, Pickle wrote apologies to his family for the way he had lived and had treated them. Pickle's behavior-change much influenced the later successful course of Buchman's witnessing at Penn State and in the Eastern college system.

The Keswick and Pickle stories illustrate Buchman's convictions about the importance of restitution as a vital part of the surrender process.

Oxford Group adherents felt likewise. Getting right with other people to get right with God was vital. Weatherhead wrote:

> Nothing is clearer in the gospels than the direct teaching that our relation to God cannot be right unless our relations with men are as right as we can make them.[220]

Garth Lean wrote:

> If you will put right what you can put right, God will put right what you can't put right. Restitution. That was the action I had to take. Wherever I could do anything to right the wrongs I had done I must do it. It has been said that you should do four things with sin—hate it, forsake it, confess it, restore for it. I had to

---

[218] Buchman, *Remaking the World*, pp. 312-15; Begbie, *Life Changers*, pp. 166-67; Benson, *The Eight Points*, pp. x-xii; Walter, *Soul Surgery*, p. 61; Russell, *For Sinners Only*, pp. 56-60; Lean, *On the Tail of a Comet*, pp. 21-32; *What Is The Oxford Group?*, p. 60; and Howard, *Frank Buchman's Secret*, pp. 22-26.

[219] Buchman, *Remaking The World*, pp. 330-45; Russell, *For Sinners Only*, pp. 189-204; Howard, *Frank Buchman's Secret*, pp. 26-30; and Lean, *On the Tail of a Comet*, pp. 33-44.

[220] Weatherhead, *Discipleship*, p. 113.

restore for mine. . . . One footnote about restitution. No on has the right to make restitution that implicates a third party.[221] The Christian confesses his own sins, not those of other people.[222]

The Oxford Group writings had much to say about restitution. Russell's *For Sinners Only*, the book, *What Is The Oxford Group?*, and Benson's *The Eight Points* all contained excellent summaries. One of the most useful, related to A.A.'s Ninth Step process, is this:

> We cannot make effective contact with God, we cannot truly worship while our hearts are choked with resentments. . . . True worship enables us to test our conduct by God's Will for us and others. It redeems from blindness, listlessness and self concern and gives us new insight into our obligations to God's other children. . . . Our task today is to look at the Sermon on the Mount not as the wild dream of a Galilean visionary, but as a piece of realism—the only plan upon which men can live together in peace and security.[223]

A number of Bible verses were cited for the restitution concept. *For Sinners Only* quoted this translation of Numbers 5:6-7:

> Speak unto the children of Israel, when a man or a woman shall commit any sin that men commit to do a trespass against the Lord, and that soul shall be guilty; Then they shall confess their sin which they have done; and he shall make restitution for his guilt in full, and add unto it the fifth part thereof, and give it to him in respect of whom he hath been guilty.[224]

---

[221] Compare the Big Book language of Step Nine, which suggests making direct amends "except when to do so would injury them or others" (p.59); and see discussion of this point at Big Book pages 79-82.

[222] Lean, *Cast Out Your Nets*, pp. 86, 90.

[223] Benson, *The Eight Points*, p. 31. Compare the Big Book's statement at page 77, "Our real purpose is to fit ourselves to be of maximum service to God and the people about us."

[224] Russell, *For Sinners Only*, pp. 119. See also, Thornton-Duesbury, *Sharing*, p. 6.

One of the most commonly cited verses is from the Sermon on the Mount in Matthew 5:23-24:

> Therefore if thou bring thy gift to the altar, and there rememberest that thy brother hath ought against thee; Leave there thy gift before the altar, and go thy way; first, be reconciled to thy brother, and then come and offer thy gift.[225]

For Sinners Only also referred to the Prodigal Son story in Luke, Chapter 15. Russell said, "Sending prodigal sons back to their earthly as well as their Heavenly Father is a specialty of the Oxford Group."[226] Russell also mentioned the conversation between Jesus and Zacchaeus recorded in Luke 19:1-10. Zacchaeus had told Jesus that if he had taken anything from any man by false accusation, he had restored the man fourfold. Jesus responded approvingly, "This day is salvation come to thy house."[227] In its discussion of restitution, *What Is The Group?* cited Acts 3:19: "Repent ye therefore, and turn again, that your sins may be blotted out" (p. 55).

In *The Eight Points of the Oxford Group*, Benson made a number of other important points:

1. Christians must take the initiative in reconciling and mending a quarrel with an enemy—"agree with thine adversary quickly" [Matthew 5:25].[228]

---

[225] Benson, *The Eight Points*, p. 30; Russell, *For Sinners Only*, p. 120; Weatherhead, *Discipleship*, 113; Shoemaker, *The Conversion of the Church*, pp. 47-48; *The Gospel According To You*, pp. 146-51; Macmillan, *Seeking And Finding*, p. 176; and DR. BOB, p. 308. Speaking from his personal experience in the Oxford Group, Willard Hunter noted in writing to the author that this verse was "big"—obviously referring to its importance to the Group.

[226] Russell, *For Sinners Only*, p. 129. See also *What Is The Oxford Group?*, pp. 63-64; and Almond, *Foundations For Faith*, p. 30.

[227] Russell, *For Sinners Only*, pp. 135. See also, Lean, *Cast Out Your Nets*, pp. 87-88; Macmillan, *Seeking and Finding*, p. 111; Almond, *Foundations For Faith*, p. 13; and Weatherhead, *Discipleship*, pp. 115-16.

[228] Benson, *The Eight Points*, p. 32. See also, Weatherhead, *Discipleship*, p. 110.

2. The evil or fault of another must be overcome with good, with forgiveness or it ends in futile, mental poisoning from anger and revenge.[229]

3. Christ died for us sinners, forgiving the very men who drove the nails through his hands and feet—the just for the unjust.[230]

4. Resentment and revenge are cheap and conventional, but forgiveness is constructive and God-like.[231]

5. Before we can get right with God, we must leave no stone unturned to get right with men.[232]

6. He that loveth not his brother whom he hath seen, cannot love God whom he hath not seen.[233]

7. Restitution is openly cutting the cord of sin which has bound us to the life of wrong we have lived in the past. It is righting to the best of our ability wrongs we have committed in the past.[234]

8. Good must be accomplished, and not just a personal release from the burden of sin at the expense of the one wronged.[235]

---

[229] Benson, *The Eight Points*, p. 33. See Romans 12:17-21.

[230] Benson, *The Eight Points*, p. 34. See Macmillan, *Seeking and Finding*, pp. 109-20. Romans 5:7-8.

[231] Benson, *The Eight Points*, pp. 34-35. See also, Allen, *He That Cometh*, p. 115; Colossians 3:13.

[232] Benson, *The Eight Points*, pp. 36-37; See also, Russell, *For Sinners Only*, p. 128; Macmillan, *Seeking and Finding*, pp. 98-99; and Hofmeyr, *How to Change*, p. 3. Matthew 5:40-41; 6:14-15.

[233] 1 John 4:20. See Benson, *The Eight Points*, pp. 36-37; Macmillan, *Seeking And Finding*, p. 99; and Dick B., *The Akron Genesis*, p. 92.

[234] Benson, *The Eight Points*, p. 39; and *What Is The Oxford Group?*, pp. 55-56.

[235] Benson, *The Eight Points*, p. 41.

And what did Sam Shoemaker say? Just this:

I want to remind you that our experience of God is all bound up
inextricably with our human relationships. "If a man love not his
brother whom he hath seen, how can he love God whom he hath
not seen" [1 John 4:20]. "If thou bring thy gift to the altar, and
there rememberest that thy brother hath ought against thee, first
go and be reconciled unto thy brother, and then come and offer
thy gift" [Matthew 5:23-24]. It is idle for us to try to be in touch
with God, or keep in touch with Him, so long as there are human
relationships which must be righted at the same time.[236]

But I am certain that the most important factor in continuance,
second only to prayer, is in a series of new relationships. First
with the family. . . . He may need to make a blanket-apology to
the entire family for impatience, for temper, for wanting his own
way, for wanting to play Providence to them all. There may be
specific wrongs to be shared with individuals. Probably heretofore
he has been confessing their sins to them; now he confesses his
own. . . . A confessing Christian is a propagating Christian.[237]

By obedience God gets us to where we begin fulfilling His plan.
. . . Here is a man guided to make restitution for his resentment
against some of his own family. If he does it fully, he reestablished
relationships with them. . . . Christ . . . said, "Thou hypocrite, cast
out first the beam out of thine own eye, then shalt thou see clearly
to put out the mote that is in thy brother's eye" [Matthew 7:5].[238]

Compare this statement in A.A.'s Big Book:

We go to him [an enemy] in a helpful and forgiving spirit,
confessing our former ill feeling and expressing our regret. Under
no condition do we criticize such a person or argue (p. 77).

---

[236] Shoemaker, *The Conversion of the Church*, pp. 47-48.

[237] Shoemaker, *The Conversion of the Church*, pp. 41-43.

[238] Shoemaker, *God's Control*, pp. 63-64. See also Allen, *He That Cometh*, p. 140;
Kitchen, *I Was A Pagan*, pp. 110-11; and Dick B., *Anne Smith's Journal*, p. 30.

Jesus Christ

15.   *Jesus Christ—The Source of Power*

> The Oxford Group believed in Jesus Christ as the Divine
> Redeemer and Way-Shower by whose transforming power
> man can be changed through surrender to Christ and
> an experience of Christ.

John 14:6 quoted Jesus Christ as follows:

> Jesus saith unto him, I am the way, the truth, and the life: no
> man cometh unto the Father, but by me.

And Oxford Group people certainly spoke of, and believed in,
Jesus Christ as the Way, the Truth, and the Life.[239] In addition,
as Savior, Lord, and God's only begotten Son.[240]

Having written *For Sinners Only*, A. J. Russell wrote *One
Thing I Know*.[241] Russell said that some, who did not read *For
Sinners Only* with care or sympathy, felt there was not enough in
it about Atonement. Russell said he was astonished. He said he
had not written that book about the "Atonement," or the "Virgin
Birth," or the Star of Bethlehem, or the "Sacraments of the
Gospels." "And so none of these chapters in our Lord's life was
dwelt upon, though 'all were, of course, accepted by the writer'."
Russell said he finally realized how little the public knew of the
Atonement and how suddenly there was a desire for more
information. He said he might have written a treatise on the

---

[239] See Brown, *The Venture of Belief*, p. 49; Foot, *Life Began Yesterday*, p. 87;
Benson, *The Eight Points*, p. 125; Shoemaker, *Religion That Works*, p. 28; *Christ and
This Crisis*, p. 39; *They're on the Way*, p. 153; and Olive Jones, *Inspired Children*, p.
150. Compare Foot, *Life Began Yesterday*, p. 87.

[240] Shoemaker, *Religion That Works*, pp. 27-29; *Christ's Words from the Cross*, p.
11; Walter, *Soul Surgery*, p. 126; Benson, *The Eight Points*, pp. 158-59, 116, 126; and
Almond, *Foundations for Faith*, pp. 14-21, 44, 56.

[241] A. J. Russell, *One Thing I Know* (New York: Harper & Brothers, 1933).

subject years ago, had he been competent to do so. But that there are some forty theories of the Atonement. He said of himself:

> Through faith in His loving sacrificial achievement on the Cross, and through the sincere endeavor attended by many failures to follow the commands of that Divine Redeemer and Way-Shower, our incomparable Lord, I know I am a new man in Christ Jesus; a new man who is still being saved from sin.[242] My theory, then, if I dare to have a theory of so mighty an event in history—Christ crucified from the foundation of the world—is no more and certainly no less than that expressed by the old hymn which is acceptable to Protestants and Catholics, High Church and Lower Church, Modernists and Fundamentalists:

> There is a green hill far away,
>   Without a city wall,
> Where the dear Lord was crucified,
>   Who died to save us all.
> We may not know, we cannot tell
>   What pains He had to bear;
> But we believe it was for us
>   He hung and suffered there.[243]

Russell said one of the most compelling reasons for writing *One Thing I Know* was his need to state, in language clear, simple, and emphatic, an unqualified belief in the divinity of Jesus Christ, and his Atonement on Calvary, and to assert a sincere desire for Christian unity.[244]

Dr. L. W. Grensted, wrote an entire book in 1933 on *The Person of Christ*.[245] Grensted was a convinced spokesman for

---

[242] Compare Ephesians 4:24.

[243] Russell, *One Thing I Know*, pp. ix-xiii.

[244] Russell, *One Thing I Know*, p. ix. In a telephone interview on February 9, 1992, Earl H., an A.A. oldtimer who has provided the author with much assistance in his research, informed the author that he had in his possession a copy of *One Thing I Know* with the signature of Anne Smith (Dr. Bob's wife).

[245] L. W. Grensted, *The Person of Christ* (New York: Harper & Brothers, 1933).

and supporter of the Oxford Group. *The Person of Christ* was on the Calvary *Evangel's* Oxford Group literature list. A quick look at the contents of his book shows Grensted dealt with the Jesus of History, the Body of Christ, the Jesus of Experience, the Manhood of Christ, the Godhead, and finally the Person of Christ. Grensted wrote the Foreword to what some call an Oxford Group "handbook." This handbook was *What Is The Oxford Group?*, at least two copies of which were owned and loaned to others by Dr. Bob.[246] Grensted concluded his Foreword with:

> Characteristically individual as this book is, it yet covers so much of the ground of the experience upon which the fellowship of the Group is based, and in a form at once so systematic and so readable, that I believe it may, under God, be used very widely to help others to bring home to them that challenge of the living Christ for which and for which alone the fellowship stands.[247]

Shoemaker's books were laced with references to and teachings about Jesus Christ. Shoemaker's *Confident Faith* had a chapter titled, "What Christ Means To Me." He commenced with John 13:13, "Ye call me Master and Lord: and ye say well; for so I am."[248] In his *The Conversion of the Church*, as well as in other books, Shoemaker spoke frequently of a "vital experience of Jesus Christ."[249] Shoemaker's *Religion That Works* had a chapter titled "The Necessity of Christ."[250] In *Realizing Religion*, Shoemaker wrote: "You need to find God. You need Jesus Christ."[251] In *Christ's Words from the Cross*, Shoemaker reviewed Jesus Christ's "Seven Last Words of Jesus on the Cross," which, Shoemaker believed, found Jesus sharing himself with us, and allowing us to

---

[246] Interview of the author with Sue Smith Windows, Dr. Bob's daughter, in Akron in June, 1991.

[247] *What Is The Oxford Group?*, Foreword by L. W. Grensted.

[248] Shoemaker, *Confident Faith*, p. 35.

[249] Shoemaker, *The Conversion of the Church*, p. 109.

[250] Shoemaker, *Religion That Works*, pp. 21-30.

[251] Shoemaker, *Realizing Religion*, p. 9.

partake of his thoughts and feelings. The seven last words (with Shoemaker's comments about them in our footnotes) were:

Luke 24:34:
Father, forgive them: for they know not what they do.[252]

Luke 23:43:
Verily I say unto thee, Today shalt thou be with me in paradise.[253]

John 19:26, 27:
Woman, behold thy son! . . . Behold thy mother.[254]

Matthew 27:46:
My God, my God, why hast thou forsaken me![255]

John 19:28:
I thirst.[256]

John 19:30:
It is finished.[257]

---

[252] At page 16, Shoemaker said, "Redemption was a part of creation, the most important part. . . . Christ came forth from God to make God known to man and reconcile man with Him—that was God's purpose in Christ. All His life, but more acutely, more intensely, uniquely, in the Cross, Christ poured out His purpose. The core of the Cross was in these words, 'Father, forgive them; for they know not what they do.' From the Cross Christ shared with us the purpose of God in creation."

[253] Shoemaker pointed out that Jesus, even in His own torment on the Cross, could think of His purpose in the restoration of men like the malefactor next to Him to complete relationship with the holy and loving God.

[254] Shoemaker said that then, in his torture on the cross, Jesus shared with his mother and his closest apostle, John, the loving relationship to him that they were then to share with each other.

[255] Shoemaker said Jesus thus opened himself to his human needs in the midst of His agony.

[256] Shoemaker pointed out that Jesus also opened Himself to human help.

[257] What was finished, stated Shoemaker, was the completion of the purpose of revelation and redemption which brought Jesus into the world. Jesus started with

(continued...)

Luke 23:46:
Father, into thy hands I commend my spirit.[258]

In his review of these seven declarations by Jesus, Shoemaker was speaking of forgiveness, unselfish and honest love, sharing, opening up for help, accepting help, following Jesus Christ, and accomplishing this by surrender as Jesus Christ himself did—all exemplified by his last words on the Cross.

In *With the Holy Spirit and with Fire*, Shoemaker spoke of what Jesus Christ actually accomplished and made available to mankind by reason of his crucifixion, death, being raised victorious from the dead, and ascending to heaven. The evidence, Shoemaker said, was in Acts 1 and 2. There Jesus promised baptism with the Holy Spirit and the receipt of "power from on high." And this actually occurred on the day of Pentecost when the Apostles were assembled and waiting as Jesus had instructed.

In 1960, Shoemaker wrote that what we are feeling for, imagining, longing for, and really praying for, is a world-wide awakening under the power of the Holy Spirit.[259] He said he had been much influenced by Dr. Henry Pitney Van Dusen's book, *Spirit, Son and Father*. Shoemaker said the book is based on the conviction that in the faith of the Early Church, the Spirit was a central, perhaps *the* central reality.

Shoemaker said Van Dusen's book helped him to realize afresh that the Holy Spirit alone explains the thing we mean by Christian experience and spiritual power.[260] Shoemaker said:

> The Christian experience of the Holy Spirit, then, holds more than awesome power and cleansing judgment. For the grace shown forth in the Cross restores and renews the life of man

---

[257] (...continued)
"Repent," then urged "Follow Me," then on the Cross indicated that all He had come for was, by the mercy of God, available for man.

[258] At the end, said Shoemaker, Jesus surrendered to God.

[259] Shoemaker, *With The Holy Spirit And With Fire*, p. 10.

[260] Shoemaker, *With The Holy Spirit And With Fire*, pp. 10-11.

through the continuing work of the Spirit . . . as "the Comforter"
. . . "His guidance" . . . the Spirit [that would] "convict the
world of sin" . . . "being used to bring faith in Christ to another
person,"
. . . [and in] the way "He brings unity and fellowship."[261]

Thus far, we have been speaking of Oxford Group ideas about
Jesus Christ as the means of man's gaining God's forgiveness, and
Jesus Christ as the source of the power that regenerates and
renews man. Also about Jesus Christ as the way to guidance by the
Holy Spirit, Jesus Christ as a means of witness, and Jesus Christ
as a central basis for unity and the fellowship of the Holy Spirit
which he made available.

There is another side of the picture—Jesus Christ as the teacher
and as the exemplar of doing God's Will. Henry Drummond's *The
Ideal Life* had a chapter on "How To Know The Will of God."
Drummond quoted Jesus from John 7:16, "My doctrine is not
Mine, but His that sent Me." Also, John 5:30, "My judgment is
just; because I seek not Mine own will, but the will of the Father
Which hath sent me." Finally, John 7:17, "If any man will do His
Will, he shall know of the doctrine, whether it be of God, or
whether I speak of myself."[262]

These latter concepts are particularly important for their
bearing on the A.A.-Oxford Group connection. For the teachings
of Jesus Christ were central in the Four Absolutes, of which we
shall write in a moment. Dr. Robert Speer's *The Principles of
Jesus* contained a chapter titled, "Jesus and the Will of God."
Speer wrote:

The ruling principle in the life of Jesus, both in its prayer and in
its service, was the will of God. Jesus conditioned His prayers on
God's Will: "not My will, but Thine be done."[263] . . . Doing
God's will was his "meat." "My meat is to do the will of Him

---

[261] Shoemaker, *With The Holy Spirit And With Fire*, pp. 29-33.

[262] Drummond, *The Ideal Life*, pp. 303-20.

[263] Luke 22:42.

that sent me, to finish His work."²⁶⁴ . . . Also, portions of John
6:38-40, particularly verse 38: "For I came down from heaven,
not to do Mine own will, but the will of Him that sent me."²⁶⁵

Henry Wright pointed to Jesus's statement in John 8:29, "for I
do always those things that please Him [God]."²⁶⁶ Wright then discussed the "four touchstones" of Jesus's principles as Dr. Speer had
reconstructed them in *The Principles of Jesus*. Wright said Speer's
four touchstones or four standards were the "Four Absolutes" taught
by Jesus and also by the Apostles concerning the will of God.²⁶⁷

What Is The Oxford Group? said this about Jesus and the Absolutes:

> The Oxford Group has four points which are the keys to the kind
> of spiritual life God wishes us to lead. . . . Jesus Christ kept to
> these four points in their fulness. . . . the Oxford Group do know
> that placing these necessary four points for a Christian life as
> absolute ones is placing Christ as the absolute example to which,
> by the help of God, we can aspire (p. 7).

So the foregoing, then, are just short-hand views of the Oxford
Group's total emphasis on Christ as Savior, Way-Shower,
Exemplar of doing, and Teacher of, God's Will. But what has all
that to do with Alcoholics Anonymous?

One can search the text of A.A.'s Big Book in vain for any
affirmative reference to Jesus Christ as Son or God. And our
reader will have to judge for himself—after reviewing the contents
of this book—just how much the literature of the Oxford Group on
Jesus Christ influenced the Big Book and the Steps.²⁶⁸

---

²⁶⁴ John 4:34.

²⁶⁵ Speer, *The Principles of Jesus*, pp. 21-24.

²⁶⁶ Wright, *The Will of God*, p. 169.

²⁶⁷ Wright, *The Will of God*, p. 165-69.

²⁶⁸ As we pointed out in *Dr. Bob's Library*, and in *Anne Smith's Journal*, and will
point out in other books to come, there were many Christian and Biblical sources of
A.A. ideas—and *not* just those derived from the Oxford Group.

Here are a few historical markers:

1. Dr. Bob said Jesus Christ's Sermon on the Mount contained the underlying spiritual philosophy of A.A.[269]

2. The Lord's Prayer—taught by Jesus—has always figured in A.A. literature and survives at the close of most A.A. meetings today.[270]

3. The Four Absolutes—culled from Jesus's teachings, particularly the teachings in the Sermon on the Mount—were much utilized by early AAs. They were practiced by Dr. Bob throughout his life; and they were—according to Bill Wilson—incorporated into Steps Six and Seven. They are still used in many parts of the United States by AAs.[271]

---

[269] *DR. BOB*, p. 228. Dr. Bob's own library contained a number of studies of the Sermon on the Mount. See Dick B., *Dr. Bob's Library*, pp. 38-40. It appears to be a common thought in A.A. that Emmet Fox's *The Sermon on the Mount* was the only book on that topic that was studied in early A.A. And it *was* much read and recommended by Dr. Bob and early AAs. See, Dick B., *Dr. Bob's Library*, pp. 35-36, 38-40; and *DR. BOB*, p. 310; and lengthy discussion in Mel B., *New Wine*, pp. 105-06, 111-14. Many thought and today think that Emmet Fox was affiliated with the Oxford Group. But he was not. In any event, Dr. Bob *himself* stressed reading the portion of the Bible itself that contains the Sermon; and he also read, studied, and loaned to others the following: Oswald Chambers, *Studies in the Sermon on the Mount* (London: Simpkin, Marshall, Ltd., n.d.); E. Stanley Jones, *The Christ of the Mount* (New York: The Abingdon Press, 1931); Glenn Clark, *The Soul's Sincere Desire* (Boston: Little, Brown & Co., 1925); and *I Will Lift Up Mine Eyes* (New York: Harper & Brothers, 1937). These, along with a good many other books that Dr. Bob, his wife, and the early AAs read, contained a great deal of study of Jesus's Sermon. See Dick B., *Dr. Bob's Library*, pp. 25-80; *Anne Smith's Journal*, pp. 79-86; and *The Akron Genesis*, pp. 84-96.

[270] *DR. BOB*, pp. 141, 148, 183; Pittman, *AA The Way It Began*, p. 197; Dick B., *Dr. Bob's Library*, pp. 12, 33-35, 39-40, 56-57, 59, 82, 87; and Mel B., *New Wine*, p. 157. As previously mentioned, "Thy will be done" (from the Lord's Prayer) is still present in the Big Book. See pp. 67, 85, 88.

[271] *DR. BOB*, pp. 54, 163; *Pass It On*, pp. 127, 172; *AA Comes of Age*, pp. 75, 161; *The Language of the Heart*, pp. 196-00; and *Co-Founders*, pp. 12-14. See also *The Four Absolutes* published by Cleveland A.A., 940 Rockefeller Building, 614 Superior Ave., N. W., Cleveland, Ohio 44113. For a discussion of Bill's comments that the Four Absolutes are incorporated in Steps Six and Seven, see Dick B., *Anne Smith's Journal*, pp. 118-19; and Kurtz, *Not-God*, pp. 242-43.

4. Not only was the Oxford Group known as "A First Century Christian Fellowship," but Dr. Bob and other Akron, Ohio members continued to refer to it in that way in the late 1930's and referred to themselves as a "Christian Fellowship."[272]

5. Anne Smith spoke frequently about Jesus Christ in her writings and Bible readings to the alcoholics with whom she and Dr. Bob worked.[273]

6. While Bill Wilson was careful to eliminate Oxford Group language about Jesus Christ from the Big Book, Bill's own language in early drafts of the Big Book shows how much Jesus Christ probably figured in pre-Big Book thinking. Bill's manuscripts spoke of being "born again," the "living God," and used other distinctly Christian words.[274]

The one reference to Jesus Christ in the Big Book text simply contains Bill Wilson's musings that he conceded to Christ the certainty of a great man, not too closely followed by those who claimed him.[275] Of all this, Dr. Ernest Kurtz observed:

Yet A.A.'s total omission of "Jesus," its toning down of even "God" to a "Higher Power" which could be the group itself, and

---

[272] We covered this point before. Here, for the reader's convenience, we suggest reference to *DR. BOB*, pp. 53-54; *Pass It On*, p. 130; our interview with Sue Windows in Akron, June 1991; and the Memo from Bob E. to Lois Wilson.

[273] See Dick B., *Anne Smith's Journal*. Anne not only recommended reading a number of books on the life of Jesus Christ, but spoke of Christ as the regenerating power that changes men. She quoted a number of Bible verses about Jesus Christ. Like the Oxford Group, she spoke of a maximum experience of Jesus Christ. Anne's references to Christ are so numerous we simply refer to the entire *Journal*.

[274] The author personally inspected draft manuscripts of the Big Book at Bill's home in Stepping Stones during the author's research visit there in October, 1991. In one manuscript, Bill said of his religious experience that he had been "born again." In another, he spoke of the "living God." As we have shown, both of these expressions were fundamental and common Bible, Christian, Oxford Group, and Shoemaker phrases. In *Lois Remembers*, Bill's wife spoke of her "joy and faith in his [Bill's] rebirth" (p. 98).

[275] Big Book, p. 11.

its changing of the "verbal" first message into hopeless helplessness rather than salvation: these ideas and practices, adopted to avoid any "religious" association, were profound changes. Since these ideas and practices were consciously embraced to deny any Oxford Group implication. . . .[276]

If Jesus Christ had actually been omitted from A.A., we might not need to discuss him at all. However, the Big Book is filled with ideas related to Jesus Christ. These include Big Book quotes from: (1) the Lord's Prayer.[277] (2) the Sermon on the Mount.[278] (3) Biblical words such as "God," "Spirit," "Power," and "Faith"—with the use of capital letters. There are quotes, without attribution, from the Book of James in the New Testament.[279] And there are other words—considering Dr. Bob's emphasis on the Sermon on the Mount and 1 Corinthians 13—that derive from the Christian writings in the Bible—words such as patience, tolerance, kindness, love, forgiveness.[280]

Spiritual Growth—Continuance

16. *Conservation—Continuance As an Idea*

The changed, surrendered, converted person must maintain and grow in his life of grace through prayer, Bible study, waiting upon God for guidance, public worship, and witness.

---

[276] Kurtz, *Not-God*, p. 50.

[277] "Thy will be done." See Matthew 6:10; Big Book, pp. 67, 88.

[278] "Love thy neighbor as thyself." See Matthew 5:43; compare James 2:8; and examine Big Book, p. 153.

[279] "Faith without works is dead" (James 2:20, 26). See Big Book, pp. 14, 88. "Father of Light." See Big Book, p. 14; compare James 1:17—"Father of lights."

[280] Patience [James 1:4; Big Book, p. 83]; Tolerance [1 Corinthians 13:4; Big Book, pp. 83, 127]; Kindness [1 Corinthians 13:4; Big Book, 83]; Love [1 Corinthians 13; Big Book, pp. 83, 127]; Forgiveness [Matthew 6:14; Big Book, p. 77].

The Oxford Group indicated a person's life-change was not complete with that person's *conversion*. The Group called for daily *growth* in the life of grace. They were speaking of the fifth of their 5 C's. Sometimes they called this "Conservation" and sometimes "Continuance."[281] We will not go into much detail here on the various aspects of "Conservation" since the individual topics it comprehends are separately discussed in our ensuing concepts.

Shoemaker made the following comments which explain the essence of Conservation:

> Conversion is the beginning, not the ending of an experience of God. That experience continues when we use all the means Jesus put at our disposal for continuation—prayer, the Scriptures, the Church and Sacraments, Christian fellowship and worship. . . . Many situations in my life are not covered by the Sermon on the Mount. I need special guidance and illumination. . . . What infinite possibilities of learning the will of God, through communion with Him, may lie ahead of us, who can dare to imagine?[282]

> [Man needs] to live this life of grace. Too much stress cannot be laid on private prayer and Bible study, and public uniting with the Church. And there is no more empowering habit in the lives of those who seek to live the Christ-life than this "fishing for men," as Jesus called it.[283]

Reconstructing Conservation from the various Oxford Group writings, there were five aspects: (1) Prayer,[284] (2) Bible

---

[281] See Walter, *Soul Surgery*, pp. 89-100; Shoemaker, *Realizing Religion*, p. 80; Begbie, *Life Changers*, p. 169-70; Lean, *On the Tail of a Comet*, p. 79; DR. BOB, p. 54; and Dick B., *Anne Smith's Journal*, pp. 102-06.

[282] Shoemaker, *Religion That Works*, p. 14, 15.

[283] Shoemaker, *Realizing Religion*, p. 82. See Matthew 4:19.

[284] Walter, *Soul Surgery*, p. 91, "First of all, then, we must guide the convert into a real and continuous and developing prayer life;" and p. 90, "Hence the importance of prayer as a daily exercise and a life-long study. In prayer we breath the tonic air of faith

(continued...)

study,[285] (3) Guidance,[286] (4) Group worship,[287] and (5) Witness.[288] Cecil Rose wrote, "Surrender goes on. It is not simply an initial act. It is a process carried deeper every day. We find out more of ourselves to give to God."[289]

Shoemaker wrote:

> We believe entirely that conversion is the experience which initiates the new life. But we are not fools enough to think that the beginning is the end. All subsequent life is a development of the relationship with God which conversion opened. For us its daily focal point is in what we call the "Quiet Time." As in all

---

[284] (...continued)
that defies every temptation to doubt and fear. In prayer our souls become assured that while *we* may fail God, He never fails us."

[285] Walter, *Soul Surgery*, p. 91, "In the second place, the new convert must learn to feed his soul, day by day, on God's living Word revealed in the Scriptures; and here, too, he cannot be left to himself, but needs and will usually welcome friendly guidance."

[286] Benson, *The Eight Points*, pp. 74-75, "Diving guidance must become the normal experience of ordinary men and women, says Dr. Buchman. Any man can pick up divine messages if he will put his receiving set in order. Definite, accurate, adequate information can come from the Mind of God to the mind of men . . . The crux of the Oxford Group Movement is its insistence upon the possibility and necessity of the guided life . . . No one can read the Bible without being impressed by the constant references to Divine Guidance." Compare Dick B., *Anne Smith's Journal*, p. 114; and Dick B., *New Light on Alcoholism*, pp. 337-38 (for Lois Wilson's own notes on Guidance).

[287] This was the particular stress of Dr. Shoemaker. See *Realizing Religion*, p. 82. As to a possible effect of Shoemaker's emphasis on "uniting with the church," Dr. Bob's daughter, Sue Smith Windows, informed the author that Dr. Bob and his wife, Anne, joined a Presbyterian Church in Akron because of Oxford Group stress on church affiliation [Personal interview with the author by Sue Windows in Akron, Ohio, June, 1991]. Later, Dr. Bob became a communicant at St. Paul's Episcopal Church in Akron, Ohio. See Dick B., *New Light on Alcoholism*, p. 20-21; and *Dr. Bob's Library*, pp. 2-3.

[288] Walter, *Soul Surgery*, p. 92, "In the third place—and here most of all we are prone to fail in this work of individual conservation—following conversion the new convert must be set to work to win others." Shoemaker and Buchman often spoke of the necessity of "giving it away to keep it." In *Realizing Religion*, Shoemaker referred to the account in Acts 3:6, "Such as I have give I thee," and Paul's statement in 1 Thessalonians 2:8, that we should give "not the gospel of God only, but also our own souls" (pp. 82-83). Shoemaker called this "fishing for men." See also, Lean, *Cast Out Your Nets*, p. 97.

[289] Rose, *When Man Listens*, p. 21.

other private devotions, we pray and read the Bible. But the distinguishing element of a Quiet Time is listening for the guidance of God. "Speak Lord, for Thy servant heareth," is the expectant mood of a Quiet Time. The validity of what we believe to be God's guidance must show itself, in the long run, by more acute moral perception, more genuine human relationships, and increasing assurance of what one ought to do every hour of the day.[290]

We talked of the daily Quiet Time, of Bible study, prayer and listening, and of the power of God to lead and guide those who are obedient enough to be led. We also talked of the need for early sharing of the experience through which he had passed and bringing others to the same place.[291]

Compare these two statements in A.A.'s Big Book:

1. The spiritual life is not a theory. We have to live it (p. 83).

2. Every day is a day when we must carry the vision of God's will into all our activities (p. 85).

17. *Daily surrender as a process*

"General" surrender to God must be accompanied by daily self-examination and surrender to get rid of newly accumulated sin and selfishness.

What Is The Oxford Group? said:

Our initial Surrender to God does not mean that henceforth we shall be asleep to the world around us; that temptations will never assail nor sins conquer us again, and that, if they do, God is not living up to His part of the compact. . . . It means that after

---

[290] Shoemaker, *Children of the Second Birth*, p. 16. See 1 Samuel 3:9.

[291] Shoemaker, *Children of the Second Birth*, pp. 148-149.

Surrender we have to work and eat and sleep and laugh and play as before, and that in the round of daily life come situations which cause reactions against our spiritual good resolutions. . . . Sin remains sin, but even if we only surrendered to God yesterday our sin of to-day does not cancel that surrender. God knows and waits. He waits to see if we will Surrender that sin of to-day to Him with as much sincerity as we surrendered our lives yesterday; to see if we will acknowledge it was lack of trust that made us fail to ask Him to take that sin away from us while it was still temptation; to see if we will confess that it was want of faith in His Guidance that made us vulnerable to spiritual weakness. . . . Our lives will be one continuous surrender: surrender to God of every difficulty that confronts us, each temptation, each spiritual struggle; laying before Him either to take away or to show to us in their proper spiritual proportions (pp. 45-46).

The Eight Points of the Oxford Group had a chapter on "Daily Checking," which said:

"Shine out O Light divine and show how far we stray." That is the prayer of a man who is not satisfied to go on living a haphazard, unverified life. When we speak of self-examination, it suggests tests. It implies the selection of standards of judgment by which we measure ourselves. . . . The saints are not people who are better than the rest, but those who are trying to be better than they are. The Group takes the four absolute standards of the life of Christ—Absolute Love, Absolute Purity, Absolute Honesty and Absolute Unselfishness. These are applied as daily tests of life in all its issues. This practice of regular self-examination in the light of Christ has proved to be of genuine practical value in our Christian development.[292]

When I came to make a daily surrender I learned what a different experience this is from a general surrender. Daily checking on the four absolutes revealed to me things I had never questioned in myself. . . . The Quiet Time was no new method of prayer to

---

[292] Benson, *The Eight Points*, pp. 44-45.

me but it became increasingly searching. I came to a daily willingness to do anything for God. I made amends where He gave me light.[293]

Shoemaker had these things to say:

The daily and hourly renewal of the crucifixion of our selves, and the implantation of the will of God where our wills used to be, comes by seeking the mind of God through listening. . . . How many of us are grown up enough to remember that the important thing in prayer is not to change the will and mind of God, but to find them.[294]

There is need for rededication day by day, hour by hour, by which progressively, in every Quiet Time, the contaminations of sin and self-will are further sloughed off (for they do have a way of collecting) and we are kept in fresh touch with the living Spirit of God. A further surrender is needed when and whenever there is found to be something in us which offends Christ, or walls us from another. We shall need, in this sense, to keep surrendering so long as we live. . . . I believe that with a God of love, there is no limit to the number of times we may come back to Him in surrender, provided only we mean it and are penitent for the past.[295]

The progress of the Christian life . . . consists of development and motion, with the direction of a clear path that is punctuated by critical periods or decisions, upon the conquest of which depends all the rest of the course. . . . And first we must say that the initial hurdle is deciding to run the Christian course at all. . . . The next hurdle for most of us arises when we begin to face ourselves honestly. . . . Next there comes a hurdle familiar . . . to us all as an experience, the hurdle of surrender to God. . . . For most people there is wrapped up in the decision to surrender

---

[293] Benson, *The Eight Points*, p. 149.
[294] Shoemaker, *The Church Can Save The World*, pp. 96-97.
[295] Shoemaker, *The Conversion of the Church*, p. 79.

to God the necessity to right all wrongs with men. . . . This is the hurdle of restitution. . . . Again: we all move forward in our Christian course by the help of other Christians. . . . [There] is a decision to keep on just when the full force of the meaning of a decision for Christ sweeps over us, and scares us with its bigness. . . . And then . . . the hurdles of fresh, vivid battle with returning, characteristic temptation.[296]

Compare these portions from A.A.'s Big Book:

Continue to watch for selfishness, dishonesty, resentment, and fear. When these crop up, we ask God at once to remove them. . . . When we retire at night, we constructively review our day. Were we resentful, selfish, dishonest or afraid? . . . After making our review we ask God's forgiveness and inquire what corrective measures should be taken. . . . As we go through the day. . . . We constantly remind ourselves we are no longer running the show, humbly saying to ourselves many times each day "Thy Will be done." . . . So we let God discipline us in the simple way we have just outlined (pp. 84-88).

18.   *Guidance—The Walk by Faith*

The Holy Spirit gives Divine Guidance to a life that is changed from sin to God. It takes normal intelligence and guides it to the fullest harmony with God's Will, both for the good of the individual and for that of his neighbor.

Frank Buchman said:

Leaders everywhere now say that the world needs a moral and spiritual awakening. . . . The problem is how. . . . Now I find when we don't know how, God will show us if we are willing. When man listens, God speaks. When man obeys, God acts. We are not out to tell God. We are out to let God tell us. And He

---

[296] Shoemaker, *The Gospel According To You*, pp. 81-91.

will tell us. The lesson the world most needs is the art of listening to God. . . . It is thoughts from God which have inspired the prophets through history.[297]

God spoke to the prophets of old. He may speak to you.[298]

By a miracle of the Spirit, God can speak to every man.[299]

Direct messages from the Mind of God to the mind of man—definite, direct, decisive. God speaks.[300]

Oxford Group writers often mentioned the God who speaks. And they couched their discussion in Biblical terms. Theologian B. H. Streeter's wrote an entire book titled, *The God Who Speaks*. Oxford Group author, Cecil Rose wrote:

> *God speaks*. That is the tremendous fact around which both the Old and New Testament are built—not that man can and may speak to God, but that God can and does speak to man. . . . We can only hope to live a life fully effective, and possessing a real sense of security and peace, if this truth that "God speaks" can be tested and found true by us. . . . *God has a plan. God speaks*. But if He is to be heard and His plan is to be known and carried out, *man must listen*. . . . The promise that our petitions will be answered is only to those who have first placed themselves in line with His Will. If God is to become for us the living, active God, at work directing our life and the world's, it is vital that we should learn how to listen. There is one condition to be fulfilled before we begin. We must be willing to hear anything God says to us.[301]

---

[297] Buchman, *Remaking The World*, p. 35-36.

[298] Buchman, *Remaking The World*, p. 41.

[299] Buchman, *Remaking The World*, p. 42.

[300] Buchman, *Remaking The World*, p. 72. Compare Lois Wilson's comments in her Oxford Group notes which echo Buchman's comments, almost verbatim. Dick B., *New Light on Alcoholism*, p. 337. For similar remarks by Anne Smith, see Dick B., *Anne Smith's Journal*, pp. 57-62.

[301] Cecil Rose, *When Man Listens*, pp. 27, 30-31.

Eleanor Napier Forde cited Romans 8:26, explaining, "It is God's Spirit Who must pray through us, bringing to our minds the people and the needs for which to intercede." Miss Forde wrote of a little girl, saying "God could talk to her." And Forde suggested tests as to possible Divine origin of thoughts, including "intuitive conviction."[302]

Oxford Group people frequently wrote about the Biblical authority for their guidance concept. They said, for example:

To Sam Shoemaker in 1920, Buchman wrote a seven-page foolscap letter, citing a formidable array of Biblical and theological authority for the practice [listening to God—listening for Guidance—receiving "luminous thoughts" from God].[303]

No one can read the Bible without being impressed by the constant references to Divine Guidance. Abraham was guided. . . . We find the same sense of guidance in Isaac, Jacob, Joseph, Moses . . . the life of David or of any of the other Old Testament heroes. . . . So also with the prophets. There are numerous passages in the Psalms. . . . We find the same evidence in the New Testament.[304]

In the New Testament a full relationship to God is described by saying that "we receive the Holy Spirit." If that phrase is vague to us, it is not vague to the writers of the New Testament. To those first Christians that gift clearly meant, not only the purifying and strengthening power of God within them, but His directing voice as well. He is the One who dictates their decisions

---

[302] Eleanor Napier Forde, *The Guidance of God* (The Oxford Group, Printed at the University Press at Oxford by John Johnson, n.d.), pp. 25, 21.

[303] Lean, *On the Tail of a Comet*, p. 75. In a footnote, Lean added, "The thoughts which arose in such times of seeking God's guidance in later years became known in the verbal shorthand of Buchman and his friends, as 'guidance,' although neither he nor they considered that all such thoughts came from God."

[304] Benson, *The Eight Points*, p. 75. See, for illustrations of Benson's points: Genesis 17; 26:2-6; 28; 35; Exodus 6; 2 Samuel 6; Psalm 105; Isaiah 7; Jeremiah 34; Ezekiel 38; Hosea 1; Malachi 3; Acts 7; 8:26; 10:4-43. See further discussion of Biblical illustrations by Almond, *Foundations For Faith*, p. 22.

in council. As their Master promised, they are given the words to say when called on to witness. Peter on the roof-top is told to go down and follow the messengers of Cornelius.[305] Philip to "get up and go south along the road from Jerusalem to Gaza;"[306] and Paul is directed not to enter Bithynia.[307] Here is a picture of men and women moving obediently under the effective guidance of God. Is God less able to guide us today?[308]

Revelation: This is the keystone in the Buchman theological arch. As far as he personally was concerned, revelation was probably in second place behind the redemption at the Cross of Christ. In later years the latter faded as an up-front public concern. The guidance of God, however, was top coinage to the end. . . . A recent book about Tournier carries this explanation that might have come out of Buchman himself: "God has a unique, detailed purpose for every man. He has prepared for this by giving specific gifts or temperaments, and it is our duty to discover as best we can what God desires for every moment of our lives. The Bible gives broad outlines of this purpose, but God also speaks through the advice of friends, circumstances of life, or the ideas that come to mind during periods of meditation."[309]

For precise Bible references to revelation, see:

1. Galatians 1:12:
    For I [the Apostle Paul] neither received it [my gospel] of man, neither was I taught it, but by the revelation of Jesus Christ.

2. 2 Timothy 3:16:
    All scripture is given by inspiration of God. . . .

---

[305] Acts 10:1-21.

[306] Acts 8:26-30.

[307] Acts 16:6-9.

[308] Rose, *When Man Listens*, p. 28.

[309] Hunter, *World Changing Through Life Changing*, pp. 135, 139.

3. 1 Corinthians 12:8:
   For to one is given by the Spirit the word of wisdom; to another the word of knowledge by the same Spirit.

4. 2 Peter 1:21:
   For the prophecy came not in old time by the will of man; but holy men of God spake as they were moved by the Holy Ghost.

5. John 14:26:
   The Comforter, which is the Holy Ghost, whom the Father will send in my name, he shall teach you all things.[310]

When Frank Buchman used words such as "God speaks," "inspiration," and "revelation," those words rested on specific Bible verses, cited by the Oxford Group, which support the idea that God can and does guide. Here are some:

Psalm 32:8:
I will instruct thee and teach thee in the way which thou shalt go. I will guide thee with mine eye.[311]

Psalm 37:5:
Commit thy way unto the Lord; Trust also in him; and he shall bring it to pass.[312]

Proverbs 3:6:
In all thy ways acknowledge him, and he shall direct thy paths.[313]

---

[310] For discussion of "inspiration" and "revelation" as used in the Bible, see *The Abingdon Bible Commentary*, pp. 26-31; and Almond, *Foundations For Faith*, p. 13.

[311] Drummond, *The Ideal Life*, p. 282; Wright, *The Will of God*, pp. 19, 131; Streeter, *The God Who Speaks*, p. 141; and Benson, *The Eight Points*, p. 80.

[312] Benson, *The Eight Points*, p. 81; Shoemaker, *The Experiment of Faith*, pp. 28-29; and *How You Can Find Happiness*, p. 149.

[313] Brown, *The Venture of Belief*, p. 40; Streeter, *The God Who Speaks*, p. 191; and Benson, *The Eight Points*, p. 81. See full citations in Dick B., *Dr. Bob's Library*, pp. 96-97.

Romans 8:14:
For as many as are led by the Spirit of God, they are the sons of God.[314]

1 Corinthians 2:9:
But as it is written, Eye hath not seen, nor ear heard, neither have entered into the heart of man, the things which God hath prepared for them that love Him.[315]

2 Corinthians 5:7:
For we walk by faith, not by sight.[316]

James 3:17:
But the wisdom that is from above is first pure, then peaceable, gentle, and easy to be intreated.[317]

What Is The Oxford Group? said of Guidance:

1. One of the Oxford Group's "four practical spiritual activities" is "Listening to, accepting, relying on God's Guidance and carrying it out in everything we do or say, great or small" (pp. 8-9).

2. Divine guidance to a life changed from Sin to God is the Holy Spirit taking a normal intelligence and directing it in the fullest harmony with His will for the good of the individual and his neighbors (p. 67).

3. Suggestions as to conduct, solutions to material and spiritual difficulties are given by daily guidance. It is God using for our best, in partnership with us, the lives we have surrendered to His care (p. 67).

---

[314] *What Is The Oxford Group?*, p. 66; and Winslow, *Why I Believe In The Oxford Group*, p. 39.

[315] *What Is The Oxford Group?*, p. 66; and Lean, *Cast Out Your Nets*, p. 30. See Dick B., *The Akron Genesis*, p. 101.

[316] *What Is The Oxford Group?*, p. 67.

[317] Wright, *The Will of God*, p. 167.

4. "Every good gift and every perfect boon is from above."[318] Life under guidance . . . is all-wise and all-embracing, building up our right God-appointed kind of ego (p. 67).

5. Divine guidance takes us away from that fear of tomorrow. . . . Not only is our to-day in God's keeping but our to-morrow; we have surrendered that to Him, too, so why fear whatever we think tomorrow must bring us as a logical sequence of to-day's events (pp. 67-68).

Benson's *The Eight Points of the Oxford Group* said:

God has a plan for every life. He will make known to us His plan day by day if we give Him a chance.[319]

God cannot do very much for us so long as we insist on playing the part of Providence to ourselves. Things begin to happen when we "let go" and "let God." . . . wait again in passive silence. . . . It is surprising how, while apparently thinking our own thoughts, difficulties are cleared away, problems solved, how doubt and uncertainty, trouble and despondence and mental disquiet give place to a sense of peace and joy. . . . There is scarcely a page of the Scriptures which does not witness to the fact of guidance. The plain promise of the Bible is that in all perplexities and anxieties we may expect illumination and direction. . . . God has a plan for every life and He will reveal it to us day by day when we fulfill the conditions. . . . So the Group insists upon absolute surrender to God—our selves, our sins, our will, time, possessions, ambitions, everything. He will guide us into His Will for us.[320]

---

[318] See James 1:17, "Every good gift and every perfect gift is from above and cometh down from the Father of lights, with Whom is no variableness, neither shadow of turning." See Big Book, p. 14, "I must turn in all things to the Father of Light who presides over us all."

[319] Benson, *The Eight Points*, pp. 65.

[320] Benson, *The Eight Points*, pp. 68, 69, 70, 76, 78.

Shoemaker had these things to say:

We are quite clear in our theology of the Holy Spirit. But we
have forgotten that the ordinary man lays hold of God through
experience, and not through definition. . . . For the Holy Spirit
sounds very vague until we know that He brings with Him
definite light. . . . God speaks in six great ways: (1) In nature
and creation; (2) In the moral law; (3) In the Scriptures; (4) In
Jesus Christ; (5) In human conscience; and (6) In history. . . .
We cannot carry on a conversation with God through nature or
moral law. We find God's general will in the Scriptures. We find
God still more directly in Jesus Christ. But human conscience is
no perfect reflector of God, and history only points to His
existence and His general will. We want to know that God can
and does speak directly to the human heart. The reason why
some of us believe in guidance, at least in theory, is that the Old
and New Testaments are full of instances of it, as specific as you
please. Men said clearly that they were guided of God in this and
that act and decision. . . . I prefer to see whether this sort of
thing is not now possible to those who put their trust in God
entirely.[321]

You can be in touch with God. We need to come to Him with a
child's openness and simplicity. God always meets such an
approach more than halfway, and takes the initiative with an open
life. We need the help of others for whom being in touch with
God is more familiar than it is for us. We need the constant
recreation of the atmosphere of "Speak, Lord, for thy servant
heareth,"[322] instead of the usual approach to God which is
"Hear Lord, for thy servant speaketh." And we need to know
that guidance is not for our private comfort or even illumination,
but that by it God means to touch some actual human situation
that needs to be touched and cured.[323]

---

[321] Shoemaker, *The Conversion of the Church*, pp. 49-50.

[322] See 1 Samuel 3:9. Shoemaker frequently cited this verse. See Dick B., *New Light on Alcoholism*, pp. 44, 103, 202, 205, 228, 270, 316.

[323] Shoemaker, *National Awakening*, p. 86.

Let it be said often, that there is no short-cut to truth which we are supposed to dig out with our minds: it is God's crystallization of truth from the facts we have and also from some facts which we cannot possibly know, but can only guess by what humanly we call a "flash of intuition." The guidance of religion is "intuition" *plus* [emphasis added]. It is not a substitute for, but a tremendous supplement to, the common processes of thought. The sustenance of the new spiritual life lies in the material which is in the Bible which is everlasting and universal; and then in God's direct messages to us, which are temporal and personal; but sometimes have widespread effects. Let man cultivate that time alone with the living God, day by day.[324]

Another most important experience of the Holy Spirit is His guidance. Dr. Van Dusen says, "If there be a Living God at all, He must desire to make His Will and purposes known to men; and a silent, receptive, expectant consciousness furnishes Him the most favorable condition for the disclosure of His thoughts to the minds of men." He goes on to say that his own "experience has been that, when I take up an attitude of openminded and responsible expectancy, thoughts and ideas and directives often came which subsequent empirical testing validated as the closest approximation to trustworthy divine guidance which is available to us." He also calls the Holy Spirit "the donor of direct and immediate instruction from God, and that leading is toward the new, the unexpected, the mandatory. . . . The Holy Spirit is the never exhausted discloser of 'new truth.'"[325] While it is not always easy to know what God is saying to us, and sometimes very easy to be dogmatic where we feel sure of our own guidance, we may be sure that the calls to the saints to take up God's work through the centuries have been received mostly through the guidance of the Holy Spirit. We who ought to be true saints but do not always manage to live in this way are yet often the

---

[324] Shoemaker, *Twice-Born Ministers*, pp. 184-85. As to the "intuitive thought" and A.A., see Big Book, p. 84 ("We will intuitively know how to handle situations which used to baffle us"); p. 86 ("Here we ask God for inspiration, an intuitive thought or decision").

[325] See John 16:13.

recipients of God's direction whenever we honestly seek it, and pray in the words of the old prayer that He may 'in all things direct and rule in our hearts.' The difficult thing about guidance is not the receiving or recognizing of it: it is the truly wanting it, so that we come to God stripped, honest, without pretense. . . . Abraham Lincoln once said, "I am satisfied that, when the Almighty wants me to do, or not to do, a particular thing He finds a way of letting me know it." I think that unless we believe that God has a will, wants to reveal it to us (subject always to our own free will), and can do so in spite of our sins, we do not believe much in much of a God. And we are not in business with Him until we are seeking His will in all matters, great and small. There is such a thing, as we shall later see, as living in the stream of the Spirit. Increasingly we can all live that way if we are determined to do so. The people I know who experience the true adventure of faith are continually seeking and finding meanings, connections, coincidence, and "signs" in events which others do not see. Carried to certain extremes this can appear like romancing with the Eternal; but true faith always seeks and sees the Hand of God in all events.[326]

There are many statements in A.A.'s Big Book which exemplify its stress on receiving guidance and direction from God. The following are two:

For we are now on a different basis; the basis of trusting and relying upon God. . . . We are in the world to play the role He assigns. Just to the extent that we do as we think he would have us, and humbly rely on Him, does He enable us to match calamity with serenity (p. 68).

We ask that we be given strength and direction to do the right thing (p. 79).[327]

---

[326] Shoemaker, *With The Holy Spirit And With Fire*, pp. 30-31.

[327] Compare Rose, *When Man Listens*, pp. 38, 19; and see just a few of the endless examples in the Big Book of the Oxford Group-Shoemaker Guidance concepts and language at pp. 14, 49, 50, 57, 68, 69, 70, 79, 83, 85, 86, 87, 98, 100.

19. *The Four Absolutes—Christ's Standards*

Absolute Honesty, Absolute Purity, Absolute Unselfishness, and Absolute Love are the essence of Jesus's teachings about the Will of God, the ideals for man's life, and the moral standards by which man's thoughts and actions may be tested for harmony with God's will.

As previously shown, the Oxford Group's Four Absolutes can be found in Frank Buchman's speeches;[328] in books about Buchman;[329] in descriptions of Oxford Group principles;[330] in Sam Shoemaker's writings;[331] in A.A. conference-approved books discussing the Oxford Group;[332] in Anne Smith's writings;[333] and in some A.A. Groups today.[334]

Almost every Oxford Group writer, including the Reverend Samuel M. Shoemaker, Jr., accepted the fact that the "Four

---

[328] Buchman, *Remaking The World*, pp. 36, 40, 96, 131.

[329] Russell, *For Sinners Only*, pp. 319-29; Howard, *Frank Buchman's Secret*, p. 29; Lean, *On the Tail of a Comet*, pp. 76-77; Spoerri, *Dynamic out of Silence*, p. 39; and Frank H. Sherry and Mahlon H. Hellerich, *The Formative Years of Frank N. D. Buchman* (Portion of book located at Frank Buchman's home at Allentown, Pennsylvania, and provided to the author by A.A. Oldtimer, Earl H.), pp. 237, 251.

[330] *What Is The Oxford Group?*, pp. 7-8; 73-118; Almond, *Foundations for Faith*, pp. 11-13; Benson, *The Eight Points*, pp. 44-57; Winslow, *Why I Believe in the Oxford Group*, pp. 24-32; Foot, *Life Began Yesterday*, p. 57; Kitchen, *I Was a Pagan*, p. 130; Hofmeyr, *How to Change*, p. 1; Viney, *How Do I Begin?*, pp. 2,3; and Howard Rose, *The Quiet Time*.

[331] Samuel M. Shoemaker, *Twice-Born Ministers*, p. 150; *The Church Can Save the World*, p. 110; *How to Become a Christian*, p. 57; *How You Can Help Other People* (New York: E. P. Dutton, 1946), p. 59; and see Helen Shoemaker, *I Stand by the Door*, pp. 24-26; and Dick B., *New Light on Alcoholism*, pp. 41, 67, 73, 130-31, 209, 211, 270-72, 315.

[332] *DR. BOB*, pp. 54, 163; *Pass It On*, pp. 114, 172; *AA Comes of Age*, pp. 68, 75, 161; *The Language of the Heart*, pp. 196-200; and *Co-Founders*, pp. 13-14.

[333] Dick B., *Anne Smith's Journal*, pp. 31-34, 59, 59-60, 64, 72, 75, 87-88, 98, 104-06, 108, 115, 116-20, 143.

[334] Mel B., *New Wine*, pp. 76, 138; and refer to the pamphlet, titled "Four Absolutes," which is available at A.A.'s Intergroup office in Akron, Ohio.

Absolutes," or "Four Standards," as they were also called, emerged directly from the research by Dr. Robert E. Speer into the heart of Jesus's teachings.[335] Speer set out to prove that Jesus taught some absolute moral standards, and he said that Jesus was the teacher of *absolute* principles.[336] Perfection was Jesus's standard.[337]

Speer provided the following Biblical documentation for the four absolute standards Jesus set up:

1. **Honesty**:

> John 8:44: "When he [the devil] speaketh a lie, he speaketh of his own: for he is a liar and the father of it."[338]

2. **Purity**:

> Matthew 5:29-30: "And if thy right eye offend thee, pluck it out, and cast it from thee: for it is profitable for thee that one of thy members should perish, and not that thy whole body should be cast into hell. And if thy right hand offend thee, cut it off, and cast it from thee , for it is profitable for thee that one of thy members should perish, and not that thy whole body should be cast into hell." [339]

---

[335] Lean, *On the Tail of a Comet*, p. 76; Spoerri, *Dynamic out of Silence*, p. 49; Samuel M. Shoemaker, *How You Can Help Other People*, p. 59; and Helen Smith Shoemaker, *I Stand By The Door*, p. 24.

[336] Speer, *The Principles of Jesus*, pp. 33-34.

[337] Speer, *The Principles of Jesus*, p. 34, citing Matthew 5:48.

[338] Speer, *The Principles of Jesus*, at page 35, said that Jesus set up an absolute standard of truth. If Satan is the father of lies, how can any lie be justifiable? Jesus did not make truthfulness depend upon its profitableness or its loss. Men must be true and speak the truth regardless of consequences.

[339] Speer, *The Principles of Jesus*, at page 35, said that Jesus set up an absolute standard of purity. He tolerated no uncleanness whatsoever. The inner chambers of imagery and desire must be pure, citing Mark 7:15 ["There is nothing from without a man, that entering into him can defile him: but the things which come out of him, those are they that defile the man"]. A hand or an eye, outer or inner sin, must be sacrificed to the claims of the kingdom of heaven, citing Matthew 5:29, 30.

3. **Unselfishness**:

Luke 14:33: "So likewise, whosoever he be of you that forsaketh not all that he hath, he cannot be my disciple."[340]

4. **Love**:

John 13:34: "A new commandment I give unto you, That ye love one another; as I have loved you, that ye also love one another."[341]

The absolute nature of these four standards is apparent from the severity of the command Jesus gave. Lies are the province of Jesus's arch foe—the devil, "the thief" who steals, kills and destroys (John 10:10). Purity was of such nature that even a significant unclean part must be "plucked out" to keep the whole pure. Giving meant giving "all." Love was a commandment to love as Jesus loved—giving up his life for love.

Henry Wright analyzed Speer's "absolute standards" and documented them with Scriptural references from the Gospels *and* the Epistles.[342] Wright first approached the standards in terms of the standards Jesus set. And we covered these above—just as Speer, their author, laid them out.

Second, Wright looked at Jesus's teachings about life lived by the absolute standards. And these are verses Wright examined:

---

[340] Speer, *The Principles of Jesus*, at page 35, said Jesus set up an absolute standard of unselfishness. Speer pointed to Mark 10:45 and Luke 22:27 to show unselfishness was his own spirit—Jesus came to minister and give his life a ransom for many. He was among his apostles to serve. In Matthew 19:29, Jesus called those who forsook houses, family, or lands for his name's sake the recipients of an hundredfold, and the inheritors of everlasting life.

[341] Speer, *The Principles of Jesus* said at page 35, Jesus set up an absolute standard of love, (citing) John 13:34. Neither dirt (Luke 16:20), nor poverty (Luke 14:13), nor social inferiority (Luke 7:39), were annulments of the law of love. He himself loved to the limit (John 13:1), and with no abatements.

[342] Wright, *The Will of God*, pp. 167-218.

1. **Honesty**:

   Luke 16:10-11: "He that is faithful in that which is least is faithful also in much; and he that is unjust in the least is unjust also in much. If therefore ye have not been faithful in the unrighteous mammon, who will commit to your trust the true riches?"[343]

2. **Purity**:

   Matthew 5:8: "Blessed are the pure in heart: for they shall see God."[344]

3. **Unselfishness**:

   Luke 9:23-24: If any man will come after me, let him deny himself, and take up his cross daily, and follow me. For whosoever will save his life shall lose it; but whosoever will lose his life for my sake, the same shall save it."[345]

4. **Love**:

   Matthew 25:41-43,45: "Depart from me, ye cursed, into the everlasting fire, prepared for the devil and his angels; for I was an hungred and ye gave me no meat; I was thirsty, and ye gave me no drink. I was a stranger, and ye took me not in; naked, and ye clothed me not; sick and in prison and ye visited me not. . . . Inasmuch as ye did it not unto one of the least of these, ye did it not to me."[346]

Finally, Wright found all four of the absolutes in the following verses:

---

[343] Wright, *The Will of God*, p. 187.

[344] Wright, *The Will of God*, p. 179. This verse from the Sermon on the Mount was often quoted in the Oxford Group and much influenced Buchman as to the need for eliminating sin from life. See Russell, *For Sinners Only*, p. 63.

[345] Wright, *The Will of God*, p. 197. See Almond, *Foundations For Faith*, p. 12.

[346] Wright, *The Will of God*, p. 207.

Mark 10:19-21:
Thou knowest the commandments, Do not commit adultery. Do not kill. Do not steal. Do not bear false witness. Defraud not. Honor thy father and mother. And he answered and said unto Him, Master, all of these have I observed from my youth. Then Jesus beholding him loved him and said unto him, One thing thou lackest: go thy way, sell whatsoever thou hast, and give to the poor, and thou shalt have treasure in heaven: and come, take up the cross, and follow me.[347]

Ephesians 4:25-5:4:
Wherefore putting away lying, speak every man truth with his neighbor. . . . And be ye kind one to another, tenderhearted, forgiving one another even as God for Christ's sake has forgiven you. . . . And walk in love as Christ also hath loved us and hath given Himself for us an offering and sacrifice to God. . . . But fornication and all uncleanness, or covetousness, let it not be once named among you, as becometh saints. Neither filthiness . . .[348]

Colossians 3:5-14:
Mortify therefore your members which are upon the earth; fornication, uncleanness, inordinate affection, evil concupiscence. But now put ye off all these. . . . Lie not one to another. . . . Put on therefore, as the elect of God . . . bowels of mercies, kindness, humbleness of mind, meekness, longsuffering. . . . Forbearing one another, and forgiving one another. . . . And above all these things put on charity [love], which is the bond of perfectness.[349]

1 Thessalonians 4:3-12:
For this is the will of God . . . that ye should abstain from fornication . . . That no man go beyond and defraud his brother in any matter . . . For ye yourselves are taught of God to love one another. That ye may walk honestly toward them that are without.[350]

---

[347] Wright, *The Will of God*, p. 167.
[348] Wright, *The Will of God*, p. 167. See Almond, *Foundations For Faith*, p. 12.
[349] Wright, *The Will of God*, p. 167.
[350] Wright, *The Will of God*, p. 167

James 3:17:
But the wisdom that is from above is first pure, then peaceable,
gentle, and easy to be intreated, full of mercy and good fruits,
without partiality and without hypocrisy.[351]

Wright said these verses contain all aspects of the walk of
honesty, unselfishness, purity, and love.

What Is The Oxford Group? treated the four absolutes as
follows:

1. Absolute purity demands a clean mind in a clean body and
    embraces clean conduct in business, in work and play,
    interest in world affairs, our use of our possessions, our
    attitudes toward relations, friends and acquaintances (p. 87).

2. Absolute unselfishness means unselfish according to the love
    we bear toward the object of our unselfishness. It is the
    sacrifice of ourselves and our interests to other people's
    interests without thought of reward (p. 97).

3. Absolute honesty means to ourselves the absolute truth, to
    others as truthful as we are to ourselves, tempered with
    common sense and kindliness (pp. 75-76).

4. Absolute love is best lived by the principles of 1 Corinthians
    13 (p. 108).[352]

The Eight Points dealt with the issue of "perfection" called for
in the Absolutes. The word "absolute" in the Oxford Group is
used to speak of perfection. But the perfection is like the
perfection of a father. God is perfect as a Father. A father is
perfect when he loves his children with perfect love. And love in
our Heavenly Father is no more an abstract, distant thing than is

---

[351] Wright, *The Will of God*, p. 167.

[352] In Almond, *Foundations For Faith*, the author said at page 12: "1 Corinthians 13
is a full exposition of this standard. See also Ephesians 4:15-16, 25, and 31-32."

love in an earthly father. Christian perfection does not imply an exemption either from ignorance or mistake or infirmities or temptations. There is no absolute perfection on earth. There is no perfection which does not admit of a continual increase.[353] Humility is essential to perfection. Nine-tenths of our misery is due to self-centeredness. To get ourselves off our hands is the essence of happiness. We do not find ourselves until we are thrown outside of ourselves into something greater than ourselves and set free. The point is that we learn to love, by receiving Christ in our hearts by faith. The love which we then have is not our love. It is the love of Christ, expressing itself in us and through us. I love; yet not I, but Christ loveth in me. It is not merely that we are trying to approximate a standard without and separate from us, but God begins to dwell in us.

To understand Benson better, see 1 John 4:10-16:

Herein is love, not that we loved God, but that He loved us, and sent His Son to be the propitiation for our sins. Beloved, if God so loved us, we ought also to love one another. No man hath seen God at any time. If we love one another, God dwelleth in us, and His love is perfected in us. Hereby we know that we dwell in Him, and He in us, because He hath given us of His Spirit. And we have seen and do testify that the Father sent the Son to be the Savior of the world. Whosoever shall confess that Jesus is the Son of God, God dwelleth in him, and he in God. And we have known and believed the love that God hath to us.

---

[353] Webster's Dictionary speaks of "perfect" and "perfection" as "being entirely without fault or defect." By this definition, there could be no "continual increase." However, Webster adds a usage: "the act or process of perfecting." This seems to be what *The Eight Points* spoke of. Further, unless one believes in the regenerating power of Christ within, which must, by the renewing of the mind, be brought into manifestation through "putting on" the mind of Christ, the *Eight Points* statement is most difficult to understand. See, therefore, Romans 12:1-2; Ephesians 3:17-19; 4:21-32; Philippians 2:5; 3:15; Colossians 3:1-16. Garth Lean wrote the author about the "perfection" issue, stating, "On perfection, the Scofield Bible may shed more light than Webster. Its note on Matthew 5, 'Be ye therefore perfect,' says: 'The word implies full development, growth into maturity or godliness, not sinless perfection'."

God is love; and he that dwelleth in love dwelleth in God, and God in him.

He assimilates us to Himself. We are not saved by the love we exercise, but by the Love we trust.[354]

Shoemaker said this about the Four Absolutes:

> I asked him whether he had had a Quiet Time about the four standards: absolute honesty, purity, unselfishness, and love. He said he had, and produced a piece of yellow fool'scap from his pocket, neatly divided into four quarters, one for each standard, on which he had written down all the places where he felt he had fallen down on them. The paper was quite full. I shared honestly with him about my own sins. He said he wanted to make a decision, and give himself completely to Christ, so we got on our knees and he did it.[355]

> [There are] Four Standards which Dr. Robert E. Speer said represented the summary of the Sermon on the Mount—Absolute Honesty, Absolute Purity, Absolute Unselfishness, and Absolute Love.[356]

> Dr. Robert E. Speer, in one of his books, had said the essence of the ethics of the Sermon on the Mount was the Four Absolutes: Honesty, Purity, Unselfishness, and Love. . . . For thousands of young and not so young folk, fumbling and groping for a way of life, they [the Four Absolutes] became a sharp challenge—clear, demanding, giving a plain starting place. The Law came before Grace. Few could feel anything but guilt before any one of the Four Absolutes. . . . Absolute purity means to find some all-consuming and high faith and purpose which takes

---

[354] Benson, *The Eight Points*, pp. 44-57.

[355] Shoemaker, *The Church Can Save The World*, p. 119-20.

[356] Shoemaker, *How to Become a Christian*, p. 57. The Rev. Harry Almond said the following verses from the Sermon on the Mount explained the Four Absolutes: (1) Honesty, Matthew 5:33-37; (2) Purity, Matthew 5:27-28; (3) Unselfishness, Matthew 5:38-42; (4) Love, Matthew 5:43 and following. Almond, *Foundations for Faith*, pp. 11-13.

up and uses one's energies. . . . Absolute unselfishness—that catches us all in a hundred places. . . . And then Absolute Love. There were many minor irritations, but the cleavage between my father and me . . . was a deep one. . . . I just knew that basic dishonesty, impurity, selfishness, want of love, and withal a kind of pervasive inferiority were holding me down.[357]

Some think the Four Absolutes in early A.A. vanished into history. But even after Wilson and his few New York AAs had left the Oxford Group in 1937 and after the Akron AAs had reluctantly parted company in 1940, the *Central Bulletin*, which was the official A.A. publication in Cleveland, Ohio, carried the Four Absolutes on its masthead. And today still finds them very much discussed and used in A.A. literature distributed in Ohio and in some other A.A. areas. Bill Wilson demonstrated the frequency of their mention in the Oxford Group, saying: "Little was heard of theology, but we heard plenty of absolute honesty, absolute purity, absolute unselfishness, and absolute love—the four principles of the Oxford Group."[358] Recall too Bill's statement, "I am always glad to say privately that some of the Oxford Group presentation and emphasis upon the *Christian message* saved my life" (emphasis added).[359] As we previously pointed out, Bill said the Four Absolutes had been incorporated into A.A.'s Sixth and Seventh Steps. Dr. Bob emphasized *Love* and Service [unselfishness], exemplified by his stress of 1 Corinthians 13 and Henry Drummond's book about it. Purity, unselfishness, and love were also comprehended in what one writer believed was Dr. Bob's "required" study of the Sermon on the Mount and the Book of James.[360] In any event, one can hardly pick up the Big Book

---

[357] Helen Shoemaker, quoting Sam Shoemaker, in *I Stand By The Door*, p. 24.

[358] *Pass It On*, p. 127.

[359] *Pass It On*, p. 171.

[360] We believe that, while Dr. Bob felt 1 Corinthians 13 and the Sermon on the Mount were "absolutely essential" for recovery, he never "required" the reading of anything (though one researcher believed that he did). See Dick B., *Dr. Bob's Library*, pp. x, 9, 12-13.

without finding, in many places, the strong emphasis placed on unselfishness, love, and honesty. And possibly even "purity," in the sense that Buchman used the phrase "pure in heart" from Matthew 5:6. Buchman was talking about removing the "blocks" to God. And so was the Big Book.[361]

20. *Quiet Time*

> The Oxford Group observed some time in early morning for quietness, creating an atmosphere where one can be susceptible to Divine Guidance and sensitive to the sway of the Spirit.

For Sinners Only said of Quiet Time: The Group said the individual was guided by God both during the Quiet Time and throughout the day in the following ways:

Through the Holy Spirit in attentive prayer by means of:
    The Scriptures.
    The Conscience.
    Luminous Thoughts.
    Cultivating The Mind of Christ.
Through reading the Bible and prayer.
Through circumstances.
Through reason.
Through Church, Group, or Fellowship.[362]

Benson said in *The Eight Points of the Oxford Group* that one of the most valuable features of Oxford Group practices is "The Quiet Time."[363] Each member is urged to devote some time in the early morning to quietness. At that time, said Benson, it is possible to have the mind illumined by unhurried reading of the

---

[361] Big Book, pp. 64, 71, 72.

[362] Russell, *For Sinners Only*, p. 94. See also, Howard Rose, *The Quiet Time*.

[363] Garth Lean wrote the author stating that it should be called "God's Art, expressed through individuals and teams."

Bible, by prayer, and by waiting upon God for guidance. Oxford Group people not only *spoke* to God. In the stillness, they gave God a chance to speak to them. They said prayer is "colloquy with God." They learned to be still and wait for God.[364] The process involved: (1) Learning stillness. (2) Eliminating "overstrain." (3) Eliminating the crowded program. "Be still and know that I am God," said Benson, meant that to know God we must be still. To be still we must know God. There must be silence in order to know God. The hurried mind and the distracted heart make a vital knowledge of God impossible. When we are ruffled, troubled about many things, in a state of agitation and flutter, we are not conscious of God; there is no receptive quietness.[365]

Compare these statements in A.A.'s Big Book:

On awakening let us think about the twenty-four hours ahead. . . . Here we ask God for inspiration, an intuitive thought or a decision. We relax and take it easy. We don't struggle. We are often surprised how the right answers come after we have tried this for a while (p. 86).

Oxford Group author Jack Winslow wrote a good deal on Quiet Time, stating:

The morning quiet time has come to mean to me a time when I seek to know God's plan for my day—when I come to Him for orders. After a time of quiet adoration and thanksgiving and the renewal of my self-surrender for His service, I ask Him for His directions, and listen receptive for them.[366]

If you wish to make your life effective and useful for God and your fellow-men, it is essential that you should put aside unhurried time every day for a morning watch with God. . . . I

---

[364] This is a reference to Psalm 46:10, "Be still and know that I am God" — which is often quoted in Oxford Group literature.

[365] See Benson, *The Eight Points*, pp. 58-73.

[366] Winslow, *Why I Believe In The Oxford Group*, p. 43

saw that I must be prepared to keep at least half an hour, day by
day, for this "morning watch." I saw that it must be something
much more than "saying prayer." There must be in it some vital
touch with the living God. I began to learn something about the
devotional study of the Bible, and to realize that through it one
could receive, as it were, a personal message from God. . . . My
experience over these years has taught me that this quiet hour
spent with God day by day is an unfailing secret of power,
progress, purpose, and peace. . . . I grow in understanding of
God as I meditate on the Bible. . . . I learnt morning by morning
to commit the day to God, to try to see His plan for each day so
far as He chose to show it, and to wait for whatever orders He
might wish to give me. . . . First, then, we should spend a few
moments in entering into stillness. . . . Our opening moments of
silent adoration pass into praise and thanksgiving. . . . From
praise and thanksgiving we pass to the renewal, day by day, of
our self-surrender to God. . . . I think it right to insert a chapter
at this point on the subject of intercession.

. . . I pass now to consider a part of the morning watch to which
most Christians devote far too little thought and time, viz, the
prayer of attention or listening.

. . . Now, at the close of all this, and before we go out into the
day's work, we must return again into the stillness, resting
quietly in the presence of God, and drinking in His peace and His
strength for the day's tasks.[367]

Shoemaker said:

I plead again for the keeping of the "Morning Watch"—coming
fresh to God with the day's plans unmade, submitting first our
spirits and then our duties to Him for the shedding of His white
light on both. To steam full-speed through icebergs is irreligious.
To start the day without one thought of our Maker is to invite
catastrophe.[368]

---

[367] Winslow, *When I Awake* (quoting from entire book).
[368] Shoemaker, *Realizing Religion*, pp. 65-66.

Something happened to the quality of my time of prayer when I moved out of the old conception of a "Morning Watch" (which had a way of slipping round till evening), to the conception of a "Quiet Time." The emphasis was in a different place. Formerly, I had sought to find my way up to God. Now I let Him find His way down to me. Listening became the dominant note. Not the exclusive note: for there was Bible study first, taking a book and studying it straight through; and there was ordinary prayer, confession, petition, thanksgiving, intercession. But the bulk of the time is listening.[369]

We can only find the possible ways out in a Quiet Time with God. The way to find out what can happen in a Quiet Time is not to discuss all the metaphysical pros and cons of divine guidance, but to sit down and have a Quiet Time! Listen to God. . . . OBEY. The essence of the giving of ourselves to God is the willingness to do what He says, and the heart of the Quiet Time is asking Him what He wants.[370]

Quiet Times do not need to be confined to morning and evening. One of the most profitable Quiet Times I ever had was one Saturday afternoon on the top of a Fifth Avenue bus. . . . I often stop in at Trinity Church, downtown, for a Quiet Time at noon, when things have gotten a bit on my nerves at the office. The early morning is the best time for Quiet Time, but not the only time.[371]

21.   *Bible Study*

God has revealed His Will for man through the Scriptures; and man must daily feed his soul on God's written Word. This is part of the Quiet Time and also Oxford Group life.

---

[369] Shoemaker, *The Conversion of the Church*, p. 60.

[370] Shoemaker, *The Church Can Save The World*, p. 126.

[371] Shoemaker, *Children of the Second Birth*, p. 97.

Henry Drummond said God gave us two helps in learning how to do His Will: (1) Christ, the Living Word; and (2) the Bible, the Written Word. He said that without Christ's Model Life, the ideal life would be incredible; but without the analysis of that life in the Word of God (the Bible), Christ's Model Life would be unintelligible.[372] Christ did the Will of God, and God's written Word—the Bible—makes the nature of his obedience intelligible.

Canon Streeter's title, *The God Who Speaks*, was almost wholly devoted to study of how God revealed His Will in the Old Testament and in the New Testament. Streeter pointed to the Bible's own testimony as to the divine guidance that God provided throughout history. Hence the Word reveals God's "general" or "universal" will; and it contains endless accounts of God's making specific facts, solutions, and directions known to those who listened.

For Sinners Only discussed prayerful study of the Bible as a means of receiving divine Guidance (p. 94).

Benson's *The Eight Points* detailed just how and what its author studied in the Bible in his Quiet Time. Benson said he preferred the life of Christ, the book of Acts or the Psalms (p. 68). He believed the mind can be illumined at the beginning of the day by unhurried reading of the Bible, by prayer, and by waiting upon God for guidance (p. 58). He cited a number of Psalms and Proverbs, which we discussed under the subject of Guidance, and which show that God will guide. He also pointed out that luminous thoughts can be checked with the mind of Christ as revealed in the New Testament (pp. 78-84).

There is scarcely a one of Shoemaker's twenty-eight major books that does not study a portion of the Bible, quote a portion of it, illustrate a point with a Bible reference, or advocate regular study of the Bible—particularly in conjunction with Quiet Time. And sometimes all of these. Shoemaker wrote:

---

[372] Drummond, *The Ideal Life*, p. 231.

Let us consider together these three great primary means which God gives for sustaining the experience when the sharp lines of conversion seem to grow dim, and we wonder whether it was real or not. First, the Bible. . . . The chief thing I want to emphasize about our use of the Bible is not so much the way each of us shall pursue our study of it, as the setting apart of a definite time each morning for this, together with prayer . . . the results will justify the effort; and granted the desire and determination to use this time daily, with the Bible open before you, you will soon make a method of study for yourself that will suit you better than anything which this book might recommend. . . . I want to give a few practical suggestions which one might follow. One should have the best, that is the most accurate translation obtainable, and it is well, to have some new translation, like Moffatt's; we are in danger of learning phrases rather than assimilating ideas, and the veneration of some for the King James Version is near to bibliolatry. It is good to have a marker where you make plenty of entries, and for this you want a wide margin, and also a fresh copy. D. L. Moody, who was noted especially for his familiarity with the Bible, "was always wearing out Bibles, covering the margins with references and notes, and allowing them to pass freely among his friends." Study one book at a time, mastering the thought of it, the plan and dominant ideas. Read what is there, not your own ideas into it. Do not read hit or miss unsystematically; do not read superstitiously, opening anywhere and expecting to find a fruitful lesson for the day; and do not dwell too much on favorite passages. . . . Read, as President Wilson urged the soldiers, long passages that will really be the road to the heart of it. One may read topically, using the concordance to seek out ideas on sin, faith, prayer, the use of money, consecration or other subjects; or biographically, as in the fascinating development of Peter from the old faults and sins found in the gospel stories of him to the might and influence of the Acts and Epistles. Read and know the Bible, and all else, including public worship, will fall in its place.[373]

---

[373] Shoemaker, *Realizing Religion*, pp. 58-62.

We find God's general will in the Scriptures. . . . [In Quiet Time,] there was Bible study first, taking a book and studying it straight through. . . . They will need constant help, suggestions about how to study the Bible, where and what to read in it. For most, the Gospels will come first.[374]

I find that reading Moffatt's Translation in the New Testament, after I have read the passage in the King James Version, is a great help to understanding it, especially in the Epistles. I recall my extreme prejudice against any translation except my beloved King James, not considering that the desire of God must be that I know the sense of the passage as well as enjoying the vehicle of it.[375]

Now guidance has got to become concrete and, in the best sense, habitual for ministers. This cannot come true without setting apart a definite time in the morning, the very first part of it, for sufficient prayer, Bible study, and listening for the Holy Spirit's direction.[376]

What about A.A. and the Bible? Without lamenting the obliteration of the Bible from mention in the pages of the Big Book, one can still perceive the very obvious omission. Almost every Oxford Group concept survived in A.A. in one form or another. But mention and discussion of the Bible as the source of the concept did not. There are only two short Big Book sentences that even hint of former use of the Bible in early A.A.:

There are many helpful books also. Suggestions about these may be obtained from one's priest, minister, or rabbi (p. 87).

And the progressive move away from the Bible is perhaps also evident by its treatment in A.A.'s conference-approved histories.

---

[374] Shoemaker, *The Conversion of the Church*, pp. 49, 60, 79.

[375] Shoemaker, *Children of the Second Birth*, p. 97.

[376] Shoemaker, *Twice-Born Ministers*, p. 184.

The Index to *DR. BOB and the Good Oldtimers*, which is often thought of as Dr. Bob's biography, contains 37 references to "The Holy Bible." Preparation and publication of the book was approved by the April, 1977 A.A. General Conference. The Index to *Pass It On*, which is considered to be Bill W.'s biography, refers to the Bible only five times. This book was published in 1984. Bill's own history of A.A., *Alcoholics Anonymous Comes of Age*, was published in 1957, just a few years after Dr. Bob died; and the Index makes no mention of the Bible. It seems that, under Bill's lead, and after Dr. Bob was gone, A.A. chose to eliminate the Bible as an official topic of discussion. But A.A.'s genesis in Bible ideas can hardly be ignored in view of the paramount position of the Bible in Oxford Group and Shoemaker writings as the source of information on the will and power of God. Nor can its dominant presence in early A.A. meetings be ignored. Nor can its significance in the following statement in *Anne Smith's Journal*:

Of course the Bible ought to be the main Source Book of all. No day ought to pass without reading it.[377]

We believe that, as the "mother" of A.A.'s "first group, Akron Number One," as Bill phrased these words,[378] Anne Smith must have passed on to the first group the foregoing Bible emphasis.

22. *Prayer*

Prayer is the natural complement of God-Direction. We cannot expect God to talk to us if we do not talk to Him. Prayer is an integral part of Quiet Time.

Canon Streeter wrote on the function of prayer, saying there a necessary interrelation between the idea of God's Plan and the

---

[377] Dick B., *Anne Smith's Journal*, pp. 79-80.
[378] *The Language of the Heart*, p. 353.

view we entertain as to the nature and function of prayer.[379] He said of the Lord's Prayer that it should not be interpreted as a fixed form of words, but rather as an outline indicating a series of mental attitudes in which God should be approached by man. These are: (1) Lifting up the heart and mind to God in adoration; (2) The desire that God's Plan should be realized on earth; and (3) A trustful mention to our Heavenly Father of the individual's material and spiritual needs. And Christ added the injunction that we "use not vain repetitions"[380] because God knows what we have need of before we ask Him.[381]

Benson's *The Eight Points* considered as a single process Quiet Time, reading the Bible slowly, praying, lingering, and waiting on God.[382] All these make us "receptive and sensitive to Divine leading. Petition is not the whole of prayer. We must practice the other great form of prayer, the openness of the soul to God so that the light and power and grace which 'cometh down from above'[383] may enter."[384] No Christian can be vital without the Bible, prayer and Guidance.[385]

What Is The Oxford Group? said:

> Prayer is the natural complement of God Direction. We cannot expect God to talk to us if we do not talk to Him. But it is not always essential continually to ask God for help in every move we make or in every problem of our lives. When we listen for His guidance during our Quiet Times, all requests asked or unasked are answered. However, real prayer receives a real

---

[379] Streeter, *The God Who Speaks*, p. 17. Compare also Roger Hicks, *The Lord's Prayer and Modern Man* (London: Blandford Press, 1967).

[380] Matthew 6:7-8.

[381] Streeter, *The God Who Speaks*, p. 18.

[382] Benson, *The Eight Points*, pp. 58-69, 79.

[383] This is a partial quotation from James 1:17, which reads, "Every good gift and every perfect gift is from above, and cometh down from the Father of lights, with whom is no variableness, neither shadow of turning." Note the reference to this verse in the Big Book at page 14.

[384] Benson, *The Eight Points*, p. 79.

[385] Benson, *The Eight Points*, p. 153.

answer in any place at any time. No supplication to God from the heart is ever lost (p. 69).

Walter stressed in *Soul Surgery* the importance of early morning prayer, saying "our own spirits are brought into tune with the infinite and made spiritually sensitive and strong and resourceful" (p. 41). He pointed to the number of great men who give an important place to believing, persistent sacrificial prayer which enables spiritual apprehension and power. He also said early morning prayer enables man to learn each day's program of procedure since God would never have us act in a haphazard manner. Such prayer transfers to our minds as much of God's perfect plan as we need to know (pp. 43-44).

Compare these comments in A.A.'s Big Book:

We shouldn't be shy on this matter of prayer. Better men than we are using it constantly. It works if we have the proper attitude and work at it (pp. 85-86).

Shoemaker said of prayer:

Whatever be one's theories about prayer, two things stand: man will pray as long as God and he exist, and the spiritual life cannot be lived without it. . . . People need to pray, and they pray. But it is an art—the art of discerning God's will—and one must learn it. For prayer is more than primitive awareness of the supernatural; for us Christians it is the communing of children with Father. . . . Obedience to the Voice which speaks in prayer must ever be the condition of hearing that Voice again. We ask for what we need, remembering that oftentimes we pray for a thing and He gives us a chance; and also that the essence of prayer is not childish asking for gifts, but the eternal questing for the disposition of God toward the ways of our life. And we are praying best when we come, quite empty of request, to bathe ourselves in His presence, and to "wait upon Him" with an open mind, concerned far more with His message to us than anything we can say to Him. . . . The prayer of confession and for forgiveness is perhaps the deepest, best prayer of all, and the one which we shall need most often if God gives us an acute sense of sin. However necessary it may be, prayer is seldom easy. . . . I have followed my own will so prayerfully and intensely that I do not know how to find another will. Sometimes the impression is vague and we are not sure it is from God. . . . Trusting Him, then, we must pray on, for we can do no other. And if we be faithful, we shall soon find that the reality of the experience of prayer far outweighs the reality of the questionings which make us doubt it.[386]

Each morning, there should be continued relation with God in prayer, and daily waiting on God in Quiet. We give in afresh to God, admitting that He has the order and answer for the day.[387]

We talked for a little on the way to keep the New Life. We talked of the daily Quiet Time, of Bible study, prayer and listening, and of the power of God to lead and guide those who are obedient enough to be led.[388]

23.   *Listening to God for Leading Thoughts and Writing Down Guidance Received*

Frank Buchman said:

Anyone can hear the words of the Lord. It is only necessary to obey the rules. The first rule is that we listen honestly for everything that may come—and if we are wise, we write it down.[389]

The Reverend Howard Rose echoed those remarks and cited Jeremiah 30:1-2:

---

[386] Shoemaker, *Realizing Religion*, pp. 63-65.

[387] Shoemaker, *National Awakening*, p. 53.

[388] Shoemaker, *Children of the Second Birth*, p. 53.

[389] Buchman, *Remaking the World*, p. 36. See also, Cecil Rose, *When Man Listens*, p. 37; and Bremer Hofmeyr, *How to Listen* (New York: Moral Re-Armament, n.d.).

The word that came to Jeremiah from the Lord, saying, Thus speaketh the LORD God of Israel, saying, Write down all the words that I have spoken unto thee in a book.[390]

For Sinners Only described a Quiet Time experience its author, A. J. Russell, had:

As Ken Twitchell announced the Quiet Time, the undergraduates fumbled for pencils and guidance books and began to "listen to God." This was not simple meditation, which may be concentration on some aspect of Christ or the Gospel, but something more: a listening for definite messages applicable to present needs. As they were committed to doing God's will, that will could be known for them at any moment of necessity. . . . Yet in the afternoon of that same day at Oxford I had my first results from the Quiet Time. . . . Ken said, "Let's try the Quiet Time." We drew out slips of paper, relaxed, listened. . . . Then, just as we were about to put our papers away, there suddenly crossed my ordinary, tumbled, human thoughts one of another order which seemed to possess luminous glow, differing sharply from the rest. . . . The new luminous thought had come so unexpectedly and with such a peculiar glow of rightness that I went to London and tried it. Within a few moments of the thought being transferred to the person in great authority whom it concerned, he rang me up on the telephone thanking me profusely. . . . So there *was* something in organized prayer for guidance, after all.[391]

What Is The Oxford Group? said:

The Oxford Group advocates our use of a pencil and note-book so that we may record every God-given thought and idea that comes to us during our time alone with Him, that no detail, however small, may be lost to us and that we may not shirk the truth about ourselves or any problem when it comes to us (p. 68).

---

[390] Rev. Howard Rose, *The Quiet Time*, p. 3.
[391] Russell, *For Sinners Only*, pp. 93-96.

The Eight Points of the Oxford Group cited these verses:

Psalm 46:10:
Be still and know that I am God.[392]

1 Samuel 3:9:
Speak LORD, for thy servant heareth.[393]

Isaiah 40:31:
But they that wait upon the Lord shall renew their strength; they shall mount up with wings as eagles; they shall run and not be weary; they shall walk and not faint.[394]

Shoemaker wrote:

Listening became the dominant note of Quiet Time. Not the exclusive note. . . . But the bulk of the time is listening. Most of us find it indispensable to have a loose-leaf notebook, in which to write down the things which come to us. We find that in

---

[392] *The Eight Points* said, at page 65, that it takes time to know God; it takes time to believe; it takes time to learn the mind of Christ. To know God requires more than a hurried nod and a passing glance. God cannot teach us if we have no time to sit in the school of stillness. Howard Rose cited Psalm 46:10 in *The Quiet Time*. See also Brown, *The Venture of Belief*, p. 37; Beverley Nichols, *The Fool Hath Said* (New York: Doubleday, Doran, 1936), pp. 134, 168; and W. E. Sangster, *God Does Guide Us* (New York: The Abingdon Press, 1934), p. 12.

[393] *The Eight Points* said, as did Shoemaker, that this does not mean, "Hear Lord, Thy servant speaketh" (p. 66). *The Eight Points* author pointed to his own practice in Quiet Time when he read the Bible, then knelt and waited in silence. He waited in self-forgetting silence, contemplating the presence of God and remembering that He is Love and He is Spirit and that limitless spiritual forces are in Him and will flow out from Him. Next, he prayed. Finally, he waited in passive silence. Then he wrote down the thoughts in his Guidance book (pp. 68-73). Howard Rose also cited 1 Samuel 3:9 in *The Quiet Time*. It was often cited in Oxford Group writings, particularly those of Shoemaker, for the proper attitude to be taken when one is ready to listen for, and obey, the will of God. See Cecil Rose, *When Man Listens*, p. 30; Foot, *Life Began Yesterday*, p. 4; Winslow, *When I Awake*, p. 48; Hofmeyr, *How to Listen*, p. 1; Shoemaker, *National Awakening*, pp. 78-88; and *God's Control*, pp. 115-16.

[394] Benson, *The Eight Points*, p. 73. Note that many Oxford Group writers made reference to this verse by mentioning "waiting upon the Lord."

trying to remember what has come before, we block what is coming now; we find it impossible to remember sometimes the things which come even in a brief Quiet Time. The Chinese have a saying that the strongest memory is weaker than the weakest ink. We do not want to forget the slightest thing that God tells us to do; and I have sometimes had a rush of detailed guidance which came almost as fast as I could write it. . . . He may give us the conviction of sin . . . and sends us to someone with restoration and apology. He may send us a verse of encouragement like, "Fear Not." "Go in thy might, have I not sent thee?" "All is well." He may warn us against a wrong course, or a tedious and time-killing person, or a tendency in ourselves. He may send us to telephone or to call someone, or tell us to write a letter, or pay a visit, or take some exercise, or read a book. Nothing which concerns our lives is alien to His interest, or to the doing of His Will. He may give us guidance about how to help someone, or tell us what is the matter with them or us.[395]

P. G. suggested a Quiet Time together. So they prayed together, opening their minds to as much of God as he understood, removing first the hindrance of self-will, allowing the Spirit to focus an impression upon the mind, like light upon a camera exposed. There and then he lifted his own life to God, giving Him entrance and sway.[396]

The man who knows God's will is the man who loves it. The man who finds out what God wants is the man who cares what God wants, who feels upon him the same kind of burdens God feels and carries. If God can count on you, He can commit His secrets to you. We have got to get on God's side before it's any use to ask what is God's plan. Drummond . . . said, "Above all things, do not touch Christianity unless you are willing to seek the Kingdom of God first."[397] "Not every one that saith unto me, 'Lord, Lord, shall enter the kingdom of heaven; but he that

---

[395] Shoemaker, *The Conversion of the Church*, pp. 60-66.
[396] Shoemaker, *Children of the Second Birth*, p. 47.
[397] Matthew 6:33.

doeth the will of my Father who is in heaven."[398] God give us
the grace to ask, "Lord, what wilt thou have me to do."[399]

Dr. Bob's wife, Anne, followed the Oxford Group practice of
writing down "leading" thoughts. She did so before, during, and
after Quiet Time periods of Bible study, prayer, and "meditation"
that she and Dr. Bob and Bill observed together during Bill's stay
with the Smiths in the summer of 1935.[400] Dr. Bob's daughter,
Sue Windows, so informed the author during a personal interview
in Akron in June of 1991. Sue also recalled that other early AAs
followed this procedure. But the Oxford Group practice of writing
down thoughts in a Guidance book never made it into the Big
Book itself. Although the author has never heard this practice
discussed in the many A.A. meetings he attends, he has certainly
encountered in recovery center talk, and even in A.A., the idea of
"keeping and writing in a daily journal." Whether this concept
springs from Oxford Group origins, we do not know.

24.   *Checking*

> Luminous thoughts received in Quiet Time may not actually
> be Divine Guidance or from God. They may involve self-
> deception. They should be checked for harmony with God's
> Will by testing them with: 1) The Four Absolutes; 2) The
> Bible; 3) Teachings of the Church; 4) Circumstances; 5)
> Willingness to obey; 6) Advice of other surrendered
> Christians.

Frank Buchman said of luminous thoughts: The second rule
[the first being honestly listening and writing down the thoughts]

---

[398] Matthew 7:21.

[399] Acts 9:6. See Shoemaker, *Religion That Works*, pp. 64-65. Shoemaker frequently
referred to this "what-wilt-thou-have-me-to-do" concept. See Shoemaker, *A Young Man's
View of the Ministry*, p. 80. Compare *Confident Faith*, p. 107

[400] See Dick B., *Anne Smith's Journal*, pp. 53-62.

is that we test the thoughts that come, to see which are from God. Buchman's first suggested test is the Bible. He stated it is steeped in the experience through the centuries of men who dared, under Divine revelation, to live experimentally with God. He pointed out that in the Bible, culminating in the life of Jesus Christ, we find the highest moral and spiritual challenge—complete honesty, purity, unselfishness and love. He pointed to another test: "What do others say who also listen to God?" He said that seeking is an unwritten law of fellowship and an acid test of one's commitment to God's plan. He said that no one can be wholly God-controlled who works alone.[401]

Henry Wright wrote a chapter entitled, "How to Find Out the Particular Will of God."[402] He examined the answers of six "modern" religious leaders. Their answers were:

1. "Do the right"—Bushnell.
2. "Love"—Mosley.
3. "Be generous, chaste, true and brave"—F. W. Robertson.
4. "Practice 1 Corinthians 13:4-6"—Drummond.
5. "Sanctify yourself, believe on Christ, and devote yourself to His program for the salvation of the world"—Speer.
6. "Follow Christ in your life"—Abbott.

Wright asked which of the foregoing should be selected as the absolute standard to recommend to all men? He pointed out how men differ as to what is right, do not always understand love, and so on. Then he asked if there were absolute standards of right and wrong. He asked how Jesus found out the particular will of God for himself. He said Jesus "did always those things that please Him [God]."[403] Wright said Jesus was therefore sure of God's presence and guidance.[404] Consequently Wright asked what *were* those things that were pleasing to God. And he proposed going

---

[401] Buchman, *Remaking The World*, p. 36.

[402] Wright, *The Will of God*, pp. 153-176.

[403] John 8:29.

[404] John 8:29 (first half).

back to the teachings of Jesus and the Apostles to reconstruct the touchstones that applied to every question.[405]

Wright began with the work of Dr. Robert E. Speer who reconstructed from the teachings of Jesus the four standards in regard to which, said Wright, Jesus never allowed himself an exception and with reference to which his teaching is absolute and unyielding. These were the Four Absolutes—honesty, purity, unselfishness, and love—of which we have already written. Wright said these were the tests to be applied by a Christian to determine the particular will of God for each step of his career. The Christian was to ask, "Is the step which I planned to take an absolutely pure one, honest one, most unselfish one, the fullest possible expression of my love?"[406] Thus emerged the most basic form of Oxford Group "checking" or "tests," not only of luminous thoughts but also of the conduct of a man's life.

For Sinners Only said, "The conditions for effective guidance were the whole-hearted giving of one's self to Jesus Christ." The tests as to whether this was being done were:

Does it [the proposed conduct] go counter to the highest standards of belief that we already possess?

Does it contradict the revelations which Christ has already made in or through the Bible?

Is it absolutely honest, pure, unselfish, loving?

Does it conflict with our real duties and responsibilities to others?

If still uncertain, wait and continue in prayer, and consult a trustworthy friend who believes in the guidance of the Holy Spirit?[407]

---

[405] Wright, *The Will of God*, pp. 165-66.

[406] Wright, *The Will of God*, p. 173.

[407] Russell, *For Sinners Only*, p. 94. See also, Cecil Rose, *When Man Listens*, pp. 34-35; and Hofmeyr, *How to Listen*, p. 2.

What Is The Oxford Group? said, "In cases of difficulty, our guidance can be 'checked up' with the teachings of the Bible or by conference with others who are also receiving guidance in Quiet Time" (p. 69).

Clarence Benson said in his book, *The Eight Points of the Oxford Group*:

> The Group witnesses that guidance comes through a careful study of the Scriptures, a clear conscience, the cultivation of the mind of Christ in all things,[408] the exercise of reason, illuminating thoughts, the circumstances of life, and through the corporate fellowship of guided lives in the Church and the Group. Guidance must be checked by the highest standards we already possess; in light of our duties and responsibilities to others; and by the Fourfold Standards of the Life of Christ. . . . The Group recognizes that guidance needs to be checked in various ways. If it is God's guidance, it will be in accord with the mind of Christ revealed in the New Testament[409] and in harmony with the four standards. . . . And because the individual may be swayed by personal facts such as lack of knowledge, the Group further emphasizes the need for checking with other surrendered Christians. With these safeguards, we may expect guidance as to what letters to write, visits to pay, restitution to make and so forth. We have to guard against thrusting our own will upon God when we pray to Him to guide us. We need also to be warned against too readily taking for granted any idea that jumps into our head as Divine inspiration. A strong impulse is not necessarily a Divine Guidance. It may arise from a strong desire or a disordered imagination. One of the commonest fears felt about simple faith in Divine guidance is that it will lead to unchecked individualism. . . . the follower of the light will be continually correcting the first perception of it by a fuller experience, and by that of others who have followed it more faithfully. When a man keeps every avenue of his being open to Divine guidance, he acquires a firm conviction that he is being led, not always

---

[408] See Philippians 2:5.

[409] See Philippians 2:5, Romans 13:14; and Galatians 3:27.

because of remarkable events but through daily hourly gifts of grace to meet every human need.[410]

Benson also pointed out that the fly leaf of Henry Drummond's Bible suggested, for knowledge of the Will of God: (1) Pray. (2) Think. (3) Talk to wise people, but don't regard their judgment as final. (4) Beware of the objections of your own will, but don't be too much afraid of it. God never unnecessarily thwarts man's nature and likings; it is a mistake to think that His will is always in the line of the disagreeable. (5) Meanwhile, do the next things, for doing God's will in small things is the best preparation for doing it in great things. (6) When decision and action are necessary, go ahead. (7) You will probably not find out until afterwards, perhaps long afterwards, that you have been led at all.[411]

Benson asked and answered this question:

When the Group speak of God's direct guidance, how do they know that what they hear is really a message from God and not only a prompting of the subconscious mind? May not this guidance be misleading and dangerous? It is possible to mistake the source of these impulses. But mistakes and dangers can be checked by applying a simple test to the guidance which we believe comes from God. He has given us the power to reason and compare. We are able to discern spiritual values, the higher from the lower, the Divine from human. God makes Himself known to the surrendered life in light of His Will for the world and His plan for our lives. Guidance is tested by the Divine scale and standard of values.[412]

Shoemaker made these comments about checking:

How then, do we know what is guidance? . . . Is not guidance simply conscience at work? "No Mummy," [said a little girl].

---

[410] Benson, *The Eight Points*, pp. 84-87.

[411] Benson, *The Eight Points*, pp. 87-88.

[412] Benson, *The Eight Points*, pp. 151-52.

"Conscience tells you the difference between right and wrong; but guidance tells you which of several right things you ought to do." Then it must be tested by the Spirit of Christ. A man steeped in the New Testament will by so much, getter better guidance than a man who is not. Guidance, if true, will never be found contrary to the New Testament. But Jesus . . . . [Jesus] also promised His Holy Spirit to "guide us into all truth."[413] Knowing the life of Jesus, His teachings, His principles and parables, His Spirit that was manifested all through all his words and acts constitutes part of the discipline and preparation which are necessary if the Holy Spirit is to find us ready to hear and understand His will; but in themselves they are not sufficient direct inspiration for our practical decisions. We meet many cases not covered by the New Testament. . . . The Holy Spirit's guidance will never be contrary to the New Testament; it will really show us what the New Testament means for us in any given case. God's Will is sometimes made clear, also by circumstances. He guides us by open and closed doors. There is always a danger here of being overwhelmed by moral obstacles, which need to be ignored and crashed through: but there are unmistakable signs sometimes in circumstances. But chiefly guidance is to be tested by the concurrence of other guided people. . . . Individualistic guidance can, and sometimes does, run off the rails into undesirable courses. And, on the other hand, if we check guidance with those who believe in guidance, they simply quench the Spirit. . . . Find a man that believes in God's guidance. Better yet, find a group that is God-guided, and check it with them. This brings in the relation between reason and guidance. Guidance is no short-cut to knowledge. . . . Every bit of human knowledge one can have about people or things will help them, provided that knowledge can be surrendered to God and He be allowed to guide it in its application. There is no room for prejudiced thought: and much so-called thought is thought with a bias, defending a point of view, rationalizing a desire. But real, honest, dispassionate thinking should precede guidance. It must come in and do all that it can. Then it must retire, and

---

[413] John 16:13.

leave the final disposition to God. . . . *Guidance far exceeds intuition.*[414] Reason, then goes as far as it can. God is greater than reason, and makes the final decision and reveals it to us through guidance. Some of you will find yourselves hung up on the problem of guidance in small things. . . . Personally, I am now content to obey my guidance and let God decide what is big and what is little. Whatever He tells me is "big" to me (emphasis added).[415]

At another [house-party], I learned still more about the pain which is involved in merging one's life into a spiritual fellowship, of thoroughly working with a group, sharing with them, being "checked" by them when it was necessary, and at times having to obey one's spiritual teacher.[416]

What about "Checking" and A.A.? Writing in *Alcoholics Anonymous Comes of Age*, Bill Wilson said:

Until the middle of 1937 we in New York had been working along-side the Oxford Groups. But in the latter part of that year we most reluctantly parted company with these great friends. . . . For example, drinkers would not take pressure in any form, excepting from John Barleycorn himself. They always had to be led, not pushed. They would not stand for the rather aggressive evangelism of the Oxford Groups. And they would not accept the principle of "team guidance" for their own personal lives. It was too authoritarian for them.[417]

Bill's discussion failed to point out, however, that the Oxford Group not only practiced "checking" by *team*, but also with other *individuals*. And there certainly were the other checks they used, such as measuring proposed conduct by "yardsticks" in the Bible

---

[414] Compare Big Book, pp. 84 and 86, which suggest that intuition alone is all that is involved.

[415] Shoemaker, *The Conversion of the Church*, pp. 51-57.

[416] Shoemaker, *Twice-Born Ministers*, p. 125.

[417] *AA Comes of Age*, p. 74.

and the teachings of Jesus Christ. However, these additional remarks by Bill are quoted in *Pass It On*:

> It was discovered that all forms of coercion, both direct and indirect, had to be dropped. We found that "checking" in the hands of amateurs too often resulted in criticism, and that resulted in resentment, which is probably the most serious problem the average alcoholic is troubled with.[418]

> While most of us believe profoundly in the principle of "guidance," it was soon apparent that to receive it accurately, considerable spiritual preparation was necessary.[419]

This second remark above is sad. For the early Akron AA did engage in just such "considerable" spiritual preparation. They read the Bible. They studied the teachings of Jesus. They adopted the Four Absolutes as guides. And, as previously shown, these are still applied in Ohio and some other A.A. areas. The early AAs prayed and had Quiet Time. These things gave them considerable spiritual preparation. Dr. Bob and many other AAs continued to study the Bible and other Christian literature for the rest of their lives.[420] Dr. Bob continued to pray and try to live by the principles of the Four Absolutes.[421] In fact, Dr. Bob stated, in his remarks at Detroit, Michigan, in 1948, that he often "checked" his views on a problem against the Four Absolutes and with others—just as the Oxford Group had taught him. Anne Smith wrote frequently about the necessity for checking.[422]

But "checking" never made it to the Big Book or the Steps. Yet remnants of "guidance" *do* exist in the Big Book and particu-

---

[418] *Pass It On*, p. 172.

[419] *Pass It On*, p. 172.

[420] See Dick B., *Dr. Bob's Library*; and *The Books Early AAs Read for Spiritual Growth*.

[421] His daughter, Sue Smith Windows, so informed the author in a personal interview in Akron, Ohio in June, 1991.

[422] Dick B., *Anne Smith's Journal*, pp. 32, 50, 63, 108, 113, 115-16, 122, 144.

larly in its Eleventh Step discussion. The Big Book speaks, as the Oxford Group did, about "intuitive" thinking.[423] But both the Oxford Group and Shoemaker (as one of their spokesmen) made it very clear that they believed Guidance was a good deal *more* than "intuitive" thinking.[424] It was revelation *received from God!* That is why Buchman, Shoemaker, and others of the Oxford Group spoke so much about the examples of Guidance in both the Old and New Testament.[425]

Recent A.A. emphasis on a "Higher Power," which has often become a "door knob," a "tree," or even the "group" has hardly left the newcomer with a "Divine" source for checking the validity of his or her "intuitive" thought as far as God's will is concerned.[426] Moreover, the newcomer is often told: "Don't think. Don't drink. Go to meetings." Such instructions might have value for the confused, detoxing member in the earliest days of sobriety. But they certainly move that newcomer far from the Oxford Group's suggestions for "checking" thoughts and guidance ideas for their conformity to the Bible, the teachings of Jesus Christ, the Four Absolutes, the Church, and the informed help of like-minded Christian believers.

---

[423] See Big Book, p. 86: "an intuitive thought or decision;" and p. 84: "we will intuitively know how to handle situations which used to baffle us."

[424] Shoemaker, *Twice-Born Ministers*, p. 184: "Let it be said often, this is no short-cut to truth which we are supposed to dig out with our minds; it is God's crystallization of truth from the facts we have and also from some facts which we cannot possibly *know*, but can only guess by what humanly we call a 'flash of intuition.' The 'guidance' of religion is 'intuition' *plus*. It is not a substitute for, but a tremendous supplement to, the common processes of thought" (emphasis added).

[425] See, for example, James 1:5, 17; John 16:13, and the many verses from Psalms and Proverbs quoted in our Oxford Group portions on Guidance, Quiet Time, and Listening.

[426] The author has personally attended A.A. meetings almost daily for six years. In these A.A. meetings and, particularly, in recovery center talk, where the author participated as a patient and in "after-care," God was often described as a "tree," a "stone," and the "group." And compare, for example, the experiences of Barnaby Conrad, *Time Is All We Have* (New York: Dell Publishing, 1986), p. 21; and Nan Robertson, *Getting Better: Inside Alcoholics Anonymous* (New York: Fawcett Crest, 1988), p. 124, 129.

The Bible, significant mention of Jesus Christ, the Four Absolutes, Church as a must, and checking with "guided" believers are words and ideas that certainly are not a part of either the Big Book or today's A.A. But note the price that has been paid. The Big Book presents this apparent quandary: "It is not probable that we are going to be inspired at all times" (p. 87). As to which we would ask, just how an AA is to determine what is and what is *not* "inspired" by God without the kind of checks provided in the Bible itself and in the teachings of religion, including the Oxford Group. How can the AA know if the "inspired" thought is guidance from God?

In fairness, we repeat these few lines—discussed all too little in today's A.A.—in which the Big Book does make *several* helpful (in fact, vital) suggestions:

> There are many helpful books also. Suggestions about these may be obtained from one's priest, minister, or rabbi. Be quick to see where religious people are right. Make use of what they offer (p. 87).

The Spiritual Experience or Awakening

25. *Knowledge of God's Will*

> Knowledge of God's Will comes to us from a study of His "universal" or "general" will as revealed in the Bible and in nature and from willingness to bend every effort in doing the general will and have God's "private" or "particular" will revealed to us by His guidance.

The Oxford Group wrote much on the importance of knowing God's will. They stressed that God had a plan and that a person's life would go well if he or she learned the plan—God's will—and harmonized his or her life with the plan. But how to know it?

There were two basic rules: (1) Study the Bible which contains God's general or universal will for man. (2) Learn how to listen

for God's "Voice" by which He reveals his particular or private
will for man. In the sections on Guidance, Prayer, Bible Study,
Quiet Time, Listening, and Checking, we have covered most of
the Oxford Group material on *how* to know God's will. Here we
simply review the Biblical principles on *where* to find it.

Oxford Group writings were clear that the Bible contains God's
Universal Will. That idea was certainly expounded by Professor
Henry Drummond in *The Ideal Life*.[427] Frank Buchman's most
significant mentor, Henry B. Wright, reiterated the details in his
The Will of God And A Man's Lifework, saying, for example:

> There is a part of God's will which every one may know. It is
> written in divine characters in two sacred books, which every
> man may read. The one of them is the Bible, the other is Nature.
> The Bible is God's will in words, in formal thoughts, in grace.
> Nature is God's will in matter and tissue and force. Nature is not
> often considered a part of God's will, but it is a part, and a great
> part, and the first part. . . . The laws of nature are the will of
> God for our bodies. As there is a will of God for our higher
> nature—the moral laws—as emphatically is there a will of God
> for the lower—the natural laws. If you would know God's will
> in the higher, therefore, you must begin with God's will in the
> lower, which simply means this—that if you want to live the ideal
> life you must begin with the ideal body. The law of moderation,
> the law of sleep, the law of regularity, the law of exercise, the
> law of cleanliness—this is the law or will of God for you.
>
> From the moral side there are three different departments of
> God's will. Foremost, and apparently most rigid of all, are the
> Ten Commandments. Now the Ten Commandments contain in a
> few sentences one of the largest known portions of God's will .
> . . the most venerable and universal expression of God's will for
> man. Following upon this there come the Beatitudes of Christ.
> This is another large portion of God's will. . . . But there is a
> third set of laws and rules which are not to be found exactly
> expressed in either of these. . . . Hence we must add to all this

---

[427] See, for example, Drummond, *The Ideal Life*, pp. 268-71.

mass of law and beatitude many more laws and many more beatitudes which lie enclosed in other texts, and in other words of Christ which have their place, like the rest. as portions of God's will.[428]

As we have already noted, Sam Shoemaker frequently wrote to the same effect, saying:

We find God's general will in the Scriptures.[429]

The sustenance of the new spiritual life lies in the material in the Bible, which is everlasting and universal; and then in God's direct messages to us, which are temporal and personal, but sometimes have widespread effects.[430]

There is a general will of God, and there is a particular will of God. All men everywhere who have lined up for the right, have been true and square and clean, have done the general will of God. One is grateful for them. But a man may do the general will of God and yet miss the particular will of God for him.[431]

The Bible from one end to the other tells us about Him [God], about His will for man and the world. Christ has proclaimed His Voice as no one else before or since. You may have trouble with the inspiration of the Scripture; I have trouble conceiving of it as possible that those words were concocted by man alone. But are you listening to them? Before there is any private revelation, we must accept and dig into and learn from this public revelation made before all men in the life and death of Jesus according to the immortal words in which that story has been enshrined for all time. But when we have done this, we may seek and expect and have personal and private revelation from Him. There are places in our lives not covered exactly by any law given in the Bible: if

---

[428] Wright, *The Will of God*, p. 137.

[429] Shoemaker, *The Conversion of the Church*, pp. 49-50.

[430] Shoemaker, *Twice-Born Ministers*, pp. 184-85.

[431] Shoemaker, *A Young Man's View of the Ministry*, p. 78.

we seek to obey the laws already written, God will give us His special will and command for us now if we ask Him.[432]

Here we need to focus on where the Oxford Group people found God's *particular* or *private* will for men and women. And the Oxford Group answer was: by *revelation*. They said that God may choose to reveal His particular will for man when man listens and obeys. The thrust of the obedience idea was said to lie in John 7:17:

> If any man will do his will, he shall know of the doctrine whether it be of God, or whether I speak of myself.

This difficult-to-understand verse was uttered by Jesus Christ. But Oxford Group writers, from the earliest Buchman mentors to Shoemaker, interpreted the verse to mean that man would receive guidance from God as to God's particular will when man was *sincerely bending his efforts* to live by what he believed to be God's general will as revealed in Scripture.

A. J. Russell said John 7:17 was Sam Shoemaker's favorite verse.[433] And have already noted the frequency of its appearance in Shoemaker writings.[434] Shoemaker shed this light on his views of the verse:

> Jesus said, "If any man willeth to do his will, he shall know." That is to say, "If any man will begin by living up to as much as he understands of the moral requisites of God, he will later, in

---

[432] Shoemaker, *Christ and This Crisis*, p. 106. See also, Shoemaker, *Realizing Religion*, pp. 58-62; *The Church Alive*, pp. 75-77; and *How to Become a Christian*, pp. 108-10.

[433] Russell, *For Sinners Only*, p. 211.

[434] Shoemaker, *A Young Man's View of the Ministry*, p. 41; *Religion That Works*, pp. 36, 46, 58; *The Church Can Save The World*, p. 110; *Living Your Life Today*, pp. 101-09; *The Experiment of Faith*, p. 36; *How To Find God*. pp. 5, 6, 15; *How You Can Help Other People*, p. 61; *The Adventure of Living Under New Management* (Grand Rapids: Zondervan, 1966), p. 46. and Dick B., *New Light on Alcoholism*, pp. 43, 101, 110, 117, 118, 121, 148, 181, 208, 227, 230, 267, 294, 298, 316.

the light of his experience, come to see straight intellectually."
. . . A moral experiment is worth ten times an intellectual
investigation in apprehending spiritual truth. Obedience is as
much the organ of spiritual understanding as reason.[435]

There is a truth which we need to learn well and to get down
deep in our bones if we are to help people: and that is the truth
contained in the verse St. John 7:17: "If any man willeth to do
His will, he shall know of the doctrine." So often we think that
if we knew God, we should live a good life. This says, Live a
good life, and you will know God! The attempt really to be rid
of our sins seems to open us to God Who hovers over us with
love all the time, and the readiness to stay in our sins seems to
blind us to His Presence and make it impossible to believe that
He exists."[436]

The soundest approach I know to religious discovery is found in
St. John's Gospel, chapter 7, verse 17; "If any man willeth to do
his will, he shall know of the doctrine." We are busy getting
"willing to do His will," and that means changing many of our
ways. The verse says clearly that this is the order: moral change,
then intellectual perception. "Blessed are the pure in heart, for
they shall see God."[437] A certain amount of "law" always
precedes "grace."[438]

There is an intriguing verse in St. John's gospel (chapter 7, verse
17, based on ASV): "If any man wills to do his (God's) will, he
shall know of the teaching, whether it is of God, or whether I

---

[435] Shoemaker, *Religion That Works*, p. 36. Shoemaker is here referring to writings
found in Bushnell, Robertson, and particularly Henry B. Wright, who said, in *The Will
of God*, "It is here that the universal will of God is connected with the particular.
Transgression of the universal will of God—the laws of nature and morality so far as
they have been revealed—is sin and sin blocks the channel of communication. In other
words, obedience to the universal will of God is the first step toward knowing the
particular will of God . . . There must be a complete renunciation of self-will" (pp. 148-
149).

[436] Shoemaker, *How You Can Help Other People*, p. 61.

[437] Matthew 5:8.

[438] Shoemaker, *The Experiment of Faith*, p. 36.

speak from myself." We might boil this down to say that Jesus implied, "Don't begin at the theological end; begin at the moral end."[439]

We believe the foregoing Shoemaker quotes came from, and conformed to, the views of Henry Drummond, Henry B. Wright, and other Oxford Group writers. All made clear the condition for knowing God's particular will—obedience to God's general will.[440] And this is where the Four Absolutes were believed to be of such importance. The absolute standards represented vital statements about moral law that were reconstructed from the teachings of Jesus. And Oxford Group people believed that endeavoring to live by these Four Absolutes was essential to receiving knowledge of God's particular will in a situation.[441]

The order of A.A.'s Steps seems to follow. Step Three meant a decision to follow God's will. Steps Four through Nine represented obedience through acting in accordance with that perceived will. That seems to be why Bill Wilson felt the Four Absolutes were incorporated into Steps Six and Seven. Step Ten required a *daily* effort to apply the surrender principles learned in Steps Four through Nine. *Then* Step Eleven placed the alcoholic in a position, "through prayer and meditation," to *improve* the relationship with God by seeking knowledge of God's will and the power to carry it out. The Bible was, by Oxford Group precepts, already the repository of knowledge of God's general will. Hence the focus, through Eleventh Step prayer and meditation, was upon receiving

---

[439] Shoemaker, *Under New Management*, p. 46.

[440] See Henry B. Wright, *The Will of God*, p. 117, citing John 7:17, and then discussing Robertson and Drummond (pp. 117-29). See also Drummond, *The Ideal Life*, 302; Brown, *The Venture of Belief*, pp. 28, 48; Cecil Rose, *When Man Listens*, p. 17; Russell, *For Sinners Only*, p. 211; and Benson, *The Eight Points*, p. 129.

[441] Reviewing the author's manuscript on April 2, 1992, Willard Hunter made the following comments: "The Oxford Group never claimed that any one could achieve any of the absolutes. As in target practice, you aim for the center of the bull's eye. They used to say, 'If you aim at nothing, you are likely to hit it.' In addition, it was clear that human struggle was of no avail. God supplied compliance with the standards in a life surrendered to God."

guidance in understanding the general will *and*, because of previous *obedience to the general will*, receiving revelation as to God's particular will if God chose to reveal it. Step Twelve represented the faith payoff that resulted from taking the foregoing steps.

Shoemaker explained:

> Surrender to God's will, which is the heart of faith, is summed up in the question, "Lord, what wilt thou have me to do?"[442] If a man says that and means it, he has settled the most momentous question of his career. It means that hypothetically and for the time being, at least, he gives up every preconceived notion of what he wants to do, every plan he ever had; lest the plan be outside the plan of his Father. So long as an "if" or a "but" remain in his mind, it cannot be surrender. We have got to wipe the slate clean, and then ask Him to write His will upon it."[443]

26.   *God consciousness*

> The end of surrendering life completely to God through the power of Christ is a total change. There is an experience—the discovery and knowledge of God, the carrying of this message to others, and a difference in the way life is lived. There is rebirth—consciousness of being in harmony with God.

One could write volumes on what it means to have a life in harmony with God, to have the estrangement removed, to be conscious of God's power and presence in daily life, to be helping others to change, and to be living life according to God's principles. Much of this was comprehended in the Oxford Group "Conservation" and "Continuance" ideas. But there were a number of expressions used to explain the end result of the life-change process. The following are some:

---

[442] See Acts 9:6; Referring to this verse, see Drummond, *The Ideal Life*, p. 306; and Shoemaker, *Confident Faith*, p. 107.

[443] Shoemaker, *A Young Man's View of the Ministry*, p. 80.

1. An "experience of God."[444]
2. A "vital experience of Jesus Christ."[445]
3. A "religious experience."[446]
4. A "spiritual experience."[447]
5. A "spiritual awakening."[448]
6. A "relationship with God."[449]
7. A sense of the "power and presence of God."[450]
8. Finding God.[451]
9. Being "in touch with God."[452]
10. "Contact" with God.[453]
11. "Conversion"[454]

---

[444] Leon, *The Philosophy of Courage or the Oxford Group Way*, p. 110; Brown, *The Venture of Belief*, pp. 24-25; Weatherhead, *How Can I Find God?*, p. 66; Shoemaker, *The Conversion of the Church*, p. 113; and *How to Become a Christian*, p. 156.

[445] Shoemaker, *The Conversion of the Church*, p. 109; *Twice-Born Ministers*, p. 10—"a complete experience of Jesus Christ;" See Benson, *The Eight Points*—"a maximum experience of Jesus Christ" (p. xviii); and Buchman, *Remaking The World*, p. x.

[446] Shoemaker, *Realizing Religion*, p. 9; *Twice-Born Ministers*, p. 156; Brown, *The Venture of Belief*, pp. 21-24; and William James, *The Varieties of Religious Experience*.

[447] Shoemaker, *Twice-Born Ministers*, pp. 10, 61.

[448] Buchman, *Remaking the World*, pp. 19, 24, 35, 54; Shoemaker, *The Conversion of the Church*, p. 124; and Walter, *Soul Surgery*, p. 82.

[449] Shoemaker, *Children of the Second Birth*, p. 16; *Christ's Words from the Cross*, p. 50; Weatherhead, *Discipleship*, p 18; Benson, *The Eight Points*, pp. 48, 92; Macmillan, *Seeking and Finding*, p. 99; and Brown, *The Venture of Belief*, p. 11.

[450] Kitchen, *I Was a Pagan*, p. 157, 68; Brown, *The Venture of Belief*, pp. 24-26, 44; and Shoemaker, *With the Holy Spirit and with Fire*, p. 27.

[451] Shoemaker, *Realizing Religion*, p. 9; *God's Control*, p. 137; *How To Find God*; Kitchen, *I Was A Pagan*, p. 94; and Weatherhead, *How Can I Find God?*.

[452] Buchman, *Remaking the World*, p. 80; Foot, *Life Began Yesterday*, p. 132; Shoemaker, *The Conversion of the Church*, pp. 47-65; *National Awakening*, pp. 78-88; *How to Become a Christian*, p. 55; and *Under New Management*, p. 66.

[453] Benson, *The Eight Points*, p. 31; and Brown, *The Venture of Belief*, p. 24, 31.

[454] Olive Jones, *Inspired Children*, p. 136; Shoemaker, *Children of the Second Birth*, p. 16; *Realizing Religion*, pp. 22-35; *Twice-Born Ministers*, p. 10; and Benson, *The Eight Points*, p. 62.

12.   "Surrender."[455]
13.   "Change."[456]
14.   "Born again."[457]
15.   "God Consciousness."[458]

William James wrote an entire book *describing* religious experiences; and the foregoing words and phrases are really shorthand expressions for the following ideas. Thus William James wrote:

[The four features of "saintliness" present in all religions are:] (1) The feeling of being part of a wider life—the conviction of the existence of an Ideal Power; (2) The person's feeling of the friendly continuity of this Power with his own life—the self having willingly surrendered its control; (3) The experience of elation and freedom which the changed life has when the confining self ceases to dominate the personality; (4) The shift of the emotional center towards love and compassion.[459]

If we practice by acting *as if* there were a God, feel *as if* we were free, consider Nature *as if* she were full of special designs,

---

[455] *What Is The Oxford Group?*, p. 40-57: Shoemaker, *Children of the Second Birth*, p. 16; Brown, *The Venture of Belief*, p. 28; and Weatherhead, *Discipleship*, pp. 15-30.

[456] Olive Jones, *Inspired Children*, p. 136; Shoemaker, *God's Control*, pp. 9, 11; *The Church Can Save The World*, pp. 124-125; *By The Power of God*, pp. 56, 10; Foot, *Life Began Yesterday*, p. 27; Begbie, *Life Changers*; See Mel B., *New Wine*, p. 23; and Dennis C. Morreim, *Changed Lives* (Minneapolis: Augsburg, 1991), p. 24.

[457] Shoemaker, *Twice-Born Ministers*, pp. 56, 10; *National Awakening*, p. 55-66; *By the Power of God*, pp. 28-33; *They're on the Way*, p. 157; *How to Find God*, p. 7; Allen, *He That Cometh*, pp. 19, 32, 48; Buchman, *Remaking the World*, p. 23; Drummond, *The Ideal Life*, p. 211; Begbie, *Life Changers*, p. 104; Allen, *He That Cometh*, pp. 19, 32, 48; and Olive Jones, *Inspired Children*, p. 136. Bill Wilson himself twice wrote in early manuscripts of the Big Book that he had "been born again" in the process of his conversion experience. See Dick B., *New Light on Alcoholism*, p. 55, n. 10.

[458] Begbie, *Life Changers*, pp. 16, 39; Leon, *The Philosophy of Courage*, pp. 110-111; Kitchen, *I Was a Pagan*, pp. 43, 75; Murray, *Group Movements Throughout the Ages*, p. 349; Shoemaker, *Twice-Born Ministers*, p. 123; and *How to Become a Christian*, p. 52.

[459] James, *The Varieties of Religious Experience*, pp. 249-50.

lay plans *as if* we were to be immortal, then we find those words do make a genuine difference in our moral life. Our faith that these objects actually exist proves to be a full equivalent in hindsight for a knowledge of what they might be if we were permitted positively to conceive them.[460]

To be converted, to be regenerated, to receive grace, to experience religion, to gain an assurance, are so many phrases which denote the process, gradual or sudden, by which a self, hitherto divided and consciously wrong, inferior and unhappy, becomes unified and consciously right, superior and happy, in consequence of its firmer hold upon religious realities.[461]

The Oxford Group had these things to say:

Now, how can we find this new quality of living? How can we capture that spirit that can change the world? It can only come from a genuine religious experience—that is valid for a change of heart, for changed social conditions, for true national security, for international understanding. It is valid because is originates in God, and issues in actual changes in human nature.[462]

---

[460] James, *The Varieties of Religious Experience*, p. 56. Sam Shoemaker once wrote an article titled "'Act As If—'The First Step Toward Faith." It appeared in the *Christian Herald* (October, 1954). The article was condensed and, in that form, appeared in the May, 1962 issue of *The Reader's Digest*. Shoemaker frequently quoted James's *Varieties*; and Dr. Charles Knippel stated that Shoemaker first read William James's book after his own conversion experience (in China, in 1918) under the pastoral care of Frank Buchman. Knippel believed that James's "act as if" thesis influenced Shoemaker and Shoemaker's "Act As If" article, and that Shoemaker's act-as-if approach left its broad mark on Wilson. See Knippel, *Samuel M. Shoemaker's Theological Influence*, pp. 132-33, 177-78. And, in both recovery center meetings and A.A. meetings, we have often heard the expression "act as if" and also the more confusing "fake it until you make it." Whether either or both of these ideas have their genesis in Wilson, Shoemaker, or William James himself, we do not know.

[461] James, *The Varieties of Religious Experience*, p. 177. This conception of a conversion or religious experience was very much accepted by Oxford Group writers, particularly Shoemaker. See Shoemaker, *Realizing Religion*, p. 22; *A Young Man's View of the Ministry*, pp. 11-12; and Walter, *Soul Surgery*, p. 80

[462] Buchman, *Remaking The World*, p. 75.

The basis of conversion is the awakening of a new self, and the vital element in this new birth is the dawning of a new affection which henceforth dominates the heart. . . . It is this passion for the Unseen and the Eternal which above all else can change the heart, and strengthen the will, and illuminate the mind. Conversion is the birth of Love. . . . God outside of us is a theory; God inside of us becomes a fact. God outside of us is an hypothesis; God inside of us is an experience. . . . God the Spirit is actuality of life, joy, peace and saving power . . . and the consciousness that Another had grasped the hand, and that thereafter freedom and strength and peace had come.[463]

Peace, direction, power—the fullness of life—await the complete surrender of ourselves to God for His purposes.[464]

The testimony of those who have been changed by conversion and themselves have become changers of human life, whatever their various theological inheritance, is, that any form of wilfulness in the mind is a vital bar to the vital consciousness of God; that as soon as the mind, with real honesty and a consuming desire for that divine consciousness, hates its sin, and turns to God, the will is new born; and, finally, that henceforth life for them becomes transfigured by a joy which seems to consist of, first, a poignant conviction of the reality of God's response to their craving; second, an entire sense of freedom from a division in personality; and third, a sense of creative power in the lives of other men, making for a like happiness with their own.[465]

The Presence of God. I find throughout the diverse testimonies of religious experiences a striking unity and identity . . . all testify to the irreducible minimum of religious experience, namely, the certainty of the "presence of God" in this universe. Men and women of all races, of different mental capacities, social and cultural backgrounds, unite throughout history in their

---

[463] Walter, *Soul Surgery*, pp. 82-83.
[464] Cecil Rose, *When Man Listens*, p. 17.
[465] Begbie, *Life Changers*, p. 21.

common witness to the reality of God. They tell of the strength of heart and of mind, of the depth of knowledge of life, of the charity and love that are poured into human beings whenever they establish contact with God. . . . Let me remind you again that the essence of religious experience is the sense of the presence of God and of His power to regenerate and guide men.[466]

Sam Shoemaker's writings are filled with similar descriptions of the reality of sensing the presence of God and what He has done; and also of the sense of peace and power and joy that come from surrender. For example, he said:

Let go! Abandon yourself to Him. Say to Him, "Not my will but Thine be done." Live it. Pray for it. Put yourself at His disposal for time and for eternity. And if your experience is anything like mine has been, you will find that Jesus gives to life a zest and a glory, a peace and a purpose, which He only can give.[467]

This experience, which I consider was my conversion, brought to me a kind of life which was entirely new to me. The fears were proved foolish. There was an integration of scattered impulses. I had victory where I never expected to have it.[468]

The Oxford Group experiment, involving belief, decision, self-examination, confession, conviction, conversion, conservation, and restitution, produced change—a change brought about by God's power and not their own. Shoemaker's *By the Power of God* explained:

---

[466] Brown, *The Venture of Belief*, pp. 24, 47.

[467] Shoemaker, *Religion That Works*, pp. 19-20. Abandon! How often that word and emphasis appear in the Big Book! At page 59, "We asked His protection and care with complete abandon." At page 63, "we could at last abandon ourselves utterly to Him." At page 164, "Abandon yourself to God as you understand God." We see Shoemaker, the Oxford Group, and Anne Smith in these phrases. See Dick B., *Anne Smith's Journal*, pp. 124-25. All emphasized surrendering as much of yourself as you understand to as much of God as you understand. The result of the experiment was an experience in which the power and presence of God were sensed.

[468] Shoemaker, *Twice-Born Ministers*, p. 55.

There may be much misgiving and great spiritual struggle: somewhere there must always be a great "giving in" that abandons self-generated power for God's power.[469]

The following comparative words from A.A.'s Big Book should be enough to indicate the influence of Oxford Group language (about the spiritual experience) on the language of A.A.:

In the face of collapse and despair, in the face of the total failure of their human resources, they found that a new power, peace, happiness, and sense of direction flowed into them (p. 50).

When many hundreds of people are able to say that consciousness of the Presence of God is today the most important fact of their lives, they present a powerful reason why one should have faith (p. 51).

In a few seconds he was overwhelmed by a conviction of the Presence of God. . . . He stood in the Presence of Infinite Power and Love. He had stepped from bridge to shore. For the first time, he lived in conscious companionship with his Creator (p. 56).

The great fact is just this, and nothing less: That we have had deep and effective spiritual experiences which have revolutionized our whole attitude toward life, toward our fellows and toward God's universe. The central fact of our lives today is the absolute certainty that our Creator has entered into our hearts and lives in a way which is indeed miraculous. He has commenced to accomplish those things for us which we could never do by ourselves (p. 25).

Next, we decided that hereafter in this drama of life, God was going to be our Director. . . . When we sincerely took such a position, all sorts of remarkable things followed. . . . As we felt new power flow in, as we enjoyed peace of mind, as we

---

[469] Shoemaker, *By The Power of God*, p. 134.

discovered we could face life successfully, as we became conscious of His presence, we began to lose our fear of today, tomorrow or the hereafter. We were reborn (pp. 62-63).

We are sure God wants us to be happy, joyous, and free (p. 133).

See to it that your relationship with Him is right, and great events will come to pass for you and countless others. This is the Great Fact for us (p. 164).

We conclude this review of the first twenty-six Oxford Group concepts—including the concept that a "spiritual awakening" occurs when the other steps are followed—with several points from Shoemaker and from the Bible.

First, in *Twice-Born Ministers*, Shoemaker said:

Such sayings as, "Ye must be born again,"[470] and "He that loseth his life for my sake . . . shall find it,"[471] and "Seek ye first the kingdom . . . and all these things shall be added,"[472] became living to me as part of my own experience. Previously I had gone just far enough into Christianity to feel the burden of the law, and not far enough to reap the joy of the Spirit. Now things were different.[473]

Shoemaker's concluding chapter in *By the Power of God*, was titled, "What Awakening Takes." These were his topics:

1. How Awakening Begins: "Often he has had a lifelong spiritual exposure to the things of the Spirit. But somewhere these must become *his own*. That may happen when he comes into contact with another person who is truly in touch with God, gives evidence of it in his own life, and provides the

---

[470] John 3:7.

[471] Matthew 10:39.

[472] Matthew 6:33.

[473] Shoemaker, *Twice-Born Ministers*, p. 56.

channel and the challenge that are needed. You never can give away what you do not possess" (p. 134).

2. Difference between Working and Being Used: "It will surprise you how much begins to happen when you stop trying to do a job for God, and just let God work through you" (p. 137).

3. An Intense Preoccupation with Individuals: "I believe the greatest unwritten portion of the Gospels is the time that Jesus spent with individual disciples" (p. 137).

4. Persons and the Gospel: "We must never confuse our message with ourselves . . . there is timeless truth here about the way God intends to use people to reach people" (p. 139).

5. New Wine and Old Bottles:[474] "What it [the Church] needs is nothing less than the fresh invasion of the Spirit in awakening" (p. 144).

6. This Is Every Christian's Business: 1. Know who Jesus Christ is. 2. Be converted to Jesus Christ through an act of dedication. 3. Be able to articulate that experience for the benefit of others. 4. Be able to relate that experience to the needs of individuals. 5. Be able to relate that faith to situations, e.g., in business, etc. (p. 146).

7. The Ultimate Objective: "There is a direct correlation between the spread of personal faith, and the spread of those deeds of helpfulness which make faith's most attractive vehicle. Men converted, men impassioned, men in touch with spiritual power, men trained in practical ways of working, all living at a revolutionary level of concern and in great concerted action with one another—this is our means to the ultimate objective, that the Kingdoms of this world shall become the Kingdom of our Lord and of His Christ" (pp. 155-56).

---

[474] See Matthew 9:17 for the pertinent verse.

Oxford Group people quoted the following relevant Bible verses:

> Verily, verily, I say unto thee, Except a man be born again, he cannot see the kingdom of God. . . . Except a man be born of water and *of* the Spirit, he cannot enter into the kingdom of God. Marvel not that I said unto thee, Ye must be born again.[475]

> But seek ye first the kingdom of God, and his righteousness; and all these things shall be added unto you.[476]

> Not every one that saith unto me, Lord, Lord, shall enter into the kingdom of heaven; but he that doeth the will of my Father which is in heaven.[477]

> And being assembled together with them, [Jesus] commanded them that they should not depart from Jerusalem, but wait for the promise of the Father, which, *saith he*, ye have heard of me.
> For John truly baptized with water; but ye shall be baptized with the Holy Ghost not many days hence. . . . Ye shall receive power, after that the Holy Ghost is come upon you: and ye shall be witnesses unto me both in Jerusalem, and in all Judaea, and in Samaria, and unto the uttermost part of the earth.[478]

> And when the day of Pentecost was fully come . . . they were all filled with the Holy Ghost, and began to speak with other tongues as the Spirit gave them utterance. . . . Then Peter said unto them, "Repent, and be baptized every one of you in the name of Jesus Christ for the remission of sins, and that ye shall receive the gift of the Holy Ghost. . . ." And when they had prayed, the place was shaken where they were assembled together; and they

---

[475] John 3:3, 5, 7. See Shoemaker, *National Awakening*, pp. 55-66; *Confident Faith*, pp. 137, 140; *God's Control*, p. 137; *Realizing Religion*, p. 35, 21; and Allen, *He That Cometh*, p. 19.

[476] Matthew 6:33. See Shoemaker, *National Awakening*, pp. 41-42; *God's Control*, p. 35; and Macmillan, *Seeking and Finding*, p. 226.

[477] Matthew 7:21. See Allen, *He That Cometh*, p. 139.

[478] Acts 1:4, 5, 8. See Benson, *The Eight Points*, pp. 90, 96, 101; and Streeter, *The God Who Speaks*, pp. 110-11.

were all filled with the Holy Ghost, and they spake the word of God with boldness. . . . And with great power gave the apostles witness of the resurrection of the Lord Jesus: and great grace was upon them all.[479]

But the fruit of the Spirit is love, joy, peace, longsuffering, gentleness, goodness, faith, meekness, temperance: against such there is no law.[480]

Now the Lord is that Spirit; and where the Spirit of the Lord is, there is liberty. But we all, with open face, beholding as in a glass the glory of the Lord are changed into the same image from glory to glory, even as by the Spirit of the Lord.[481]

Fellowship with God and Believers, and Witness by Life and Word

27. *Fellowship*

The Oxford Group was first called "A First Century Christian Fellowship." They endeavored to maintain the fellowship of the Holy Spirit—one of mutual sacrifice to win all men to the fellowship of the love of God revealed by Jesus Christ.

---

[479] Acts 2:1, 4, 38; 4:31, 33. See Shoemaker, *Religion That Works*, pp. 66-76; and Macmillan, *Seeking and Finding*, pp. 162-63.

[480] Galatians 5:22-23. See Walter, *Soul Surgery*, p. 54; and Streeter, *The God Who Speaks*, p. 111.

[481] 2 Corinthians 3:17-18. Streeter, *The God Who Speaks*, pp. 109-11. Compare the "Third Step Prayer" in the Big Book, p. 63: "God, I offer myself to Thee . . . Relieve me of the bondage of self, that I may better do Thy will. Take away my difficulties, that victory over them may bear witness to those I would help of Thy Power, Thy Love, and Thy Way of Life. May I do Thy will always!" The foregoing presents A.A.'s Third Step hope, and we suggest that the Twelfth Step "awakening" is a recognition of the truth of Buchman's statement "God comes to us when we ask Him." See Begbie, *Life Changers*, p. 37, and the statement at page 57 of the Big Book: "But He [God] has come to all who have honestly sought Him."

We have already discussed Frank Buchman's formation of what he and his friends called "A First Century Christian Fellowship."[482] Buchman had said, "It is . . . an attempt to get back to the beliefs and methods of the Apostles."[483] He said, "We not only accept their beliefs, but are also decided to practice their methods."[484] And Buchman stated in detail the "elemental beliefs of a First Century Christianity," namely:

1. The possibility of immediate and continued fellowship with the Holy Spirit—*guidance.*
2. The proclamation of a redemptive gospel—*personal, social, and national salvation.*
3. The possession of fulness of life—rebirth, and *an ever-increasing power and wisdom.*
4. The propagation of their life by individuals to individuals—*personal religion.*

Buchman said the foregoing beliefs produce an effective method of propagation

Love for the sinners.
Hatred of the sin.
Fearless dealing with sin.
The presentation of Christ as the cure for sin.
The sharing and giving of self, with and for others.[485]

Pointing to the following, powerful *fellowship* concepts, Begbie said Oxford Group people were more concerned with testifying to

---

[482] Though the name became "Oxford Group," the name "A First Century Christian Fellowship" was much used at first. Clark, *The Oxford Group,* p. 35; Begbie, *Life Changers,* pp. 107,122; Olive Jones, *Inspired Children,* p. ix; Shoemaker, *Twice-Born Ministers,* pp. 23, 46, 90; *Calvary Church Yesterday and Today,* p. 270; Hunter, *World Changing Through Life Changing,* p. 40; Lean, *On the Tail of a Comet,* p. 97; and *Pass It On,* p. 130.

[483] Lean, *On the Tail of a Comet,* p. 97.

[484] Begbie, *Life Changers,* p. 122.

[485] Begbie, *Life Changers,* p. 122.

real experiences (brought about by God's power through Christ), than with teaching an abstract ethical doctrine:

1. Guidance.[486]
2. Salvation.[487]
3. Rebirth and the availability of God's power and wisdom through it.[488]
4. Individual, personal witness to others.[489]

Except for the word "salvation," these concepts pop up over and over in A.A. words, practices, and history. The Big Book

---

[486] Rose said, in *When Man Listens*, "We shall, then, need to keep in close touch with those spiritual children of ours, helping them to see the fuller implications of their surrender, and particularly planning with them daring action; for fellowship is found most of all when we step into God-guided action together" (p. 53). A.A.'s "Tradition Two" states: "For our group purpose there is but one ultimate authority—a loving God as He may express Himself in our group conscience. Our leaders are but trusted servants; they do not govern." We believe this Tradition contains a very strong residual of the Oxford Group's Guidance idea that the Holy Spirit can and does operate in a fellowship of like-minded Christian believers. Tradition Two assumes that God actually expresses himself to and through the group in the way that Shoemaker and other writers mentioned when they were speaking of the concept of "koinonia."

[487] Winslow's *Why I Believe in the Oxford Group* said (quoting from Romans 1:16-17): "The Oxford Group has no new Gospel to proclaim. . . . that which the Apostles taught in the first Christian age, and which the Christian Church has taught from their days until ours. The Gospel is 'the power of God unto salvation to all who believe;' and no new Gospel can take its place" (p. 17). See also Macmillan, *Seeking and Finding*, pp. 139-51. We believe the Oxford Group was speaking of "spiritual wholeness"—the whole package of "God in Christ in you" made available to believers on the day of Pentecost. See John 3:16; John 10:10; Luke 24:47-49; Acts 1:5, 8; 2:1-4; 4:8-32; Romans 10:9-10; Ephesians 1:19; 2:8; Colossians 1:27, 2:9-10. After Pentecost, Peter boldly preached in Acts 4:12, "Neither is there salvation in any other [than Jesus Christ]: for there is none other name under heaven given among men, whereby we must be saved."

[488] Brown, *The Venture of Belief*, "[T]he essence of religious experience is the sense of the presence of God and of His power to regenerate and guide men" (p. 47).

[489] Winslow said the Oxford Group was "held together by the spiritual bond of a common self-surrender to Christ and a common determination to win the world to His allegiance, and . . . [exhibited] a quality of fellowship which . . . [gave] a new vision for what the Church of Christ might be." Winslow, *Why I Believe in the Oxford Group*, p. 19.

talks about the guidance of God; so did Dr. Bob and Bill.[490] The Big Book uses the word "reborn," talks of "transformation," and speaks in one way or another about God's wisdom as contrasted to man's.[491] And A.A.'s Twelfth Step idea of "carrying the message" certainly bespeaks Witness.

The Oxford Group fellowship generated witness. Fresh from his recovery through the Oxford Group, Ebby Thacher felt compelled to seek out his friend, Bill. And Bill, fresh from his Oxford Group indoctrination in New York, felt compelled to search out another alcoholic (Dr. Bob as it turned out) when things were going badly and a drink was in prospect. And Bill and Dr. Bob, both having compared notes on Oxford Group service ideas, immediately went about Akron "oxidizing," after their long discussion on Mother's Day, 1935.[492]

What Is The Oxford Group? had this to say about fellowship: The Oxford Group offers Fellowship in Christ to the world, reborn souls to Churches, a sane, practical Christianity to put right the spiritual and material problems which confront us (p. 129).

In his chapter, "Lo! Here is Fellowship," Benson wrote:

"One man is not man." We need each other to realize ourselves. The story of human life on this planet is the record of man's slow learning of life's law of fellowship. . . . Living to himself, man is weak, poor, joyless, limited. In fellowship he becomes strong, rich, happy and expansive. It brings him to a greater fulness of life and a comradeship of spirit which mean personal enrichment to all. . . . Loneliness is the most terrible tragedy of the human spirit. . . . One of the greatest things the Oxford Group Movement is doing is to make fellowship possible. . . . Fellowship is one of the great words of the New Testament as it is also one of the great facts of Christian history. Now the New Testament makes it quite clear that fellowship is in the Holy Spirit. . . . It

---

[490] See, for example, Big Book, page 86; *DR. BOB*, p. 314; and *Pass It On*, p. 172,

[491] See Big Book, pp. 63, 569-70, 100.

[492] *DR. BOB* suggests at page 78 that "Oxidizing" was probably short for "Oxfordizing."

refers to fellowship with the Holy Spirit.[493] But even more, it means fellowship with one another in and through the Holy Spirit. It refers to a certain quality, intensity and power of fellowship which is created by the presence of the Holy Spirit in a group of people and by His action upon them. . . . Jesus . . . gathered . . . a fellowship of mutual service through sacrifice, and their task was to win all men to the fellowship of the love of God revealed by Jesus Christ. . . . This close, intimate communion with Christ drew them to each other in mutual affection and mutual helpfulness, each seeking to share with the other his own resources in Christ Jesus.[494]

Benson, the author, also said there are heartfelt needs the pulpit cannot meet. Sermons and books without fellowship are dead letters. The mind is haunted by fears, doubts, and failures. He said:

Suppose you could talk heart to heart with sympathetic souls who have had those very experiences and found a remedy, what strength and hope would come into your life. Well, that is exactly the spiritual climate which the Groups provide. . . . Through the power of fellowship separate personalities blend in a society of friends that has a characteristic quality and a power of concerned action which increase the potentialities of individuals.[495]

Benson emphasized the following verses on fellowship:

1 John 1:3:
That which we have seen and heard declare we unto you, that ye also may have fellowship with us; and truly our fellowship is with the Father, and with His Son, Jesus Christ.[496]

---

[493] See, for example, 2 Corinthians 13:14: "The grace of the Lord Jesus Christ, and the love of God, and the communion of the Holy Ghost, be with you all, Amen."

[494] Benson, *The Eight Points*, pp. 102-06.

[495] Benson, *The Eight Points*, pp. 108-09.

[496] The following quote this verse: Benson, *The Eight Points*, p. 112; Anne Smith (See Dick B., *Anne Smith's Journal*, pp. 71, 120, 130); and Thornton-Duesbury, *Sharing*, p. 3.

Philippians 1:3-5, 12:
I thank my God upon every remembrance of you, Always in every prayer of mine for you all making request with joy, For your fellowship in the gospel from the first day until now.
But I would ye should understand, brethren, that the things which happened unto me have fallen out rather unto the furtherance of the gospel.[497]

Mark 10:45:
For even the Son of man came not to be ministered unto, but to minister, and to give His life a ransom for many.[498]

Galatians 3:28:
There is neither Jew nor Greek, there is neither bond nor free, there is neither male nor female: for ye are all one in Christ Jesus.[499]

Matthew 18:15-19:
Moreover if thy brother shall trespass against thee, go and tell him his fault between thee and him alone . . . But if he will not hear thee, then take with thee one or two more, that in the mouth of two or three witnesses every word may be established. And if he shall neglect to hear them, tell it unto the church. Verily I say unto you, Whosoever ye shall bind on earth shall be bound in heaven: and whatsoever ye shall loose on earth shall be loosed in heaven. Again I say unto you, That if two of you shall agree on earth as touching anything that they shall ask, it shall be done for them of my Father Which is in heaven.[500]

---

[497] Benson, *The Eight Points*, cited, at page 112, the above two verses from Philippians.

[498] Benson, *The Eight Points*, p. 112, said this verse was "the national anthem of the Kingdom of fellowship."

[499] Benson, *The Eight Points*, p. 106;

[500] Weatherhead, *Discipleship*, said, citing the foregoing at page 73, "I think we ought to feel that a unanimous finding of such a group is the mind of God concerning the situation. I believe that is implied in the New Testament."

Matthew 18:20:
For where two or three are gathered together in My name, there am I in the midst of them.[501]

Ephesians 2:19-22:
Now therefore ye are no more strangers and foreigners, but fellow citizens with the saints and of the household of God; and are built upon the foundation of the apostles and prophets, Jesus Christ himself being the chief corner stone; In Whom all the building fitly framed together groweth into an holy temple in the Lord: In whom ye also are builded together for an habitation of God through the Spirit.[502]

There are several important ideas that found favor in the Oxford Group concerning "Fellowship" and which derived from the foregoing and other Bible verses: (1) There was Fellowship with God and with His son, Jesus Christ.[503] (2) There was a fellowship of believing people which was empowered by the Holy Ghost.[504] (3) There was a communion with the Holy Spirit.[505] (4) All believers had the common bond of being members of a living body whose head was Jesus Christ himself.[506] (5) There was no discrimination once all had the common bond.[507] (6) There was a "corporate" experience where the Holy Spirit is found through the group-experience of like-minded believers.[508] (7) God had a unique presence in the Group itself both by the fellowship tie of the spirit and by the Holy Spirit's ability to guide the group itself whose individuals received the spirit of God

---

[501] Benson, *The Eight Points*, p. 109.

[502] These are verses speaking of the body of Christ about which Shoemaker taught when he was speaking of the Fellowship of the Holy Spirit. See Shoemaker, *Religion That Works*, pp. 66-76.

[503] Thornton-Duesbury, *Sharing*, p. 3.

[504] Shoemaker, *Religion That Works*, p. 67.

[505] Shoemaker, *How To Find God*, p. 21.

[506] Day, *The Principles of the Group*, p. 9.

[507] Winslow, *Why I Believe in the Oxford Group*, p. 53.

[508] Shoemaker, *Religion That Works*, p. 67.

through their new birth.[509] (8) There was a unity in the fellowship that ended loneliness and encouraged commonality in purpose, in sharing with others, and in distribution of necessities.[510] (9) There was a focus on teamwork.[511] (10) There was a common mission of changing lives to change the world to Christ.[512] (11) There was an emphasis on service.[513]

Shoemaker wrote:

Somewhere the new church will have a group for the sharing of experience, a working "koinonia." As those who are won increase, there will be need for a meeting where they see and hear one another, where those who are discouraged are lifted up again, where those who have had victories can share them with others, where new people can declare themselves. At first, this will be small. It grows out of changed lives. Convert people, and the group will develop as you relate them.[514]

There would be plenty of diversity of experience, opinion and background amongst them to divide them hopelessly, unless they had a major unifying principle. That principle is the guidance of God, the Voice of Christ made new to them each day. Because they have Him, and put and keep Him first, they do not have disagreement, division, disunity.[515]

It has been my belief for several years that the surest sign of spiritual awakening in our time is the emergence of the small spiritual group. It is as if, in a day of widespread loneliness and fear, the Holy Spirit were saying to us that the characteristic manifestation of His life and power would not be just in changed

---

[509] Benson, *The Eight Points*, p. 105, 113.

[510] Benson, *The Eight Points*, pp. 106-07.

[511] Day, *The Principles of the Group*, pp. 9-10.

[512] *What Is The Oxford Group?*, p. 12.

[513] Benson, *The Eight Points*, p. 110.

[514] Shoemaker, *The Conversion of the Church*, pp. 114-15.

[515] Shoemaker, *The Gospel According To You*, p. 190.

individuals, but in individuals found in relation to other individuals from the first. . . . In that sense, we may be on the brink of a real, permanent Christian revival; but it will work slowly and surely in small groups. These are nothing new in the life of the Church. Even in the ancient Jewish church, there were small societies of friends who met weekly for devotion and charity. . . . You can't organize them . . . they come about through the impact of life upon life. The group cannot and will not do everything. Its strength will be in fairly direct proportion to what is happening to its members outside as well as inside the meetings. . . . Dr. Elton Trueblood . . . says there are five elements in common that are found in these informal groups: A primary emphasis on commitment; an unequivocal belief in the "priesthood of all believers;" . . . an emphasis on the reality in fellowship; an emphasis on work—daily work—at the job level; an unapologetic acceptance of spiritual discipline.[516]

The Spirit can communicate His truth to a spiritual fellowship of believers in ways He cannot communicate to individuals: it is another phase of Christ's meaning when He said that "where two or three are gathered together in my name, there am I in the midst of them."[517] He is wherever a believer is; but He is present in heightened reality in the fellowship.[518]

28. *Witness by Life and Word*

Sharing with others by personal evangelism the fruits of a life changed and changing lives is essential. The Oxford Group is witness for Christ—having a conviction of the existence of a living Christ and proof of God's forgiveness and the power of the Holy Spirit.

Frank Buchman said that personal knowledge of Christ is not a thing to be folded away and secretly treasured; it is to be put to

---

[516] Shoemaker, *With The Holy Spirit and With Fire*, pp. 109-18.

[517] Matthew 18:20.

[518] Shoemaker, *Religion That Works*, pp. 72-73.

work for others. He apparently coined a phrase, part of which became well known to AAs: "The best way to keep an experience of Christ is to *pass it on.*"[519] Shoemaker turned the "pass it on" idea into a different expression, part of which also became well known to AAs: "You have to give it away to keep it." Anne Smith often taught this concept.[520]

Shoemaker wrote:

The only way to keep religion is to give it away. Give what you can right away; it will increase as you give it.[521]

The best way to keep what you have is to give it away, and no substitute has ever been found for personal Christian witness.[522]

We must begin giving away what we have, or we shall lose it. One of the first impulses after we hear a good story is to find someone to tell it to. And one of the first impulses after we have had a real Christian experience is to want to impart it to others.[523]

Get them into the stream of God's will and God's grace, till they ask Him to use them to help reconcile others. They will not keep this unless they give it away. That is a spiritual law—for them and for us.[524]

Oxford Group people cited a number of Bible verses for Christian witness:

---

[519] Buchman, *Remaking the World*, p. x (emphasis added).

[520] Dick B., *Anne Smith's Journal*, pp. 65, 69, 72-73, 85, 121, 138.

[521] Shoemaker, *One Boy's Influence*, p. 15.

[522] Shoemaker, *They're On The Way*, p. 159.

[523] Shoemaker, *How to Become a Christian*, p. 80.

[524] Shoemaker, *The Church Alive*, p. 139. See also Shoemaker's interesting comment about Alcoholics Anonymous and "Twelfth Step Work" in Shoemaker, *By The Power of God*, p. 102.

And we are His witnesses of these things; and so is also the Holy Ghost, Whom God hath given to them that obey Him.[525]

Having therefore obtained help of God, I continue unto this day, witnessing both to small and great, saying none other things than those which the prophets and Moses did say should come; That Christ should suffer, and that He should be the first that should rise from the dead, and should shew light unto the people, and to the Gentiles.[526]

Now then we are ambassadors for Christ, as though God did beseech you by us: we pray you in Christ's stead, be ye reconciled to God.[527]

In the mouth of two or three witnesses shall every word be established.[528]

For the life was manifested, and we have seen it, and bear witness, and shew unto you that eternal life, which was with the Father, and was manifested unto us.[529]

Oxford Group people said, about witnessing to deliverance:

For we must remember that the love of Christ, which we are called to share, is an active love. He was not content to live a life of "silent witness" and hope for the best. He went out seeking men. When we are filled with the same kind of love we shall do as He did. Life-changing is not a matter of special commission nor of special gifts. It is a matter of how much real love for people we have, how much we want them to find the one complete answer to their need, and how much of God we have

---

[525] Acts 5:32. *What Is The Oxford Group?*, p. 36.

[526] Acts 26:22-23. *What Is The Oxford Group?*, p. 26.

[527] 2 Corinthians 5:20. *What Is The Oxford Group?*, p. 35. See Sangster, *God Does Guide Us*, p. 23.

[528] 2 Corinthians 13:1. *What Is The Oxford Group?*, p. 26.

[529] 1 John 1:2. *What Is The Oxford Group?*, p. 38.

ourselves to share with them. . . . Life-changing is simply normal Christian living. It is doing Christ's work. If our aim falls below that level we are failing Him.[530]

God has liberated me from the tyranny of fear and from these particular sins which before I could not conquer, and life is so full of the joy of freedom, that if you would permit, I long to tell you by what methods God's healing came. It is this type of evangelism which sent St. Paul coursing through Asia Minor.[531]

Let the new convert understand at the outset, what many of us had to learn after many years, at painful cost, that the only way to live a normal buoyant, developing Christian life is to be constantly a missionary of Christ to others.[532]

Moreover, it meant a relentless crusade to induce other men and women not only to believe in the possibility of living the victorious life, but to live it.[533]

We can all be witnesses for Christ, all of us who are aware of what the power of Christ has done for us. . . . This message must be one not only of hope but of concrete proof of the Christ who was manifested unto us. It means telling others of our own experiences in Sin, of our Surrender, and after; of the power of God guidance in our lives and the spiritual strength given us to overcome our present difficulties, in accordance with the needs of those to whom we witness.[534]

And now compare these words in A.A.'s Big Book:

Life will take on new meaning. To watch people recover, to see them help others, to watch loneliness vanish, to see a fellowship

---

[530] Cecil Rose, *When Man Listens*, pp. 54-55.

[531] Allen, *He That Cometh*, pp. 202-03.

[532] Walter, *Soul Surgery*, p. 93.

[533] Russell, *For Sinners Only*, p. 62.

[534] *What Is The Oxford Group?*, p. 37.

grow about you, to have a host of friends—this is an experience you will not want to miss.[535]

Outline the program of action, explaining how you made a self-appraisal, how you straightened out your past and why you are endeavoring to be helpful to him. . . . Make it plain he is under no obligation to you, that you hope only that he will try to help other alcoholics when he escapes his own difficulties.[536]

Never talk down to an alcoholic from any moral or spiritual hilltop; simply lay out the kit of spiritual tools for his inspection. Show him how they worked with you. Offer him friendship and fellowship. Tell him if he wants to get well you will do anything to help.[537]

Helping others is the foundation stone of your recovery. A kindly act once in a while isn't enough. You have to act the Good Samaritan every day, if need be.[538]

Your job now is to be at the place where you may be of maximum helpfulness to others.[539]

---

[535] Big Book, p. 89.

[536] Big Book, p. 94.

[537] Big Book, p. 95.

[538] Big Book, p. 97. Oxford Group writers often spoke of the "Good Samaritan." For the Biblical account of the "Good Samaritan," see Luke 10:25-37.

[539] Big Book, p. 102.

7

Oxford Group Traces in A.A.'s Twelve Steps and Big Book Language

Principal Ideas in the Twelve Steps

Powerless, the Unmanageable Life and Step One

[Step One: We admitted we were powerless over alcohol—that our lives had become unmanageable.][1]

There is little to say about the Oxford Group's use of the expression "powerless" in relation to alcohol. A number of Bill Wilson's Oxford Group friends, such as Hazard, Cornell, Kitchen, and Clapp, were relieved of their alcoholism. All sought help from God and often called Him a "Power." Sam Shoemaker, who had helped each of these men, wrote: "It [sin] makes a gap between myself and the Ideal which I am *powerless* to bridge. . . . Only God, therefore, can deal with sin. He must contrive to do for us what *we have lost the power to do ourselves*" (emphasis added).[2]

---

[1] In this chapter and elsewhere in the book, *The Twelve Steps of Alcoholics Anonymous* are reprinted with permission of Alcoholics Anonymous World Services, Inc.

[2] Samuel M. Shoemaker, *If I Be Lifted Up* (New York: Fleming H. Revell, 1931), pp. 131, 133.

And Oxford Group people wrote much about the need for *finding* "Power" which, to them, referred to their separation from God and *powerlessness* over sin, resentment, fear, and so on.[3]

The *unmanageable life* was an entirely different matter. It often marked the beginning of the Oxford Group surrender prayer.

In his well-known Oxford Group book, *For Sinners Only*, A. J. Russell described the prayer from Dr. Frank Buchman's story about "Victor," and how Victor surrendered and had his life changed. Russell told at some length how Frank Buchman had converted Victor at a schoolboys' camp in the Himalayas. Russell recounted the following conversation between Buchman and Victor:

> [Buchman said:] What we need is faith. When we are perfectly willing to forsake sin and follow Christ, then joy and release come. What we want to do is to get in touch with Him and turn our lives over to Him. Where should we go to do it? At once the lad replied: "There is only one place—on our knees." The lad prayed—one of those powerful, simple prayers which are so quickly heard by Him Who made the eye and the ear: "*O Lord, manage me, for I cannot manage myself*" (emphasis added).[4]

Variations of this "Victor story" were told again and again in Oxford Group writings.[5]

---

[3] See Theophil Spoerri, *Dynamic out of Silence: Frank Buchman's Relevance Today* (London: Grosvenor Books, 1976), p. 25; Stephen Foot, *Life Began Yesterday* (New York: Harper & Brothers, 1935); pp. 5-6, 8-9, 22, 29-35, 47, 62, 67, 80; and Harold Begbie, *Life Changers* (London: Mills & Boon, 1932), p. 22. See Anne Smith's comment on the subject in Dick B., *Anne Smith's Journal, 1933-1939: A.A.'s Principles of Success* (San Rafael, CA: Paradise Research Publications, 1994), p. 22. Also see some comparative thoughts from Shoemaker in Samuel M. Shoemaker, *Courage to Change: The Christian Roots of the 12-Step Movement*. Compiled and edited by Bill Pittman and Dick B. (Michigan: Fleming H. Revell, 1994), pp. 25-30.

[4] See A. J. Russell, *For Sinners Only* (London: Hodder & Stoughton, 1932), p. 79.

[5] See Peter Howard, *Frank Buchman's Secret* (New York: Doubleday & Co., 1961), pp. 41-44; Spoerri, *Dynamic out of Silence*, pp. 34-37; Garth Lean, *On the Tail of a Comet: The Life of Frank Buchman* (Colorado Springs; Helmers & Howard, 1988), pp.

(continued...)

There was a similar surrender story and prayer involving Shoemaker. And Sam's "unmanageable" prayer came to be called "Charlie's Prayer." Shoemaker's long-time associate and assistant minister gave this account:

> One morning, as the two [Shoemaker and a poorly educated "east-sider" named Charlie] chatted in the rectory hallway, "it" happened. No one knows what the rector said on that occasion, but new life came to Charlie, and those who heard about Charlie's prayer could never forget it. It was a classic, a simple plea in eight words: *"God, manage me, 'cause I can't manage myself"* (emphasis added).[6]

Dr. Bob's wife, Anne Smith, several times suggested use of a virtually identical prayer.[7]

Recall: The Big Book's First Step language reads as follows:

> . . . that *our lives had become unmanageable* (p. 59, emphasis added).

The foregoing step language is followed by the A.A. Big Book's well-known "a,b,c's," which are:

> Our description of the alcoholic, the chapter to the agnostic, and our personal adventures before and after make clear three pertinent ideas: (a) That we were alcoholic *and could not manage our own lives.* (b) That probably no human power could have relieved our alcoholism. (c) That God could and would if He were sought (p. 60, emphasis added).

---

[5] (...continued)
112-13; and Cecil Rose, *When Man Listens* (New York: Oxford University Press, 1937), pp. 19-22.

[6] See Irving Harris, *The Breeze of the Spirit: Sam Shoemaker and the Story of Faith-at-Work* (New York: The Seabury Press, 1978), p. 10. See also Samuel M. Shoemaker, *How to Find God.* Reprint from *Faith at Work* Magazine, n.d., p. 6; and *How You Can Help Other People* (New York: E. P. Dutton & Co., 1946), p. 60.

[7] Dick B., *Anne Smith's Journal*, pp. 19-21.

A Power Greater Than Ourselves and Step Two

[Step Two: Came to believe that a Power greater than ourselves could restore us to sanity.]

In a chapter in *Life Began Yesterday*, which he titled "The Solution," Oxford Group writer, Stephen Foot, devoted a page to that solution, stating:

> There is at work in the world to-day a *Power* that has for many generations been neglected by masses of mankind, a *Power* that can change human nature—*that is the message of this book*. It is like the great power of the Niagara Falls, which existed for millenniums before man inhabited the earth. Then for thousands of years man lacked the knowledge to use the power and so it ran to waste. To-day, harnessed, it is bringing light into thousands of homes. So with this *Power* by which human nature can be changed. I have felt it in my own life and seen it at work in the lives of others; it is at work all over the world to-day, and through this *Power* problems are being solved (emphasis added).[8]

In one of the earliest, popular Oxford Group books, Harold Begbie wrote:

> The future of civilization, rising at this moment from the ruins of materialism, would seem to lie in an intelligent use by man of this ultimate source of spiritual *Power* (emphasis added).[9]

In the Big Book chapter, "There is a Solution," Bill Wilson said that will-power alone would not solve problems (pp. 22, 44). He made it clear that the solution lay in a relationship with God.[10] For those who doubted the existence of God, Bill wrote

---

[8] Foot, *Life Began Yesterday*, p. 22.

[9] Begbie, *Life Changers*, p. 22.

[10] See Big Book, pp. 29, 13, 28, 100, 164.

his chapter, "We Agnostics." He wrote it to enable agnostics to find and establish a relationship with what Bill and some Oxford Group people had described as a "Power", which they *all*, including Bill Wilson, called "God."[11] Thus Bill wrote:

> Lack of power, that was our dilemma. We had to find a power by which we could live, and it had to be a *Power greater than ourselves*. Obviously. But where and how were we to find this Power? Well, that's exactly what this book is about. Its main object is to enable you to find a Power greater than yourself which will solve your problem. . . . And it means, of course, that we are *going to talk about God* (p. 45).

> We found that as soon as we were able to lay aside prejudice and express even a willingness to believe in a *Power greater than ourselves*, we commenced to get results, even though it was impossible for any of us to fully define or comprehend that *Power, which is God* (p. 46, emphasis added).

As can be seen, Wilson used and emphasized the idea of "willingness to believe" as one means for finding a power greater than ourselves. And so did the Oxford Group.[12]

Anne Smith spoke much about the need for a power stronger than ourselves.[13] Sam Shoemaker wrote about "a Force outside himself, greater than himself" and "a vast Power outside themselves."[14]

---

[11] For example, one long-time Oxford Group writer said: "Only the Power which raised Jesus Christ from the dead can, and will, raise us from our old nature and begin to form in us the new." K. D. Belden, *Reflections on Moral Re-Armament* (London: Grosvenor Books, 1983), p. 42.

[12] See, for example, K. D. Belden, *Meeting Moral Re-Armament* (London: Grosvenor, 1979), p. 28

[13] Dick B., *Anne Smith's Journal*, pp. 22, 23, 68.

[14] Dick B., *New Light on Alcoholism: The A.A. Legacy from Sam Shoemaker* (Corte Madera, CA: Good Book Publishing Company, 1994), pp. 179-80.

Shoemaker often pointed to the need for a *relationship* with this Power (God).[15] Thus, in *Children of the Second Birth*, he wrote:

> We believe entirely that conversion is the experience which initiates the new life. But we are not fools enough to think that the beginning is the end! All subsequent life is a development of the relationship with God which conversion opened (p. 16).

The Decision to Surrender to God As You Understand Him and Step Three

> [Step Three: Made a decision to turn our will and our lives over to the care of God, *as we understood Him.*]

Alcoholics Anonymous, the Oxford Group, and Rev. Sam Shoemaker all emphasized, in their writings, that the *path* to a relationship with God involved attaining a spiritual experience. But the path *began* with a *decision* to entrust the care of one's life to God by surrendering to God.

Our own discussion of surrender will be divided into three parts: (1) The decision. (2) God *as you understand Him.* (3) The surrender itself.

1. *The decision*

Oxford Group people stated that one must start his or her path to a relationship with God by making a *decision* to surrender. One basic primer, *What Is The Oxford Group?*, said:

> The Oxford Group initial act of Surrender is not, in any way, an outward and visible ceremony we feel we must shrink from; it is a simple *decision* put into simple language, spoken aloud to God,

---

[15] Samuel M. Shoemaker, *Realizing Religion* (New York: Association Press, 1923), p. 42; *Confident Faith* (New York: Fleming H. Revell, 1932), p. 110; *Christ's Words from the Cross* (New York: Fleming H. Revell, 1933), p. 49; and *National Awakening* (New York: Harper & Brothers, 1936), p. 13.

in front of a witness, at any time in any place, that we have *decided* to forget the past in God and to give our future into His keeping. Nothing more need be added; . . . (emphasis added).[16]

Anne Smith also stressed beginning with a decision.[17]

Embodying this *decision* in Step Three, the Big Book said:

Made a decision to turn our will and our lives over to the care of God *as we understood Him* (p. 59, italics in original).

Being convinced, *we were at Step Three*, which is that we decided to turn our will and our life over to God as we understood Him (p. 60, italics in original).

This is the how and why of it. First of all, we had to quit playing God. It didn't work. Next, we *decided* that hereafter in this drama of life, God was going to be our Director (p. 62, emphasis added).

Though our *decision* was a vital and crucial step, it could have little permanent effect unless at once followed by a strenuous effort to face, and to be rid of, the things in ourselves which had been blocking us (p. 64, emphasis added).

2. *God as you understand Him*

A.A. legend has it that Jim B. (an AA and former atheist), authored the concept of "God as we understood Him" as it is

---

[16] The Layman with a Notebook, *What Is The Oxford Group?* (London: Oxford University Press, 1933), p. 47. See also Henry B. Wright, *The Will of God and a Man's Lifework* (New York: Young Men's Christian Association Press, 1909), pp. 43-114; Ebenezer Macmillan, *Seeking and Finding* (New York: Harper & Brothers, 1933), p. 273; Samuel M. Shoemaker, *Children of the Second Birth* (New York: Fleming H. Revell, 1927), pp. 175-87; *Religion That Works* (New York: Fleming H. Revell, 1928), pp. 46-47); *If I Be Lifted Up*, p. 93; *The Conversion of the Church* (New York: Fleming H. Revell, 1932), pp. 39-40, 77; and *The Church Can Save the World* (New York: Harper & Brothers, 1938), p. 120.

[17] Dick B., *Anne Smith's Journal*, p. 25.

expressed in A.A.'s Twelve Steps.[18] Bill Wilson acknowledged
there had been a controversy over use of the word "God" when
the Twelve Steps were being adopted, but we are not aware that
Bill himself ever affirmed Jim B.'s claim that he (Jim) was the
author of God *as we understood Him*.[19] In fact, in two different
early accounts of his first visits with his friend and sponsor (Ebby
Thacher), Bill indicated that Ebby himself had suggested to Bill in
1934 that Bill should surrender himself to God *as Bill understood
Him*.[20] The Oxford Group and Sam Shoemaker had frequently
spoken of "surrendering as much of yourself as you understand to
as much of God as you understand."[21] Hence Ebby's suggestion
to Bill was quite consistent with what Ebby must have heard in the
Oxford Group prior to the existence of A.A. Further, there was a
similar surrender idea in vogue at this time; and Stephen Foot
wrote:

---

[18] See, for example, Jim B.'s own statement of this claim in Jim's Big Book story
at page 248. Jim B. made the same claim on page 5 of a document he wrote, titled
Evolution of Alcoholics Anonymous. A copy was supplied to the author by Eddie S., an
oldtimer from Colorado.

[19] See, for example, Bill's account in *Alcoholics Anonymous Comes of Age* (New
York: Alcoholics Anonymous World Services, 1957), pp. 17, 166-67; and Ruth Hock's
account in *Pass It On* (New York: Alcoholics Anonymous World Services, 1984), p.
199.

[20] See Bill Wilson, *Original Story*, a thirty-four page document located at the archives
at Bill's Home at Stepping Stones. Each line of the document is numbered; and the
author was permitted to copy and retain a copy of the document. On page 30, Bill stated:
"This is what my friend [Ebby Thacher] suggested I do: Turn my face to God as I
understand Him and say to Him with earnestness—complete honesty and abandon—that
I henceforth place my life at His disposal and Direction forever" (lines 989-92). See also
W. W., "The Fellowship of Alcoholics Anonymous," *Quarterly Journal of Studies on
Alcohol* (Yale University, 1945): pp. 461-73, in which Bill is quoted on page 463 as
saying that Ebby Thacher told him, "So, call on God as you understand God. Try
prayer."

[21] See Shoemaker, *Children of the Second Birth*, pp. 27, 47; *How to Become a
Christian* (New York: Harper & Brothers, 1953), p. 72; *How to Find God*, p. 6; "In
Memoriam" (Princeton, The Graduate Council, June 10, 1956), pp. 2-3; and Dick B.,
New Light on Alcoholism, pp. 45, 350.

Life began for me with a surrender of all that I know of self, to all that I knew of God.[22]

Are you prepared to do His will, let the cost be what it may? That is surrender of all one knows of self to all one knows of God.[23]

Anne Smith twice used this surrender-to-all-one-knows-of-God language in her Journal.[24]

3. *Surrender of the will to God's direction*

Sam Shoemaker wrote:

[Of a parishioner:] She surrendered to God her groundless fears, and with them turned over to Him her life for His direction.[25]

[Quoting a minister Shoemaker described as "The Militant Mystic":] That night I decided to "launch out into the deep:" and with the decision to cast my will and my life on God, there came an indescribable sense of relief, of burdens dropping away.[26]

The Big Book's "Third Step Prayer" and discussion reads in part:

God, I offer myself to Thee—to build with me and to do with me as Thou wilt. Relieve me of the bondage of self, that I may better do Thy will. Take away my difficulties, that victory over them may bear witness to those I would help of Thy Power, Thy Love, and Thy Way of life. May I do Thy will always (p. 63)!

---

[22] Foot, *Life Began Yesterday*, pp. 12-13.

[23] Foot, *Life Began Yesterday*, p. 175. See also James D. Newton, *Uncommon Friends* (New York: Harcourt Brace, 1987), p. 154.

[24] Dick B., *Anne Smith's Journal*, pp. 25, 95.

[25] Shoemaker, *Children of the Second Birth*, p. 82.

[26] Samuel M. Shoemaker, *Twice-Born Ministers* (New York: Fleming H. Revell, 1929), p. 184.

Self-examination, the Moral Inventory and Step Four

[Step Four: Made a searching and fearless moral inventory of ourselves.]

1. *Looking for your own fault or part*

In her Journal, Anne Smith quoted parts of the following verses from the Sermon on the Mount, which had been quoted in the Oxford Group and apparently followed in A.A.[27] The verses emphasized looking for your own fault, your own part in a bad relationship with another human being. Matthew 7:1-5 said:

> Judge not, that ye be not judged. For with what judgment ye judge, ye shall be judged: and with what measure ye mete, it shall be measured to you again. And why beholdest thou the mote [speck] that is in thy brother's eye, but considerest not the beam [log] that is in thine own eye? Or how wilt thou say to thy brother, Let me pull out the mote out of thine eye; and, behold, a beam *is* in thine own eye? Thou hypocrite, first cast out the beam out of thine own eye; and then shalt thou see clearly to cast out the mote out of thy brother's eye.[28]

As we've covered before, the Oxford Group was big on identifying your own fault in a situation.[29]

A.A.'s Big Book said:

---

[27] Dick B., *Anne Smith's Journal*, p. 31.

[28] For Oxford Group writings citing these verses, see Geoffrey Allen, *He That Cometh* (New York: The Macmillan Company, 1932), pp. 81, 140; Victor Kitchen, *I Was a Pagan* (New York: Harper & Brothers, 1934), pp. 110-11; Shoemaker, *The Church Can Save the World*, pp. 81-121; and *God's Control* (New York: Fleming H. Revell, 1939), pp. 62-72. The verses were also cited in Oswald Chambers, *My Utmost for His Highest* ((London: Simpkin Marshall, 1927), pp. 169-74, a devotional used by Oxford Group people. Compare Russell, *For Sinners Only*, pp. 309-16.

[29] Spoerri, *Dynamic out of Silence*, pp. 25-26; Frank Buchman, *Remaking The World* (London: Blandford, 1961), p. 46; and Benson, *The Eight Points*, p. 28.

First, we searched out the flaws in our make-up which caused our failure (p. 64).

Putting out of our minds the wrongs others had done, we resolutely looked for our own mistakes. Where had we been selfish, dishonest, self-seeking and frightened? Though a situation had not been entirely our fault, we tried to disregard the other person involved entirely. Where were we to blame? The inventory was ours, not the other man's (p. 67).

Where had we been selfish, dishonest, or inconsiderate? Whom had we hurt? Did we unjustifiably arouse jealousy, suspicion or bitterness? Where were we at fault . . . (p. 69)?

2. *Applying a moral test in your self-examination*

The Oxford Group stressed the importance of "making the moral test." H. A. Walter's *Soul Surgery* was one of the earliest Oxford Group "texts." Dr. Bob used Walter's book a great deal.[30] And Walter said that the concept, "make the moral test," came from Frank Buchman's and Sherwood Eddy's "Ten Suggestions for Personal Work."[31] Anne Smith specifically mentioned Sherwood Eddy's ten suggestions in her Journal.[32] And this moral test meant examining one's life to see how it measured up to the Oxford Group's Four Absolutes—honesty, purity, unselfishness, and love.[33]

---

[30] Dick B., *Dr. Bob's Library* (San Rafael, CA: Paradise Research Publications, 1994), pp. 25, 78. In his 1992 visit to Stepping Stones (the Bill Wilson home at Bedford Hills in New York), the author found a copy of *Soul Surgery* in the copy of Anne Smith's Journal of which the Stepping Stones archives has custody.

[31] H. A. Walter, *Soul Surgery*, 6th ed (Oxford at the University Press, 1940—the earliest edition being published in 1919), pp. 43-44.

[32] Dick B., *Anne Smith's Journal*, pp. 30-32, 72, 98, 99.

[33] See C. Rose, *When Man Listens*, pp. 18-19; Olive Jones, *Inspired Children* (New York: Harper & Brothers, 1933), pp. 47-68; *Inspired Youth* (New York: Harper & Brothers, 1938), p. 41; and Hallen Viney, *How Do I Begin?* (Copyright, 1937 by The Oxford Group), pp. 2-4.

3. *Making a written inventory*

An Oxford Group moral self-examination meant writing down on a piece of paper the items in a person's life which showed where that person had fallen short of the standards set by Jesus Christ in the Sermon on the Mount and elsewhere. The standards could also be found in other New Testament writings. As we have previously shown, Sam Shoemaker summarized the self-examination technique as follows:

> It would be a very good thing if you took a piece of foolscap paper and wrote down the sins you feel guilty of. Don't make them up—there will be plenty without that. . . . One of the simplest and best rules for self-examination that I know is to use the Four Standards which Dr. Robert E. Speer said represented the summary of the Sermon on the Mount—Absolute Honesty, Absolute Purity, Absolute Unselfishness, and Absolute Love. Review your life in their light. Put down everything that doesn't measure up. Be ruthlessly, realistically honest.[34]

The Four Absolutes as a test for moral behavior had much vitality in early A.A. Thus *DR. BOB and the Good Oldtimers* stated:

> At the core of the program were the "four absolutes": absolute honesty, absolute unselfishness, absolute purity, and absolute love. (In 1948, Dr. Bob recalled the absolutes as "the only yardsticks" Alcoholics Anonymous had in the early days, before the Twelve Steps. He said he still felt they held good and could be extremely helpful when he wanted to do the right thing and the answer was not obvious. "Almost always, if I measure my decision carefully by the yardsticks of absolute honesty, absolute unselfishness, absolute purity, and absolute love, and it checks up

---

[34] Shoemaker, *How to Become a Christian*, pp. 56-57. See also Shoemaker, *The Conversion of the Church*, pp. 30-34; *Twice-Born Ministers*, p. 182; *God's Control*, pp. 104-05; and see Belden, *Meeting Moral Re-Armament*, p. 17.

pretty well with those four, then my answer can't be very far out of the way," he said. The absolutes are still published and widely quoted at A.A. meetings in the Akron-Cleveland area).[35]

A.A.'s Big Book followed the Oxford Group lead on the subject of an inventory. It spoke of a *moral* inventory (p. 59). It spoke of the necessity for a *written* inventory—getting the facts about grudges, fears, sex conduct, and harms "on paper" (pp. 64, 68, 69, 70, 75). And it was insistent that the examination look for "our own mistakes . . . our faults . . . our wrongs" (pp. 67-69).

Confession, Sharing with Another and Step Five

[Step Five: Admitted to God, to ourselves, and to another human being the exact nature of our wrongs.]

1. Confession of Faults

A.A.'s Fifth Step requires the confidential sharing of faults and clearly originated with the Bible verse in James 5:16 which reads:

Confess *your* faults one to another, and pray one for another, that ye may be healed. The effectual fervent prayer of a righteous man availeth much.[36]

The Book of James was a favorite in early A.A.[37] James was considered so important that some early AAs suggested "The

---

[35] *DR. BOB and the Good Oldtimers* (New York: Alcoholics Anonymous World Services, Inc., 1980), p. 54, 163. See also *Alcoholics Anonymous Comes of Age*, pp. 68, 75, 161; *Pass It On*, p. 127, 171-73; *The Language of the Heart* (New York: The A.A. Grapevine, Inc., 1988), pp. 196-200; Richmond Walker, *For Drunks Only* (MN: Hazelden, n.d.), Preface, p. 3; p. 6; and Mel B., *New Wine: The Spiritual Roots of the Twelve Step Miracle* (MN: Hazelden, 1991), pp. 21, 41, 64, 76, 95, 98, 138, 139.

[36] See Dick B., *The Akron Genesis of Alcoholics Anonymous* (CA: Good Book Publishing Co., 1994), pp. 192-97, for a discussion of the impact of James 5:13-16 on the procedures early Akron AAs followed for prayer, healing, confession, and surrender.

[37] *DR. BOB*, pp. 71, 96; and *Pass It On*, pp. 128, 138n, 147, 195.

James Club" as a name for the A.A. Fellowship.[38] A.A. literature strongly suggests that James 5:16 was the foundation for its
Fifth Step.[39] That the James verse was in fact the root of A.A.'s
confession Step is borne out by the fact that the Oxford Group
often cited James 5:16 in connection with its "sharing for
confession."[40] So did Sam Shoemaker.[41] And Anne Smith three
times mentioned this verse in connection with admitting one's
faults or sins.[42]

2. *Honesty with self, with God, and with another*

The Fifth Step concept of being honest with God, with another,
and with yourself, in your admission of shortcomings, was also a
well established Oxford Group principle.[43]

Conviction, Readiness to Be Changed and Step Six

[Step Six: Were entirely ready to have God remove all these
defects of character.]

The Oxford Group's "Five C's" were mentioned in *DR. BOB and
the Good Oldtimers* and other books about early A.A.[44]
They—Confidence, Confession, Conviction, Conversion, and

---

[38] *Pass It On*, p. 147.

[39] *Pass It On*, p. 128.

[40] J. P. Thornton-Duesbury, *Sharing* (Pamphlet of The Oxford Group, published at
Oxford University Press, n.d.), p. 5; Sherwood Sunderland Day, *The Principles of The
Group* (Oxford: Oxford University Press, n.d.), p. 6; and *What Is The Oxford Group?*,
pp. 29, 31.

[41] Shoemaker, *The Conversion of the Church*, p. 35.

[42] Dick B., *Anne Smith's Journal*, pp. 36-40.

[43] Shoemaker, *The Church Can Save The World*, pp. 110-12; and Dick B., *Anne
Smith's Journal*, p. 39.

[44] As to the Five C's, see Walter, *Soul Surgery*, pp. 21, 24, 28-29; and Shoemaker,
Realizing Religion, pp. 79-80. As to A.A.'s mention of them, see *DR. BOB*, p. 54;
Walker, *For Drunks Only*, pp. 45-46; and *The 7 Points of Alcoholics Anonymous*, Rev.
ed. (Seattle: Glen Abbey, 1989), pp. 91-93.

Continuance—were the heart of the Oxford Group's life-changing art. And A.A.'s own steps parallel these concepts.[45]

A.A.'s Sixth Step concerned "repentance," or "willingness to be changed." Some, including this author, believe that the Oxford Group's "Conviction" idea was codified in A.A.'s Sixth Step.[46]

The Big Book treats *conviction* in two installments: First, it suggests a *review* of Steps One through Five after the Fifth Step confession has been completed. It asks if anything has been omitted. It uses the metaphor of building a foundation—using a figure of speech similar to that Anne Smith used.[47] Second, the Big Book sets forth the actual Sixth Step process:

> We have emphasized willingness as being indispensable. Are we now ready to let God remove from us all the things which we have admitted are objectionable? Can He now take them all—every one? If we still cling to something we will not let go, we ask God to help us to be willing (p. 76).

As we have said, "willingness" was rooted in John 7:17.

Surrender of Sins, God's Removal and Step Seven

[Step Seven: Humbly asked Him to remove our shortcomings.]

Both Anne Smith and the Oxford Group suggested God can *remove* sins or shortcomings.[48] And the idea of *humility*—humbly asking

---

[45] See Chapter Six, *supra.* Confidence had to do with Fifth Step sharing, and the Twelfth Step concept of working with others. Confession with the Fifth Step. Conviction with the Sixth Step. Conversion with the Third and Seventh Steps. And Continuance with A.A.'s so-called "maintenance" steps—Ten, Eleven, and Twelve—which are dedicated to maintaining and growing in the spiritual condition achieved by taking A.A.'s first nine steps.

[46] See Mel B., *New Wine*, pp. 34-35.

[47] For this figurative material, see Big Book, page 75; and Dick B., *Anne Smith's Journal*, p. 42.

[48] Allen, *He That Cometh*, p. 147; Kitchen, *I Was a Pagan*, p. 73; and Dick B., *Anne Smith's Journal*, pp. 46-47.

God's help in such a problem—was a common one in the Bible and in Sam Shoemaker's thinking.[49]

The life-change, transformation, or conversion that took place when one "surrendered" and "gave his life to God" was much discussed and probably little understood in early A.A. But Oxford Group founder, Frank Buchman, made it simple for his followers. He spoke of "Sin, Jesus Christ, and the result, a miracle."[50]

The miracle of the conversion seemingly could not, and did not need to, be explained. Sam Shoemaker wrote in his first book:

> What you want is simply a vital religious experience. You need to find God. You need Jesus Christ.[51]

Dr. Carl Jung, who was credited by AAs as the source of their common spiritual solution (a conversion experience), wrote Bill Wilson, stating that the highest religious experience could be described as "the union with God." Jung quoted Psalm 42:1: "As the hart panteth after the water brooks, so panteth my soul after thee, O God."[52]

For those Oxford Group people who chose to speak in New Testament terms, surrender and conversion were rooted in John 3:3-8—being born again of the spirit.[53]

---

[49] James 4:10 states: "Humble yourselves in the sight of the Lord, and he shall lift you up." Writing in A.A.'s *Grapevine* about the Seventh Step, many years after the Twelve Steps were written, Shoemaker said: "We need help, grace, the lift of a kind of divine derrick." *Best of the Grapevine, Volume II* (New York: The AA Grapevine, Inc., 1986), p. 130.

[50] Frank Buchman often said, "Sin is the disease. Jesus Christ is the cure. The result is a miracle." See H. W. Bunny Austin, *Frank Buchman As I Knew Him* (London: Grosvenor Books, 1975), p. 10; Peter Howard, *Frank Buchman's Secret* (Garden City, NY: Doubleday & Co., 1961), p. 130; and Walter, *Soul Surgery*, p 86.

[51] Shoemaker, *Realizing Religion*, p. 9.

[52] *Pass It On*, pp. 384-85.

[53] See Henry Drummond, *The Ideal Life* (New York: Hodder & Stoughton, 1897), p. 211; Buchman, *Remaking The World*, p. 23; Begbie, *Life Changers*, p. 104; Allen, *He That Cometh*, pp. 19-43; Jones, *Inspired Children*, p. 136; Samuel M. Shoemaker, *National Awakening*, pp. 55, 57, 58; *Twice-Born Ministers*, pp. 56, 10; and *By The Power of God* (New York: Harper & Brothers, 1954), pp. 28-33.

In its "Seventh Step Prayer," the Big Book stated:

My Creator, I am now willing that you should have all of me, good and bad. I pray that you now *remove* from me every single defect of character which stands in the way of my usefulness to you and my fellows. Grant me strength, as I go out from here, to do your bidding. Amen (p. 76, emphasis added).

In an earlier discussion of surrender, the Big Book spoke of conformity with God's will, utilization of His power, and the resultant rebirth. It stated:

Being all powerful, He provided what we needed if we kept close to Him and performed His work well. . . . As we felt new power flow in, as we enjoyed peace of mind, as we discovered we could face life successfully, as we became conscious of His presence, we began to lose our fear of today, tomorrow or the hereafter. We were *reborn* (p. 63, emphasis added).[54]

Restitution, Amends and Steps Eight and Nine

[Step Eight: Made a list of all persons we had harmed, and became willing to make amends to them all.]

Anne Smith's Journal spoke of making a list.[55] Oxford Group people frequently spoke of "restitution," but at least one writer specifically used the word "amends."[56] A number of verses from the Bible were quoted in connection with restitution. Many came from the Sermon on the Mount. But the starting point seemed to

---

[54] See Dick B., *The Akron Genesis*, pp. 328-30, for a discussion of the language Bill Wilson actually used in earlier Big Book drafts. Bill said, "For sure, I'd been born again." Compare the remarks of Bill's friend, Victor Kitchen, in *I Was a Pagan*. Kitchen spoke of the sensation of release and freedom for all who face and confess their sins and then said a surrender prayer similar to that in the Big Book, concluding, "We were reborn into life. . . ." (pp. 66-68).

[55] Dick B., *Anne Smith's Journal*, p. 48.

[56] Benson, *The Eight Points*, p. 35.

be Jesus's statement: "Agree with thine adversary quickly, whiles thou art in the way with him. . . ."[57] Again, the concept of "willingness" was involved; and we have already discussed the importance in the Oxford Group and to Shoemaker of John 7:17 as far as "willingness" to obey God's will was concerned.[58]

[Step Nine: Made direct amends to such people wherever possible, except when to do so would injure them or others.]

The Big Book specifically acknowledges the Oxford Group origins of "restitution to those harmed."[59] The Oxford Group felt that God's guidance was necessary in determining what atonement constitutes, the right time to make it, the form it should take, and to whom it should be made.[60] As we have previously mentioned, the Group cited a number of Bible verses which urged making things right.[61] The concept of doing this, *practicing forgiveness*, was stressed in the Oxford Group and in A.A.[62]

The Big Book said, as to amends (Steps Eight and Nine):

> We have a list of all persons we have harmed and to whom we are willing to make amends. . . . We subjected ourselves to a drastic self-appraisal. Now we go out to our fellows and repair the damage done in the past. If we haven't the will to do this, we ask until it comes. . . . At the moment we are trying to put our lives in order. But this is not an end in itself. Our real purpose is to fit ourselves to be of maximum service to God and the people about us (pp. 76-77).

---

[57] Matthew 5:25. See Weatherhead, *Discipleship*, p. 112; and Benson, *The Eight Points*, p. 32.

[58] And see, for example, Brown, *The Venture of Belief*, pp. 27-29.

[59] Big Book, p. xvi.

[60] *What Is The Oxford Group?*, p. 62. See Big Book, pp. 79, 80, 82, 83.

[61] (1) Numbers 5:6-7. See *Russell, For Sinners Only*, p. 119. (2) Matthew 5:23-24. See Benson, *The Eight Points*, p. 30. (3) Luke 19:1-9. See Almond, *Foundations For Faith*, p. 13. (4) Luke 15:10-32. See *What Is The Oxford Group?*, pp. 62-64.

[62] Benson, *The Eight Points*, pp. 34-36. Big Book, p. 77.

Although these reparations take innumerable forms, there are some general principles which we find guiding. Reminding ourselves that we have decided to go to any lengths to find a spiritual experience, we ask that we be given strength and direction to do the right thing, no matter what the personal consequences may be. We may lose our position or reputation or face jail, but we are willing. We have to be (p. 79).

Continued Inventory, Daily Surrender and Step Ten

[Step Ten: Continued to take personal inventory and when we were wrong promptly admitted it.]

A.A.'s Tenth Step speaks to the vital importance of *maintaining* the spiritual condition achieved through taking the previous nine steps. It stresses helpfulness to others.[63] It also challenges alcoholics "to *grow* in understanding and effectiveness." It says, "This is not an overnight matter. It should continue for our lifetime" (emphasis above is ours).[64]

Step Ten seems rooted in Oxford Group "Conservation," "Continuance," and "Daily Surrender" ideas, as contrasted to the basic and General Surrender of self that, in their A.A. counterparts, can be found in Steps Three, Seven, or both.[65]

For the Oxford Group and Sam Shoemaker, this involved the concept of "continuance" or "conservation"—the so-called fifth of the "5 C's." In the Oxford Group/Shoemaker circles, in which early AAs were traveling, there were five aspects of "continuance": (1) Prayer; (2) Bible study; (3) Guidance; (4) Group worship; and (5) Witness. They were part of the continuing process of "Daily surrender."

---

[63] At the close of the Tenth Step instructions on page 84, the Big Book says: "Then we resolutely turn our thoughts to someone we can help."

[64] See Big Book, pp. 84-85.

[65] See Nell Wing, *Grateful to Have Been There: My 42 Years with Bill and Lois, and the Evolution of Alcoholics Anonymous* (Illinois: Parkside Publishing, 1992), p. 21—"Daily Practice." See also Dick B., *Anne Smith's Journal*, pp. 49-53.

We repeat these Oxford Group statements about *daily* surrender, daily inventory and amends, and daily spiritual contact:

Our lives will be one continuous surrender: surrender to God of every difficulty that confronts us, each temptation, each spiritual struggle, laying before Him either to take away or to show to us in their proper spiritual proportions.[66]

When I came to make a daily surrender I learned what a different experience this is from a general surrender. Daily checking on the four absolutes revealed to me things I had never questioned in myself. . . . I came to a daily willingness to do anything for God. I made amends where He gave me light.[67]

There is need for rededication day by day, hour by hour, by which progressively, in every Quiet Time, the contaminations of sin and self-will are further sloughed off (for they do have a way of collecting) and we are kept in fresh touch with the living Spirit of God. A further surrender is needed when and whenever there is found to be something in us which offends Christ, or walls us from another. We shall need, in this sense, to keep surrendering as long as we live.[68]

The Big Book's instructions for taking the step are very specific. They state AAs should:

Continue to watch for selfishness, dishonesty, resentment, and fear.[69] When these crop up, we ask God at once to remove them.[70] We discuss them with someone immediately and make amends quickly if we have harmed anyone.[71] Then we resolutely

---

[66] *What Is The Oxford Group?*, p. 46.

[67] Benson, *The Eight Points*, p. 149.

[68] Shoemaker, *The Conversion of the Church*, p. 79.

[69] Recall that Frank Buchman asked: "What is the disease? Isn't it fear, dishonesty, resentment, selfishness?" Buchman, *Remaking The World*, p. 38.

[70] The Steps Six and Seven process.

[71] The Steps Five, Eight and Nine process.

turn our thoughts to someone we can help.[72] Love and tolerance of others is our code (p. 84).[73]

It is easy to let up on the spiritual program of action and rest on our laurels. We are headed for trouble if we do, for alcohol is a subtle foe. We are not cured of alcoholism. What we really have is a daily reprieve contingent on the maintenance of our spiritual condition. Every day is a day when we must carry the vision of God's will into all of our activities. "How can I best serve Thee—Thy will (not mine) be done." These are thoughts which must go with us constantly. We can exercise our will power along this line all we wish. It is the proper use of the will (p. 85).

Quiet Time, Prayer, Bible Study, Listening, God's Will, Guidance and Step Eleven

[Step Eleven: Sought through prayer and meditation to improve our conscious contact with God *as we understood Him*, praying only for knowledge of His will for us and the power to carry that out.]

Prayer, Bible study, spiritual reading, listening for guidance, and Quiet Time were vital in early A.A.[74] In our review of the twenty-eight Oxford Group principles, we documented the role of these practices in the Oxford Group itself. We have shown from Bill Wilson's comments in *The Language of the Heart*, that Bill specifically acknowledged that A.A. got its ideas for Quiet Time, prayer, meditation, and guidance from the Oxford Group.[75] The

---

[72] The Step Twelve process.

[73] The practice of principles Dr. Bob and other early AAs stressed as coming from the Sermon on the Mount, 1 Corinthians 13, and the Book of James.

[74] See our lengthy review of this subject from the perspective of Anne Smith's teachings and what went on in early Akron A.A. Dick B., *Anne Smith's Journal*, pp. 53-64.

[75] *The Language of the Heart*, pp. 298, 196-97. See *DR. BOB*, pp. 131, 135-36.

Oxford Group often spoke of the necessity for establishing "contact with God."[76] And Oxford Group writer, Stephen Foot, used language about that contact, which seemed to have been incorporated into the Eleventh Step verbatim. Foot said, "I will ask God to show me His purpose for my life and claim from Him *the power to carry that purpose out*" (emphasis added).[77]

We believe the Big Book's instructions for taking the Eleventh Step can be divided into four parts. Its four sets of instructions for taking this Step might be categorized in the following manner.

First, those things the AA is to do each evening as he or she constructively reviews the day (p. 86). In effect, AAs are to review how well they practiced the Tenth Step during their daily surrender process. The review questions are: (1) "Were we resentful, selfish, dishonest or afraid?" [a Step Four question]; (2) "Do we owe an apology?" [a Step Nine question]; (3) "Have we kept something to ourselves which should be discussed with another person at once?" [a Step Five question]; (4) "Were we kind and loving toward all? What could we have done better? Were we thinking of ourselves most of the time? Or were we thinking of what we could do for others, of what we could pack into the stream of life?" [Steps Four, Six, Seven and Twelve questions] . . . (5) "After making our review we ask God's forgiveness and inquire what corrective measures should be taken." While these hardly seem to qualify as "prayer and meditation," they are part of A.A.'s Eleventh Step instructions. We have seen from all the twenty-eight Oxford Group principles how frequently the Group posed tests for determining how well a person was conducting daily surrender and quiet time activities.

Second, the Eleventh Step places great focus on how one commences the day (pp. 86-87). Recall that Anne Smith spoke of living "one day at a time."[78] The Big Book suggests, "On awakening, let us think about the twenty-four hours ahead. We

---

[76] See, for example, Foot, *Life Began Yesterday*, p. 13.

[77] Foot, *Life Began Yesterday*, p. 11.

[78] Dick B., *Anne Smith's Journal*, p. 51.

consider our plans for the day." It then suggests three different approaches: (1) That we ask God to direct our thinking and keep the thought-life clear of wrong motives. [This certainly coincides with Oxford Group emphasis on, and discussion of guidance, quiet time, prayer, listening for leading thoughts, and checking.] (2) That we ask God for inspiration, an intuitive thought or a decision when facing "indecision." [Compare our Oxford Group discussion of Guidance.] (3) That we be shown all through the day what the next step is to be, that our needs be supplied in that regard, and that our actions be free from selfish ends. [Again, Oxford Group teachings comprehend this subject matter.]

Third, the Eleventh Step process covers what the author has often described as the Big Book's "lost paragraph;" and, more optimistically, the "growth paragraph." We call this the *growth* paragraph because Bill Wilson frequently spoke of A.A. as a "spiritual kindergarten."[79] In the Big Book's "spiritual growth" paragraph, Bill wrote as follows:

If circumstances warrant, we ask our wives or friends to join us in morning meditation. If we belong to a religious denomination which requires a definite morning devotion, we attend to that also. If not members of religious bodies, we sometimes select and memorize a few set prayers which emphasize the principles we have been discussing. There are many helpful books also. Suggestions about these may be obtained from one's priest, minister, or rabbi. Be quick to see where religious people are right. Make use of what they offer (p. 87).

We believe many portions of our book demonstrate the Oxford Group and Anne Smith's influence on the foregoing paragraph. Anne's whole family, and those—including Bill Wilson—who visited her home, were involved in a great deal of morning meditation. Anne and Dr. Bob maintained membership in a religious denomination for most of the period from 1935 to the end

---

[79] See, for example, *As Bill Sees It*, p. 95; and Ernest Kurtz, *Shame and Guilt. Characteristics of the Dependency Cycle* (Minnesota: Hazelden, 1981), p. 12.

of their lives.[80] Anne suggested specific prayers in her Journal. She recommended and used the Bible, many spiritual books, and daily Bible devotionals as part of the daily inspirational reading. And she suggested seeking help from others as to the materials which should be read. Recall also our quote from Sam Shoemaker's letter on the occasion of Calvary Church's break with Frank Buchman. Shoemaker said he felt the early Oxford Group stress was on work within the churches.

Finally, the Big Book speaks of the action to be taken throughout the day when agitated or in doubt. Essentially, it recommends seeking the guidance of God and surrendering to Him many times throughout the day, saying, "Thy will be done" (pp. 87-88). As we have shown, the Oxford Group teachings paralleled all aspects of these latter suggestions.

The Spiritual Awakening, Witness, Practice of Principles and Step Twelve

[Step Twelve: Having had a spiritual awakening as the result of these steps, we tried to carry this message to alcoholics, and to practice these principles in all our affairs.]

We believe A.A.'s Twelfth Step can and should be viewed as having three "parts." They are: (1) The spiritual awakening achieved through taking the preceding eleven steps. (2) The obligation to witness to others by "passing on" the message of how one received this deliverance through what God has done for that person. (3) The actual living of a changed life by "practicing the principles"—the principles learned from taking the Twelve Steps of recovery. And we will discuss the Oxford Group's contribution to these Twelve Step ideas by separately discussing each of the Twelfth Step's three "parts."

---

[80] See Dick B., *Dr. Bob's Library: Books for Twelve Step Growth* (San Rafael, CA: Paradise Research Publications, 1994), p. 3.

1. *The spiritual awakening*[81]

As we have shown, Professor William James, the Oxford Group, and Reverend Sam Shoemaker had many expressions for the "vital religious experience" or "conversion" which took place when a person surrendered his or her life to God, took the steps of confession, conviction, conversion, restitution, and continuance, and then experienced the fruits of the changed life. The religious experience was variously described as: (1) An experience of God. (2) A vital experience of Jesus Christ. (3) A religious experience. (4) A spiritual experience. (5) A spiritual awakening. (6) A relationship with God. (7) A sense of the power and presence of God. (8) Finding God. (9) Being in touch with God. (10) Contact with God. (11) Conversion. (12) Surrender. (13) Change. (14) Born again. (15) God Consciousness.

Compare the following ideas in A.A.'s Big Book:

There was a sense of victory, followed by such a peace and serenity as I had never known. There was utter confidence. I felt lifted up, as though the great clean wind of a mountain top blew through and through. God comes to most men gradually, but His impact on me was sudden and profound (Bill's Story, p. 14).

The great fact is just this, and nothing less: That we have had deep and effective spiritual experiences which have revolutionized our whole attitude toward life, toward our fellows and toward God's universe (p. 25).

[It] is true that our first printing gave many readers the impression that these personality changes, or religious experiences, must be in the nature of sudden and spectacular upheavals. Happily for

---

[81] The phrase "spiritual awakening" is an Oxford Group phrase. Buchman frequently spoke of a "spiritual awakening." See, for example, Frank N. D. Buchman, *Remaking the World* (London: Blandford Press, 1991), pp. 5, 24, 28. So did Shoemaker; and Shoemaker wrote an entire book, titled, *National Awakening*. Shoemaker also devoted a chapter of another book to the elements of awakening. See Shoemaker, *By the Power of God*, and its chapter IX—"What Awakening Takes" (pp. 133-54).

everyone, this conclusion is erroneous. . . . Most of our experiences are what the psychologist William James calls the "educational variety" because they develop slowly over a period of time. . . . With few exceptions our members find they have tapped an unsuspected inner resource which they presently identify with their own conception of a Power greater than themselves. Most of us think this awareness of a Power greater than ourselves is the essence of a spiritual experience. Our more religious members call it "God-consciousness" (pp. 571-72).[82]

In the face of collapse and despair, in the face of the total failure of their human resources, they found that a new power, peace, happiness, and sense of direction flowed into them. . . . When many hundreds of people are able to say that the consciousness of the Presence of God is today the most important fact of their lives, they present a powerful reason why one should have faith (pp. 50-51).[83]

In a few seconds he was overwhelmed by a conviction of the Presence of God. . . . He stood in the Presence of Infinite Power and Love. He had stepped from bridge to shore. For the first time, he lived in conscious companionship with his Creator (p. 56).

We will suddenly realize that God is doing for us what we could not do for ourselves (p. 84).[84]

Much has already been said about receiving strength, inspiration, and direction from Him who has all knowledge and power. If we have carefully followed directions, we have begun to sense the flow of His Spirit into us. To some extent we have become God-conscious (p. 85).

---

[82] See Chapter Six for our discussion of the twenty-eight Oxford Group principles, the discussion of "God Consciousness," and the frequency with which Oxford Group people used that phrase.

[83] See the latter part of this chapter containing quotes from the Oxford Group writings and from the Big Book which show the frequency with which Oxford Group people referred to consciousness of the power and presence of God in their lives.

[84] There are many Oxford Group quotes which speak of God's doing for people what they could not do for themselves. Compare Samuel M. Shoemaker, *If I Be Lifted Up*, pp. 161-62.

Ask Him in your morning meditation what you can do each day for the man who is still sick. The answers will come, if your own house is in order. But obviously you cannot transmit something you haven't got. See to it that your relationship with Him is right, and great events will come to pass for you and countless others. This is the Great Fact for us (p. 164).

2. *Witness—giving it away to keep it*

The second Twelfth Step idea comprehends *service* by carrying the message—passing it on—giving it away to keep it—witnessing. We covered these points in our discussion of fellowship, witnessing, and service.

A large part of Anne Smith's Journal was devoted to discussing service to others, life-changing, and "witnessing." Anne said:

Giving Christianity away is the best way to keep it.[85]

We can't give away what we haven't got.[86]

In one of his earliest pamphlets—one which Anne quoted in her spiritual journal—Sam Shoemaker spoke of "giving it away to keep it."[87] The following, from a much later Shoemaker book, exemplified this concept of "passing it on." Shoemaker wrote:

The best way to keep what you have is to give it away, and no substitute has ever been found for personal Christian witness.[88]

Compare the following thoughts from A.A.'s Big Book:

He [Bill Wilson] suddenly realized that in order to save himself he must carry his message to another alcoholic (p. xvi).

---

[85] Dick B., *Anne Smith's Journal*, p. 69.

[86] Dick B., *Anne Smith's Journal*, p. 69.

[87] Samuel M. Shoemaker, *One Boy's Influence* (New York: Association Press, 1925), p. 15.

[88] Samuel M. Shoemaker, Jr., *They're on The Way* (New York: E. P. Dutton, 1951), p. 159. See also Dick B., *New Light on Alcoholism: The A.A. Legacy from Sam Shoemaker* (CA: Good Book Publishing, 1994), p. 274.

My friend [Bill Wilson's sponsor, Ebby Thacher] had emphasized
. . . [that it was] imperative to work with others as he had
worked with me. Faith without works was dead, he said. And
how appallingly true for the alcoholic! For if an alcoholic failed
to perfect and enlarge his spiritual life through work and self-
sacrifice for others, he could not survive the certain trials and
low spots ahead (p. 15).

Practical experience shows that nothing will so much insure
immunity from drinking as intensive work with other alcoholics.
It works when other activities fail. This is our *twelfth suggestion*:
Carry this message to other alcoholics! (p. 89).

And be careful not to brand him as an alcoholic (p. 92).[89]

Keep his attention focussed mainly on your personal experience.
. . . Tell him exactly what happened to you. Stress the spiritual
feature freely (pp. 92-93).

It is important for him to realize that your attempt to pass this on
to him plays a vital part in your own recovery (p. 94).

You will be most successful with alcoholics if you do not exhibit
any passion for crusade or reform. Never talk down to an alcoholic from any moral or spiritual hilltop; simply lay out the
spiritual tools for his inspection. Show him how they worked
with you. Offer him friendship and fellowship. Tell him if he
wants to get well you will do anything to help (p. 95).

Helping others is the foundation stone of your recovery (p. 97).

The minute we put our work on a service plane, the alcoholic commences to rely upon our assistance rather than upon God. . . . we
simply do not stop drinking so long as we place dependence upon
other people ahead of dependence on God. Burn the idea into the

---

[89] See Dick B., *Anne Smith's Journal*, p. 69, where we quote Anne as follows:
"Share with people—don't preach, don't argue. Don't talk up nor down to people. Talk
to them, and share in terms of their own experience, speak on their level."

consciousness of every man that he can get well regardless of any-one. The only condition is that he trust God and clean house (p. 98).

Remind the prospect that his recovery is not dependent upon people. It is dependent upon his relationship with God (p. 100).[90]

Give freely of what you find and join us (p. 164).

3. *Living the changed life; practicing the spiritual principles*

Many claim Anne Smith's "favorite" Bible verse was "Faith with-out works is dead."[91] The verse certainly wound up in A.A.'s Big Book (pp. 14, 76, 88). And Anne wrote much about *living* by spiritual principles.

The Big Book really does not define the "principles" or describe the "works" in any orderly fashion. But we think the following are *among* the principles it insists should be practiced: (1) Relying upon God (pp. 46, 50, 51-53, 68, 80, 98, 100, 120, 292); (2) Being rigorously honest (pp. 58, 64, 67, 69, 73, 84, 86); (3) Eliminating selfishness and self-centeredness (pp. 62, 63, 69, 84. 86); (4) Eliminating resentment, jealousy, and envy (pp. 64-67, 84, 86, 145); (5) Eliminating fear (pp. 67-68, 84, 86, 145); (6) Practicing patience, tolerance, kindliness, understanding, love, forgiveness, and helpfulness to others (pp. 20, 77, 83, 84, 97, 118, 153, 292). Other Twelfth Step principles embody the ideas of humility, forgiveness, and service—plus such other Oxford Group concepts as overcoming the bondage of self, confession, restitution, reconciliation, guidance, and so on.[92]

---

[90] We have already documented frequently the number of times in which both the Oxford Group and the Big Book emphasized *relationship with God*.

[91] See Nell Wing, *Grateful To Have Been There*, pp. 70-71; *DR. BOB*, p. 71; and *Pass It On*, p. 147. See Dick B., *Anne Smith's Journal*, pp. v, 54, 74.

[92] See, for example, *What Is The Oxford Group?*, which spoke of the four absolute ideals in the Sermon on the Mount and four practical activities—sharing of sins and as witness, surrendering your life to God's direction, making restitution, and relying on God

(continued...)

The Oxford Group's "Four Absolutes"—honesty, purity, unselfishness, and love—are not mentioned as "absolutes" in the Big Book. But they were "yardstick" principles by which early AAs measured their conduct.[93] And the concepts of honesty, unselfishness, and love are very much a part of A.A. thinking.

The Oxford Group neither could, nor tried to, lay special claim on God, the Bible, Jesus Christ, or the Holy Spirit; nor did they see themselves as a sect or religion. In fact, they proclaimed, whether warranted or not, a universality and compatibility with all Christian churches and religions. And as we take this brief look at Oxford Group traces in A.A.'s Big Book and Twelve Steps, we do not say that Oxford Group spiritual principles could not and cannot be found elsewhere. Bill Wilson himself said:

> The basic principles which the Oxford Groupers had taught were
> ancient and universal ones, the common property of mankind.[94]

And, of course, they *were*! Many of the Oxford Group principles came from the Old Testament—certainly not just the province of Christianity. And most Oxford Group principles came from the New Testament—certainly the province of all Christianity—Roman Catholic, Protestant, and other.

---

[92] (...continued)
for guidance. These, it said, were the means of living the "simple tenets of Christianity" (pp. 8-9). Of equal importance were the principles of 1 Corinthians 13, which were the subject of Drummond's *The Greatest Thing in the World*, and arrested the attention of Dr. Bob and so many Oxford Group writers such as Benson (*The Eight Points*, p. 47). Shoemaker's *Confident Faith* spoke of the kind of relationship which comes to pass between those who find themselves cooperating with God. Those whose lives are integrated into the same great plan of God, who work together with complete honesty and accord, knowing all there is to be known about one another, dealing in the truth with love, and sharing in the work of making God and His holy spirit a reality to other people (p. 184). Bill's secretary, Nell Wing, said very simply that Bill took "Daily Practice" from the Oxford Group. Wing, *Grateful to have been there*, pp. 20-21.

[93] *DR. BOB*, p. 54.

[94] *AA Comes of Age*, p. 39. Compare *Twelve Steps and Twelve Traditions*, p. 16.

In making the foregoing statement about "ancient and universal" principles, Bill was obviously looking to broaden A.A.'s base. And he was safe—though the Oxford Group was the specific tutor—in pointing to Judeo-Christian origins. But when we point to Oxford Group traces in the Big Book and the Twelve Steps, we are pointing to the same source that A.A.'s co-founders did.

Oxford Group people often spoke of the beatitude, "Blessed are the pure in heart, for they shall see God."[95] And the Big Book, along with the Oxford Group, was concerned with removing the "blocks" to God, which "shut ourselves off from the sunlight of the Spirit."[96]

In this picturesque language, we see the necessity for "cleansing" by removing "blocks" in order to let God *in*. And 1 John 1:7 was a verse that Frank Buchman often mentioned in this context. The verse reads:

> But if we walk in the light, as he is in the light, we have fellowship one with another, and the blood of Jesus Christ his Son cleanseth us from all sin.[97]

And we close by mentioning Bill's coverage of the "cleansing" idea when he said, on page 98 of the Big Book, that the only condition of getting well "is that he [the alcoholic] trust in God and clean house."

So we believe that the practice of spiritual principles began, in Oxford Group and A.A. parlance, with a "clean house"—a cleansing that was possible only through the power of God.

---

[95] Matthew 5:8.

[96] Big Book, pp. 64, 66, 71; and Dick B., *Anne Smith's Journal*, p. 93.

[97] Howard, *Frank Buchman's Secret*, p. 109; Belden, *Reflections on Moral Re-Armament*, p. 51; Almond, *Foundations for Faith*, p. 15; and Phillimore, *Just for Today*, p. 7. See also, 1 Corinthians 6:9-11, which were some other verses that meant a great deal to Frank Buchman: "And such were some of you: but ye are washed, but ye are sanctified, . . ." Howard, *Frank Buchman's Secret*, p. 40; Almond, *Foundations for Faith*, pp. 10-11; and Spoerri, *Dynamic out of Silence*, p. 46.

Principal Oxford Group Ideas Which Can Be Found in A.A.'s Basic Text, the Big Book

We have examined the basic Oxford Group ideas which influenced and can be traced to the language in A.A.'s twelve suggested steps of recovery. And we shortly will look at specific language which Bill Wilson seems to have taken from specific Oxford Group ideas or books and incorporated in the Big Book and other A.A. literature. However, the Big Book itself stands as the basic text for recovery in A.A. It contains the "instructions," or "directions," or "suggestions" as to how the newcomer is to "take" the steps. The Big Book therefore contains the details about recovery. And, just as Oxford Group ideas can be traced into step language and into Big Book language, so the basic ideas themselves can be found in broad outline in the Big Book. These are some of those basic ideas.

As to God

1. *God is*

We have pointed to the frequency with which the Big Book used the name "God," pronouns describing Him, and Biblical names for Him (such as Creator, Maker, Father, Spirit). And the Big Book offered its readers the same choice that Sam Shoemaker offered his readers. *God either is or isn't.* The Big Book said:

> When we became alcoholics, crushed by a self-imposed crisis we could not postpone or evade, we had to fearlessly face the proposition that either God is everything or else He is nothing. God either is, or He isn't. What was our choice to be?[98]

Using almost identical language, Sam Shoemaker had previously written:

---

[98] Big Book, p. 53.

Faith is not sight: it is a high gamble. There are only two
alternatives here. God is, or He isn't. You leap one way or the
other. It is a risk to take to bet everything you have on God.[99]

2. *Find God now!*

The Big Book offered a vital suggestion to the hopeless alcoholic:

But there is One who has all power—that One is God. May you
find Him now![100]

The Oxford Group and Shoemaker had offered the same suggestion. Thus Shoemaker had written:

What you want is simply a vital religious experience. You need
to find God.[101]

3. *Start with your own understanding of God*

To the searcher who was confused about the nature of God, the
Big Book and the Oxford Group suggested that that person start by
choosing his or her own conception of God *for a beginning*. The
Big Book said:

When, therefore, we speak to you of God, we mean your own
conception of God. . . . At the start, this was all we needed to

---

[99] Shoemaker, *Confident Faith*, p. 187. Recall that Dr. Bob owned, studied and
loaned out this book. See also Hebrews 11:6; Shoemaker, *Religion That Works*, p. 88;
The Gospel According To You, pp. 47, 29, 31; *National Awakening*, p. 40; Leslie D.
Weatherhead, *How Can I Find God?* (London: Fleming H. Revell, 1934), p. 72; and
Philip Leon, *The Philosophy of Courage or The Oxford Group Way* (New York: Oxford
University Press, 1939), p. 19. The foregoing writings of Shoemaker and Weatherhead
quote or paraphrase Hebrews 11:6, which states the necessity for believing that God *is*
if one is to come to God and to please God.

[100] Big Book, p. 59.

[101] Shoemaker, *Realizing Religion*, p. 9. See also Shoemaker, *How To Find God*;
Weatherhead, *How Can I Find God?*; and Kitchen, *I Was A Pagan*, p. 94.

commence spiritual growth, to effect our first conscious relation with God as we understood Him.[102]

Oxford Group people had previously suggested commencing with your *own* knowledge or understanding of God. Foot wrote about:

Surrender of all one knows of self to all one knows of God.[103]

4. *Aim at establishing a relationship with God*

The Big Book and the Oxford Group both said the real objective was establishing a *relationship with God*. The Big Book stated:

Each individual, in the personal stories, describes in his own language and from his own point of view the way he established his relationship with God.[104]

The relationship-with-God language appeared often in Oxford Group writings.[105] And it was used by Anne Smith.[106]

---

[102] Big Book, p. 47.

[103] Foot, *Life Began Yesterday*, p. 175. Shoemaker spoke of the "dim" God, quoting Horace Bushnell, and saying: "Begin honestly where you are. Horace Bushnell once said, 'Pray to the dim God, confessing the dimness for honesty's sake.' I was a man who prayed his first real prayer in these words: 'O God, if there be a God, help me now because I need it.' God sent him help. He found faith. He found God" (Shoemaker, *How to Find God*, Reprint from *Faith at Work* magazine, n.d., p. 6. Shoemaker used the expression "surrendering as much of himself as he knows to as much of God as he knows" (Shoemaker, *How to Become a Christian*, p. 72). But Shoemaker also wrote of surrendering to God *as you understand Him*. See Shoemaker, *Children of the Second Birth*, pp. 25, 47; and *The Gospel According to You*, p. 128. Anne Smith used this concept in her Journal. Dick B., *Anne Smith's Journal*, pp. 26-27. Willard Hunter commented to the author that this expression (surrender to as much of God as you know) was "big" with Sam Shoemaker in his writing and in his life-changing; it led directly, said Hunter, to "God as we understood Him."

[104] Big Book, p. 29; and see pages 28, 13, 56, 164.

[105] Shoemaker, *Children of the Second Birth*, p. 16; *Christ's Words from the Cross*, p. 49; *Confident Faith*, pp. 183-84; *How to Become a Christian*, p. 56; Walter, *Soul Surgery*. p. 79; Benson, *The Eight Points*, pp. 48, 92; Brown, *The Venture of Belief*, p. 11; Macmillan, *Seeking and Finding*, p. 99; and Weatherhead, *Discipleship*, p. 18.

We believe the essence of the relationship was believing in, finding, and doing the will of God, as expressed by the words of the Lord's Prayer—*Thy will be done.* And that idea along with the exact words—Thy will be done—was commonplace in the Big Book and in Oxford Group writings.[107] Also the idea of being of maximum service to God.[108]

The Oxford Group experiment of faith placed the emphasis on *do* with the result—*know.* We will say more in a moment about John 7:17. The important point here is that believing in God; seeking Him by doing His will; and listening for His direction, where His will is not known, all result in an experience of God—*experiencing the power and presence of God.* The Big Book and the Oxford Group used almost identical expressions in that respect.[109]

The Barriers or Blocks to God

As time went on in A.A., its founders began thinking of alcoholism as involving a spiritual malady as well as a disease of the body (an allergy) and a disease of the mind (an obsession to drink). Bill Wilson put it this way:

> Of course, we have since found that these awful conditions of mind and body invariably bring on the third phase of our malady. This is the sickness of the spirit; a sickness for which there must

---

[106] (...continued)

[106] Dick B., *Anne Smith's Journal*, pp. 22-24.

[107] In the Big Book, see pages 67, 85, 88, 63. In Oxford Group writings, see, for example, Wright, *The Will of God*, pp. 43-114; *What Is The Oxford Group?*, pp. 47-48; Brown, *The Venture of Belief*, pp. 26, 29-30; Shoemaker, *Children of the Second Birth*, pp. 175-87, 58; and Robert H. Murray, *Group Movements Throughout the Ages* (New York: Harper & Brothers, 1935), p. 349.

[108] Big Book, p. 77. And see Dick B., *Anne Smith's Journal*, p. 37, and other examples of "maximum" cited in that title.

[109] Big Book, pp. 14, 51, 56, 63, 162. Brown, *The Venture of Belief*, pp. 21-26; Rose, *When Man Listens*, p. 17; Leon, *The Philosophy of Courage*, pp. 112-13; Weatherhead, *Discipleship*, p. 17; Shoemaker, *The Conversion of the Church*, p. 113; and *How to Become a Christian*, p. 156.

necessarily be a spiritual remedy. We AAs recognize this in the first five words of Step Twelve of the recovery program. These words are: "Having had a spiritual awakening. . . ." Here we name the remedy for our threefold sickness of body, mind, and soul. Here we declare the necessity for that all important spiritual awakening.[110]

Liquor and bottles were said merely to be symptoms or symbols of the underlying problem.[111] Selfishness—self-centeredness—was proclaimed as the root of the alcoholic's troubles.[112] And the Big Book described the problem in its totality as *focus on self.*[113] Over many pages, the problem was given such names as excesses of self-will, self-propulsion, selfishness, self-centeredness, ego-centricity, self-seeking, self-pity, and self-delusion.[114]

As we have shown, the Oxford Group sometimes defined sin as selfishness. And AAs originally referred to "sin" in their steps. Corollary words, which defined sin as focus on self and self-centeredness, can be found with much frequency in Oxford Group writings.[115] Buchman, Shoemaker, and many Oxford Group writers spoke of ego-centricity in terms of getting rid of the big "I" of self.[116] Both the Big Book and Oxford Group writers

---

[110] *The Language of the Heart*, p. 297.

[111] Big Book, pp. 64, 103.

[112] Big Book, p. 62.

[113] Big Book, p. 62.

[114] Big Book, pp. 14, 15, 21, 60-62, 64, 68, 69, 71, 84, 86, 87, 88.

[115] Buchman, *Remaking The World*, pp. 3, 24, 28, 38, 71, 79, 95, 104, 128; Russell, *For Sinners Only*, pp. 317, 324-329, Begbie, *Life Changers*, pp. 17, 87; *What Is The Oxford Group?* pp. 97-105; Leon, *The Philosophy of Courage*, pp. 41-53, 146; Cecil Rose, *When Man Listens*, pp. 41, 54, 67; Shoemaker, *God's Control*, pp. 21, 30, 57-58, 69, 98; *Confident Faith*, pp. 97-98, 106, 144-45; *Twice-Born Ministers*, pp. 26, 76, 103, 113, 116, 154; *Christ's Words From The Cross*, p. 35; and *If I Be Lifted Up*, pp. 60-61, 166.

[116] Russell, *For Sinners Only*, p. 60; Shoemaker, *If I Be Lifted Up*, p. 28; *What Is The Oxford Group?*, pp. 23-24; Spoerri, *Dynamic out of Silence*, p. 36; and Weatherhead, *How Can I Find God?*, p. 84. See the interesting article by Harry M. Tiebout, M.D., entitled, "When the Big 'I' Becomes Nobody." *Best of the Grapevine* (New York: The AA Grapevine, Inc., 1985), pp. 129-33.

specifically referred to "resentment, selfishness, dishonesty, and fear" as the most common and objectionable manifestations of self that needed to be eliminated.[117] As we previously detailed, these manifestations of ego were said by the Big Book and by the Oxford Group writers to be the barriers or blocks to a relationship with God.

Elimination or Destruction of the Barriers through Self-surrender

1. *The Turning Point.* "We stood at the *turning point*," said the Big Book at page 59. Then it set forth the steps its authors took in order to abandon themselves to God—to surrender themselves to His care and protection. The expression "turning point" was possibly first heard by the Oxford Group through the following much-quoted language of William James:

> But since, in any terms, the crisis described is the throwing of our conscious selves upon the mercy of the powers which, whatever they may be, are more ideal than we are actually, and make for our redemption, you see why self-surrender has been and always must be regarded as the vital turning-point of religious life, so far as the religious life is spiritual and no affair of outer works and ritual and sacraments.[118]

As we've mentioned, William James and his "turning point" expression were cited many times in Oxford Group writings, particularly those of Shoemaker.[119]

The following points were made in the Oxford Group and in the Big Book as to where the surrender process must begin:

---

[117] Big Book, pp. 64, 67, 68, 69, 71, 84-88. See Buchman, *Remaking The World*, pp. 3, 24, 28, 38; Shoemaker, *Confident Faith*, pp. 97-98; *God's Control*, pp. 9, 57-58, 87; and *Twice-Born Ministers*, pp. 76, 182.

[118] James, *The Varieties of Religious Experience*, pp. 195-96.

[119] Shoemaker, *Realizing Religion*, p. 30; *Religion That Works*, p. 48; *God's Control*, p. 138; and *Christ's Words From The Cross*, p. 51.

It was necessary to be honest.[120]

It was necessary to be willing.[121]

It was necessary to begin with childlike humility.[122]

As shown in the footnotes to the foregoing three points, the concepts of honesty, willingness, and humility are often repeated in the Big Book.

2. *Realize that you are not God.* An important ingredient transmitted by the Oxford Group to the Big Book was the concept that self is *not* God and that God *is* God.[123]

3. *Identify your ego-centricity.* In the matter of self-examination, the Oxford Group's idea of taking a business inventory seemed to spill over directly into the Big Book.[124] So also, the correlative idea of making a written list of shortcomings which, in the case of the Big Book, involved resentments, fears,

---

[120] Big Book, pp. 58, 65, 73-74; Brown, *The Venture of Belief*, pp. 28, 32-33; Shoemaker, *Christ's Words from the Cross*, pp. 11-12; *Twice-Born Ministers*, pp. 50-51;and *God's Control*, p. 9. See Dick B., *New Light on Alcoholism*, p. 343, for Bill Wilson's April, 1953, memo on the "Original AA Steps," in which Wilson emphasizes the importance of "honesty" in two of the six steps.

[121] Big Book, pp. 46-47, 57, 58, 76, 570. It was here that John 7:17 entered the picture. And we will not repeat the discussion, but "willingness" was a necessary in the surrender process. See Brown, *The Venture of Belief*, pp. 27-29, 48; Belden, *Meeting Moral Re-Armament*, p. 28; and Shoemaker, *Religion That Works*, pp. 45-46, 58, 64.

[122] Big Book, pp. 13, 52-53, 57, 62, 68, 73, 76, 88. See Brown, *The Venture of Belief*, pp. 29, 32; Allen, *He That Cometh*. pp. 45-68; Shoemaker, *National Awakening*, pp. 78-88; *Confident Faith*, p. 72; and *The Church Can Save the World*. p. 55. See Tiebout, *Best of the Grapevine*, p. 132.

[123] Big Book, p. 62. See Shoemaker, stating in *National Awakening* at page 48, "God is God, and self is not God—that is the heart of it." See also, Shoemaker, *God's Control*, p. 21. Benson wrote in *The Eight Points*, at page 69: "Things begin to happen when we 'let go' and 'let God.' He is God—not you."

[124] Big Book, p. 64. See our previous discussion of Cecil Rose, *When Man Listens*, pp. 17-19; and Benson, *The Eight Points*, at page 44.

sex conduct and harms; and, in Oxford Group approaches, a testing of conduct against the Four Absolutes of Honesty, Purity, Unselfishness and Love.[125] And in both the Big Book and Oxford Group writings, there was to be a "moral test."[126]

Daily Spiritual Growth

As we have shown, the Oxford Group called for daily growth in one's relationship with God. This involved Guidance, Quiet Time, Bible study, two-way prayer, checking, application of the Four Absolutes, fellowship, and sharing by witness. The author has little doubt that we have traced all of these—save for Bible study and checking—into the Big Book, but not in any precise language. We say the ideas *are* traceable because Bill Wilson specifically stated that such concepts as guidance, prayer, and meditation came from the Oxford Group, along with such Oxford Group ideas as fellowship and of the sharing experience, strength, and hope.[127] Also, recall Bill's assertion that the Four Absolutes were incorporated into Steps Six and Seven. We will not review the Oxford Group writings again; but we will call attention to the location of some Oxford Group *continuance* and spiritual growth ideas in the Big Book, however modified their form became:

1. *Guidance*. Guidance ideas start in Bill's Story and can be found throughout the Big Book.[128] Asking God for direction is an ever-present idea in the Big Book.

---

[125] See Shoemaker, *How to Become a Christian*, pp. 56-57; and Belden, *Meeting Moral Re-Armament*, pp. 17, 19.

[126] In the Big Book, it was spoken of as a "moral inventory" (pp. 59). Henry Drummond, Frank Buchman, and other Oxford Group writers spoke of making the "moral test" (Walter, *Soul Surgery*, pp. 43-44, 48), as did Anne Smith in her Journal. Dick B., *Anne Smith's Journal*, pp. 30-32, 72, 98, 99.

[127] See, for example, Irving Harris, *The Breeze of the Spirit* (New York: The Seabury Press, 1978), pp. 19-20.

[128] Big Book, pp. 10, 13, 49, 50, 57, 59, 68, 69, 70, 79, 80, 83, 85, 86, 87, 100, 164.

2. *Prayer.* The Big Book's emphasis on prayer is not confined to the Eleventh Step. There are one or more prayers mentioned in connection with almost every Step.[129]

3. *Morning meditation and devotions.* While the Oxford Group Quiet Time is not mentioned as such, the practice of turning in the morning to God for inspiration, direction, and strength is.[130]

4. *Seeking help from the religious.* AAs today talk much about *spirituality* in contrast to *religion.*[131] And the Big Book's own hearkening back to the early days of turning to the clergy for help is therefore often overlooked. But the Big Book comments are there. The Oxford Group had no hostility to organized religion and, as with Calvary Church, for example, worked within the church itself. Similarly, the Big Book displayed no hostility to religion and, in fact, several times encouraged seeking help from religion.[132]

5. *Putting things in God's hands (letting go and letting God).*[133]

---

[129] Big Book, pp. 13, 46, 56, 63, 67, 68, 69, 70, 75, 76, 79, 80, 81, 82, 83, 84, 85, 86, 87, 88, 100, 117, 120, 158, 164.

[130] Big Book, pp. 86-87.

[131] See Ernest Kurtz and Katherine Ketcham, *The Spirituality of Imperfection: Modern Wisdom from Classic Stories* (New York: Bantam Books, 1992), p. 25: "The fellowship of Alcoholics Anonymous presents itself as 'spiritual rather than religious.'" Conceding this idea, Mel B. stated in *New Wine: The Spiritual Roots of the Twelve Step Miracle* (MN: Hazelden, 1991), p. 5: "AA members have always issued disclaimers when discussing God: Typical is, 'Our program is spiritual, not religious.' If pressed for what the program's actual definition of *spiritual* is, however, it's doubtful that many AA members could explain."

[132] Big Book, pp. xiv, xx, 1, 9, 11, 19, 28, 87, 131-32.

[133] Big Book, pp. 100, 120, 124. Oxford Group writers did refer to putting things in God's hands. Kitchen, *I Was a Pagan*, p. 108; and Shoemaker, *With the Holy Spirit and With Fire*, p. 31; but more familiar to AAs is their expression, "Let go and let God." See Shoemaker, *Twice-Born Ministers*, pp. 106, 20; and Benson, *The Eight Points*, p. 68.

6. *Faith without works is dead.*[134]

7. *Fellowship* and *Fellowship of the Spirit.*[135]

8. *Sharing experience, strength, and hope.*[136]

A Spiritual Experience or Awakening

There are several Big Book expressions concerning "spiritual experience" and "spiritual awakening" that may have come from Bill's and Dr. Bob's Oxford Group exposure. Frank Buchman often used the very words "spiritual awakening."[137] As we have shown, these and other Oxford Group words such as contact with God, the power and presence of God, the living God, and God as the Great Reality were common place in early A.A.[138] Also that God had done for the alcoholic what he could not do for himself.[139] And particularly "God Consciousness."[140]

---

[134] Big Book, pp. 14, 88, 93; *What Is The Oxford Group?*, p. 36; and Dick B., *Anne Smith's Journal*, pp. v, 54, 74.

[135] Big Book, pp. xiii, xv, xix, xxiii, 94, 96, 152, 159, 161, 163, 164. See Shoemaker, *Religion That Works*, containing an entire chapter entitled "The Fellowship of the Holy Ghost" (pp. 66-76).

[136] Big Book, pp. xii, xxii, 29, 58. See Day, *The Principles of the Group*, p. 7; Shoemaker, *Calvary Church Yesterday and Today*, where Dr. Shoemaker reports on the meetings in Calvary Hall where "was found the sharing of spiritual experience by ordinary individuals, confronted with common problems and situations of life . . . the emphasis was on the will being given to God, and on what He could do to guide and use a life so given to Him" (p. 245).

[137] Buchman, *Remaking The World*, pp. 19, 24, 35, 54.

[138] Big Book, pp. 28, 46, 47, 51, 55, 56, 59, 63, 85, 87, 130, 161, 162, 569, 570. And see, for example: (1) "Living God": Buchman, *Remaking the World*, p. 107; Foot, *Life Began Yesterday*, p. 161; (2) "the joy of conscious fellowship with God and with those to whom He is the one great Living Reality": Shoemaker, *Confident Faith*, pp. 189-190. (3) "contact with God": Benson, *The Eight Points*, p. 31.

[139] Big Book, pp. 11, 25, 57, 84, 100. See, for example, Shoemaker, *If I Be Lifted Up*, "Do not marvel at what God has done *through* you, for you may wind up marvelling at you; but marvel at what God has done *for* you . . . " (p. 34).

Service

The Big Book highly emphasized the importance of—the *necessity for*—thinking of, helping, and working with others.[141]

The Principles of the Four Absolutes

We might start with the direct quote in the Big Book from the Sermon on the Mount—one of Dr. Bob's favorite portions from the Good Book: "Love thy neighbor as thyself."[142] The principles of honesty, unselfishness, and love can be found throughout the Big Book.[143] And we believe the "purity" idea possibly exists at least in the "clean house" idea of the Big Book.[144]

Parallels Between Oxford Group and Big Book Language

There are remarkable similarities between words and phrases in Oxford Group literature and those in A.A.'s Big Book. The

---

[140] (...continued)

[140] Big Book, pp. 13, 51, 85, 569-570. See, for example, Shoemaker, *Twice-Born Ministers*, p. 123, and the other books cited in our discussion of God-consciousness.

[141] Big Book, pp. 14-15, 20, 84, 89-103, 159. See Day, *The Principles of the Group*, pp. 7-8; Harris, *The Breeze of the Spirit*, p. 19; Thornton-Duesbury, *Sharing*, pp. 6-8; and Shoemaker, *Realizing Religion*, p. 83. Reverend Howard J. Rose concludes his little pamphlet, *The Quiet Time*, stating: "The more general results of the Quiet Time are . . . A Christ-centered and unified life, issuing in joyous, spontaneous, God-directed service" (p. 4). Benson wrote in *The Eight Points*, at page 110: "The strength of fellowship comes from the fact that to men of limited view and partial capacity there is given immense enrichment of personal power and service. Sharing their lives and dedication to a common aim give added strength."

[142] Big Book, p. 153. See Matthew 5:43; Leviticus 19:18; James 2:8 (called in James "the royal law").

[143] Big Book, pp. xxvii, 13, 26, 28, 32, 44, 47, 55, 57, 58, 63, 64, 65, 67, 70, 73, 83, 117, 140, 145, 570; 20. 70, 84, 89, 90, 94, 95, 97, 100, 102, 131, 161, 162; 67, 70, 84, 86, 118, 122, 127, 153.

[144] Big Book, p. 98. See also James 4:8, "Draw nigh to God, and he will draw nigh to you. Cleanse *your* hands, ye sinners; and purify *your* hearts, ye double minded."

similarities would be of less significance if Bill Wilson had not attributed almost every A.A. idea to the Oxford Group and if A.A. biographies and histories had not re-affirmed the link. We do not say that the following Oxford Group language directly found its way to the Big Book, but the reader will see striking parallels. We have gone through thousands of pages of Oxford Group language. We've also reviewed the Big Book page by page for similarities. And we have set out below quotes from Oxford Group books, largely in the chronological order that their parallels appear in the Big Book. The full titles for the Oxford Group books we cite can be found in our Bibliography.

1. I've got religion.[145]
2. A vast Power outside themselves.[146]
3. A Force outside himself, greater than himself.[147]
4. A power within yet coming from outside myself—a power far stronger than I was.[148]
5. A Personal God.[149]
6. New power and direction came to her when she started listening to God.[150]
7. Love of God.[151]
8. Marvel at what God has done for you.[152]

---

[145] Shoemaker, *Children of the Second Birth*, pp. 118, 165. Big Book, p. 9.

[146] Shoemaker, *A Young Man's View of the Ministry*, p. 42. Big Book: "Power greater than ourselves," pp. 10, 46, 47, 59.

[147] Shoemaker, *If I Be Lifted Up*, p. 176. See also, Kitchen, *I Was a Pagan*, p. 78; Big Book, *supra*, pp. 10, 45, 46, 47, 59.

[148] Kitchen, *I Was a Pagan*, p. 63. See Big Book, pp. 10, 36, 47, 59.

[149] Shoemaker, *Children of the Second Birth*, p. 61. Big Book, pp. 10, 12: "a God personal to me."

[150] Foot, *Life Began Yesterday*, p. 112. Big Book, p. 10: "When they talked of a God . . . who was love, superhuman strength and direction. . . ."

[151] *What Is The Oxford Group?*, p. 112; Allen, *He That Cometh*, p. 219. Big Book, p. 10: "God. . . who was love."

[152] Shoemaker, *If I Be Lifted Up*, pp. 13, 84; Big Book, pp. 11, 84: "God is doing for us what we could not do for ourselves."

9. Surrender of all one knows of self to all one knows of God.[153]

10. God-consciousness.[154]

11. Relationship with God.[155]

12. Self was the centre of my life, not God.[156]

13. Willingness to believe.[157]

14. Willingness.[158]

15. God comes to us when we ask Him.[159]

16. They prayed together, opening their minds to *as much of God as he understood.*[160]

17. She surrendered to God . . . and . . . turned over to Him her life for His direction.[161]

18. To give up sin men must do four things: Hate, Forsake, Confess, Restore.[162]

---

[153] Foot, *Life Began Yesterday*, pp. 175, 12-13; Big Book, p. 12: "Why don't you choose your own conception of God?"

[154] Kitchen, *I Was a Pagan*, pp. 28, 41, 75, 96, 28; Begbie, *Life Changers*, p. 39. Big Book, pp. 13, 85, 570.

[155] Shoemaker, *Children of the Second Birth*, p. 16; Kitchen, *I Was a Pagan*, p. 113; Benson, *The Eight Points of the Oxford Group*, pp. 48, 92. Big Book, pp. 13, 28, 29, 100, 164.

[156] Foot, *Life Began Yesterday*, p. 9; Begbie, *Life Changers*, p. 17. Big Book, p. 14: "It meant destruction of self-centeredness. I must turn in all things to the Father of Light." See James 1:17.

[157] Brown, *The Venture of Belief*, p. 26. Big Book, p. 12: "It was only a matter of being willing to believe."

[158] Brown, *The Venture of Belief*, p. 36. Big Book, p. 12.

[159] Begbie, *Life Changers*, p. 37. Big Book, p. 12: "I had needed and wanted God. There had been a humble willingness to have Him with me—and He came."

[160] Shoemaker, *Children of the Second Birth*, pp. 25, 47; *The Gospel According to You*, p. 128; Big Book, p. 67, 88, 13: "I humbly offered myself to God, as I then understood Him, to do with me as He would."

[161] Shoemaker, *Children of the Second Birth*, p. 82. Big Book, p. 13: "I placed myself unreservedly under His care and direction." The Shoemaker language is very similar to the language of A.A.'s Third Step as it was written in the multi-lith copy that preceded publication of the First Edition of the Big Book.

[162] Shoemaker, *Children of the Second Birth*, p. 94. Big Book, p. 13: "I ruthlessly faced my sins and became willing to have my new-found Friend take them away, root and branch."

19. Have you looked back into your life and carefully considered *every wrong* you have ever done to anyone and *endeavored to set it right?*[163]

20. *Listen to the guidance of the Holy Spirit,* said the Group, and you will hear Him saying, "Be ye reconciled one towards another." I began to listen.[164]

21. Witness is Sharing with others the main reasons and the concrete results of our surrender to God. . . . "*Faith apart from works,*" said St. James, "*is barren.*"[165]

22. Design for living.[166]

23. Coming so wholly into the *confidence* of the one we seek to help along the avenue of personal friendship that we know his verdict in his own case.[167]

24. Wretched man that I am! Who shall deliver me from the body of this death?[168]

25. By the grace of God.[169]

26. The Solution.[170]

---

[163] Russell, *For Sinners Only*, p. 128. Big Book, p. 13: "We made a list of people I had hurt. . . . I expressed my entire willingness to approach these individuals admitting my wrong. . . . I was to right all such matters to the utmost of my ability."

[164] Russell, *For Sinners Only*, p. 135. Big Book, p. 13: "I was to sit quietly when in doubt, asking only for direction and strength to meet my problems as He would have me."

[165] *What Is The Oxford Group?*, p. 36. Big Book, p. 14: "Particularly was it imperative to work with others as he had worked with me. Faith without works is dead, he said."

[166] Kitchen, *I Was a Pagan*, p. 167. Big Book, pp. 15, 28.

[167] Walter, *Soul Surgery*, p. 30. Big Book, p. 18: "But the ex-problem drinker who has found the solution . . . can generally win the entire confidence of another alcoholic. . . . Until such an understanding is reached, little or nothing can be accomplished."

[168] This quotation is from Romans 7:24. See Shoemaker, *Religion That Works*, p. 45. Big Book, p. 24: "unable, at certain times, to bring into our consciousness with sufficient force the memory of the suffering and humiliation of even a week or a month ago . . . beyond human aid."

[169] Begbie, *Life Changers*, p. 17. Big Book, p. 25: "But for the grace of God . . ."

[170] Foot, *Life Began Yesterday*, p. 21. Big Book, pp. 17, 25: "There is a solution."

27. Be ready to confess your own shortcomings honestly and humbly.[171]
28. Spiritual experience.[172]
29. In God's hands, and awaits His wise direction . . .[173]
30. Higher Power.[174]
31. This Power by which human nature can be changed . . . and through this Power problems are being solved.[175]
32. There is at work in the world today a Power that has for many generations been neglected by masses of mankind.[176]
33. I made the surrender of my will to the Divine purpose, as a calm, resolute, intelligent and reasonable act of submission to the Power controlling the world.[177]
34. He made a decision to surrender to God.[178]
35. Peace, direction, power—the fulness of life—await the complete surrender of ourselves to God for His purposes.[179]

---

[171] Walter, *Soul Surgery*, p. 57. Big Book, p. 25: "the self-searching, the leveling of our pride, the confession of shortcomings which the process requires for its successful consummation."

[172] Shoemaker, *Twice-Born Ministers*, pp. 61, 10. Big Book, pp. 17, 29: "spiritual experience."

[173] Kitchen, *I Was a Pagan*, p. 108. Big Book, pp. 28, 100, 120, 124.

[174] Kitchen, *I Was a Pagan*, p. 85. Big Book, pp. 43, 100.

[175] Foot, *Life Began Yesterday*, p. 22. Big Book, p. 45: "But where and how were we to find this Power?"

[176] Foot, *Life Began Yesterday*, p. 22; "I could not quite make out just what this secret or power *was*" See Kitchen, *I Was a Pagan*, p. 28. Big Book, p. 45: "Well, that's exactly what this book is about. Its main object is to enable you to find a Power greater than yourself which will solve your problem."

[177] Foot, *Life Began Yesterday*, p. 30. Big Book, p. 45: "And it means, of course, that we are going to talk about God."

[178] Foot, *Life Began Yesterday*, p. 44; "I surrender Thee my entire life, O God," Kitchen, *I Was a Pagan*, p. 67. Big Book, p. 46: "It was impossible for any of us to fully define or comprehend that Power, which is God."

[179] Cecil Rose, *When Man Listens*, p. 17. Big Book, p. 50, 46: "We began to be possessed of a new sense of power and direction, provided we took other simple steps."

36. I had, in other words, actually to *become* God-conscious.[180]

37. Refusal to believe is as much a decision as the willingness to believe.[181]

38. A man had simply to step out of his own light to become immediately and keenly conscious of the presence of God.[182]

39. "I was keen on self-management—a self-determinist—the captain of my own soul. . . . *And there is the real secret of all human difficulty.* . . . I—the *self-sufficient* V. C. Kitchen—would continue to live outside the law of fellowship."[183]

40. God-sufficiency.[184]

41. God is, or He isn't.[185]

42. He is the all-pervading Reality.[186]

43. Conscious of the presence and the companionship of God.[187]

---

[180] Kitchen, *I Was a Pagan*, p. 41. Big Book, p. 47: "At the start, this was all we needed . . . to effect our first conscious relation with God as we understood Him."

[181] Cecil Rose, *When Man Listens*, p. 27. Big Book, p. 47: "Am I even willing to believe that there is a Power greater than myself."

[182] Kitchen, *I Was a Pagan*, p. 43. Big Book, p. 51: "Many hundreds of people are able to say that the consciousness of the Presence of God is today the most important fact of their lives."

[183] Kitchen, *I Was a Pagan*, pp. 39, 61. Big Book, pp. 52: "We agnostics and atheists were sticking to the idea that self-sufficiency would solve our problems."

[184] Shoemaker, *If I Be Lifted Up*, pp. 106-07. Big Book, p. 52-53: "Others showed us that 'God-sufficiency' worked with them. . . ."

[185] Shoemaker, *Confident Faith*, p. 187. Big Book, p. 53: "God either is, or He isn't."

[186] Streeter, *The God Who Speaks*, p. 12; Shoemaker, *The Gospel According To You*, p. 47: The great thing that all of us long for in religion is the reality of the Presence of God. See also, Begbie, *Life Changers*, p. 104. Big Book, p. 55: "He was there. He was as much a fact as we were. We found the Great Reality deep down within us."

[187] Begbie, *Life Changers*, p. 16. Big Book, p. 56: "He lived in conscious companionship with his Creator."

44. Creator.[188]
45. Maker.[189]
46. Director.[190]
47. Father.[191]
48. Infinite Power.[192]
49. Spirit.[193]
50. I then and there admitted my inability to quit [drinking] of my own will and asked God to take charge of the matter. . . . God simply lifted that desire entirely out of my life.[194]
51. God floods in when a man is honest.[195]
52. We must surrender our wills to a greater Will, and that will set us free.[196]
53. We must be absolutely honest with ourselves.[197]
54. How did I accomplish the self-deflation. . . ?[198]

---

[188] Brown, *The Venture of Belief*, p. 25; Begbie, *Life Changers*, p. 16; and Streeter, *The God Who Speaks*, p. 109. Big Book, pp. 13, 25, 28, 56, 68, 72, 75, 76, 80, 83, 158, 161.

[189] Benson, *The Eight Points of the Oxford Group*, p. 73. Big Book, p. 57.

[190] Streeter, *The God Who Speaks*, p. 10; Big Book, p. 62: "God was going to be our Director."

[191] *What Is The Oxford Group?*, p. 48; Shoemaker, *The Conversion of the Church*, p. 49. Big Book, p. 62.

[192] Brown, *The Venture of Belief*, p. 25. Big Book, p. 68.

[193] Walter, *Soul Surgery*, p. 27. Big Book, p. 85.

[194] Kitchen, *I Was a Pagan*, p. 74. Big Book, p. 57: "Save for a few brief moments of temptation the thought of drink has never returned. . . God had restored his sanity. . . He humbly offered himself to his Maker—then he knew."

[195] Begbie, *Life Changers*, p. 103. Big Book, p. 57: "Even so has God restored us all to our right minds. . . . He has come to all who have honestly sought Him."

[196] Foot, *Life Began Yesterday*, p. 35. Big Book, p. 57: "When we drew near to Him, He disclosed Himself to us!"

[197] *What is the Oxford Group?*, p. 77. Big Book, p. 58: "Those who do not recover are people . . . who are constitutionally incapable of being honest with themselves."

[198] Kitchen, *I Was a Pagan*, p. 47. Big Book, p. 58: "Some of us have tried to hold on to our old ideas and the result was nil until we let go absolutely. Remember that we deal with alcohol—cunning, baffling, powerful. Without help it is too much for us."

55. Let go! Abandon yourself to Him. Say to Him, "Not my will but Thine be done."[199]

56. It was this power of the Spirit flowing into me that . . . gave me not only the courage [but also] the strength . . . I needed.[200]

57. You need to find God.[201]

58. My real education did not begin till the day I found God.[202]

59. The crisis of self-surrender has always been and must always be regarded as the vital *turning* point of the religious life.[203]

60. Abandon yourself to Him.[204]

61. O Lord, manage me, for I cannot manage myself.[205]

62. The first action is mental action, it is a decision of the will to make a *decision*—one decides that one has not controlled one's life particularly well hitherto, and therefore it had better be put under new management.[206]

63. He made his decision.[207]

---

[199] Shoemaker, *Religion That Works*, p. 19. Big Book, p. 58: "The result was nil until we let go absolutely."

[200] Kitchen, *I Was a Pagan*, pp. 78-79; Big Book, p. 59: "But there is One who has all power—that One is God."

[201] Shoemaker, *Realizing Religion*, p. 9; Big Book, p. 59: "But there is One who has all power—that One is God. May you find Him now!"

[202] Kitchen, *I Was a Pagan*, p. 94; Big Book, p. 59: "May you find Him now!"

[203] Shoemaker, *Realizing Religion*, p. 30; Begbie, *Life Changers*, p. 126; For the frequent references by Shoemaker to "the turning point," see Dick B., *New Light on Alcoholism*, p. 41; Big Book, p. 59: "We stood at the turning point."

[204] Shoemaker, *Religion that Works*, p. 19; Big Book, p. 59: "We asked His protection and care with complete abandon."

[205] Russell, *For Sinners Only*, p. 79; Howard, *Frank Buchman's Secret*, pp. 41-44; and Harris, *The Breeze of the Spirit*, p. 10. For the many usages of the "manage me" prayer, see Dick B., *Anne Smith's Journal*, pp. 20-22; Big Book, p. 59: "We admitted . . . that our lives had become unmanageable."

[206] Foot, *Life Began Yesterday*, p. 10; Big Book, p. 59: "Made a decision to turn our will and our lives over to the care of God *as we understood Him.*"

[207] Shoemaker, *Children of the Second Birth*, p. 125; Big Book, p. 59: "Made a decision."

64. The decision to cast my will and my life on God.[208]
65. [Man needs to] devote his soul to self-examination, to self examination of the most solemn and searching kind.[209]
66. We are bidden by Frank Buchman to "make the moral test."[210]
67. The first step for me was to be honest with God, the next to be honest with men.[211]
68. If a person is honest with himself and with God, he will be honest also with us.[212]
69. God . . . satisfied unsound desire by *removing* the desire itself.[213]
70. He was wounded for our transgressions. He was bruised for our iniquities; the chastisement of our peace was upon Him, and with His stripes we are healed. . . . Be ready to confess your own shortcomings honestly and humbly.[214]
71. How can anyone who professes to love God and his neighbor as himself, as all Christians must do, allow a wrong he has done to anyone to go unrighted?[215]

---

[208] Shoemaker, *Twice-Born Ministers*, p. 134. Big Book, p. 60: "Being convinced, we were at Step Three, which is that we decided to turn our will and our life over to God as we understood Him."

[209] Drummond, *The Ideal Life*, p. 316. Big Book, p. 59: "Made a fearless and searching moral inventory of ourselves."

[210] Walter, *Soul Surgery*, pp. 43-44. Big Book, p. 59: "moral inventory of ourselves."

[211] Foot, *Life Began Yesterday*, p. 11. Big Book, p. 59: "Admitted to God, to ourselves, and to another human being the exact nature of our wrongs."

[212] Shoemaker, *The Gospel According to You*, p. 38. Big Book, p. 59: "Admitted to God, to ourselves, and to another human being. . . ."

[213] Kitchen, *I Was a Pagan*, p. 73. Big Book, p. 59: "Were entirely ready to have God remove all these defects of character."

[214] Walter, *Soul Surgery*, p. 57 (citing Isaiah 53:4, 5). Big Book, p. 59: "Humbly asked Him to remove our shortcomings."

[215] Russell, *For Sinners Only*, p. 128. Big Book, p. 59: "and became willing to make amends to them all."

72. I discovered four things which needed putting right in my life. . . . There was a restitution which I would not make.[216]

73. Every person I have wronged I have seen and made restitution to him, in so far as I was able.[217]

74. In order to leave nothing undone in the attempt to make things right with people I had wronged, I wrote fourteen letters of confession of specific wrong.[218]

75. Spiritual awakening.[219]

76. Contact with God is the necessary fundamental condition, and that is made through prayer and listening. . . .[220]

77. I will ask God to show me His purpose for my life and claim from Him the power to carry that purpose out.[221]

78. God is and is a Rewarder of them that seek Him.[222]

79. Opening their minds to as much of God as he understood, removing first the hindrance of *self-will*.[223]

80. Selfish and self-centered.[224]

---

[216] Shoemaker, *Twice-Born Ministers*, p. 92. Big Book, p. 59: "Made a list of all persons we had harmed."

[217] Russell, *For Sinners Only*, p. 128. Big Book, p. 59: "Made direct amends to such people wherever possible, except when to do so would injure them or others."

[218] Shoemaker, *Twice-Born Ministers*, p. 166. Big Book, p. 59: "Made direct amends to such people wherever possible. . . ."

[219] Buchman, *Remaking the World*, pp. 19, 24, 35, 54; and Shoemaker, *The Conversion of the Church*, p. 124. Big Book, p. 60: "Having had a spiritual awakening . . ."

[220] Foot, *Life Began Yesterday*, p. 13. Big Book, p. 59: "Sought through prayer and meditation to improve our conscious contact with God. . . . "

[221] Foot, *Life Began Yesterday*, p. 11. Big Book, p. 59: "Praying only for knowledge of His will for us and the power to carry that out."

[222] Shoemaker, *Religion That Works*, p. 68; *The Gospel According To You*, p. 47. Big Book, p. 60: "God could and would if He were sought."

[223] Shoemaker, *Children of the Second Birth*, p. 47. Big Book, p. 60: "Any life run on self-will can hardly be a success."

[224] Kitchen, *I Was a Pagan*, p. 103. Big Book, p. 61: "Our actor is self-centered—ego centric."

81. That is what the Oxford Group is working for, changed lives, God-centered in place of self-centered.[225]
82. Self-will seems the blackest sin of all.[226]
83. For most men, the world is centered in self, which is misery.[227]
84. Self was at the bottom of many of these actions.[228]
85. There is a good deal of sorrow in our life of our own making.[229]
86. A very large part of human misery is of our own making.[230]
87. When you blow away the clouds of your self-pity, self-will, self-centeredness, all that you will find left is a universe of opportunity, with God to help you, and a miserable, petty little self sitting down in the midst of it, refusing to play.[231]
88. God showed me, however, that it was not only possible to be honest in advertising, but to be unselfish, loving and pure.[232]
89. An experience of God means . . . a new charge of strength flowing into the will . . . a new direction and a new power

---

[225] Foot, *Life Began Yesterday*, p. 47. Big Book, p. 62: "Selfishness—self centeredness! That, we think, is the root of our troubles."

[226] Shoemaker, *Realizing Religion*, pp. 31-32. Big Book, p. 52: "Our troubles . . . arise out of ourselves, and the alcoholic is an extreme example of self-will run riot."

[227] Shoemaker, *Realizing Religion*, p. 11. Big Book, p. 62: "We alcoholics must be rid of this selfishness. We must, or it kills us! God makes that possible. And there often seems no way of entirely getting rid of self without His aid."

[228] Foot, *Life Began Yesterday*, p. 9. Big Book, p. 62: "We have made decisions based on self which later placed us in a position to be hurt."

[229] Shoemaker, *Confident Faith*, p. 149. Big Book, p. 62: "So our troubles, we think, are basically of our own making."

[230] Shoemaker, *The Gospel According to You*, p. 38. Big Book, p. 103: "After all, our problems were of our own making. Bottles were only a symbol."

[231] Shoemaker, *God's Control*, p. 57. Big Book, p. 62: "Neither could we reduce our self-centeredness much by wishing or trying on our own Power. We had to have God's help."

[232] Kitchen, *I Was a Pagan*, p. 120. Big Book, p. 63: "Being all powerful, He provided what we needed, if we kept close to Him and performed His work well."

to choose correctly and rightly . . . [and] a new affection—strengthened, invigorated, cleansed.[233]

90. Where He [God] guides, He provides.[234]

91. We were reborn into life. . . . I know what is meant by "The Peace that Passeth All Understanding."[235]

92. All anxiety and fear has flown out the window never to return. God has time and time again vindicated this faith in Him by taking care of our needs as each need has arisen.[236]

93. I surrender Thee my entire life, O God. I have made a mess of it, trying to run it myself. You take it—the whole thing—and run it for me, according to Your will and plan.[237]

94. When I gave my life to God, however, He freed me from this bondage.[238]

95. She saw how definite sin was blocking her from Christ.[239]

96. If, then, I want God to take control of my life, the first thing I must do is produce the books. A good way to begin this

---

[233] Kitchen, *I Was a Pagan*, p. 104. Big Book, p. 63: "We felt new power flow in . . . we enjoyed peace of mind . . . we discovered we could face life successfully . . . we became conscious of His presence."

[234] Shoemaker, *Children of the Second Birth*, p. 160. Big Book, p. 63: "Being all powerful, He provided what we needed, if we kept close to Him and performed His work well."

[235] Foot, *Life Began Yesterday*, p. 68. Big Book, p. 63: "We were reborn."

[236] Kitchen, *I Was a Pagan*, p. 121. Big Book, p. 63: "As we became conscious of His presence, we began to lose our fear of today, tomorrow or the hereafter."

[237] Kitchen, *I Was a Pagan*, p. 67. Big Book, p. 63; "God, I offer myself to Thee—to build with me and to do with me as Thou wilt. . . . Take away my difficulties, that victory over them may bear witness to those I would help of Thy Power, Thy Love, and Thy Way of life. May I do Thy will always!"

[238] Kitchen, *I Was a Pagan*, p. 145. Big Book, p. 145: "Relieve me of the bondage of self, that I may better do Thy will."

[239] Shoemaker, *Twice-Born Ministers*, p. 32; and *They're On The Way*, p. 154. Big Book, p. 64: "Our decision . . . could have little permanent effect unless at once followed by a strenuous effort to face, and be rid of, the things in ourselves which had been blocking us; p. 71: "God can remove whatever self-will has blocked you off from Him."

examination of the books is to test my life beside the Sermon on the Mount.[240]

97. If when a trader finds his way into the bankruptcy court, it is revealed that for years he has not taken stock, he is very severely censured.[241]

98. I found that self crept into almost everything. . . . And . . . this selfishness has as surely shut me off from a true consciousness of God.[242]

99. The thing which is striking about much of the misery one sees is that it is *spiritual* misery. . . . The root of the malady is estrangement from God.[243]

100. What is our real problem? . . . Isn't it fear, dishonesty, resentment, selfishness?[244]

101. Selfishness, fear, resentment, pride, do not live in the air. They live in men.[245]

102. Any remnant of resentment, hatred or grudge blocks God out effectively.[246]

---

[240] Rose, *When Man Listens*, pp. 17-18. Big Book, p. 64: "Taking a commercial inventory is a fact-finding and a fact-facing process. . . We did exactly the same thing with our lives."

[241] Benson, *The Eight Points*, p. 44. Big Book, p. 64: "A business which takes no regular inventory usually goes broke. . . We took stock honestly. First, we searched out the flaws in our make-up which caused our failure."

[242] Kitchen, *I Was a Pagan*, p. 46; Foot, *Life Began Yesterday*, p. 9: "Self was at the bottom of many of these actions. . . . Self was the centre of my life, not God." Big Book, p. 64: "Being convinced that self, manifested in various ways, was what had defeated us, we considered its common manifestations."

[243] Shoemaker, *Realizing Religion*, pp. 4-5. Big Book, p. 64: "all forms of spiritual disease . . . we have been spiritually sick. . . . When the spiritual malady is overcome, we straighten out mentally and physically."

[244] Buchman, Remaking The World, p. 38. Big Book, p. 64: "Resentment is the 'number one' offender. . . . In dealing with resentments, we set them on paper."

[245] Rose, *When Man Listens*, p. 41. Big Book, p. 64: "We asked ourselves why we were angry."

[246] Macmillan, *Seeking and Finding*, p. 98; Shoemaker, *Twice-Born Ministers*, p. 182; Benson, *The Eight Points*, p. x (grudges). Big Book, p. 65: "On our grudge list we set opposite each name our injuries."

103. I ceased struggling to pull myself *up* and stepped out of the way so that His light could shine *down* to me.[247]
104. Thy will be done.[248]
105. It means confessing our part in the sinning. Blaming others and thereby making excuses for ourselves is not sharing, but is sheer selfishness.[249]
106. Moral recovery starts when everyone admits his own faults instead of spot-lighting the other fellow's.[250]
107. Fear may be the great paralyser; its effect a negation of action and not a stimulus.[251]
108. The root problems in the word today are dishonesty, selfishness and fear—in men, and consequently in nations.[252]
109. Hundreds . . . have fallen ill, some . . . have committed suicide, because they had no faith to substitute for fear: and fear literally ate the heart out of them. And its antidote is faith in God. The emotion of worship, of trust, of faith, is strong enough to offset fear.[253]

---

[247] Kitchen, *I Was a Pagan*, pp. 48; see also, pp. 42, 44, 46. Big Book, p. 66: "When harboring such feelings we shut ourselves off from the sunlight of the Spirit."

[248] Wright, *The Will of God* pp., 50-51; Macmillan, *Seeking and Finding*, p. 273; *What Is The Oxford Group?*, pp. 46-48; Shoemaker, *Children of the Second Birth*, pp. 175-87; *If I Be Lifted Up*, p. 93; and *How To Find God*, p. 10. Big Book, p. 67, 88.

[249] Benson, *The Eight Points*, p. 28. Big Book, p. 67: "We resolutely looked for our own mistakes. . . . Where were we to blame? . . . When we saw our faults we listed them."

[250] Buchman, *Remaking the World*, p. 46. Big Book, p. 67: "Though a situation had not been entirely our fault, we tried to disregard the other person entirely. . . . We admitted our wrongs honestly."

[251] Foot, *Life Began Yesterday*, p. 31. Big Book, p. 67: "The word 'fear' is bracketed. . . . This short word somehow touches about every aspect of our lives. It was an evil and corroding thread; the fabric of our existence was shot through with it."

[252] Buchman, *Remaking the World*, p. 28. Big Book, pp. 67-68: "But did not we, ourselves set the ball rolling? Sometimes we think fear ought to be classed with stealing. It seems to cause more trouble."

[253] Shoemaker, *Confident Faith*, p. 172. Big Book, p. 68: "For we are now on a different basis; the basis of trusting and relying upon God. We trust infinite God rather than our finite selves."

110. God . . . is not only the answer to disharmony in sex relations; not only our Guide, Counsellor and Friend. . . . He is Judge, Provider and Stabilizer.[254]

111. It takes the power of God to *remove* these fears and mental conditions.[255]

112. Putting our sins and spiritual problems into words to another makes us absolutely honest with God.[256]

113. One of God's most effective ways of introducing us to ourselves is to send us another person, whom we can trust, to tell them the whole truth about our lives as far as we know it.[257]

114. We greatly need to come out into the open—to take off the mask and drop the pose, and to be our real selves, honest about our mistakes and sins, frank about our thoughts and intentions, willing to let other people know us.[258]

115. I have found that to deal drastically with sins it is necessary to share them completely with someone in whom we have confidence.[259]

---

[254] Kitchen, *I Was a Pagan*, p. 104. Big Book, p. 69: "In meditation, we ask God what we should do about each [sex] matter. The right answer will come, if we want it. God alone can judge our sex situation. . . . [W]e let God be the final judge. . . . We earnestly pray for the right idea, for guidance . . . for sanity . . . for the strength to do the right thing."

[255] Kitchen, *I Was a Pagan*, p. 143. Big Book, p. 71: "We hope you are convinced now that God can remove whatever self-will has blocked you off from Him."

[256] *What Is The Oxford Group?*, p. 32. Big Book, p. 72: "We have admitted to God, to ourselves, and to another human being the exact nature of our defects."

[257] Rose, *When Man Listens*, p. 49. Big Book, p. 73: "But they had not learned enough of humility, fearlessness and honesty, in the sense we find it necessary, until they told someone else *all* their life story."

[258] Rose, *When Man Listens*, p. 43. Big Book, p. 73-74: "They took inventory all right, but hung on to some of the worst items in stock. They only *thought* they had lost their egoism and fear; they only *thought* they had humbled themselves. . . . We must be entirely honest with somebody if we expect to live long and happily in this world."

[259] Brown, *The Venture of Belief*, pp. 33-34. Big Book, p. 74: "We think well before we choose the person or persons with whom to take this intimate and confidential step. . . . We search our acquaintance for a close-mouthed, understanding friend."

116. They are prepared to pocket their pride, risk their reputation, hazard their material interests for the sake of living in the open with their fellows.[260]

117. One human soul going out to another in all humility . . .so completely and fearlessly that for once in his life a man can know the immense relief of being absolutely honest without reservation or concealment.[261]

118. I believe that there is no other sure way to a full "surrender" to God.[262]

119. To summarize the various stages of spiritual adventure: first, the will to believe; second, the honest facing and sharing of all conscious sin; third, the complete surrender of self to God; and, fourth, the willingness to obey His will.[263]

120. God cannot take over my life unless I am *willing*.[264]

121. I then and there admitted my inability to quit of my own will and asked God to take charge of the matter.[265]

122. It takes the power of God to *remove* the desire for these indulgences.[266]

123. My concern must be to try to be more worthy of this daily sacrament of being alive. I cannot do this unless I "wait on

---

[260] Rose, *When Man Listens*, p. 44. Big Book, p. 75: "We pocket our pride and go to it, illuminating every twist of character, every dark cranny of the past."

[261] Brown, *The Venture of Belief*, p. 35. Big Book, p. 75: "Once we have taken this step, withholding nothing, we are delighted. We can look the world in the eye. We can be alone at perfect peace and ease."

[262] Brown, *The Venture of Belief*, p. 35. Big Book, p. 75: "We feel we are on the Broad Highway, walking hand in hand with the Spirit of the Universe."

[263] Brown, *The Venture of Belief*, p. 36. Big Book, p. 76: "We have emphasized complete willingness as being indispensable. Are we now ready to let God remove from us all the things we have admitted are objectionable."

[264] Rose, *When Man Listens*, p. 17. Big Book, p. 76: "If we still cling to something we will not let go, we ask God to help us be willing."

[265] Kitchen, *I Was a Pagan*, p. 74. Big Book, p. 75: "My Creator, I am now willing that you should have all of me, good and bad."

[266] Kitchen, *I Was a Pagan*, p. 143. Big Book, p. 76: "I pray that you now remove from me every single defect of character which stands in the way of my usefulness to you and my fellows."

God" and seek humbly and confidently to ascertain His will in my life.[267]

124. A further point in the moral challenge which the Oxford Group presents is that known as restitution, viz. putting right, as far as in our power, wrongs committed in the past.[268]

125. If while we hesitate we realize that God is really with us and that an act of restitution . . . is necessary, our hand, God-guided, without hesitation creeps up to the post box and the letter goes beyond our recalling, to carry out one more act of atonement that will set us free from our past selves.[269]

126. Voluntary confession and restitution bring home the seriousness of wrong-doing more effectively than any other curative method.[270]

127. These first steps of restitution are absolutely necessary if I am to start the new life clear with God and other people. . . . [The] great task that is waiting: to cooperate with God and to ask God to make us fit for Him to use.[271]

128. [T]he same series of exceedingly simple steps. First, they said, that I would have to make clean contact. . . . To get my contact points clean, they said, I would have to face up to my sins. . . .[272]

---

[267] Brown, *The Venture of Belief*, p. 40. Big Book, p. 76: "Grant me strength, as I go out from here, to do your bidding."

[268] Winslow, *Why I Believe in the Oxford Group*, p. 31. Big Book, p. 76: "Now we go out to our fellows and repair the damage done in the past."

[269] *What Is The Oxford Group?*, p. 59. Big Book, p. 76: "If we haven't the will to do this, we ask until it comes."

[270] Russell, *For Sinners Only*, p. 124. Big Book, p. 76: "We subjected ourselves to a drastic self-appraisal. . . . We attempt to sweep away the debris which has accumulated out of our effort to live on self-will and run the show ourselves."

[271] Rose, *When Man Listens*, p. 20. Foot, *Life Began Yesterday*, p. 98. Big Book, p. 77: "At the moment we are trying to put our lives in order. But this is not an end in itself. Our real purpose is to fit ourselves to be of maximum service to God and the people about us."

[272] Kitchen, *I Was a Pagan*, p. 56. Big Book, p. 77: "We are there to sweep off our side of the street. . . ."

129. There will be a great many things I can never put right now.[273]

130. Peace, direction, power—the fullness of life—await the complete surrender of ourselves to God for His purposes.[274]

131. We are giving a far more adequate picture of Christ's power by sharing the thing from which He has saved us than we should by making no mention of our own problems and their solution. . . . Frequently, for example, a father has won the confidence of his boy by telling him something of the conflicts of his own youth and what Christ has done for him.[275]

132. "I went to a theological student who seemed to me to be troubled, to be suffering, and confessed to him my own secret sin—impurity. The . . . student came to life, confessed his secret sin to me, and ended our talk by saying, 'Prayer is going to mean something now.'"[276]

133. There is a hunger for fellowship with God and man, and there are many who have found that hunger satisfied in themselves and in others, along this double road of confession and witness.[277]

134. The answer is a God-guided, released life with constant outgo into the lives of needy people. An experience that is not shared dies or becomes twisted and abnormal.[278]

---

[273] Rose, *When Man Listens*, p. 20. Big Book, p. 83: "There may be some wrongs we can never fully right."

[274] Rose, *When Man Listens*, p. 17. Big Book, p. 83: "We are going to know a new freedom and a new happiness."

[275] Thornton-Duesbury, *Sharing*, pp. 7-8. Big Book, p. 83: "We will not regret the past nor wish to shut the door on it."

[276] Begbie, *Life Changers*, p. 103. Big Book, p. 84: "No matter how far down the scale we have gone, we will see how our experience can benefit others."

[277] Thornton-Duesbury, *Sharing*, p. 10. Big Book, p. 84: "That feeling of uselessness and self-pity will disappear."

[278] Day, *The Principles of the Oxford Group*, p. 8. Big Book, p. 84: "We will lose interest in selfish things and gain interest in our fellows. Self-seeking will slip away."

135. The most remarkable result of all . . . all anxiety and fear has flown out of the window never to return.[279]

136. The fourth signpost is an intuitive conviction that a course of action is inherently right, the certainty that, hard as it may be, there can be no other way.[280]

137. Expressional activity . . . does mean using one's spiritual muscles to maintain spiritual health.[281]

138. The deepest thing in the Christian religion is not anything we can do for God, it is what God has already done for us.[282]

139. There is need for rededication day by day, hour by hour, by which progressively, in every Quiet Time, the contaminations of sin and self-will are further sloughed off (for they do have a way of collecting).[283]

140. What is the disease? Isn't it fear, dishonesty, resentment, selfishness? We talk about freedom and liberty, but we are slaves to ourselves.[284]

141. That is what the Oxford Group is working for, changed lives, God-centered in place of self-centered, and the change continuing every day under the guidance of His Holy Spirit.[285]

---

[279] Kitchen, *I Was a Pagan*, p. 121. Big Book, p. 84: "Fear of people and of economic insecurity will leave us."

[280] Forde, *The Guidance of God*, p. 21. Big Book, p. 84: "We will intuitively know how to handle situations which used to baffle us."

[281] Day, *The Principles of the Oxford Group*, p. 8. Big Book, p. 84: "Our whole attitude and outlook upon life will change." See also Belden, *Meeting Moral Re-Armament*, p. 20.

[282] Shoemaker, *If I Be Lifted Up*, pp. 161-62. Big Book, p. 84: "We will suddenly realize that God is doing for us what we could not do for ourselves."

[283] Shoemaker, *The Conversion of the Church*, p. 79. Big Book, p. 84: "We continue to take personal inventory and continue to set right any new mistakes as we go along."

[284] Buchman, *Remaking The World*, p. 38. Big Book, p. 84: "Continue to watch for selfishness, dishonesty, resentment, and fear."

[285] Foot, *Life Began Yesterday*, p. 47. Big Book, p. 84: "We have entered the world of the Spirit. Our next function is to grow in understanding and effectiveness."

142. Our job, whether it be in business or society, is to serve the world as God shall direct.[286]
143. Nevertheless, not my will, but Thy will be done.[287]
144. Those who have entered in . . . tell us that we may expect another prize—a new conviction that God exists and a new understanding of His will, as well as a new strength and happiness in His free service. If any man willeth to do his will, he shall know . . . [John 7:17].[288]
145. Christ does not merely teach men what to do, he gives them power to do it.[289]
146. Paul has undergone a revolutionary internal change . . . the result of the indwelling of a living spirit—divine and identical with the risen Jesus.[290]
147. I "emerged" into God-consciousness.[291]
148. Experience shows that the individual is guided by God, both during the quiet time and throughout the day.[292]
149. We must be relaxed from all tension, of haste or unbelief, or too impatient seeking.[293]

---

[286] Foot, *Life Began Yesterday*, p. 60. Big Book, p. 85: "Every day is a day when we must carry the vision of God's will into all of our activities. 'How can I best serve Thee—Thy will (not mine) be done.'"

[287] Shoemaker, *If I Be Lifted Up*, p. 93; *A Young Man's View of the Ministry*, p. 70. Big Book, p. 85: "Thy will (not mine) be done."

[288] Streeter, *The God Who Speaks*, p. 126. Big Book, p. 85: "Much has already been said about receiving strength, inspiration, and direction from Him who has all knowledge and power."

[289] Streeter, *The God Who Speaks*, p. 151. Big Book, p. 85: "If we have carefully followed directions, we have begun to sense the flow of His Spirit into us."

[290] Streeter, *The God Who Speaks*, p. 92. Big Book, p. 85: "to sense the flow of His Spirit into us."

[291] Kitchen, *I Was a Pagan*, p. 43; Begbie, *Life Changers*, p. 39. Big Book, p. 85: "To some extent we have become God-conscious."

[292] Rose, *The Quiet Time*, p. 1. Big Book, p. 86: "We consider our plans for the day. Before we begin, we ask God to direct our thinking."

[293] Shoemaker, *The Conversion of the Church*, p. 50. Big Book, p. 86: "We relax and take it easy."

150. "Be still and know that I am God." . . . The hurried mind and the distracted heart make a vital knowledge of God impossible.[294]

151. Where I used to plan the day . . . I now simply ask God's guidance on the day.[295]

152. They tell of the strength of heart and mind, of the depth of knowledge of life, of the charity and love that are poured into human beings whenever they establish contact with God.[296]

153. It meant letting go of your own plans and desires for your own life, and trusting that God could run it better than yourself.[297]

154. We talked of daily Quiet Time, of Bible study, prayer and listening, and of the power of God to lead and guide those who are obedient enough to be led.[298]

155. Spiritual growth, however, was . . . to enter into new forms of usefulness for man and God.[299]

156. Buchman . . . forbade his people to speak or write "one inch" beyond their experiences.[300]

---

[294] Benson, *The Eight Points*, p. 63. Big Book, p. 86: "We don't struggle. We are often surprised how the right answers come after we have tried this for a while."

[295] Kitchen, *I Was a Pagan*, p. 123. Big Book, p. 86: "Here we ask God for inspiration, an intuitive thought or a decision."

[296] Brown, *The Venture of Belief*, p. 24. Big Book, p. 87: "having just made conscious contact with God."

[297] Shoemaker, *Children of the Second Birth*, pp. 74, 187. Big Book, pp. 87-88: "We constantly remind ourselves we are no longer running the show, humbly saying to ourselves many times each day 'Thy will be done.'"

[298] Shoemaker, *Children of the Second Birth*, pp. 148-49. Big Book, p. 87: "We usually conclude . . . with a prayer that we be shown all through the day what our next step is to be, that we be given whatever we need to take care of such problems."

[299] Kitchen, *I Was a Pagan*, p. 168. Big Book, p. 77: "Our real purpose is to fit ourselves to be of maximum service to God and the people about us."

[300] Hunter, *World Changing Through Life Changing*, p. 111. Big Book, p. 92: "Keep his attention focussed mainly on your personal experience."

157. Tell Queen Sophie how God changed your life.[301]
158. The best way to keep an experience of Christ is to pass it on.[302]
159. Having therefore obtained help of God, I continue unto this day, witnessing both to small and great.[303]
160. Recognize . . . the man in need who is longing to *find* God.[304]
161. The willingness to obey His will.[305]
162. They have "got something." That is an evasive phrase for saying they believe in and trust God.[306]
163. If you will throw the onus of decision off yourself and on to Him, giving Him only a ready and obedient will, you will be amazed at the way things work out for you.[307]
164. It works.[308]
165. If they listen to us instead of to God, they will depend on us instead of Him.[309]

---

[301] From the story Ellie Newton told the author, when Ellie asked Frank Buchman what she should say to a queen. Big Book, p. 93: "Tell him exactly what happened to you."

[302] Buchman, *Remaking The World*, p. x. Big Book, p. 94: "It is important for him to realize that your attempt to pass this on to him plays a vital part in your own recovery."

[303] The Biblical reference is Acts 26:22. *What is the Oxford Group?*, p. 26. Big Book, p. 94: "Make it plain that he is under no obligation to you, that you hope only that he will try to help other alcoholics when he escapes his own difficulties."

[304] Kitchen, *I Was a Pagan*, p. 99. Big Book, p. 95: "If he is to find God, the desire must come from within."

[305] Brown, *The Venture of Belief*, p 36. Big Book, p. 93: "The main thing is that he be willing to believe in a Power greater than himself and that he live by spiritual principles."

[306] Shoemaker, *Religion That Works*, p. 34. Big Book, p. 98: "The only condition is that he trust in God and clean house."

[307] Shoemaker, *Religion That Works*, p. 62. Big Book, p. 100: "We realize that the things which came to us when we put ourselves in God's hands were better than anything we could have planned."

[308] Nichols, *The Fool Hath Said*, p. 171; Benson, *The Eight Points*, pp. 28-29, 118; and Big Book, p. 88: "It works—it really does."

[309] Rose, *When Man Listens*, p. 62. Big Book, p. 98: "We simply do not stop drinking so long as we place dependence upon other people ahead of dependence on God."

166. All testify to the irreducible minimum of religious experience, namely, the certainty of the "presence of God" in this universe.[310]

167. Here were students who were being brought . . . to a new and abiding consciousness of God's presence and His claims upon their lives.[311]

168. Misery of our own making.[312]

169. First Things First.[313]

170. Many did hesitate to call this force the "power of God."[314]

171. An experience that is not shared dies or becomes twisted and abnormal.[315]

172. The person with an experience of God and a poor technique will make fewer mistakes in the end than the person with a high technique and no God.[316]

173. New power and new direction came to her when she started listening to God.[317]

---

[310] Brown, *The Venture of Belief*, p. 24. Big Book, p. 25: "The central fact of our lives today is the absolute certainty that our Creator has entered into our hearts and lives in a way which is indeed miraculous."

[311] Shoemaker, *Twice Born Ministers*, p. 123. Big Book, p. 130: "This dream world has been replaced by a great sense of purpose, accompanied by a growing consciousness of the power of God in our lives."

[312] Shoemaker, *The Gospel According to You*, p. 103. Big Book, p. 133: "We made our own misery. God didn't do it."

[313] Macmillan, *Seeking and Finding*, p. 17. Big Book, p. 135: "First Things First."

[314] Kitchen, *I Was a Pagan*, p. 16. "consciousness of the power of God in our lives."

[315] Shoemaker, *God's Control*, p. 21. Big Book, p. 157: "The two friends spoke of their spiritual experience and told him about the course of action they carried out."

[316] Forde, *The Guidance of God*, p. 8. Big Book, p. 164: "Ask Him in your morning meditation what you can do each day for the man who is still sick. The answers will come, if your own house is in order. But obviously you cannot transmit something you haven't got."

[317] Foot, *Life Began Yesterday*, p. 112. Big Book, p. 158: "The lawyer gave his life to the care and direction of his Creator, and said he was perfectly willing to do anything necessary. . . . He had begun to have a spiritual experience."

174. The conception of God . . . left on the mind by the Book of Genesis is that of the transcendent Creator who in the beginning made heaven and earth.[318]

175. Somewhere a great Reality is born, which brings a new discovery of God and new tides of life.[319]

176. A vital living Presence Who could actually be "felt."[320]

177. All subsequent life is a development of the relationship with God which conversion opened.[321]

178. Let go! Abandon yourself to Him.[322]

179. The New Testament makes it quite clear that fellowship is in the Holy Spirit. . . . It refers to a certain quality, intensity and power of fellowship . . . created by the presence of the Holy Spirit in a group of people.[323]

180. Fellowship is of the essence of the Group.[324]

181. Spirit of the universe.[325]

182. We are told that conversion is "gradual or sudden."[326]

183. Nine-tenths of our misery is due to self-centeredness. To get ourselves off our hands is the essence of happiness.[327]

---

[318] Streeter, *The God Who Speaks*, p. 71. Big Book, p. 161, "They had visioned the Great Reality—the loving and All Powerful Creator."

[319] Shoemaker, *National Awakening*, pp. 23, 46-47. Big Book, p. 161: "They had visioned the Great Reality."

[320] Kitchen, *I Was a Pagan*, p. 68: Big Book, p. 162: "Many of us have felt . . . the Presence and Power of God within its walls."

[321] Shoemaker, *Children of the Second Birth*, p. 16. Big Book, p. 164: "See to it that your relationship with Him is right, and great events will come to pass for you and countless others."

[322] Shoemaker, Religion That Works, p. 19. Big Book, p. 164: "Abandon yourself to God as you understand God."

[323] Benson, *The Eight Points*, p. 105. Big Book, p. 164: "We shall be with you in the Fellowship of the Spirit."

[324] Murray, *Group Movements Throughout the Ages*, p. 349. Big Book, pp. 152, 153, 162: "It is a fellowship in Alcoholics Anonymous. . . . Thus we find the fellowship, and so will you. . . . Some day we hope that every alcoholic who journeys will find a Fellowship of Alcoholics Anonymous at his destination."

[325] Nichols, *A Fool Hath Said*, p. 28; Big Book, p. 46.

[326] Shoemaker, *Realizing Religion*, p. 27. Compare Big Book, p. 569.

[327] Benson, *The Eight Points*, p. 56. Big Book, p. 14: "It meant destruction of self-centeredness."

184. They recognize that the [sex] instinct is at bottom a God- given one.[328]

185. It is the way of young-mindedness to treat one's spiritual defects as a problem, not a fate.[329]

186. And we must honestly ask ourselves where lies our final security; whether it lies in people and things or whether it lies in God.[330]

187. God in mercy strip us this day of the last vestiges of self reliance, and help us to begin anew trusting to nothing but His grace.[331]

---

[328] Begbie, *Life Changers*, p. 176. Big Book, p. 69: "We remembered always that our sex powers were God-given and therefore good . . ."

[329] Shoemaker, *Twice Born Ministers*, p. 36. Big Book, p. 76: "I pray that you now remove from me every single defect of character which stands in the way of my usefulness to you and my fellows."

[330] Shoemaker, *National Awakening*, p. 35. Big Book, p. 68: "Wasn't it because that self-reliance failed us. . . . We are now on a different basis. . . . We trust infinite God rather than our finite selves."

[331] Shoemaker, *If I Be Lifted Up*, p. 166. Big Book, p. 68: ". . . Self-reliance failed us."

8

Conclusion

We have covered a lot of ground as far as the Oxford Group and Alcoholics Anonymous are concerned. We believe this has not been done before. It is a first. And we believe our readers can reach some solid conclusions about A.A.'s Oxford Group origins.

The first conclusion is that A.A.'s own "Conference Approved" histories were correct when they made the following statements:

[T]he famous [Big Book] fifth chapter, "How It Works" . . . *was heavy with Oxford Group principles. . . .* (emphasis added).[1]

Criticism and rejection notwithstanding, Lois and Bill did not become immediately disillusioned with *the Oxford Group* or with *its principles, from which Bill borrowed freely* (emphasis added).[2]

This was the beginning of A.A.'s "flying blind period." They had the Bible, and *they had the precepts of the Oxford Group.* They also had their own instincts. *They were working, or working out the A.A. program*—the Twelve

---

[1] *Pass It On* (New York: Alcoholics Anonymous World Services, 1984), pp. 196-97.

[2] *Pass It On*, p. 169.

Steps—without quite knowing how they were doing it (emphasis added).[3]

[Bill Wilson wrote:] There came next to the lectern [in 1955] a figure that not many A.A.'s had seen before, the Episcopal clergyman *Sam Shoemaker. It was from him that Dr. Bob and I in the beginning had absorbed most of the principles that were afterward embodied in the Twelve Steps of Alcoholics Anonymous*, steps that express the heart of A.A.'s way of life (emphasis added).[4]

[Bill also wrote:] Where did the early AAs find the material for the remaining ten Steps? Where did we learn about moral inventory, amends for harm done, turning wills and lives over to God? Where did we learn about meditation and prayer *and all the rest of it? The spiritual substance of our remaining ten Steps came straight from Dr. Bob's and my own earlier association with the Oxford Groups. . . .* (emphasis added).[5]

Our title is replete with demonstrations that Oxford Group ideas, practices, and language permeate the pages of A.A. literature and A.A.'s Twelve Steps—to a degree scarcely realized by A.A. supporters, students, and critics. We believe our title makes the similarities crystal clear.

The second conclusion should be that a knowledge of Oxford Group principles, practices, and phrases can materially help people understand A.A.'s Big Book, Twelve Steps, and ideas. When a person with little or no understanding of alcoholism, Alcoholics Anonymous, or A.A.'s spiritual program of recovery enters A.A.'s doors, that person unexpectedly hears many Biblical,

---

[3] *DR. BOB and the Good Oldtimers* (New York: Alcoholics Anonymous World Services, 1980), p. 96.

[4] *Alcoholics Anonymous Comes of Age* (New York: Alcoholics Anonymous World Services, 1957), pp. 38-39.

[5] *The Language of the Heart. Bill W.'s Grapevine Writings* (New York: The AA Grapevine, Inc., 1988), p. 198.

religious, and "spiritual" expressions. There is talk of God. There is talk of "God as we understood Him," of a "Power greater than ourselves," and of a "Higher Power." There is talk of a "decision," a "moral" inventory, confession, "character defects," "willingness," change, "turning it over," amends, prayer and meditation, a spiritual awakening, a "message," and spiritual principles.

Consider what happens when a newcomer to A.A., who has no knowledge of A.A.'s religious roots, encounters such expressions as those mentioned in the preceding paragraph. Sam Shoemaker forecast the possibilities both before A.A. began and during the years he watched A.A. progress. First, there is a strong temptation for the bewildered entrant to use the expressions without comprehending them at all, or to adopt "absurd modern names for God," or to concoct their own "god."[6] There can be what Shoemaker called "childish nonsense," when confused and defeated people desperately turn to God for help, but expect Him "to acquiesce in . . . half-baked prayers."[7] There certainly is a possibility that people disdaining organized religion but suffering from spiritual misery will, as Shoemaker put it, "make" their "own religion," expecting it to cure a spiritual malady which comes from "estrangement from God."[8] Finally, there is a very real possibility that many will simply develop personal, private, or irrelevant definitions for the religious and spiritual words and phrases they hear.[9] Such results, of course, ignore the very

---

[6] See Sam Shoemaker, "The Spiritual Path of A.A.," *The A.A. Grapevine* (November, 1960), pp. 11-12. Shoemaker adverted to "crude attempts" which involved "absurd" names for God. Shoemaker made these observations in his speech before the international A.A. convention at Long Beach in July, 1960.

[7] See the remarks of Sam Shoemaker to the international A.A. convention at St. Louis, Missouri, in July, 1955. *Alcoholics Anonymous Comes of Age* (New York: Alcoholics Anonymous World Services, 1957), p. 265.

[8] See Samuel M. Shoemaker, Jr., *Realizing Religion* (New York: Association Press, 1923), pp. 2, 4-5.

[9] In his remarks to A.A.'s 1960 International Convention, Shoemaker advised the assembled AAs: "What we have to deal with is the God that really is, not with our
(continued...)

religious origins, wisdom, and teachings of religion from which the A.A. concepts came.

When an AA hears "Faith without works is dead," what will be the meaning assigned to that sentence? The author has heard some weird ones. When an AA hears about the "Creator," "Maker," "fellowship of the Spirit," and "Father of light," what will these words mean to that person? The author has heard "Creator" turned into the "Big Dipper;" the "fellowship of the Spirit" become "Good Orderly Direction;" and the "Maker" become "Ralph." And can a dictionary alone adequately explain to the newcomer the meaning these expressions had when A.A.'s Big Book was written and when early AAs were achieving remarkable successes?

As to our second conclusion—that Oxford Group history can substantially help in an understanding of Twelve Step ideas—Bill Wilson's own statement about the clergy [and hence the Oxford Group origins] can be most helpful:

> Some AAs say, "I don't need religion, because AA is my religion." As a matter of fact, I used to take this tack myself. After enjoying this simple and comfortable view for some years I finally awoke to the probability that there might be sources of spiritual teaching, wisdom, and assurance outside AA. I recalled that preacher Sam [Shoemaker] probably had a lot to do with the vital spiritual experience that was my first gift of faith. He had also taught me principles by which I could survive and carry on. . . . Though still rather gun-shy about clergymen and their theology I finally went back to them—the place where AA came from. If they had been able to teach me the principles on which I could recover, then perhaps they might now be

---

[9] (...continued)
human concepts of Him. It is much better to pray to the God that is, He with no name, we with no words, than to pray to your own creation of God, with words prettier than a poem, but fictitious." Shoemaker, "The Spiritual Path of A.A.," *supra*, p. 11.

able to tell me more about growth in understanding, and in belief.[10]

Bill could, and probably should, have added that Sam Shoemaker was totally involved in the Oxford Group when AAs were learning their spiritual ideas; that both Shoemaker and Oxford Group founder, Dr. Frank Buchman, were staunch Bible students and teachers; and that both taught their ideas from the Bible—something that our title should make quite obvious.

The third conclusion we hope our readers will reach is that AAs, Twelve Step programs, and the recovery field need an historical lift. The successes of yesterday are not even closely approximated today as hordes of people and new ideas pour into the recovery arena. This does not mean that people cannot and do not recover today. It does suggest that those who are seeking recovery can profit from a long hard look at what the early AAs did and where they obtained their recovery ideas. The author has done this. Neither he nor the more than sixty men he has sponsored have been prompted to seek out an Oxford Group affiliation. But many of us have been strengthened in our search for accurate information about God, the power of God, the will of God, and the abundant life God can make available. And we have done this *within* the rooms of A.A. and with confidence because we know we are utilizing the same Biblical resources early AAs used when they were learning and practicing Oxford Group principles and achieving a degree of success we want.

Two of Frank Buchman's favorite verses from the Bible might be of special value to AAs and other Twelve Step people who wish to learn what God can do for believers. Ephesians 3:20-21 state about God:

Now unto him that is able to do exceeding abundantly above all that we ask or think, according to the power that worketh

---

[10] *The Language of the Heart*, pp. 178-79.

in us. Unto him *be* glory in the church by Christ Jesus throughout all ages, world without end. Amen.[11]

May these verses from Ephesians offer the same inspiration to our readers that they provided to Dr. Frank N. D. Buchman, his First Century Christian Fellowship, and the early AAs who belonged to it.

The End

---

[11] As to Frank Buchman's frequent references to these verses, see, for example, Theophil Spoerri, *Dynamic out of Silence: Frank Buchman's Relevance today* (London: Grosvenor Books, 1976), p. 135; Miles G. W. Phillimore, *Just for Today* (privately published pamphlet, published after Buchman's Lake Tahoe, California "conference" in 1940, and given by Phillimore to his friends), p. 13; and Harry J. Almond, *Foundations for Faith* (London: Grosvenor, 1980), p. 60.

Bibliography

Publications by or about the Oxford Group & Oxford Group People

A Day in Pennsylvania Honoring Frank Nathan Daniel Buchman in Pennsburg and Allentown. Oregon: Grosvenor Books, 1992.

Allen, Geoffrey Francis. *He That Cometh.* New York: The Macmillan Company, 1933.

Almond, Harry J. *Foundations for Faith.* 2d ed. London: Grosvenor Books, 1980.

——. *Iraqi Statesman: A Portrait of Mohammed Fadhel Jamali.* Salem, OR: Grosvenor Books, 1993.

Austin, H. W. "Bunny". *Frank Buchman As I Knew Him.* London: Grosvenor Books, 1975.

——. *Moral Re-Armament: The Battle for Peace.* London: William Heineman, 1938.

Begbie, Harold. *Life Changers.* New York: G. P. Putnam's Sons, 1927.

——. *Souls in Action.* New York: Hodder & Stoughton, 1911.

——. *Twice-Born Men.* New York: Fleming H. Revell, 1909.

Belden, David C. *The Origins and Development of the Oxford Group (Moral Re-Armament).* D. Phil. Dissertation, Oxford University, 1976.

Belden, Kenneth D. *Is God Speaking-Are We Listening?* London: Grosvenor Books, 1987.

——. *Meeting Moral Re-Armament.* London: Grosvenor Books, 1979.

——. *Reflections on Moral Re-Armament.* London: Grosvenor Books, 1983.

——. *The Hour of the Helicopter.* Somerset, England: Linden Hall, 1992.

Bennett, John C. *Social Salvation.* New York: Charles Scribner's Sons, 1935.

Benson, Clarence Irving. *The Eight Points of the Oxford Group.* London: Humphrey Milford, Oxford University Press, 1936.

Blair, David. *For Tomorrow-Yes!* Compiled and edited from David Blair's Notebook by Jane Mullen Blair & Friends. New York: Exposition Press, 1981.

Blake, Howard C. *Way to Go: Adventures in Search of God's Will.* Burbank, CA: Pooh Stix Press, 1992.

Braden, Charles Samuel. *These Also Believe.* New York: The Macmillan Company, 1949.

Brown, Philip Marshall. *The Venture of Belief.* New York: Fleming H. Revell, 1935.

Buchman, Frank N. D. *Remaking the World.* London: Blandford Press, 1961.

—— and Sherwood Eddy. *Ten Suggestions for Personal Work* (not located).

——. *The Revolutionary Path.* London: Grosvenor, 1975.

Bundy, David D. *Keswick: A Bibliographic Introduction to the Higher Life Movements.* Wilmore, Kentucky: B. L. Fisher Library of Asbury Theological Seminary, 1975.
———. "Keswick and the Experience of Evangelical Piety." Chap. 7 in *Modern Christian Revivals.* Urbana, IL: University of Illinois Press, 1992.
Campbell, Paul and Peter Howard. *Remaking Men.* New York: Arrowhead Books, 1954.
Cantrill, Hadley. *The Psychology of Social Movements.* New York: John Wiley & Sons, Inc., 1941.
Clapp, Charles, Jr. *The Big Bender.* New York: Harper & Row, 1938.
———. *Drinking's Not the Problem.* New York: Thomas Y. Crowell, 1949.
Clark, Walter Houston. *The Oxford Group: Its History and Significance.* New York: Bookman Associates, 1951.
Crothers, Susan. *Susan and God.* New York: Harper & Brothers, 1939.
Day, Sherwood Sunderland. *The Principles of the Group.* Oxford: University Press, n.d.
Dayton, Donald W., ed. *The Higher Christian Life: Sources for the Study of the Holiness, Pentecostal and Keswick Movements.* New York: Garland Publishing, 1984.
Dinger, Clair M. *Moral Re-Armament: A Study of Its Technical and Religious Nature in the Light of Catholic Teaching.* Washington, D.C.: The Catholic University of America Press, 1961.
"Discord in Oxford Group: Buchmanites Ousted by Disciple from N.Y. Parish House." *Newsweek.* November 24, 1941.
Driberg, Tom. *The Mystery of Moral Re-Armament: A Study of Frank Buchman and His Movement.* New York: Alfred A. Knopf, 1965.
du Maurier, Daphne. *Come Wind, Come Weather.* London: Heinemann, 1941.
Eister, Allan W. *Drawing Room Conversion.* Durham: Duke University Press, 1950.
Entwistle, Basil, and John McCook Roots. *Moral Re-Armament: What Is It?* Pace Publications, 1967.
Ferguson, Charles W. *The Confusion of Tongues.* Garden City: Doubleday, Doran Company, Inc., 1940.
Foot, Stephen. *Life Began Yesterday.* New York: Harper & Brothers, 1935.
Forde, Eleanor Napier. *The Guidance of God.* Oxford: Printed at the University Press, 1930.
Frank Buchman-80. Compiled by His Friends. London: Blandford Press, 1958.
Gordon, Anne Wolrige. *Peter Howard: Life and Letters.* London: The Oxford Group, 1969.
Grensted, L. W. *The Person of Christ.* New York: Harper & Brothers, 1933.
Grogan, William. *John Riffe of the Steelworkers.* New York: Coward—McCann, 1959.
Hamilton, Loudon. *MRA: How It All Began.* London: Moral Re-Armament, 1968.
Hamlin, Bryan T. *Moral Re-Armament and Forgiveness in International Affairs.* London: Grosvenor, 1992.
Harris, Irving. *An Outline of the Life of Christ.* New York: The Oxford Group, 1935.
———. *Out in Front: Forerunners of Christ. A Study of the Lives of Eight Great Men.* New York: The Calvary Evangel, 1942.
———. *The Breeze of the Spirit: Sam Shoemaker and the Story of Faith at Work.* New York: The Seabury Press, 1978.
Harrison, Marjorie. *Saints Run Mad.* London: John Lane, Ltd., 1934.
Henderson, Michael. *A Different Accent.* Richmond, VA: Grosvenor Books USA, 1985.

——. *All Her Paths Are Peace: Women Pioneers in Peacemaking*. CT: Kumerian Press, 1994.

——. *Hope for a Change: Commentaries by an Optimistic Realist*. Salem, OR: Grosvenor Books, 1991.

——. *On History's Coattails: Commentaries by an English Journalist in America*. Richmond, VA: Grosvenor USA, 1988.

Henson, Herbert Hensley. *The Group Movement*. London: Oxford University Press, 1933.

Hicks, Roger. *How to Read the Bible*. London: Moral Re-Armament, n.d.

——. *Letters to Parsi*. London: Blandford Press, 1960.

——. *The Endless Adventure*. London: Blandford Press, 1964.

——. *The Lord's Prayer and Modern Man*. London: Blandford Press, 1967.

Hofmeyr, Bremer. *How to Change*. New York: Moral Re-Armament, n.d.

——. *How to Listen*. New York: Moral Re-Armament, n.d.

Holmes-Walker, Wilfrid. *New Enlistment* (no data available).

Howard, Peter. *Frank Buchman's Secret*. Garden City: New York: Doubleday & Company, Inc., 1961.

——. *Innocent Men*. London: Heinemann, 1941.

——. *That Man Frank Buchman*. London: Blandford Press, 1946.

——. *The World Rebuilt*. New York. Duell, Sloan & Pearce, 1951.

Hunter, T. Willard, with assistance from M.D.B. *A.A.'s Roots in the Oxford Group*. New York: A.A. Archives, 1988.

——. *Press Release*. Buchman Events/Pennsylvania, October 19, 1991.

——. *AA & MRA: "It Started Right There": Behind the Twelve Steps and the Self-help Movement*. OR: Grosvenor Books, 1994.

——. *"The Oxford Group's Frank Buchman."* July, 1978. Founders Day archives, maintained by Gail L. in Akron, Ohio.

——. *The Spirit of Charles Lindbergh: Another Dimension*. Lanham, MD: Madison Books, 1993.

——. *Uncommon Friends' Uncommon Friend*. A tribute to James Draper Newton, on the occasion of his eighty-fifth birthday. (Pamphlet, March 30, 1990).

——. *World Changing Through Life Changing*. Thesis, Newton Center, Mass: Andover-Newton Theological School, 1977.

Hutchinson, Michael. *A Christian Approach to Other Faiths*. London: Grosvenor Books, 1991.

——. *The Confessions*. (privately published study of St. Augustine's *Confessions*).

Jones, Olive M. *Inspired Children*. New York: Harper & Brothers, 1933.

——. *Inspired Youth*. New York: Harper & Brothers, 1938.

Kitchen, V. C. *I Was a Pagan*. New York: Harper & Brothers, 1934.

Koenig, His Eminence Franz Cardinal. *True Dialogue*. Oregon: Grosvenor USA, 1986.

Laun, Ferdinand. *Unter Gottes Fuhring*. The Oxford Group, n.d.

Lean, Garth. *Cast Out Your Nets*. London: Grosvenor, 1990.

——. *Frank Buchman: A Life*. London: Constable, 1985.

——. *Good God, It Works*. London: Blandford Press, 1974.

——, and Morris Martin. *New Leadership*. London: William Heinemann, Ltd., 1936.

———. *On the Tail of a Comet: The Life of Frank Buchman.* Colorado Springs: Helmers & Howard, 1988.

Leon, Philip. *The Philosophy of Courage or the Oxford Group Way.* New York: Oxford University Press, 1939.

"Less Buchmanism." *Time,* November 24, 1941.

Macintosh, Douglas C. *Personal Religion.* New York: Charles Scribner's Sons, 1942.

Mackay, Malcolm George. *More than Coincidence.* Edinburgh: The Saint Andrew Press, 1979.

Macmillan, Ebenezer. *Seeking and Finding.* New York: Harper & Brothers, 1933.

Margetson, The Very Reverend Provost. *The South African Adventure.* The Oxford Group, n.d.

Martin, Morris H. *The Thunder and the Sunshine.* Washington D.C.: MRA, n.d.

———. *Born to Live in the Future.* n.l.: Up With People, 1991.

Mowat, R. C. *Modern Prophetic Voices: From Kierkegaard to Buchman.* Oxford: New Cherwel Press, 1994.

———. *The Message of Frank Buchman.* London: Blandford Press, 1951.

———. *Report on Moral Re-Armament.* London: Blandford Press, 1955.

Moyes, John S. *American Journey.* Sydney: Clarendon Publishing Co., n. d.

Murray, Robert H. *Group Movements Throughout the Ages.* New York: Harper & Brothers. 1935.

Newton, Eleanor Forde. *I Always Wanted Adventure.* London: Grosvenor, 1992.

Newton, James D. *Uncommon Friends: Life with Thomas Edison, Henry Ford, Harvey Firestone, Alexis Carrel, & Charles Lindbergh.* New York: Harcourt Brace, 1987.

Nichols, Beverley. *The Fool Hath Said.* Garden City: Doubleday, Doran & Company, 1936.

Orglmeister, Peter. *An Ideology for Today.* Pamphlet, 1965.

Petrocokino, Paul. *The New Man for the New World.* Cheshire: Paul Petrocokino, n.d.

Phillimore, Miles. *Just for Today.* Privately published pamphlet, 1940.

Pollock, J. C. *The Keswick Story: The Authorized History of the Keswick Convention.* Chicago: Moody Press, n.d.

Raynor, Frank D., and Leslie D. Weatherhead. *The Finger of God.* London: Group Publications, Ltd., 1934.

Reynolds, Amelia S. *New Lives for Old.* New York: Fleming H. Revell, 1929.

Roots, John McCook. *An Apostle to Youth.* Oxford: The Oxford Group, 1928.

Rose, Cecil. *When Man Listens.* New York: Oxford University Press, 1937.

Rose, Howard J. *The Quiet Time.* New York: Oxford Group at 61 Gramercy Park, North, 1937.

Russell, Arthur J. *For Sinners Only.* London: Hodder & Stoughton, 1932.

———. *One Thing I Know.* New York: Harper & Brothers, 1933.

Sangster, W. E. *God Does Guide Us.* New York: The Abingdon Press, 1934.

Selbie, W. B. *Oxford and the Groups.* Oxford: Basie Blackwell, 1934.

Sherry, Frank H., and Mahlon H. Hellerich. *The Formative Years of Frank N. D. Buchman.* (Reprint of article at Frank Buchman home in Allentown, Pennsylvania).

Smith, J. Herbert. *The Meaning of Conversion.* N.p., n.d.

Spencer, F. A. M. *The Meaning of the Groups.* London: Metheun & Co., Ltd., 1934.

Spoerri, Theophil. *Dynamic out of Silence: Frank Buchman's Relevance Today.* Translated by John Morrison. London: Grosvenor Books, 1976.

Streeter, Burnett Hillman. *The God Who Speaks.* London: Macmillan & Co., Ltd., 1943.

Suenens, Rt. Rev. Msgr. *The Right View of Moral Re-Armament.* London: Burns and Oates, 1952.

The Bishop of Leicester, Chancellor R. J. Campbell and the Editor of the "Church of England Newspaper." *Stories of our Oxford House Party.*, July 17, 1931.

The Layman with a Notebook. *What Is the Oxford Group?* London: Oxford University Press, 1933.

Thornhill, Alan. *One Fight More.* London: Frederick Muller, 1943.

———. *The Significance of the Life of Frank Buchman.* London: Moral Re-Armament, 1952.

———. *Best of Friends: A Life of Enriching Friendships.* United Kingdom, Marshall Pickering, 1986.

Thornton-Duesbury, J. P. *Sharing.* The Oxford Group, n.d.

———. *The Open Secret of MRA.* London: Blandford, 1964.

"Calvary's Eviction of Buchman." *Time Magazine*, November 24, 1941.

Twitchell, Kenaston. *Do You Have to Be Selfish.* New York: Moral Re-Armament, n.d.

———. *How Do You Make Up Your Mind.* New York: Moral Re-Armament, n.d.

———. *Regeneration in the Ruhr.* Princeton: Princeton University Press, 1981.

———. *Supposing Your Were Absolutely Honest.* New York: Moral Re-Armament, n.d.

———. *The Strength of a Nation: Absolute Purity.* New York: Moral Re-Armament, n.d.

Van Dusen, Henry P. "Apostle to the Twentieth Century: Frank N. D. Buchman." *Atlantic Monthly* 154 (July 1934).

———. "The Oxford Group Movement." *Atlantic Monthly.* 154 (August 1934).

Viney, Hallen. *How Do I Begin?* The Oxford Group, 61 Gramercy Park, New York., 1937.

Vrooman, Lee. *The Faith That Built America.* New York: Arrowhead Books, Inc., 1955.

Walter, Howard A. *Soul Surgery: Some Thoughts on Incisive Personal Work.* 6th. ed. Oxford: at the University Press by John Johnson, 1940.

Weatherhead, Leslie D. *Discipleship.* London: Student Christian Movement Press, 1934.

———. *How Can I Find God?* London: Fleming H. Revell, 1934.

———. *Psychology and Life.* New York: Abingdon Press, 1935.

Williamson, Geoffrey. *Inside Buchmanism.* New York: Philosophical Library, Inc., 1955.

Winslow, Jack C. *Church in Action* (no data available to author).

———. *Vital Touch with God: How to Carry on Adequate Devotional Life.* The Evangel, 8 East 40th St., New York, n.d.

———. *When I Awake.* London: Hodder & Stoughton, 1938.

———. *Why I Believe in the Oxford Group.* London: Hodder & Stoughton, 1934.

Books by or about Oxford Group Mentors

Bushnell, Horace. *The New Life.* London: Strahan & Co., 1868.

Chapman, J. Wilbur. *Life and Work of Dwight L. Moody.* Philadelphia, 1900.

Cheney, Mary B. *Life and Letters of Horace Bushnell*. New York: Harper & Brothers, 1890.

Drummond, Henry. *Essays and Addresses*. New York: James Potts & Company, 1904.

———. *Natural Law in the Spiritual World*. Potts Edition.

———. *The Changed Life*. New York: James Potts & Company, 1891.

———. *The Greatest Thing in the World and Other Addresses*. London: Collins, 1953.

———. *The Ideal Life*. New York: Hodder & Stoughton, 1897.

———. *The New Evangelism*. New York: Hodder & Stoughton, 1899.

Edwards, Robert L. *Of Singular Genius, of Singular Grace: A Biography of Horace Bushnell*. Cleveland: The Pilgrim Press, 1992.

Findlay, James F., Jr. *Dwight L. Moody American Evangelist*. Chicago, University of Chicago Press, 1969.

Fitt, Emma Moody, *Day by Day with D. L. Moody*. Chicago: Moody Press, n.d.

Goodspeed, Edgar J. *The Wonderful Career of Moody and Sankey in Great Britain and America*. New York: Henry S. Goodspeed & Co., 1876.

Guldseth, Mark O. *Streams*. Alaska: Fritz Creek Studios, 1982.

Hopkins, C. Howard. *John R. Mott, a Biography*. Grand Rapids: William B. Erdmans Publishing Company, 1979.

James, William. *The Varieties of Religious Experience*. New York: First Vintage Books/The Library of America, 1990.

Meyer, F. B. *The Secret of Guidance*. New York: Fleming H. Revell, 1896.

Moody, Paul D. *My Father: An Intimate Portrait of Dwight Moody*. Boston: Little Brown, 1938.

Moody, William R. *The Life of D. L. Moody*. New York: Fleming H. Revell, 1900.

Mott, John R. *The Evangelisation of the World in This Generation*. London, 1901.

Pollock, J. C. *Moody: A Biographical Portrait of the Pacesetter in Modern Mass Evangelism*. New York: Macmillan, 1963.

Smith, George Adam. *The Life of Henry Drummond*. New York: McClure, Phillips & Co., 1901.

Speer, Robert E. *Studies of the Man Christ Jesus*. New York: Fleming H. Revell, 1896.

———. *The Marks of a Man*. New York: Hodder & Stoughton, 1907.

———. *The Principles of Jesus*. New York: Fleming H. Revell Company, 1902.

Stewart, George, Jr. *Life of Henry B. Wright*. New York: Association Press, 1925.

Wright, Henry B. *The Will of God and a Man's Lifework*. New York: The Young Men's Christian Association Press, 1909.

Publications by or about Samuel Moor Shoemaker, Jr.

Shoemaker, Samuel Moor, Jr. "A 'Christian Program.'" In *Groups That Work: The Key to Renewal . . . for Churches, Communities, and Individuals*. Compiled by Walden Howard and the Editors of *Faith at Work*. Michigan: Zondervan, 1967.

———. "Act As If." *Christian Herald*. October, 1954.

———. "And So from My Heart I Say . . ." *The A.A. Grapevine*. New York: The A.A. Grapevine, Inc., September, 1948.

———. . . . *And Thy Neighbor*. Waco, Texas: Word Books, 1967.

———. *A Young Man's View of the Ministry*. New York: Association Press, 1923.

———. *Beginning Your Ministry*. New York: Harper & Row Publishers, 1963.

———. *By the Power of God*. New York: Harper & Brothers, 1954.

———. *Calvary Church Yesterday and Today*. New York: Fleming H. Revell, 1936.

———. *Children of the Second Birth*. New York: Fleming H. Revell, 1927.

———. *Christ and This Crisis*. New York: Fleming H. Revell, 1943.

———. *Christ's Words from the Cross*. New York: Fleming H. Revell, 1933.

———. *Confident Faith*. New York: Fleming H. Revell, 1932.

———. *Extraordinary Living for Ordinary Men*. Michigan: Zondervan, 1965.

———. *Faith at Work*. A symposium edited by Samuel Moor Shoemaker. Hawthorne Books, 1958.

———. *Faith at Work* magazine, frequent articles in.

———. *Freedom and Faith*. New York: Fleming H. Revell, 1949.

———. *God and America*. New York: Book Stall, 61 Gramercy Park North, New York, n.d.

———. *God's Control*. New York: Fleming H. Revell, 1939.

———. *How to Become a Christian*. New York: Harper & Brothers, 1953.

———. "How to Find God." Reprint from *Faith at Work* Magazine, n.d.

———. *How to Help People*. Cincinnati: Forward Movement Publications, 1976.

———. *How You Can Find Happiness*. New York: E. P. Dutton & Co., 1947.

———. *How You Can Help Other People*. New York: E. P. Dutton & Co., 1946.

———. *If I Be Lifted Up*. New York: Fleming H. Revell, 1931.

———. *In Memoriam: The Service of Remembrance*. Princeton: The Graduate Council, Princeton University, June 10, 1956.

———. *Living Your Life Today*. New York: Fleming H. Revell, 1947.

———. *Morning Radio Talk No. 1, by Reverend Samuel M. Shoemaker*, American Broadcasting Co., one-page transcript of program for October 4, 1945.

———. *National Awakening*. New York: Harper & Brothers, 1936.

———. *One Boy's Influence*. New York: Association Press, 1925.

———. *Realizing Religion*. New York: Association Press, 1923.

———. *Religion That Works*. New York: Fleming H. Revell, 1928.

———. *Revive Thy Church*. New York: Harper & Brothers, 1948.

———. *Sam Shoemaker at His Best*. New York: Faith At Work, 1964.

———. *So I Stand by the Door and Other Verses*. Pittsburgh: Calvary Rectory, 1958.

———. *The Breadth and Narrowness of the Gospel*. New York: Fleming H. Revell, 1929.

———. *The Calvary Evangel, monthly articles in*. New York. Calvary Episcopal Church.

———. *The Church Alive*. New York: E. P. Dutton & Co., Inc., 1951.

———. *The Church Can Save the World*. New York: Harper & Brothers, 1938.

———. *The Conversion of the Church*. New York: Fleming H. Revell, 1932.

———. "The Crisis of Self-Surrender." *Guideposts*. November, 1955.

———. *The Experiment of Faith*. New York: Harper & Brothers. 1957.

———. *The Gospel According to You*. New York: Fleming H. Revell, 1934.

———. *The James Houston Eccleston Day-Book: Containing a Short Account of His Life and Readings for Every Day in the Year Chosen from His Sermons*. Compiled by Samuel M. Shoemaker, Jr. New York: Longmans, Green & Co., 1915.

————. "The Spiritual Angle." *The A.A. Grapevine*. New York: The A.A. Grapevine, Inc., October, 1955.

————. "The Way to Find God." *The Calvary Evangel* (August, 1935).

————. *They're on the Way*. New York: E. P. Dutton, 1951.

————. "Those Twelve Steps As I Understand Them." *Best of the Grapevine: Volume II*. New York: The A.A. Grapevine, Inc., 1986.

————. *Twice-Born Ministers*. New York: Fleming H. Revell, 1929.

————. *Under New Management*. Grand Rapids: Zondervan Publishing House, 1966.

————. *What the Church Has to Learn from Alcoholics Anonymous*. Reprint of 1956 sermon. Available at A.A. Archives, New York.

————. *With the Holy Spirit and with Fire*. New York: Harper & Brothers, 1960.

"Buchman Religion Explained to 1,000." *New York Times*. May 27, 1931.

"Campus Calls by Dr. Shoemaker Foster Chain of Religious Cells." *New York Tribune*. February 25, 1951.

Centennial History: Calvary Episcopal Church, 1855-1955. Pittsburgh: Calvary Episcopal Church, 1955.

"Church Ejects Buchman Group." *New York Times*. November 8, 1941.

"Crusaders of Reform." *Princeton Alumni Weekly*. June 2, 1993.

Cuyler, John Potter, Jr. *Calvary Church in Action*. New York: Fleming H. Revell, 1934.

Day, Sherwood S. "Always Ready: S.M.S. As a Friend." *The Evangel* (New York: Calvary Church, July-August, 1950).

Get Changed; Get Together; Get Going: A History of The Pittsburgh Experiment. Pittsburgh: The Pittsburgh Experiment, n.d.

Harris, Irving. *The Breeze of the Spirit*. New York: The Seabury Press, 1978.

————. "S.M.S.—Man of God for Our Time." *Faith At Work* (January-February, 1964).

"Houseparties Across the Continent." *The Christian Century*. August 23, 1933.

Knippel, Charles Taylor. *Samuel M. Shoemaker's Theological Influence on William G. Wilson's Twelve Step Spiritual Program of Recovery (Alcoholics Anonymous)*. Dissertation. St. Louis University, 1987.

"Listening to God Held Daily Need." *New York Times*. December 4, 1939.

Norton-Taylor, Duncan. "Businessmen on Their Knees." *Fortune*. October, 1953.

Olsson, Karl A. "The History of Faith at Work" (five parts). *Faith at Work News*. 1982-1983.

Peale, Norman Vincent. "The Unforgettable Sam Shoemaker." *Faith At Work*. January, 1964.

————. "The Human Touch: The Estimate of a Fellow Clergyman and Personal Friend." *The Evangel* (New York: Calvary Church, July-August, 1950).

Pitt, Louis W. "New Life, New Reality: A Brief Picture of S.M.S.'s Influence in the Diocese of New York." *Faith at Work*, July-August, 1950.

"Pittsburgh Man of the Year." *Pittsburgh Post Gazette*. January 12, 1956.

Sack, David Edward. *Sam Shoemaker and the "Happy Ethical Pagans."* Princeton, New Jersey: paper prepared in the Department of Religion, Princeton University, June, 1993.

"Sam Shoemaker and Faith at Work." Pamphlet on file at Faith At Work, Inc., 150 S. Washington St., Suite 204, Falls Church, VA 22046.

Schwartz, Robert. "Laymen and Clergy to Join Salute to Dr. S. M. Shoemaker." *Pittsburgh Press*. December 10, 1961.

Shoemaker, Helen Smith. *I Stand by the Door*. New York: Harper & Row, 1967.

"Sees Great Revival Near." *New York Times*. September 8, 1930.

"Soul Clinic Depicted by Pastor in Book." *New York Times*. August 5, 1927.

"Ten of the Greatest American Preachers." *Newsweek*. March 28, 1955.

The Pittsburgh Experiments Groups. Pittsburgh: The Pittsburgh Experiment, n.d.

Tools for Christian Living. Pittsburgh: The Pittsburgh Experiment, n.d.

"Urges Church Aid Oxford Group." *New York Times*. January 2, 1933, p. 26.

Wilson, Bill. "I Stand by the Door." *The A.A. Grapevine*. New York: The A.A. Grapevine, Inc., February, 1967.

Woolverton, John F. "Evangelical Protestantism and Alcoholism 1933-1962: Episcopalian Samuel Shoemaker, The Oxford Group and Alcoholics Anonymous." *Historical Magazine of the Protestant Episcopal Church* 52 (March, 1983).

Alcoholics Anonymous

Publications About

A Guide to the Twelve Steps of Alcoholics Anonymous. Akron: A.A. of Akron, n.d.

A Program for You: A Guide to the Big Book's Design for Living. Minnesota: Hazelden, 1991.

Alcoholics Anonymous. (multilith volume). New Jersey: Works Publishing Co., 1939.

Alcoholics Anonymous: An Interpretation of Our Twelve Steps. Washington, D.C.: "The Paragon" Creative Printers, 1944.

A Manual for Alcoholics Anonymous. Akron: A.A. of Akron, n.d.

B., Dick. *Anne Smith's Journal, 1933-1939: A.A.'s Principles of Success*. San Rafael, CA: Paradise Research Publications, 1994.

———. *Design for Living: The Oxford Group's Contribution to Early A.A.* San Rafael, CA: Paradise Research Publications, 1995.

———. *Dr. Bob's Library: Books for Twelve Step Growth*. San Rafael, CA: Paradise Research Publications, 1994.

———. *New Light on Alcoholism: The A.A. Legacy from Sam Shoemaker*. Corte Madera, CA: Good Book Publishing Company, 1994.

———. *The Akron Genesis of Alcoholics Anonymous: An A.A.-Good Book Connection*. Corte Madera, CA: Good Book Publishing Company, 1994.

———. *The Books Early AAs Read for Spiritual Growth*. San Rafael, CA: Paradise Research Publications, 1994.

———, and Bill Pittman. *Courage to Change: The Christian Roots of the 12-Step Movement*. Grand Rapids, MI: Fleming H. Revell, 1994.

B., Jim. *Evolution of Alcoholics Anonymous*. New York: A.A. Archives.

B. Mel. *New Wine: The Spiritual Roots of the Twelve Step Miracle*. Minnesota: Hazelden, 1991.

Bishop, Charles, Jr. *The Washingtonians & Alcoholics Anonymous*. WV: The Bishop of Books, 1992.

————, and Bill Pittman. *To Be Continued . . . . . The Alcoholics Anonymous World Bibliography: 1935-1994*. Wheeling W. VA: The Bishop of Books, 1994.

Bufe, Charles. *Alcoholics Anonymous: Cult or Cure*. San Francisco: Sharp Press, 1991.

C., Stewart. *A Reference Guide To The Big Book of Alcoholics Anonymous*. Seattle: Recovery Press, 1986.

Central Bulletin, Volumes I-II. Cleveland: Central Committee, Oct. 1942-Sept. 1944.

Clapp, Charles, Jr. *Drinking's Not the Problem*. New York: Thomas Y. Crowell, 1949.

Cutten, C. B. *The Psychology of Alcoholism*. New York: Scribner's & Sons, 1907.

Conrad, Barnaby. *Time Is All We Have*. New York: Dell Publishing, 1986.

Darrah, Mary C. *Sister Ignatia: Angel of Alcoholics Anonymous*. Chicago: Loyola University Press, 1992.

Doyle, Paul Barton. *In Step with God*. Tennessee: New Directions, 1989.

E., Bob. *Handwritten note to Lois Wilson on pamphlet entitled "Four Absolutes."* (copy made available to the author at Founders Day Archives Room in Akron, Ohio, in June, 1991).

————. Letter from Bob E. to Nell Wing. Stepping Stones Archives.

First Steps: Al-Anon . . . 35 Years of Beginnings. New York: Al-Anon Family Group Headquarters, 1986.

Ford, John C. *Depth Psychology, Morality and Alcoholism*. Massachusetts: Weston College, 1951.

Gray, Jerry. *The Third Strike*. Minnesota: Hazelden, 1949.

Hunter, Willard, with assistance from M. D. B. *A.A.'s Roots in the Oxford Group*. New York: A.A. Archives, 1988.

K., Mitch. "How It Worked: The Story of Clarence H. Snyder and the Early Days of Alcoholics Anonymous in Cleveland, Ohio." New York, 1991-1992.

Kessell, Joseph. *The Road Back: A Report on Alcoholics Anonymous*. New York: Alfred A. Knopf, 1962.

Knippel, Charles T. *Samuel M. Shoemaker's Theological Influence on William G. Wilson's Twelve Step Spiritual Program of Recovery*. Ph. D. dissertation. St Louis University, 1987.

Kurtz, Ernest. *Not-God: A History of Alcoholics Anonymous*. Expanded Edition. Minnesota: Hazelden, 1991.

————. *Shame and Guilt: Characteristics of the Dependency Cycle*. Minnesota: Hazelden, 1981.

————, and Katherine Ketcham. *The Spirituality of Imperfection: Modern Wisdom from Classic Stories*. New York: Bantam Books, 1992.

McQ, Joe. *The Steps We Took*. Arkansas: August House Publishing, 1990.

Morreim, Dennis C. *Changed Lives: The Story of Alcoholics Anonymous*. Minneapolis: Augsburg Fortress, 1991.

Morse, Robert M., M.D., and Daniel K. Flavin, M.D. "The Definition of Alcoholism." *The Journal of the American Medical Association*. August 26, 1992, pp. 1012-14.

Peale, Norman Vincent. *The Power of Positive Thinking*. New York: Prentice-Hall, 1952.

Pittman, Bill. *AA The Way It Began*. Seattle: Glen Abbey Books, 1988.

Poe, Stephen E. and Frances E. *A Concordance to Alcoholics Anonymous*. Nevada: Purple Salamander Press, 1990.

Playfair, William L., M.D. *The Useful Lie*. Illinois: Crossway Books, 1991.

Robertson, Nan. *Getting Better Inside Alcoholics Anonymous*. New York: William Morrow & Co., 1988.

Second Reader for Alcoholics Anonymous. Akron: A.A. of Akron, n.d.

Seiberling, John F. "Origins of Alcoholics Anonymous." (A transcript of remarks by Henrietta B. Seiberling: transcript prepared by Congressman John F. Seiberling of a telephone conversation with his mother, Henrietta, in the spring of 1971): *Employee Assistance Quarterly*, 1985, (1), pp. 8-12.

Sikorsky, Igor I., Jr. *AA's Godparents*. Minnesota: CompCare Publishers, 1990.

Smith, Bob and Sue Smith Windows. *Children of the Healer*. Illinois: Parkside Publishing Corporation, 1992.

Spiritual Milestones in Alcoholics Anonymous. Akron: A.A. of Akron, n.d.

Stafford, Tim. "The Hidden Gospel of the 12 Steps." *Christianity Today*, July 22, 1991.

The Four Absolutes. Cleveland: Cleveland Central Committee of A.A., n. d.

Thomsen, Robert. *Bill W*. New York: Harper & Row, 1975.

Walker, Richmond. *For Drunks Only*. Minnesota: Hazelden, n.d.

———. *The 7 Points of Alcoholics Anonymous*. Seattle: Glen Abbey Books, 1989.

Wilson, Bill. *How The Big Book Was Put Together*. New York: A.A. Archives. Transcript of Bill Wilson Speech delivered in Fort Worth, Texas, 1954.

———. *Bill Wilson's Original Story*. N.d. Stepping Stones Archives. Bedford Hills, New York, a manuscript whose individual lines are numbered 1 to 1180.

———. "Main Events: Alcoholics Anonymous Fact Sheet by Bill." November 2, 1954. Archives Room. Stepping Stones Archives. Bedford Hills, New York.

———. "The Fellowship of Alcoholics Anonymous." *Quarterly Journal of Studies on Alcohol*. Yale University, 1945, pp. 461-73.

———. *W. G. Wilson Recollections*. Bedford Hills, New York: Stepping Stones Archives, September 1, 1954 transcript of Bill's dictations to Ed B.

Wilson, Jan R., and Judith A. Wilson. *Addictionary: A Primer of Recovery Terms and Concepts from Abstinence to Withdrawal*. New York: Simon and Schuster, 1992.

Wilson, Lois. *Lois Remembers*. New York: Al-Anon Family Group Headquarters, 1987.

———. Article in *The Junction* [New York A.A. newsletter for June, 1985].

Windows, Sue Smith. (daughter of AA's Co-Founder, Dr. Bob). Typewritten Memorandum entitled, *Henrietta and early Oxford Group Friends, by Sue Smith Windows*. Delivered to the author of this book by Sue Smith Windows at Akron, June, 1991.

Wing, Nell. *Grateful to Have Been There: My 42 Years with Bill and Lois, and the Evolution of Alcoholics Anonymous*. Illinois: Parkside Publishing Corporation, 1992.

Publications Approved by Alcoholics Anonymous

Alcoholics Anonymous. 3rd Edition. New York: Alcoholics Anonymous World Services, Inc., 1976.

Alcoholics Anonymous. 1st Edition. New Jersey: Works Publishing, 1939.

Alcoholics Anonymous Comes of Age. New York: Alcoholics Anonymous World Services, Inc., 1979,

As Bill Sees It: The A.A. Way of Life . . . selected writings of A.A.'s Co-Founder. New York: Alcoholics Anonymous World Services, Inc., 1967.

Best of the Grapevine. New York: The A.A. Grapevine, Inc., 1985.

Best of the Grapevine, Volume II. New York: The A.A. Grapevine, Inc., 1986.

Came to Believe. New York: Alcoholics Anonymous World Services, Inc., 1973.

Daily Reflections. New York: Alcoholics Anonymous World Services, Inc., 1991.

DR. BOB and the Good Oldtimers. New York: Alcoholics Anonymous World Services, Inc., 1980.

Members of the Clergy Ask about Alcoholics Anonymous. New York: Alcoholics Anonymous World Services, 1961, 1979-revised 1992, according to 1989 Conference Advisory Action.

Pass It On. New York: Alcoholics Anonymous World Services, Inc., 1984.

The A.A. Grapevine: "RHS"—issue dedicated to the memory of the Co-Founder of Alcoholics Anonymous, DR. BOB. New York: A.A. Grapevine, Inc., 1951.

The A.A. Service Manual. New York: Alcoholics Anonymous World Services, Inc., 1990-1991.

The Co-Founders of Alcoholics Anonymous: Biographical Sketches; Their Last Major Talks. New York: Alcoholics Anonymous World Services, Inc., 1972, 1975.

The Language of the Heart. Bill W.'s Grapevine Writings. New York: The A.A. Grapevine, Inc., 1988.

Twelve Steps and Twelve Traditions. New York: Alcoholics Anonymous World Services, Inc., 1953.

The Bible—Versions of and Books About

Authorized King James Version. New York: Thomas Nelson, 1984.

Bullinger, Ethelbert W. *A Critical Lexicon and Concordance to the English and Greek New Testament.* Michigan: Zondervan, 1981.

Burns, Kenneth Charles. "The Rhetoric of Christology: A Content Analysis of Texts Which Discuss Titus 2:13." Master's thesis, San Francisco State University, 1991.

Harnack, Adolph. *The Expansion of Christianity in the First Three Centuries.* New York: G. P. Putnam's Sons, Volume I, 1904; Volume II, 1905.

Jukes, Andrew. *The Names of GOD in Holy Scripture.* Michigan: Kregel Publications, 1967.

Moffatt, James. *A New Translation of the Bible.* New York: Harper & Brothers, 1954.

New Bible Dictionary. 2nd Edition. Wheaton, Illinois: Tyndale House Publishers, 1987.

Revised Standard Version. New York: Thomas Nelson, 1952.

Serenity: A Companion for Twelve Step Recovery. Nashville: Thomas Nelson, 1990.

Strong, James. *The Exhaustive Concordance of the Bible.* Iowa: Riverside Book and Bible House, n.d.

The Abingdon Bible Commentary. New York: Abingdon Press, 1929.

The Companion Bible. Michigan: Zondervan Bible Publishers, 1964.

The Revised English Bible. Oxford: Oxford University Press, 1989.

Vine, W. E. *Vine's Expository Dictionary of Old and New Testament Words.* New York: Fleming H. Revell, 1981.

Young's Analytical Concordance to the Bible. New York: Thomas Nelson, 1982.
Zodhiates, Spiros. *The Hebrew-Greek Key Study Bible.* 6th ed. AMG Publishers, 1991.

Spiritual Literature-Non-Oxford Group

Kempis, Thomas à. *The Imitation of Christ.* Georgia: Mercer University Press, 1989.
Allen, James. *As a Man Thinketh.* New York: Peter Pauper Press, n.d.
——. *Heavenly Life.* New York: Grosset & Dunlap, n.d.
Barton, George A. *Jesus of Nazareth.* New York: The Macmillan Company, 1922.
Brother Lawrence. *The Practice of the Presence of God.* Pennsylvania: Whitaker House, 1982.
Carruthers, Donald W. *How to Find Reality in Your Morning Devotions.* Pennsylvania: State College, n.d.
Chambers, Oswald. *Studies in the Sermon on the Mount.* London: Simpkin, Marshall, Ltd., n.d.
Clark, Glenn. *Clear Horizons.* Vol 2. Minnesota: Macalester Park Publishing, 1941.
——. *Fishers of Men.* Boston: Little, Brown, 1928.
——. *God's Reach.* Minnesota: Macalester Park Publishing, 1951.
——. *How to Find Health through Prayer.* New York: Harper & Brothers, 1940.
——. *I Will Lift Up Mine Eyes.* New York: Harper & Brothers, 1937.
——. *The Lord's Prayer and Other Talks on Prayer from The Camps Farthest Out.* Minnesota: Macalester Publishing Co., 1932.
——. *The Man Who Talks with Flowers.* Minnesota: Macalester Park Publishing, 1939.
——. *The Soul's Sincere Desire.* Boston: Little, Brown, 1925.
——. *Touchdowns for the Lord. The Story of "Dad" A. J. Elliott.* Minnesota: Macalester Park Publishing Co., 1947.
——. *Two or Three Gathered Together.* New York: Harper & Brothers, 1942.
Daily, Starr. *Recovery.* Minnesota: Macalester Park Publishing, 1948.
Eddy, Mary Baker. *Science and Health with Key to the Scriptures.* Boston: Published by the Trustees under the Will of Mary Baker G. Eddy, 1916.
Fillmore, Charles. *Christian Healing.* Kansas City: Unity School of Christianity, 1936.
——, and Cora Fillmore. *Teach Us to Pray.* Lee's Summit, Missouri: Unity School of Christianity, 1950.
Fosdick, Harry Emerson. *A Great Time to Be Alive.* New York: Harper & Brothers, 1944.
——. *As I See Religion.* New York: Grosset & Dunlap, 1932.
——. *On Being a Real Person.* New York: Harper & Brothers, 1943.
——. *The Man from Nazareth.* New York: Harper & Brothers, 1949.
——. *The Manhood of the Master.* London: Student Christian Association, 1924.
——. *The Meaning of Prayer.* New York: Association Press, 1915.
——. *The Meaning of Service.* London: Student Christian Movement, 1921.
Fox, Emmet. *Alter Your Life.* New York: Harper & Brothers, 1950.
——. *Find and Use Your Inner Power.* New York: Harper & Brothers, 1937.
——. *Power through Constructive Thinking.* New York: Harper & Brothers, 1932.
——. *Sparks of Truth.* New York: Grosset & Dunlap, 1941.

———. *The Sermon on the Mount*. New York: Harper & Row, 1934.

———. Pamphlets: *Getting Results by Prayer* (1933); *The Great Adventure* (1937); *You Must Be Born Again* (1936).

Glover, T. R. *The Jesus of History*. New York: Association Press, 1930.

Gordon, S. D. *The Quiet Time*. London: Fleming, n.d.

Heard, Gerald. *A Preface to Prayer*. New York: Harper & Brothers, 1944.

Hickson, James Moore. *Heal the Sick*. London: Methuen & Co., 1925.

James, William. *The Varieties of Religious Experience*. New York: First Vintage Press/The Library of America Edition, 1990.

Jones, E. Stanley. *Abundant Living*. New York: Cokesbury Press, 1942.

———. *Along the Indian Road*. New York: Abingdon Press, 1939.

———. *Christ and Human Suffering*. New York: Abingdon Press, 1930.

———. *Christ at the Round Table*. New York: Abingdon Press, 1928.

———. *The Choice Before Us*. New York: Abingdon Press, 1937.

———. *The Christ of Every Road*. New York: Abingdon Press, 1930.

———. *The Christ of the American Road*. New York: Abingdon-Cokesbury Press, 1944.

———. *The Christ of the Indian Road*. New York: Abingdon Press, 1925.

———. *The Christ of the Mount*. New York: Abingdon Press, 1930.

———. *Victorious Living*. New York: Abingdon Press, 1936.

———. *Way to Power and Poise*. New York: Abingdon Press, 1949.

Jung, Dr. Carl G. *Modern Man in Search of a Soul*. New York: Harcourt Brace Jovanovich, 1933.

Kagawa, Toyohiko. *Love: The Law of Life*. Philadelphia: The John C. Winston Company, 1929.

Laubach, Frank. *Prayer (Mightiest Force in the World)*. New York: Fleming H. Revell, 1946.

Layman, Charles M. *A Primer of Prayer*. Nashville: Tidings, 1949.

Lieb, Frederick G. *Sight Unseen*. New York: Harper & Brothers, 1939.

Ligon, Ernest M. *Psychology of a Christian Personality*. New York: Macmillan, 1935.

Link, Dr. Henry C. *The Rediscovery of Man*. New York: Macmillan, 1939.

Lupton, Dilworth. *Religion Says You Can*. Boston: The Beacon Press, 1938.

Moseley, J. Rufus. *Perfect Everything*. Minnesota: Macalester Publishing Co., 1949.

Oursler, Fulton. *Happy Grotto*. Declan and McMullen, 1948.

———. *The Greatest Story Ever Told*. New York: Doubleday, 1949.

Parker, William R. and Elaine St. Johns. *Prayer Can Change Your Life*. New ed. New York: Prentice Hall, 1957.

Peale, Norman Vincent. *The Art of Living*. New York: Abingdon Press, 1937.

Rawson, F. L. *The Nature of True Prayer*. Chicago: The Marlowe Company, n.d.

Sheean, Vincent. *Lead Kindly Light*. New York: Random House, 1949.

Sheen, Fulton J. *Peace of Soul*. New York: McGraw Hill, 1949.

Sheldon, Charles M. *In His Steps*. Nashville, Broadman Press, 1935.

Silkey, Charles Whitney. *Jesus and Our Generation*. Chicago: University of Chicago Press, 1925.

Speer, Robert E.. *Studies of the Man Christ Jesus*. New York: Fleming H. Revell, 1896.

Stalker, Rev. James. *The Life of Jesus Christ*. New York: Fleming H. Revell, 1891.

The Confessions of St. Augustine. Translated by E. B. Pusey. A Cardinal Edition. New York: Pocket Books, 1952.

The Fathers of the Church. New York: CIMA Publishing, 1947.

Trine, Ralph Waldo. *In Tune with the Infinite*. New York: Thomas H. Crowell, 1897.

———. *The Man Who Knew*. New York: Bobbs Merrill, 1936.

Weatherhead, Leslie D. *Discipleship*. New York: Abingdon Press, 1934.

———. *How Can I Find God?* New York: Fleming H. Revell, 1934.

———. *Psychology and Life*. New York: Abingdon Press, 1935.

Werber, Eva Bell. *Quiet Talks with the Master*. L.A.: De Vorss & Co., 1942.

Williams, R. Llewelen, *God's Great Plan, a Guide to the Bible*. Hoverhill Destiny Publishers, n.d.

Willitts, Ethel R. *Healing in Jesus Name*. Chicago: Ethel R. Willitts Evangelists, 1931.

Bible Devotionals

Chambers, Oswald. *My Utmost for His Highest*. London: Simpkin Marshall, Ltd., 1927.

Clark, Glenn, *I Will Lift Up Mine Eyes*. New York: Harper & Brothers, 1937.

Dunnington, Lewis L. *Handles of Power*. New York: Abingdon-Cokesbury Press, 1942.

Fosdick, Harry Emerson. *The Meaning of Prayer*. New York: Association Press, 1915.

Holm, Nora Smith. *The Runner's Bible*. New York: Houghton Mifflin Company, 1915.

Jones, E. Stanley. *Abundant Living*. New York: Abingdon-Cokesbury Press, 1942.

———. *Victorious Living*. New York: Abingdon Press, 1936.

The Upper Room: Daily Devotions for Family and Individual Use. Quarterly. 1st issue: April, May, June, 1935. Edited by Grover Carlton Emmons. Nashville: General Committee on Evangelism through the Department of Home Missions, Evangelism, Hospitals, Board of Missions, Methodist Episcopal Church, South.

The Two Listeners. *God Calling*. Edited by A. J. Russell. Australia: DAYSTAR, 1953.

Tileston, Mary W. *Daily Strength for Daily Needs*. Boston: Roberts Brothers, 1893.

Index

A

A.A. Archives 12, 36, 371, 376, 377, 378, 379
A.A. General Services xiv, xix, 20, 43, 137
Abandon yourself 161, 278, 345, 361
Acts 3:6 221
Acts 3:19 171, 207
Acts 4:12 285
Acts 8:26 228
Acts 8:26-30 228
Acts 9:6 258, 273
Acts 10:1-21 228
Acts 13:22 159
Acts 14:15 151
Acts 16:6-9 228
Acts 19:18 187
Agnostics 161, 301, 343
Agree with thine adversary quickly 207, 314
Air (two-way prayer) 76, 165, 220, 350
Akron Beacon Journal 98, 129
Alexander, Jack 4, 26
Allen, James (*As a Man Thinketh*) 21
Almond, Harry xvii, xviii, 42, 43, 45, 56, 57, 104, 130, 131, 141, 162, 177, 187, 207, 210, 227, 229, 235, 238-240, 242, 314, 327, 368, 369
Amends 16, 28, 206, 224, 313, 314, 316, 346, 347, 364, 365
American leader (of the Oxford Group) 109, 110
Amos, Frank B. 3, 123, 142
Anger 208
Apology 101, 191, 204, 205, 209, 257, 318
Apostle James 12
Art (Soul Surgery) 39, 48, 55, 63, 69, 72, 78, 159, 173-175, 184, 226, 244, 253, 311, 314, 382
As Bill Sees It 319, 380
Atheists 161, 343
Atonement 43, 210, 211, 314, 354
Attentive prayer 244
Austin, H. W. (*Frank Buchman As I Knew Him*) 43, 46, 47, 54, 55, 65, 69, 73, 80, 85, 104, 175, 177, 312, 369
Awakening 60-63, 90, 108, 116, 153, 156, 160, 161, 163, 182, 191, 194, 196, 200, 203, 214, 225, 232, 245, 254, 256, 267, 274, 275, 277, 280-283, 290, 302, 312, 318, 320, 321, 329, 332, 334, 337, 347, 361, 362, 365, 375

B

D

G

S

Inquiries, orders, and requests for
catalogs and discount schedules
should be addressed to:

Dick B.
c/o Good Book Publishing Company
2747 South Kihei Road, #D-110
Kihei, Maui, Hawaii 96753
1-808-874-4876

About the Author

Dick B. writes books on the spiritual roots of Alcoholics Anonymous. And they show how the basic and highly successful Biblical ideas used by early AAs can be valuable tools for success in today's A.A. His research can also help the religious and recovery communities work more effectively with alcoholics, addicts, and others involved in Twelve Step programs.

The author is an active, recovered member of Alcoholics Anonymous; a retired attorney; and a Bible student. He has sponsored more than sixty men in their recovery from alcoholism. Consistent with A.A.'s traditions of anonymity, he uses the pseudonym "Dick B."

He has had seven titles published: *New Light on Alcoholism: The A.A. Legacy from Sam Shoemaker*; *The Books Early AAs Read for Spiritual Growth*; *The Akron Genesis of Alcoholics Anonymous*; *Design for Living: The Oxford Group's Contribution to Early A.A.*; *Anne Smith's Journal*; *Dr. Bob's Library*; and *Courage to Change* (with Bill Pittman). The books have been the subject of newspaper articles, and have been reviewed in *Library Journal, Bookstore Journal, For A Change, The Living Church, Sober Times, Episcopal Life*, and *Recovery News*.

Dick is the father of two married sons (Ken and Don) and a grandfather. As a young man, he did a stint as a newspaper reporter. He attended the University of California, Berkeley, where he received his A.A. degree, majored in economics, and was elected to Phi Beta Kappa in his Junior year. In the United States Army, he was an Information-Education Specialist. He received his A.B. and J.D. degrees from Stanford University, and was Case Editor of the Stanford Law Review. Dick became interested in Bible study in his childhood Sunday School and was much inspired by his mother's almost daily study of Scripture. He joined, and later became president of, a Community Church affiliated with the United Church of Christ. By 1972, he was studying the origins of the Bible and began traveling abroad in pursuit of that subject. In 1979, he became much involved in a Biblical research, teaching, and fellowship ministry. In his community life, he was president of a merchants' council, Chamber of Commerce, church retirement center, and homeowners' association. He served on a public district board and was active in a service club.

In 1986, he was felled by alcoholism, gave up his law practice, and began recovery as a member of the Fellowship of Alcoholics Anonymous. In 1990, his interest in A.A.'s Biblical/Christian roots was sparked by his attendance at A.A.'s International Convention in Seattle. He has traveled widely; researched at archives, and at public and seminary libraries; interviewed scholars, historians, clergy, A.A. "old-timers" and survivors; and participated in programs on A.A.'s roots.

The author is the owner of Good Book Publishing Company, writes a newsletter, and has several works in progress. Much of his research and writing is done in collaboration with his older son, Ken, who holds B.A., B.Th., and M.A. degrees. Ken has been a lecturer in New Testament Greek at a Bible college and a lecturer in Fundamentals of Oral Communication at San Francisco State University. Ken is a computer specialist.

Dick is a member of the American Historical Association, Maui Writers Guild, American Society of Journalists and Authors, National Writers Association, and The Authors' Guild. He is available for conferences, panels, seminars, and interviews.

Catalog & Order Sheet

How to Order Dick B.'s Books
on the Spiritual Roots of Alcoholics Anonymous
Directly from the Author

Order Form

Qty.

Send:

    __ New Light on Alcoholism (Sam Shoemaker)   @ $19.95 ea. $____

    __ Design for Living (Oxford Group & A.A.)   @ $17.95 ea. $____

    __ The Akron Genesis of Alcoholics Anonymous   @ $16.00 ea. $____

    __ Anne Smith's Journal, 1933-1939   @ $14.00 ea. $____

    __ Dr. Bob's Library   @ $12.00 ea. $____

    __ Books Early AAs Read for Spiritual Growth   @ $ 9.00 ea. $____

Shipping and Handling   Shipping and Handling $____
    Add 10% of retail price (minimum $2.90)

Sales Tax   Sales Tax (Cal.) $____
    California residents add Sales Tax

                                       Total Enclosed $____

Name: _____ (as it appears on your credit card, if using one)

Address: _____

City: _____ State: __ Zip: _____

Tel.: _____ **Credit Card:** MC VISA (please circle one) Exp. ____

CC Acct. #: _____ Signature _____

Special Discount Value for You!

If purchased separately, the author's six titles normally sell for $88.90, plus Shipping and Handling. Using this Order Form, you may purchase **sets of all six titles for only $81.00 per set,** and the author will pay the Shipping and Handling for you!

Please mail this Order Form, with your check, money order, or credit card authorization, to: Dick B., 2747 South Kihei Road, #D-110, Kihei, HI 96753. Please make your check or money order payable to **"Dick B."** in U.S. dollars drawn on a U.S. bank. If you have any questions, please phone: 1-808-874-4876.